W9-AXG-018

RALPH WALDO EMERSON.

Photogravure after a painting by J. Jaeger.

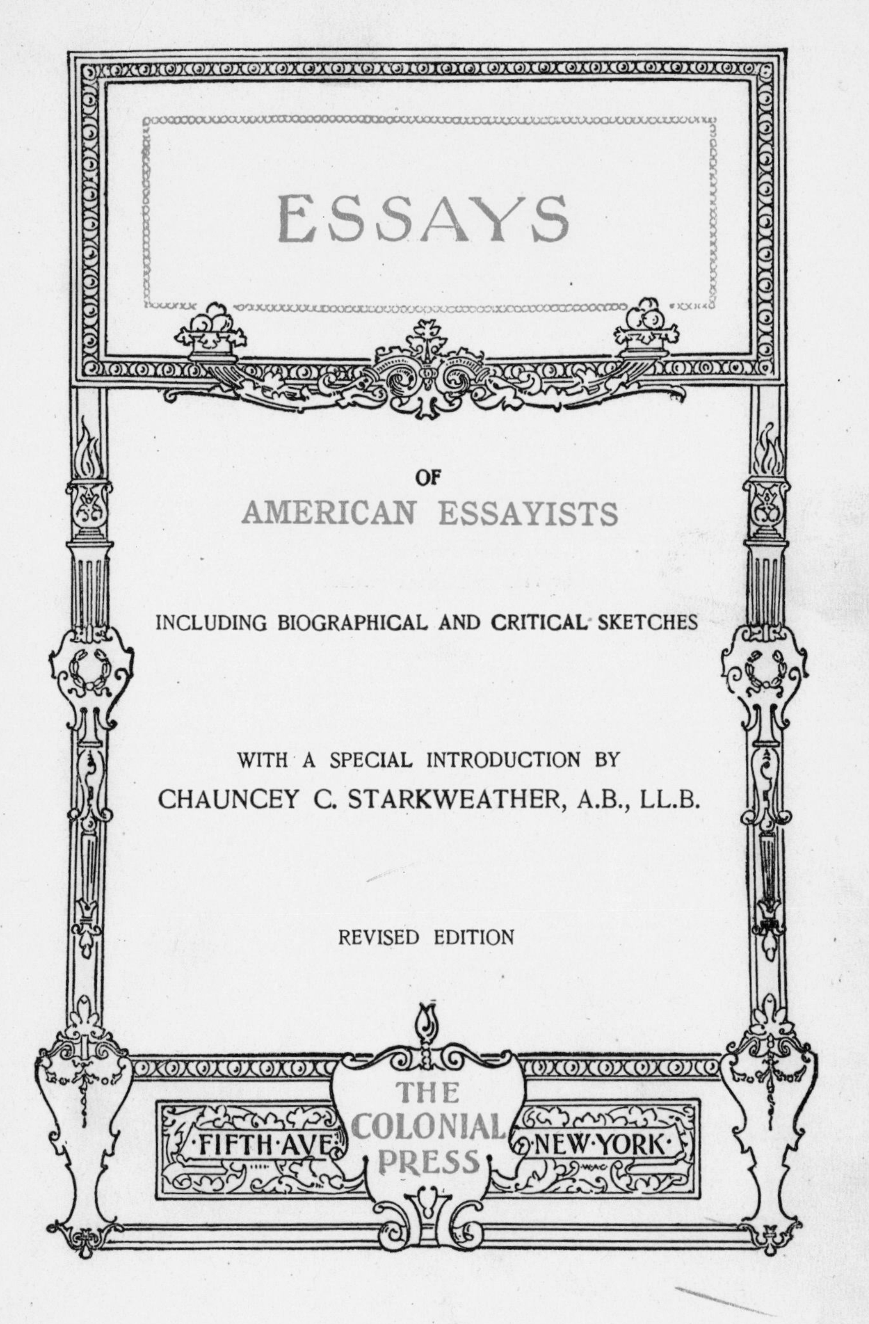

ESSAYS

OF

AMERICAN ESSAYISTS

INCLUDING BIOGRAPHICAL AND CRITICAL SKETCHES

WITH A SPECIAL INTRODUCTION BY

CHAUNCEY C. STARKWEATHER, A.B., LL.B.

REVISED EDITION

FIFTH AVE THE COLONIAL PRESS NEW YORK

SPECIAL INTRODUCTION

THE earliest American essayists were the clergymen. Those first days of the great republic were religious days. And although the pulpit was eminently spiritual, and fervid, and the devil was duly excoriated, and lessons of faith and humility were inculcated, yet those hour-long homilies were not all theology. Ethics, and manners, and social and national progress were discussed in sermons, which were in reality well-rounded essays. So that the influence of the pulpit became not only moral, but intellectual and even literary, as well. And the lecturers who came later, what was their mission but to spread the influence of the essay? Apart from polemics and in addition to politics and partisanship, they presented to well-filled halls throughout the country essays, essays, nothing but essays. And now the magazines, which visit every fireside, continue the cult and keep it well apace with poetry and fiction, far surpassing the former indeed in worth and quality. The essay then has ever been near to the American heart, has ever basked in public favor. And from the contingencies of our early days it could start full-panoplied and well-equipped. It had the culture of France and England as a fulcrum, and proceeded by main force to lift the taste of our early citizens from the merely utilitarian and the grubbing commonplace to a conception of the graceful and the beautiful. It was necessarily formative and educational. Its task was premeasured, foreordered. Those among the first essayists who were not in the pulpit might well have been, for they were ethical guides and pathfinders. And the statesmen and historians and poets who came to swell the list; they all wore the robe of the prophet and the teacher, even when dallying with lighter themes. It is well for our literature that the essayists have spoken. For whether one points to poetry or fiction or history or theology or science, in no category will he find an achievement of supremacy excelling that which the essayists have attained. Take even the greatest exemplars of our poetry and fiction, Poe and Hawthorne, in their lonely majesty of leadership. Their essays fall not far short of their lyrics and romances. To use a geographical metaphor, Poe's life was bounded on the north by sorrow, on the east by poverty, on the south by aspiration and on the west by calumny; his genius was unbounded. There are literary hyenas still prowling about his grave. But his pensive brow wears the garland of immortality. His soul was music and his very life-blood was purest art. His ear caught the cadences of that higher harmony which poets hear above the world's turmoil. In spite of detraction he is safely enshrined in memory while poetry shall live. Young poets will always have tears and roses for his grave.

And dreamy, inquisitve Hawthorne, probing and searching the human heart! There is the majesty of the seer about him. He takes one by the hand and leads him through enchanted palaces of art and whispers of the mysteries of life, and discloses the well-springs of character and motive. A favorite of the gods was he, dwelling high upon Olympus. Fancy his life at Salem among those quiet folk; shall we call them pygmies?

Bryant's style was pure and cold as a rivulet among his native hills. He was Nature's adept, knowing the language of flower and field and forest, the interpreter of natural beauty. A sweet, unruffled, high-bred quietude possessed him. He had the direct simplicity of Burns, with the lofty dignity of Wordsworth. He respected himself and his fellow-man, and dwelt ever " near to Nature's heart."

In Emerson the essay touched its highest pinnacle. Here is a teacher sent from God. His influence upon the people was incalculable and still is immeasurable. He had a high lesson for the people, and he taught it. His wisdom was needed. His exhortative utterances helped to stimulate the plodding common soul and raise it to loftier regions of thought and action. " Hitch your wagon to a star;" there is a dictum one could not by any chance forget. It burns into the memory and becomes a part of it. It is not merely remembered, it is assimilated, incorporated, absorbed. Emerson was a preacher in his essays. Humanity, morality, patriotism, these were his burdens, and he bore them to the end. He made the rostrum a second pulpit. He made culture a religion. He delved into the eternal verities, and refined the gold of thought for the many. He threshed and winnowed and garnered the golden grain of progress and high thinking, and gave it to the people. To-day hardly an essayist will dispute his leadership. His works will remain a storehouse of Christian ethics and promptings to high endeavor and a noble philosophy.

"A sweet and gentle soul," Emerson called Longfellow. To be loved by the young, ah, that is a great thing! Before the stress of the decades has wearied the heart and dimmed with tears the eyes expectant, to be then the chosen friend of youth, pure and holy in its Heavenly aspirations and its turnings toward the light! So is it with Longfellow, who sang in lute-tones, bard of the gentle, the musing, the refined. He was not sublime, he was more—he was human. The youth of the future will hold him to their hearts, as it gladly does in these current days of storm and stress.

Readers of the rising generation will never realize the extraordinary influence of Mrs. Stowe. Her cry was an evangel, a clarion-call, a battle hymn. The North and the South, reading her words, saw the camp-fires afar, heard the tread of serried columns, felt the onset of marshalled hosts. Into forty languages her book was translated. It was a golden bugle sounding the charge, but its notes have long since been hushed into the diapason of God-given fraternal peace, happy, forgiving national union and joyous concord.

Holmes was a born essayist. If Pope "lisped in numbers, for the numbers came," so the smiling philosopher of the breakfast-table wrote essays as naturally as the sun shines or the waters flow. Brilliant as a poet and novelist, able and beloved as a technical instructor, yet it was those cheery, bonny, playful papers, filled with the keenest wit and deepest feeling, recurring from month to month, essays in all but strict form, which endeared him to all hearts and made him indeed an autocrat.

"A gentleman of the old school;" how often do we hear this term misapplied! But it fits Curtis as gracefully as the folds of a toga enwrapped the form of a Roman senator. Here are courtliness and stately ease. Here is urbanity as dignified as an old court minuet. Here is a suggestion of the modern equivalent to "ruffs and cuffs, and farthingales and things." A sweet serenity and perfect taste pervade his pages, a charm like the odor of lavender which lingers about an ancient, forgotten, garret-hidden escritoire.

It is difficult for the present writer to speak of Whitman. In the first place, it seems to him something like praising Shakespeare, which appears not altogether a novel thing to do. And in the second place, he realizes that the "Whitman cult" is somewhat in advance of the times. But it is his belief that the coming centuries will place Walt Whitman high on the list of glorious names, the first voice of a united, crystallized, original America, a bard who sang democracy, our great citizenship, God-love, and the comradeship of the throbbing, suffering, hoping, majestic human heart.

Chauncey C. Starkweather

CONTENTS

ILLUSTRATIONS

THE WAY TO WEALTH

—

MORALS OF CHESS

—

BY

BENJAMIN FRANKLIN

BENJAMIN FRANKLIN

1706—1790

Benjamin Franklin was a statesman, a scientist, a philosopher, a philanthropist, and a man of affairs as well as a man of letters. In each capacity he achieved something more than ordinary success. Of a career so many-sided only a brief summary can here be given. He was born at Boston in 1706, and was the youngest of seventeen children. His father, a tallow-chandler, was a practical man, but to provide anything beyond an ordinary school education for his youngest son was beyond his means. Thus we find Franklin at the age of twelve apprenticed to his brother James, who printed and published the Boston "Gazette," the second newspaper published in America. At this period he was an eager reader, and whatever he read impressed him deeply, especially a volume of "The Spectator," which led him to cultivate Addison's delightful style. In a short time he began a series of anonymous contributions to his brother's paper, but the latter proving too hard a master he ran away and went to Philadelphia, where he began life for himself. A trip to London followed, but he was soon back in Philadelphia, and established himself as a printer in 1726.

Three years later he became the publisher and proprietor of the "Pennsylvania Gazette." For this publication Franklin, who was almost its sole contributor, wrote a large number of essays in the Addisonian vein. In 1732 he founded "Poor Richard's Almanac." This publication immediately attained a large circulation, and gave Franklin both fame and wealth. Its humor was genuine and irresistible, but what gave the work its greatest popularity and its enduring fame was the collection of wise saws and homely proverbs. While he did not claim entire originality for this work, it is conceded that the homely epigrammatic form that constitutes its chief charm was entirely his own. In 1758, during a period of unusual financial depression, Franklin made selections from this work, and published them in the form of a sermon by "Father Abraham." This was at once received with universal favor, was published in numerious editions in English, went through thirty editions in French, and was also translated into many other languages. It is best known under the title "The Way to Wealth," and is thoroughly characteristic of Franklin's style.

During this period the many-sidedness of Franklin's activity was amazing. He founded the Philadelphia library, the first subscription library in America; was one of the chief organizers of the educational institution afterwards known as the University of Pennsylvania; became Deputy Postmaster-General in 1753, and as such greatly improved the postal system of the colonies; and finally made his immortal discoveries in electricity. The work of Franklin in behalf of American independence is a matter of history. As early as 1754 he proposed a union of the colonies against the French and Indians. From 1757 to 1775 he was, except for a few months, the agent of Pennsylvania in England. From 1776 to 1785 he represented the American colonies in France, first as the agent of the revolutionary government, later as Minister of the United States. His work in this capacity was in its bearing and final results equalled only by that of Washington's armies. He was one of the signers of the Declaration of Independence, the treaty of alliance with France, and the treaty of peace. While in France he resumed literary work, and wrote for the amusement of his friends his charming "Bagatelles," of which "The Morals of Chess" is a good example. During this period he wrote his unfinished "Autobiography," the most important of his larger works. He continued active and influential till his death, in 1790, at the age of eighty-four.

THE WAY TO WEALTH

COURTEOUS reader, I have heard that nothing gives an author so great pleasure as to find his works respectfully quoted by others. Judge, then, how much I must have been gratified by an incident I am going to relate to you. I stopped my horse lately where a great number of people were collected at an auction of merchants' goods. The hour of the sale not being come, they were conversing on the badness of the times; and one of the company called to a plain, clean, old man, with white locks, "Pray, Father Abraham, what think you of the times? Will not these heavy taxes quite ruin the country? How shall we ever be able to pay them? What would you advise us to?" Father Abraham stood up and replied, "If you would have my advice, I will give it you in short; for 'A word to the wise is enough,' as Poor Richard says." They joined in desiring him to speak his mind, and gathering round him, he proceeded as follows:

"Friends," said he, "the taxes are indeed very heavy, and, if those laid on by the government were the only ones we had to pay, we might more easily discharge them; but we have many others, and much more grievous to some of us. We are taxed twice as much by our idleness, three times as much by our pride, and four times as much by our folly; and from these taxes the commissioners cannot ease or deliver us by allowing an abatement. However, let us hearken to good advice, and something may be done for us; 'God helps them that help themselves,' as Poor Richard says.

"I. It would be thought a hard government, that should tax its people one-tenth part of their time, to be employed in its service; but idleness taxes many of us much more; sloth, by bringing on diseases, absolutely shortens life. 'Sloth, like rust, consumes faster than labor wears; while the used key is always bright,' as Poor Richard says. 'But dost thou love life, then do not squander time, for that is the stuff life is made of,' as Poor Richard says. How much more than is necessary do we spend in sleep, forgetting, that 'The sleeping fox catches no poultry'; and that 'There will be sleeping enough in the grave,' as Poor Richard says.

"'If time be of all things the most precious, wasting time must be,' as Poor Richard says, 'the greatest prodigality'; since, as he elsewhere tells us, 'Lost time is never found again; and what we call time enough, always proves little enough.' Let us then up and be doing, and doing to the purpose; so by diligence shall we do more with less perplexity. 'Sloth makes all things difficult, but industry all easy'; and 'He that riseth late must trot all day, and shall scarce overtake his business at night'; while 'Laziness travels so slowly, that Poverty soon overtakes him. Drive thy business, let not that drive thee'; and 'Early to bed, and early to rise, makes a man healthy, wealthy, and wise,' as Poor Richard says.

"So what signifies wishing and hoping for better times? We may make these times better, if we bestir ourselves. 'Industry need not wish, and he that lives upon hopes will die fasting. There are no gains without pains; then help, hands, for I have no lands'; or, if I have, they are smartly taxed. 'He that hath a trade hath an estate; and he that hath a calling, hath an office of profit and honor,' as Poor Richard says; but then the trade must be worked at, and the calling followed, or neither the estate nor the office will enable us to pay our taxes. If we are industrious, we shall never starve; for, 'At the workingman's house hunger looks in, but dares not enter.' Nor will the bailiff or the constable enter, for 'Industry pays debts, while despair increaseth them.' What though you have found no treasure, nor has any rich relation left you a legacy, 'Diligence is the mother of good luck, and God gives all things to industry. Then plough deep while sluggards sleep, and you shall have corn to sell and to keep.' Work while it is called to-day, for you know not how much you may be hindered to-morrow. 'One to-day is worth two to-morrows,' as Poor Richard says; and further, 'Never leave that till to-morrow which you can do to-day.' If you were a servant, would you not be ashamed that a good master should catch you idle? Are you then your own master? Be ashamed to catch yourself idle, when there is so much to be done for yourself, your family, your country, and your king. Handle your tools without mittens; remember, that 'The cat in gloves catches no mice,' as Poor Richard says. It is true there is much to be done, and perhaps you are weak-handed; but stick to it steadily, and you will see great effects; for 'Constant dropping wears away stones'; and 'By diligence and patience the mouse ate in two the cable'; and 'Little strokes fell great oaks.'

"Methinks I hear some of you say, 'Must a man afford himself no leisure?' I will tell thee, my friend, what Poor Richard says: 'Employ thy time well, if thou meanest to gain leisure; and, since thou art not sure of a minute, throw not away an hour.' Leisure is time for doing something useful; this leisure the diligent man will obtain, but the lazy man never; for 'A life of leisure and a life of laziness are two things. Many, without labor, would live by their wits only, but they break for want of stock'; whereas, industry gives comfort, and plenty, and respect. 'Fly pleasures, and they will follow you. The diligent spinner has a large shift; and now I have a sheep and a cow, everybody bids me good morrow.'

"II. But with our industry we must likewise be steady, settled, and careful, and oversee our own affairs, with our own eyes, and not trust too much to others; for, as Poor Richard says,

> 'I never saw an oft-removed tree,
> Nor yet an oft-removed family,
> That throve so well as those that settled be.'

And again, 'Three removes are as bad as a fire'; and again, 'Keep thy shop, and thy shop will keep thee'; and again, 'If you would have your business done, go; if not, send.' And again,

> 'He that by the plough would thrive,
> Himself must either hold or drive.'

And again, 'The eye of a master will do more work than both his hands'; and again, 'Want of care does us more damage than want of knowledge'; and again, 'Not to oversee workmen is to leave them your purse open.' Trusting too much to others' care is the ruin of many; for 'In the affairs of this world men are saved, not by faith, but by the want of it'; but a man's own care is profitable; for, 'If you would have a faithful servant, and one that you like, serve yourself. A little neglect may breed great mischief; for want of a nail the shoe was lost; for want of a shoe the horse was lost; and for want of a horse the rider was lost, being overtaken and slain by the enemy; all for want of a little care about a horseshoe nail.'

"III. So much for industry, my friends, and attention to one's own business; but to these we must add frugality, if we would make our industry more certainly successful. A man may, if he knows not how to save as he gets, keep his nose all his life to the grindstone, and die not worth a groat at last. 'A fat kitchen makes a lean will'; and

> 'Many estates are spent in the getting,
> Since women for tea forsook spinning and knitting,
> And men for punch forsook hewing and splitting.'

'If you would be wealthy, think of saving as well as of getting. The Indies have not made Spain rich, because her outgoes are greater than her incomes.'

"Away then with your expensive follies, and you will not then have so much cause to complain of hard times, heavy taxes, and chargeable families; for

> 'Women and wine, game and deceit,
> Make the wealth small and the want great.'

And further, 'What maintains one vice would bring up two children.' You may think, perhaps, that a little tea, or a little punch now and then, diet a little more costly, clothes a little finer, and a little entertainment now and then, can be no great matter; but remember, 'Many a little makes a mickle.' Beware of little expenses; 'A small leak will sink a great ship,' as Poor Richard says; and again, 'Who dainties love, shall beggars prove'; and moreover, 'Fools make feasts, and wise men eat them.'

"Here you are all got together at this sale of fineries and knick-knacks. You call them goods; but, if you do not take care, they will prove evils to some of you. You expect they will be sold cheap, and perhaps they may for less than they cost; but, if you have no occasion for them, they must be dear to you. Remember what Poor Richard says: 'Buy what thou hast no need of, and ere long thou shalt sell thy necessaries.' And again, 'At a great pennyworth pause a while.' He means, that perhaps the cheapness is apparent only, and not real; or the bargain, by straitening thee in thy business, may do thee more harm than good. For in another place he says, 'Many have been ruined by buying good pennyworths.' Again, 'It is foolish to lay out money in a purchase of repentance'; and yet this folly is practised every day at auctions, for want of minding the 'Almanac.'[1] Many a one, for the sake of finery on the back, has gone with a hungry belly and half-starved their families. 'Silks and satins, scarlet and velvets, put out the kitchen fire,' as Poor Richard says.

"These are not the necessaries of life; they can scarcely be called the conveniences; and yet, only because thy look pretty, how many want to have them! By these, and other extravagances, the genteel are reduced to poverty, and forced to borrow of those whom they formerly despised, but who, through industry and frugality, have maintained their standing; in which case it appears plainly, that 'A ploughman on his legs is higher than a gentleman on his knees,' as Poor Richard says. Perhaps they have had a small estate left them, which they knew not the getting of; they think, 'It is day, and will never be night'; that a little to be spent out of so much is not worth minding; but 'Always taking out of the meal-tub, and never putting in, soon comes to the bottom,' as Poor Richard says; and then, 'When the well is dry, they know the worth of water.' But this they might have known before, if they had taken his advice. 'If you would know the value of money, go and try to borrow some; for he that goes a-borrowing goes a-sorrowing,' as Poor Richard says; and indeed so does he that lends to such people, when he goes to get it in again. Poor Dick further advises and says,

> 'Fond pride of dress is sure a very curse;
> Ere fancy you consult, consult your purse.'

And again, 'Pride is as loud a beggar as Want, and a great deal more saucy.' When you have bought one fine thing, you must

[1] This refers to "Poor Richard's Almanac," which was published by Benjamin Franklin under the nom de plume of Richard Saunders. "Poor Richard's Almanac" was issued in 1732 and published annually for about twenty-five years. It attained great popularity.—EDITOR.

buy ten more, that your appearance may be all of a piece; but Poor Dick says, 'It is easier to suppress the first desire, than to satisfy all that follow it.' And it is as truly folly for the poor to ape the rich, as for the frog to swell in order to equal the ox.

> 'Vessels large may venture more,
> But little boats should keep near shore.'

It is, however, a folly soon punished; for as Poor Richard says, 'Pride that dines on vanity, sups on contempt. Pride breakfasted with Plenty, dined with Poverty, and supped with Infamy.' And, after all, of what use is this pride of appearance, for which so much is risked, so much is suffered? It cannot promote health, nor ease pain; it makes no increase of merit in the person; it creates envy; it hastens misfortune.

"But what madness must it be to run in debt for these superfluities? We are offered, by the terms of this sale, six months' credit, and that, perhaps, has induced some of us to attend it, because we cannot spare the ready money, and hope now to be fine without it. But, ah! think what you do when you run in debt; you give to another power over your liberty. If you cannot pay at the time, you will be ashamed to see your creditor; you will be in fear when you speak to him; you will make poor, pitiful, sneaking excuses, and, by degrees, come to lose your veracity, and sink into base, downright lying; for 'The second vice is lying, the first is running in debt,' as Poor Richard says; and again, to the same purpose, 'Lying rides upon Debt's back': whereas a free-born Englishman ought not to be ashamed nor afraid to see or speak to any man living. But poverty often deprives a man of all spirit and virtue. 'It is hard for an empty bag to stand upright.'

"What would you think of that prince, or of that government, who should issue an edict forbidding you to dress like a gentleman or gentlewoman, on pain of imprisonment or servitude? Would you not say that you were free, have a right to dress as you please, and that such an edict would be a breach of your privileges, and such a government tyrannical? And yet you are about to put yourself under such tyranny, when you run in debt for such dress! Your creditor has authority, at his pleasure, to deprive you of your liberty, by confining you in jail till you shall be able to pay him. When you have got your bargain, you may, perhaps, think little of payment; but, as Poor Richard says, 'Creditors have better memories than debtors; creditors are a superstitious sect, great observers of set days and times.' The day comes round before you are aware, and the demand is made before you are prepared to satisfy it; or, if you bear your debt in mind, the term, which at first seemed so long, will, as it lessens, appear extremely short. Time will seem to have added wings to his heels as well as his shoulders. 'Those have a short Lent who owe money to be paid at Easter.' At present, perhaps, you may think yourselves in thriving circumstances, and that you can bear a little extravagance without injury; but

> 'For age and want save while you may;
> No morning sun lasts a whole day.'

Gain may be temporary and uncertain, but ever, while you live, expense is constant and certain; and 'It is easier to build two chimneys, than to keep one in fuel,' as Poor Richard says; so, 'Rather go to bed supperless than rise in debt.'

> 'Get what you can, and what you get hold;
> 'Tis the stone that will turn all your lead into gold.'

And, when you have got the philosopher's stone, sure you will no longer complain of bad times, or the difficulty of paying taxes.

"IV. This doctrine, my friends, is reason and wisdom; but, after all, do not depend too much upon your own industry, and frugality, and prudence, though excellent things; for they may all be blasted, without the blessing of Heaven; and, therefore, ask that blessing humbly, and be not uncharitable to those that at present seem to want it, but comfort and help them. Remember, Job suffered, and was afterwards prosperous.

"And now, to conclude, 'Experience keeps a dear school, but fools will learn in no other,' as Poor Richard says, and scarce in that; for, it is true, 'We may give advice, but we cannot give conduct.' However, remember this, 'They that will not be counselled, cannot be helped'; and further, that, 'If you will not hear Reason, she will surely rap your knuckles,' as Poor Richard says."

Thus the old gentleman ended his harangue. The people heard it, and approved the doctrine; and immediately practised the contrary, just as if it had been a common sermon; for the auction opened, and they began to buy extravagantly. I found the good man had thoroughly studied my "Almanacs," and digested all I had dropped on these topics during the course of twenty-five years. The frequent mention he made of me must have tired anyone else; but my vanity was wonderfully delighted with it, though I was conscious that not a tenth part of the wisdom was my own, which he ascribed to me, but rather the gleanings that I had made of the sense of all ages and nations. However, I resolved to be the better for the echo of it; and, though I had at first determined to buy stuff for a new coat, I went away resolved to wear my old one a little longer. Reader, if thou wilt do the same, thy profit will be as great as mine.

MORALS OF CHESS

PLAYING at chess is the most ancient and most universal game known among men; for its original is beyond the memory of history, and it has, for numberless ages, been the amusement of all the civilized nations of Asia, the Persians, the Indians, and the Chinese. Europe has had it above a thousand years; the Spaniards have spread it over their part of America; and it has lately begun to make its appearance in the United States. It is so interesting in itself as not to need the view of gain to induce engaging in it; and thence it is seldom played for money. Those, therefore, who have leisure for such diversions, cannot find one that is more innocent; and the following piece, written with a view to correct (among a few young friends) some little improprieties in the practice of it, shows at the same time that it may, in its effects on the mind, be not merely innocent, but advantageous, to the vanquished as well as the victor.

The game of chess is not merely an idle amusement. Several very valuable qualities of the mind, useful in the course of human life, are to be acquired or strengthened by it, so as to become habits, ready on all occasions. For life is a kind of chess, in which we have often points to gain, and competitors or adversaries to contend with, and in which there is a vast variety of good and evil events, that are in some degree the effects of prudence or the want of it. By playing at chess, then, we may learn—

I. *Foresight,* which looks a little into futurity, and considers the consequences that may attend an action; for it is continually occurring to the player, "If I move this piece, what will be the advantage of my new situation? What use can my adversary make of it to annoy me? What other moves can I make to support it, and to defend myself from his attacks?"

II. *Circumspection,* which surveys the whole chessboard, or scene of action; the relations of the several pieces and situations, the dangers they are respectively exposed to, the several possibilities of their aiding each other, the probabilities that the adversary may make this or that move, and attack this or the other piece, and what different means can be used to avoid his stroke, or turn its consequences against him.

III. *Caution,* not to make our moves too hastily. This habit is best acquired by observing strictly the laws of the game; such as, "If you touch a piece, you must move it somewhere; if you set it down, you must let it stand"; and it is therefore best that these rules should be observed, as the game thereby becomes more the image of human life, and particularly of war; in which, if you have incautiously put yourself into a bad and dangerous position, you cannot obtain your enemy's leave to withdraw your troops, and place them more securely, but you must abide all the consequences of your rashness.

And, lastly, we learn by chess the habit of not being discouraged by present appearances in the state of our affairs, the habit of hoping for a favorable change, and that of persevering in the search of resources. The game is so full of events, there is such a variety of turns in it, the fortune of it is so subject to sudden vicissitudes, and one so frequently, after long contemplation, discovers the means of extricating one's self from a supposed insurmountable difficulty, that one is encouraged to continue the contest to the last, in hopes of victory by our own skill, or at least of getting a stale-mate,[1] by the negligence of our adversary. And whoever considers, what in chess he often sees instances of, that particular pieces of success are apt to produce presumption, and its consequent inattention, by which the losses may be recovered, will learn not to be too much discouraged by the present success of his adversary, nor to despair of final good fortune upon every little check he receives in the pursuit of it.

That we may therefore be induced more frequently to choose this beneficial amusement, in preference to others which are not attended with the same advantages, every circumstance which may increase the pleasures of it should be regarded; and every action or word that is unfair, disrespectful, or that in any way may give uneasiness, should be avoided, as contrary to the im-

[1] When the King is so situated that he cannot move without going into check, and is not in check at the time, it is termed stale mate, which counts as a drawn game.

mediate intention of both the players, which is to pass the time agreeably.

Therefore, first, if it is agreed to play according to the strict rules, then those rules are to be exactly observed by both parties, and should not be insisted on for one side, while deviated from by the other, for this is not equitable.

Secondly, if it is agreed not to observe the rules exactly, but one party demands indulgences, he should then be as willing to allow them to the other.

Thirdly, no false move should ever be made to extricate yourself out of difficulty, or to gain an advantage. There can be no pleasure in playing with a person once detected in such unfair practice.

Fourthly, if your adversary is long in playing, you ought not to hurry him, or express any uneasiness at his delay. You should not sing, nor whistle, nor look at your watch, nor take up a book to read, nor make a tapping with your feet on the floor, or with your fingers on the table, nor do anything that may disturb his attention. For all these things displease; and they do not show your skill in playing, but your craftiness or your rudeness.

Fifthly, you ought not to endeavor to amuse and deceive your adversary, by pretending to have made bad moves, and saying, that you have now lost the game, in order to make him secure and careless, and inattentive to your schemes; for this is fraud and deceit, not skill in the game.

Sixthly, you must not, when you have gained a victory, use any triumphing or insulting expression, nor show too much pleasure; but endeavor to console your adversary, and make him less dissatisfied with himself, by every kind of civil expression that may be used with truth, such as, "You understand the game better than I, but you are a little inattentive"; or, "You play too fast"; or, "You had the best of the game, but something happened to divert your thoughts, and that turned it in my favor."

Seventhly, if you are a spectator while others play, observe the most perfect silence. For, if you give advice, you offend both parties, him against whom you give it, because it may cause the loss of his game, him in whose favor you may give it, because, though it be good, and he follows it, he loses the pleasure he might have had, if you had permitted him to think until it had occurred to himself. Even after a move or moves, you must not, by replacing the pieces, show how they might have been placed better; for that displeases, and may occasion disputes and doubts about their true situation. All talking to the players lessens or diverts their attention, and is therefore unpleasing. Nor should you give the least hint to either party, by any kind of noise or motion. If you do, you are unworthy to be a spectator. If you have a mind to exercise or show your judgment, do it in playing your own game, when you have an opportunity, not in criticising, or meddling with, or counselling the play of others.

Lastly, if the game is not to be played rigorously, according to the rules above mentioned, then moderate your desire of victory over your adversary, and be pleased with one over yourself. Snatch not eagerly at every advantage offered by his unskilfulness or inattention; but point out to him kindly, that by such a move he places or leaves a piece in danger and unsupported; that by another he will put his king in a perilous situation, etc. By this generous civility (so opposite to the unfairness above forbidden) you may, indeed, happen to lose the game to your opponent; but you will win, what is better, his esteem, his respect, and his affection, together with the silent approbation and good-will of impartial spectators.

SELF-CULTURE

BY

WILLIAM ELLERY CHANNING

WILLIAM ELLERY CHANNING

1780—1842

The greatest organizer of the Unitarian movement in America, William Ellery Chaning, was born at Newport, Rhode Island, in 1780. He was prepared for college under the tuition of his uncle, the Rev. Henry Channing, and entered Harvard in 1794. He was precocious as a boy, and later thorough as a student, but of a delicate constitution. When only twenty-three years old he became pastor of the Federal Street Church in Boston, and in a few years had won a wide fame for eloquence, and put himself at the head of the Unitarian party in the schism of the Congregational Church. In 1822 Channing made an extended tour in Europe, bringing back with him perhaps more of the spirit of Old World culture than any American that had been abroad.

Not only were his pulpit discourses powerful and stimulating far beyond those of any of his contemporaries, still in bondage to the narrow theology of the Mathers, but his published writings on topics other than divinity were widely read and appreciated. In his essay on "Self-Culture" Channing advocated the study of foreign literature, and insisted strongly on the importance of a more thorough culture. He looked upon self-culture as a religious duty, and pointed out and defined the connection between moral and intellectual culture. In his admirable essays on Napoleon, Milton and Fénelon, Dr. Channing contributed to American literature critical essays of genuine merit. These articles, which were first published in the "Christian Examiner," broadened the literary horizon of many American thinkers, and thus incited many to the attainment of that culture for which Channing so earnestly pleaded.

Dr. Channing was a friend of the father of Emerson, and a classmate and friend of the father of Longfellow. His influence on the minds of his contemporaries was remarkable, and can only be appreciated at the present day by remembering what a dearth of real literary ability there was in this country in his time. In 1830 Dr. Channing published "Discourses, Reviews, and Miscellanies." In later collections of his works many additional articles were printed, bringing the complete edition of his works up to six volumes. He died at Bennington, Vermont, in 1842.

SELF-CULTURE

MY RESPECTED FRIENDS: By the invitation of the committee of arrangements for the Franklin Lectures I now appear before you to offer some remarks introductory to this course.[1] My principal inducement for doing so is my deep interest in those of my fellow-citizens for whom these lectures are principally designed. I understood that they were to be attended chiefly by those who are occupied by manual labor; and, hearing this, I did not feel myself at liberty to decline the service to which I had been invited. I wished by compliance to express my sympathy with this large portion of my race. I wished to express my sense of obligation to those from whose industry and skill I derive almost all the comforts of life. I wished still more to express my joy in the efforts they are making for their own improvement, and my firm faith in their success. These motives will give a particular character and bearing to some of my remarks. I shall speak occasionally as among those who live by the labor of their hands. But I shall not speak as one separated from them. I belong rightfully to the great fraternity of working men. Happily in this community we all are bred and born to work; and this honorable mark, set on us all, should bind together the various portions of the community.

I have expressed my strong interest in the mass of the people; and this is founded, not on their usefulness to the community, so much as on what they are in themselves. Their condition is indeed obscure; but their importance is not on this account a whit the less. The multitude of men cannot, from the nature of the case, be distinguished; for the very idea of distinction is, that a man stands out from the multitude. They make little noise and draw little notice in their narrow spheres of action; but still they have their full pro-

[1] This essay was originally delivered at Boston in September, 1838, as an introductory address to the Franklin Lectures.

portion of personal worth and even of greatness. Indeed every man, in every condition, is great. It is only our own diseased sight which makes him little. A man is great as a man, be he where or what he may. The grandeur of his nature turns to insignificance all outward distinctions. His powers of intellect, of conscience, of love, of knowing God, of perceiving the beautiful, of acting on his own mind, on outward nature, and on his fellow-creatures—these are glorious prerogatives. Through the vulgar error of undervaluing what is common we are apt indeed to pass these by as of little worth. But as in the outward creation, so in the soul, the common is the most precious. Science and art may invent splendid modes of illuminating the apartments of the opulent; but these are all poor and worthless compared with the common light which the sun sends into all our windows, which he pours freely, impartially over hill and valley, which kindles daily the eastern and western sky; and so the common lights of reason, and conscience, and love, are of more worth and dignity than the rare endowments which give celebrity to a few. Let us not disparage that nature which is common to all men; for no thought can measure its grandeur. It is the image of God, the image even of his infinity, for no limits can be set to its unfolding. He who possesses the divine powers of the soul is a great being, be his place what it may. You may clothe him with rags, may immure him in a dungeon, may chain him to slavish tasks. But he is still great. You may shut him out of your houses; but God opens to him heavenly mansions. He makes no show indeed in the streets of a splendid city; but a clear thought, a pure affection, a resolute act of a virtuous will, have a dignity of quite another kind, and far higher than accumulations of brick and granite and plaster and stucco, however cunningly put together, or though stretching far beyond our sight. Nor is this all. If we pass over this grandeur of our common nature, and turn our thoughts to that comparative greatness, which draws chief attention, and which consists in the decided superiority of the individual to the general standard of power and character, we shall find this as free and frequent a growth among the obscure and unnoticed as in more conspicuous walks of life. The truly great are to be found everywhere, nor is it easy to say in what condition they spring up most plentifully. Real greatness has nothing to do with a man's sphere. It does not lie in the magnitude of his outward agency, in the extent of the effects which he produces. The greatest men may do comparatively little abroad. Perhaps the greatest in our city at this moment are buried in obscurity. Grandeur of character lies wholly in force of soul, that is, in the force of thought, moral principle, and love, and this may be found in the humblest condition of life. A man brought up to an obscure trade, and hemmed in by the wants of a growing family, may, in his narrow sphere, perceive more clearly, discriminate more keenly, weigh evidence more wisely, seize on the right means more decisively, and have more presence of mind in difficulty, than another who has accumulated vast stores of knowledge by laborious study; and he has more of intellectual greatness. Many a man who has gone but a few miles from home understands human nature better, detects motives and weighs character more sagaciously, than another who has travelled over the known world, and made a name by his reports of different countries. It is force of thought which measures intellectual, and so it is force of principle which measures moral greatness, that highest of human endowments, that brightest manifestation of the Divinity. The greatest man is he who chooses the right with invincible resolution, who resists the sorest temptations from within and without, who bears the heaviest burdens cheerfully, who is calmest in storms, and most fearless under menace and frowns, whose reliance on truth, on virtue, on God, is most unfaltering; and is this a greatness which is apt to make a show, or which is most likely to abound in conspicuous station? The solemn conflicts of reason with passion; the victories of moral and religious principle over urgent and almost irresistible solicitations to self-indulgence; the hardest sacrifices of duty, those of deep-seated affection and of the heart's fondest hopes; the consolations, hopes, joys, and peace of disappointed, persecuted, scorned, deserted virtue—these are of course unseen; so that the true greatness of human life is almost wholly out of sight. Perhaps in our presence, the most heroic deed on earth is done in some silent spirit, the loftiest purpose cherished, the most generous sacrifice made, and we do not suspect it. I believe this greatness to be most common among the multitude, whose names are never heard. Among common people will be found more of hardship borne manfully, more of unvarnished truth, more of religious trust, more of that generosity which gives what the giver needs himself, and more of a wise estimate of life and death, than among the more prosperous. And even in regard to influence over other beings, which is thought the peculiar prerogative of distinguished station, I believe that the difference between the conspicuous and the obscure does not amount to much. Influence is to be measured, not by the extent of surface it covers, but by its kind. A man may spread his mind, his feelings, and opinions, through a great extent; but if his mind be a low one, he manifests no greatness. A wretched artist may fill a city with daubs, and by a false, showy style achieve a reputation; but the man of genius, who leaves behind him one grand picture, in which immortal beauty is embodied, and which is silently to spread a true taste in his art, exerts an incomparably higher influence. Now the noblest influence on earth is that exerted on character; and he who puts forth this does a great work, no matter how narrow or obscure his sphere. The father and mother of an unnoticed family, who, in their seclusion, awaken the mind of one child to the idea and love of perfect goodness, who awaken in him a strength of will to repel all temptation, and who send him out prepared to profit by the conflicts of life, surpass in influence a Napoleon breaking the world to his sway. And not only is their work higher in kind; who knows but that they are doing a greater work even as to extent of surface than the conqueror? Who knows but that the being whom they inspire with holy and disinterested principles may communicate himself to others; and that, by a spreading agency, of which they were the silent origin, improvements may spread through a nation, through the world? In these remarks you will see why I feel and express a deep interest in the obscure, in the mass of men. The distinctions of society vanish before the light of these truths. I attach myself to the multitude, not because they are voters and have political power; but because they are men, and have within their reach the most glorious prizes of humanity.

In this country the mass of the people are distinguished by possessing means of improvement, of self-culture, possessed nowhere else. To incite them to the use of these is to render them the best service they can receive. Accordingly, I have chosen for the subject of this lecture Self-Culture, or the care which every man owes to himself, to the unfolding and perfecting of his nature. I consider this topic as particularly appropriate to the introduction of a course of lectures, in consequence of a common disposition to regard these and other like means of instruction as able of themselves to carry forward the hearer. Lectures have their use. They stir up many who, but for such outward appeals, might have slumbered to the end of life. But let it be remembered that little is to be gained simply by coming to this place once a week, and giving up the mind for an hour to be wrought upon by a teacher. Unless we are roused to act upon ourselves, unless we engage in the work of self-improvement, unless we purpose strenuously to form and elevate our own minds, unless what we hear is made a part of ourselves by conscientious reflection, very little permanent good is received.

Self-culture, I am aware, is a topic too extensive for a single discourse, and I shall be able to present but a few views which seem to me most important. My aim will be, to give first the idea of self-culture, next its means, and then to consider some objections to the leading views which I am now to lay before you.

Before entering on the discussion, let me offer one remark. Self-culture is something possible. It is not a dream. It has foundations in our nature. Without this conviction the speaker will but declaim, and the hearer listen without profit. There are two powers of the human soul which make self-culture possible—the self-searching and the self-forming power. We have first the faculty of turning the mind on itself; of recalling its past, and watching its present operations; of learning its various capacities and susceptibilities, what it can do and bear, what it can enjoy and suffer; and of thus learning in general what our nature is, and what it was made for. It is worthy of observation that we are able to discern not only what we already are, but what we may become, to see in ourselves germs and promises of a growth to which no bounds can be set, to dart beyond what we have actually gained to the idea of perfection as the end of our being. It is by this self-comprehending power that we are distinguished from the brutes, which give no signs of looking into themselves. Without this there would be no self-culture, for we should not know the work to be done; and one reason why self-culture is so little proposed is, that so few penetrate into their own nature. To most men their own spirits are shadowy, unreal, compared with what is outward. When they happen to cast a glance inward, they see there only a dark, vague chaos. They distinguish, perhaps, some violent passion, which has driven them to injurious excess; but their highest powers hardly attract a thought; and thus multitudes live and die as truly strangers to themselves as to countries of which they have heard the name, but which human foot has never trodden.

But self-culture is possible, not only because we can enter into and search ourselves. We have a still nobler power, that of acting on, determining, and forming ourselves. This is a fearful as well as glorious endowment, for it is the ground of human responsibility. We have the power not only of tracing our powers, but of guiding and impelling them; not only of watching our possessions, but of controlling them; not only of seeing our faculties grow, but of applying to them means and influences to aid their growth. We can stay or change the current of thought. We can concentrate the intellect on objects which we wish to comprehend. We can fix our eyes on perfection, and make almost everything speed towards it. This is, indeed, a noble prerogative of our nature. Possessing this, it matters little what or where we are now, for we can conquer a better lot, and even be happier for starting from the lowest point. Of all the discoveries which men need to make, the most important, at the present moment, is that of the self-forming power treasured up in themselves. They little suspect its extent, as little as the savage apprehends the energy which the mind is created to exert on the material world. It transcends in importance all our power over outward nature. There is more of divinity in it than in the force which impels the outward universe; and yet how little we comprehend it! How it slumbers in most men unsuspected, unused! This makes self-culture possible, and binds it on us as a solemn duty.

I. I am first to unfold the idea of self-culture; and this, in its most general form, may easily be seized. To cultivate anything, be it a plant, an animal, a mind, is to make grow.

Growth, expansion, is the end. Nothing admits culture but that which has a principle of life, capable of being expanded. He, therefore, who does what he can to unfold all his powers and capacities, especially his nobler ones, so as to become a well-proportioned, vigorous, excellent, happy being, practices self-culture.

This culture, of course, has various branches corresponding to the different capacities of human nature; but, though various, they are intimately united, and make progress together. The soul, which our philosophy divides into various capacities, is still one essence, one life; and it exerts at the same moment, and blends in the same act, its various energies of thought, feeling, and volition. Accordingly, in a wise self-culture, all the principles of our nature grow at once by joint, harmonious action, just as all parts of the plant are unfolded together. When, therefore, you hear of different branches of self-improvement, you will not think of them as distinct processes going on independently of each other, and requiring each its own separate means. Still a distinct consideration of these is needed to a full comprehension of the subject, and these I shall proceed to unfold.

First, self-culture is moral, a branch of singular importance. When a man looks into himself, he discovers two distinct orders or kinds of principles, which it behooves him especially to comprehend. He discovers desires, appetites, passions, which terminate in himself, which crave and seek his own interest, gratification, distinction; and he discovers another principle, an antagonist to these, which is impartial, disinterested, universal, enjoining on him a regard to the rights and happiness of other beings, and laying on him obligations which must be discharged, cost what they may, or however they may clash with his particular pleasure or gain. No man, however narrowed to his own interest, however hardened by selfishness, can deny that there springs up within him a great idea in opposition to interest, the idea of duty, that an inward voice calls him, more or less distinctly, to revere and exercise impartial justice and universal good-will. This disinterested principle in human nature we call sometimes reason, sometimes conscience, sometimes the moral sense or faculty. But, be its name what it may, it is a real principle in each of us, and it is the supreme power within us, to be cultivated above all others, for on its culture the right development of all others depends. The passions indeed may be stronger than the conscience, may lift up a louder voice; but their clamor differs wholly from the tone of command in which the conscience speaks. They are not clothed with its authority, its binding power. In their very triumphs they are rebuked by the moral principle, and often cower before its still, deep, menacing voice. No part of self-knowledge is more important than to discern clearly these two great principles, the self-seeking and the disinterested; and the most important part of self-culture is to depress the former, and to exalt the latter, or to enthrone the sense of duty within us. There are no limits to the growth of this moral force in man, if he will cherish it faithfully. There have been men, whom no power in the universe could turn from the right, by whom death in its most dreadful forms has been less dreaded than transgression of the inward law of universal justice and love.

In the next place, self-culture is religious. When we look into ourselves we discover powers which link us with this outward, visible, finite, ever-changing world. We have sight and other senses to discern, and limbs and various faculties to secure and appropriate the material creation. And we have, too, a power which cannot stop at what we see and handle, at what exists within the bounds of space and time, which seeks for the infinite, uncreated cause, which cannot rest till it ascend to the eternal, all-comprehending mind. This we call the religious principle, and its grandeur cannot be exaggerated by human language; for it marks out a being destined for higher communion than with the visible universe. To develop this is eminently to educate ourselves. The true idea of God, unfolded clearly and livingly within us, and moving us to adore and obey him, and to aspire after likeness to him, is the noblest growth in human, and, I may add, in celestial natures. The religious principle and the moral are intimately connected, and grow together. The former is indeed the perfection and highest manifestation of the latter. They are both disinterested. It is the essence of true religion to recognize and adore in God the attributes of impartial justice and universal love, and to hear him commanding us in the conscience to become what we adore.

Again. Self-culture is intellectual. We cannot look into

ourselves without discovering the intellectual principle, the power which thinks, reasons, and judges, the power of seeking and acquiring truth. This, indeed, we are in no danger of overlooking. The intellect being the great instrument by which men compass their wishes, it draws more attention than any of our other powers. When we speak to men of improving themselves, the first thought which occurs to them is, that they must cultivate their understanding, and get knowledge and skill. By education, men mean almost exclusively intellectual training. For this, schools and colleges are instituted, and to this the moral and religious discipline of the young is sacrificed. Now I reverence, as much as any man, the intellect; but let us never exalt it above the moral principle. With this it is most intimately connected. In this its culture is founded, and to exalt this is its highest aim. Whoever desires that his intellect may grow up to soundness, to healthy vigor, must begin with moral discipline. Reading and study are not enough to perfect the power of thought. One thing above all is needful, and that is, the disinterestedness which is the very soul of virtue. To gain truth, which is the great object of the understanding, I must seek it disinterestedly. Here is the first and grand condition of intellectual progress. I must choose to receive the truth, no matter how it bears on myself. I must follow it, no matter where it leads, what interests it opposes, to what persecution or loss it lays me open, from what party it severs me, or to what party it allies. Without this fairness of mind, which is only another phrase for disinterested love of truth, great native powers of understanding are perverted and led astray; genius runs wild; "the light within us becomes darkness." The subtlest reasoners, for want of this, cheat themselves as well as others, and become entangled in the web of their own sophistry. It is a fact well known in the history of science and philosophy, that men, gifted by nature with singular intelligence, have broached the grossest errors, and even sought to undermine the grand primitive truths on which human virtue, dignity, and hope depend. And, on the other hand, I have known instances of men of naturally moderate powers of mind who, by a disinterested love of truth and their fellow-creatures, have gradually risen to no small force and enlargement of thought. Some of the most useful teachers in the pulpit and in schools have owed their power of enlightening others, not so much to any natural superiority as to the simplicity, impartiality, and disinterestedness of their minds, to their readiness to live and die for the truth. A man who rises above himself looks from an eminence on nature and providence, on society and life. Thought expands, as by a natural elasticity, when the pressure of selfishness is removed. The moral and religious principles of the soul, generously cultivated, fertilize the intellect. Duty, faithfully performed, opens the mind to truth, both being of one family, alike immutable, universal, and everlasting.

I have enlarged on this subject, because the connection between moral and intellectual culture is often overlooked, and because the former is often sacrificed to the latter. The exaltation of talent, as it is called, above virtue and religion, is the curse of the age. Education is now chiefly a stimulus to learning, and thus men acquire power without the principles which alone make it a good. Talent is worshipped; but, if divorced from rectitude, it will prove more of a demon than a god.

Intellectual culture consists, not chiefly, as many are apt to think, in accumulating information, though this is important, but in building up a force of thought which may be turned at will on any subjects on which we are called to pass judgment. This force is manifested in the concentration of the attention, in accurate, penetrating observation, in reducing complex subjects to their elements, in diving beneath the effect to the cause, in detecting the more subtle differences and resemblances of things, in reading the future in the present and especially in rising from particular facts to general laws or universal truths. This last exertion of the intellect, its rising to broad views and great principles, constitutes what is called the philosophical mind, and is especially worthy of culture. What it means, your own observation must have taught you. You must have taken note of two classes of men, the one always employed on details, on particular facts, and the other using these facts as foundations of higher, wider truths. The latter are philosophers. For example, men had for ages seen pieces of wood, stones, metals falling to the ground. Newton seized on these particular facts, and rose to the idea that all matter tends, or is attracted, towards all matter, and then defined the law according to which this attraction or force acts at different distances, thus giving us a grand principle, which, we have reason to think, extends to and controls the whole outward creation. One man reads a history, and can tell you all its events, and there stops. Another combines these events, brings them under one view, and learns the great causes which are at work on this or another nation, and what are its great tendencies, whether to freedom or despotism, to one or another form of civilization. So, one man talks continually about the particular actions of this or another neighbor; whilst another looks beyond the acts to the inward principle from which they spring, and gathers from them larger views of human nature. In a word, one man sees all things apart and in fragments, whilst another strives to discover the harmony, connection, unity of all. One of the great evils of society is, that men, occupied perpetually with petty details, want general truths, want broad and fixed principles. Hence many, not wicked, are unstable, habitually inconsistent, as if they were overgrown children rather than men. To build up that strength of mind which apprehends and cleaves to great universal truths, is the highest intellectual self-culture; and here I wish you to observe how entirely this culture agrees with that of the moral and the religious principles of our nature, of which I have previously spoken. In each of these, the improvement of the soul consists in raising it above what is narrow, particular, individual, selfish, to the universal and unconfined. To improve a man is to liberalize, enlarge him in thought, feeling, and purpose. Narrowness of intellect and heart, this is the degradation from which all culture aims to rescue the human being.

Again. Self-culture is social, or one of its great offices is to unfold and purify the affections which spring up instinctively in the human breast, which bind together husband and wife, parent and child, brother and sister; which bind a man to friends and neighbors, to his country, and to the suffering who fall under his eye, wherever they belong. The culture of these is an important part of our work, and it consists in converting them from instincts into principles, from natural into spiritual attachments, in giving them a rational, moral, and holy character. For example, our affection for our children is at first instinctive; and if it continue such, it rises little above the brute's attachment to its young. But when a parent infuses into his natural love for his offspring moral and religious principle; when he comes to regard his child as an intelligent, spiritual, immortal being, and honors him as such, and desires first of all to make him disinterested, noble, a worthy child of God and the friend of his race, then the instinct rises into a generous and holy sentiment. It resembles God's paternal love for his spiritual family. A like purity and dignity we must aim to give to all our affections.

Again. Self-culture is practical, or it proposes, as one of its chief ends, to fit us for action, to make us efficient in whatever we undertake, to train us to firmness of purpose and to fruitfulness of resource in common life, and especially in emergencies, in times of difficulty, danger, and trial. But passing over this and other topics for which I have no time, I shall confine myself to two branches of self-culture which have been almost wholly overlooked in the education of the people, and which ought not to be so slighted.

In looking at our nature, we discover, among its admirable endowments, the sense or perception of beauty. We see the germ of this in every human being, and there is no power which admits greater cultivation; and why should it not be cherished in all? It deserves remark, that the provision for this principle is infinite in the universe. There is but a very minute portion of the creation which we can turn into food and clothes, or gratification for the body; but the whole creation may be used to minister to the sense of beauty. Beauty is an all-pervading presence. It unfolds in the numberless flowers of the spring. It waves in the branches of the trees and the green blades of grass. It haunts the depths of the earth and sea, and gleams out in the hues of the shell and the precious stone. And not only these minute objects, but the ocean, the mountains, the clouds, the heavens, the stars, the rising and setting sun, all overflow with beauty. The universe is its temple; and those men who are alive to it cannot lift their eyes without feeling themselves encompassed with it on every side. Now this beauty is so precious, the enjoyments it gives are so refined and pure, so congenial with our tenderest and noble feelings, and so akin to worship, that it is painful to think of the multitude of men as living in the midst of it, and living almost as blind to it as if, instead of this fair earth and glorious sky, they were tenants of a dungeon. An infinite joy is lost to the world by the want of culture of this spiritual endowment. Suppose that I were to visit a cottage, and to see its walls lined with the choicest pictures of Raphael, and every spare nook filled with statues of the most exquisite workmanship, and that I were to learn that neither man, woman, nor child ever cast an eye at these miracles of art, how should I feel their privation!—how should I want to open their eyes, and to help them to comprehend and feel the loveliness and grandeur which in vain courted their notice! But every husbandman is living in sight of the works of a diviner artist; and how much would his existence be elevated could he see the glory which shines forth in their forms, hues, proportions, and moral expression! I have spoken only of the beauty of nature; but how much of this mysterious charm is found in the elegant arts, and especially in literature! The best books have most beauty. The greatest truths are wronged if not linked with beauty, and they win their way most surely and deeply into the soul when arrayed in this their natural and fit attire. Now no man receives the true culture of a man in whom the sensibility to the beautiful is not cherished; and I know of no condition in life from which it should be excluded. Of all luxuries, this is the cheapest and most at hand; and it seems to me to be most important to those conditions where coarse labor tends to give a grossness to the mind. From the diffusion of the sense of beauty in ancient Greece, and of the taste for music in modern Germany, we learn that the people at large may partake of refined gratifications which have hitherto been thought to be necessarily restricted to a few.

What beauty is, is a question which the most penetrating minds have not satisfactorily answered; nor, were I able, is this the place for discussing it. But one thing I would say; the beauty of the outward creation is intimately related to the lovely, grand, interesting attributes of the soul. It is the emblem or expression of these. Matter becomes beautiful to us when it seems to lose its material aspect, its inertness, finiteness, and grossness, and by the ethereal lightness of its forms and motions seems to approach spirit; when it images to us pure and gentle affections; when it spreads out into a vastness which is a shadow of the Infinite; or when in more awful shapes and movements it speaks of the Omnipotent. Thus outward beauty is akin to something deeper and unseen, is the reflection of spiritual attributes; and of consequence the way to see and feel it more and more keenly is to cultivate those moral, religious, intellectual, and social principles of which I have already spoken, and which are the glory of the spiritual nature; and I name this that you may see, what I am anxious to show, the harmony which subsists among all branches of human culture, or how each forwards and is aided by all.

There is another power, which each man should cultivate according to his ability, but which is very much neglected in the mass of the people, and that is, the power of utterance. A man was not made to shut up his mind in itself; but to give it voice and to exchange it for other minds. Speech is one of our grand distinctions from the brute. Our power over others lies not so much in the amount of thought within us as in the power of bringing it out. A man of more than ordinary intellectual vigor may, for want of expression, be a cipher, without significance, in society. And not only does a man influence others, but he greatly aids his own intellect by giving distinct and forcible utterance to his thoughts. We understand ourselves better, our conceptions grow clearer, by the very effort to make them clear to another. Our social rank, too, depends a good deal on our power of utterance. The principal distinction between what are called gentlemen and the vulgar lies in this, that the latter are awkward in manners, and are especially wanting in propriety, clearness, grace, and force of utterance. A man who cannot open his lips without breaking a rule of grammar, without showing in his dialect or brogue or uncouth tones his want of cultivation, or without darkening his meaning by a confused, unskilful mode of communication, cannot take the place to which, perhaps, his native good sense entitles him. To have intercourse with respectable people, we must speak their language. On this account, I am glad that grammar and a correct pronunciation are taught in the common schools of this city. These are not trifles; nor are they superfluous to any class of people. They give a man access to social advantages, on which his improvement very much depends. The power of utterance should be included by all in their plans of self-culture.

I have now given a few views of the culture, the improvement, which every man should propose to himself. I have all along gone on the principle that a man has within him capacities of growth which deserve and will reward intense, unrelaxing toil. I do not look on a human being as a machine, made to be kept in action by a foreign force, to accomplish an unvarying succession of motions, to do a fixed amount of work, and then to fall to pieces at death, but as a being of free spiritual powers; and I place little value on any culture but that which aims to bring out these, and to give them perpetual impulse and expansion. I am aware that this view is far from being universal. The common notion has been that the mass of the people need no other culture than is necessary to fit them for their various trades; and, though this error is passing away, it is far from being exploded. But the ground of a man's culture lies in his nature, not in his calling. His powers are to be unfolded on account of their inherent dignity, not their outward direction. He is to be educated because he is a man, not because he is to make shoes, nails, or pins. A trade is plainly not the great end of his being, for his mind cannot be shut up in it; his force of thought cannot be exhausted on it. He has faculties to which it gives no action, and deep wants it cannot answer. Poems, and systems of theology and philosophy, which have made some noise in the world, have been wrought at the work-bench and amidst the toils of the field. How often, when the arms are mechanically plying a trade, does the mind, lost in reverie or day-dreams, escape to the ends of the earth! How often does the pious heart of woman mingle the greatest of all thoughts, that of God, with household drudgery! Undoubtedly a man is to perfect himself in his trade, for by it he is to earn his bread and to serve the community. But bread or subsistence is not his highest good; for, if it were, his lot would be harder than that of the inferior animals, for whom nature spreads a table and weaves a wardrobe, without a care of their own. Nor was he made chiefly to minister to the wants of the community. A rational, moral being cannot, without infinite wrong, be converted into a mere instrument of others' gratification. He is necessarily an end, not a means. A mind, in which are sown the seeds of wisdom, disinterestedness, firmness of purpose, and piety, is worth more than all the outward material interests of a world. It exists for itself, for its own perfection, and must not be enslaved to its own or others' animal wants. You tell me that a liberal culture is needed for men who are to fill high stations, but not for such as are doomed to vulgar labor. I answer, that man is a greater name than president or king. Truth and goodness are equally precious in whatever sphere they are found. Besides, men of all conditions sustain equally the relations which give birth to the highest virtues and demand the highest powers. The laborer is not a mere laborer. He has close, tender, responsible connections with God and his fellow-creatures. He is a son, husband, father, friend, and Christian. He belongs to a home, a country, a church, a race; and is such a man to be cultivated only for a trade? Was he not sent into the world for a great work? To educate a child perfectly requires profounder thought, greater wisdom, than to govern a State; and for this plain reason, that the interests and wants of the latter are more superficial, coarser, and more obvious than the spiritual capacities, the growth of thought and feeling, and the subtle laws of the mind, which must all be studied and comprehended before the work of education can be thoroughly performed; and yet to all conditions this greatest work on earth is equally committed by God. What plainer proof do we need that a higher culture than has yet been dreamed of is needed by our whole race?

II. I now proceed to inquire into the means by which the self-culture just described may be promoted; and here I know not where to begin. The subject is so extensive, as well as important, that I feel myself unable to do any justice to it, especially in the limits to which I am confined. I beg you to consider me as presenting but hints, and such as have offered themselves with very little research to my own mind.

And, first, the great means of self-culture, that which includes all the rest, is to fasten on this culture as our great end, to determine deliberately and solemnly that we will make the most and the best of the powers which God has given us. Without this resolute purpose, the best means are worth little, and with it the poorest become mighty. You may see thousands, with every opportunity of improvement which wealth can gather, with teachers, libraries, and apparatus, bringing nothing to pass, and others, with few helps, doing wonders; and simply because the latter are in earnest, and the former not. A man in earnest finds means, or, if he cannot find, creates them. A vigorous purpose makes much out of little, breathes power into weak instruments, disarms difficulties, and even turns them into assistances. Every condition has means of progress, if we have spirit enough to use them. Some volumes have recently been published, giving examples or histories of "knowledge acquired under difficulties;" and it is most animating to see in these what a resolute man can do for himself. A great idea, like this of self-culture, if seized on clearly and vigorously, burns like a living coal in the soul. He who deliberately adopts a great end, has, by this act, half accomplished it, has scaled the chief barrier to success.

One thing is essential to the strong purpose of self-culture now insisted on; namely, faith in the practicableness of this culture. A great object, to awaken resolute choice, must be seen to be within our reach. The truth, that progress is the very end of our being, must not be received as a tradition, but comprehended and felt as a reality. Our minds are apt to pine and starve, by being imprisoned within what we have already attained. A true faith, looking up to something better, catching glimpses of a distant perfection, prophesying to ourselves improvements proportioned to our conscientious labors, gives energy of purpose, gives wings to the soul; and this faith will continually grow, by acquainting ourselves with our own nature, and with the promises of divine help and immortal life which abound in revelation.

Some are discouraged from proposing to themselves improvement, by the false notion that the study of books, which their situation denies them, is the all-important and only sufficient means. Let such consider that the grand volumes, of which all our books are transcripts—I mean nature, revelation, the human soul, and human life—are freely unfolded to every eye. The great sources of wisdom are experience and observation; and these are denied to none. To open and fix our eyes upon what passes without and within us is the most fruitful study. Books are chiefly useful as they help us to interpret what we see and experience. When they absorb men, as they sometimes do, and turn them from observation of nature and life, they generate a learned folly, for which the plain sense of the laborer could not be exchanged but at great loss. It deserves attention that the greatest men have been formed without the studies which at present are thought by many most needful to improvement. Homer, Plato, Demosthenes, never heard the name of chemistry, and knew less of the solar system than a boy in our common schools. Not that these sciences are unimportant; but the lesson is, that human improvement never wants the means, where the purpose of it is deep and earnest in the soul.

The purpose of self-culture, this is the life and strength of all the methods we use for our own elevation. I reiterate this principle on account of its great importance; and I would add a remark to prevent its misapprehension. When I speak of the purpose of self-culture, I mean that it should be sincere. In other words, we must make self-culture really and truly our end, or choose it for its own sake, and not merely as a means or instrument of something else. And here I touch a common and very pernicious error. Not a few persons desire to improve themselves only to get property and to rise in the world; but such do not properly choose improvement, but something outward and foreign to themselves; and so low an impulse can produce only a stinted, partial, uncertain growth. A man, as I have said, is to cultivate himself because he is a man. He is to start with the conviction that there is something greater within him than in the whole material creation, than in all the worlds which press on the eye and ear; and that inward improvements have a worth and dignity in themselves quite distinct from the power they give over outward things. Undoubtedly a man is to labor to better his condition, but first to better himself. If he knows no higher use of his mind than to invent and drudge for his body, his case is desperate as far as culture is concerned.

In these remarks, I do not mean to recommend to the laborer indifference to his outward lot. I hold it important that every man in every class should possess the means of comfort, of health, of neatness in food and apparel, and of occasional retirement and leisure. These are good in themselves, to be sought for their own sakes; and, still more, they are important means of the self-culture for which I am pleading. A clean, comfortable dwelling, with wholesome meals, is no small aid to intellectual and moral progress. A man living in a damp cellar or a garret open to rain and snow, breathing the foul air of a filthy room, and striving without success to appease hunger on scanty or unsavory food, is in danger of abandoning himself to a desperate, selfish recklessness. Improve, then, your lot. Multiply comforts, and, still more, get wealth if you can by honorable means, and if it do not cost too much. A true cultivation of the mind is fitted to forward you in your worldly concerns, and you ought to use it for this end. Only, beware lest this end master you; lest your motives sink as your condition improves; lest you fall victims to the miserable passion of vying with those around you in show, luxury, and expense. Cherish a true respect for yourselves. Feel that your nature is worth more than everything which is foreign to you. He who has not caught a glimpse of his own rational and spiritual being, of something within himself superior to the world and allied to the Divinity, wants the true spring of that purpose of self-culture on which I have insisted as the first of all the means of improvement.

I proceed to another important means of self-culture; and this is the control of the animal appetites. To raise the moral and intellectual nature, we must put down the animal. Sensuality is the abyss in which very many souls are plunged and lost. Among the most prosperous classes what a vast amount of intellectual life is drowned in luxurious excesses! It is one great curse of wealth, that it is used to pamper the senses; and among the poorer classes, though luxury is wanting, yet a gross feeding often prevails, under which the spirit is whelmed. It is a sad sight to walk through our streets and to see how many countenances bear marks of a lethargy and a brutal coarseness, induced by unrestrained indulgence. Whoever would cultivate the soul must restrain the appetites. I am not an advocate for the doctrine that animal food was not meant for man; but that this is used among us to excess, that as a people we should gain much in cheerfulness, activity, and buoyancy of mind, by less gross and stimulating food, I am strongly inclined to believe. Above all, let me urge on those who would bring out and elevate their higher nature to abstain from the use of spirituous liquors. This bad habit is distinguished from all others by the ravages it makes on the reason, the intellect; and this effect is produced to a mournful extent, even when drunkenness is escaped. Not a few men, called temperate, and who have thought themselves such, have learned, on abstaining from the use of ardent spirits, that for years their minds had been clouded, impaired by moderate drinking, without their suspecting the injury. Multitudes in this city are bereft of half their intellectual energy by a degree of indulgence which passes for innocent. Of all the foes of the working class, this is the deadliest. Nothing has done more to keep down this class, to destroy their self-respect, to rob them of their just influence in the community, to render profitless the means of improvement within their reach, than the use of ardent spirits as a drink. They are called on to withstand this practice, as they regard their honor, and would take their just place in society. They are under solemn obligations to give their sanction to every effort for its suppression. They ought to regard as their worst enemies (though unintentionally such), as the enemies of their rights, dignity, and influence, the men who desire to flood city and country with distilled poison. I lately visited a flourishing village, and on expressing to one of the respected inhabitants the pleasure I felt in witnessing so many signs of progress, he replied that one of the causes of the prosperity I witnessed was the disuse of ardent spirits by the people. And this reformation we may be assured wrought something higher than outward prosperity. In almost every family so improved, we cannot doubt that the capacities of the parent for intellectual and moral improvement were enlarged, and the means of education made more effectual to the child. I call on workingmen to take hold of the cause of temperance as peculiarly their cause. These remarks are the more needed in consequence of the efforts made far and wide to annul at the present moment a recent law for the suppression of the sale of ardent spirits in such quantities as favor intemperance. I know that there are intelligent and good men who believe that, in enacting this law, government transcended its limits, left its true path, and established a precedent for legislative interference with all our pursuits and pleasures. No one here looks more jealously on government than myself. But I maintain that this is a case which stands by itself, which can be confounded with no other, and on which government, from its very nature and end, is peculiarly bound to act. Let it never be forgotten that the great end of government, its highest function, is, not to make roads, grant charters, originate improvements, but to prevent or repress crimes against individual rights and social order. For this end it ordains a penal code, erects prisons, and inflicts fearful punishments. Now, if it be true that a vast proportion of the crimes which government is instituted to prevent and repress have their origin in the use of ardent spirits; if our poor-houses, work-houses, jails, and penitentiaries, are tenanted in a great degree by those whose first and chief impulse to crime came from the distillery and dram-shop; if murder and theft, the most fearful outrages on property and life, are most frequently the issues and consummation of intemperance, is not government bound to restrain by legislation the vending of the stimulus to these terrible social wrongs? Is government never to act as a parent, never to remove the causes or occasions of wrong-doing? Has it but one instrument for repressing crime; namely, public, infamous punishment—an evil only inferior to crime? Is government a usurper, does it wander beyond its sphere, by imposing restraints on an article which does no imaginable good, which can plead no benefit conferred on body or mind, which unfits the citizen for the discharge of his duty to his country, and which, above all, stirs up men to the perpetration of most of the crimes from which it is the highest and most solemn office of government to protect society?

I come now to another important measure of self-culture, and this is, intercourse with superior minds. I have insisted on our own activity as essential to our progress; but we were not made to live or advance alone. Society is as needful to us as air or food. A child doomed to utter loneliness, growing up without sight or sound of human beings, would not put forth equal power with many brutes; and a man, never brought into contact with minds superior to his own, will probably run one and the same dull round of thought and action to the end of life.

It is chiefly through books that we enjoy intercourse with superior minds, and these invaluable means of communication are in the reach of all. In the best books great men talk to us, give us their most precious thoughts, and pour their souls into ours. God be thanked for books. They are the voices of the distant and the dead, and make us heirs of the spiritual life of past ages. Books are the true levellers. They give to all who will faithfully use them the society, the spiritual presence, of the best and greatest of our race. No matter how poor I am. No matter though the prosperous of my own time will not enter my obscure dwelling. If the sacred writers will enter and take up their abode under my roof; if Milton will cross my threshold to sing to me of paradise, and Shakespeare to open to me the worlds of imagination and the workings of the human heart, and Franklin to enrich me with his practical wisdom, I shall not pine for want of intellectual companionship, and I may become a cultivated man though excluded from what is called the best society in the place where I live.

To make this means of culture effectual a man must select good books, such as have been written by right-minded and strong-minded men, real thinkers, who, instead of diluting by repetition what others say, have something to say for themselves, and write to give relief to full, earnest souls; and these works must not be skimmed over for amusement, but read with fixed attention and a reverential love of truth. In selecting books we may be aided much by those who have studied more than ourselves. But, after all, it is best to be determined in this particular a good deal by our own tastes. The best books for a man are not always those which the wise recommend, but oftener those which meet the peculiar wants, the natural thirst of his mind, and therefore awaken interest and rivet thought. And here it may be well to observe, not only in regard to books, but in other respects, that self-culture must vary with the individual. All means do not equally suit us all. A man must unfold himself freely, and should respect the peculiar gifts or biases by which nature has distinguished him from others. Self-culture does not demand the sacrifice of individuality. It does not regularly apply an established machinery, for the sake of torturing every man into one rigid shape, called perfection. As the human countenance, with the same features in us all, is diversified without end in the race, and is never the same in any two individuals, so the human soul, with the same grand powers and laws, expands into an infinite variety of forms, and would be woefully stinted by modes of culture requiring all men to learn the same lesson or to bend to the same rules.

I know how hard it is to some men, especially to those who spend much time in manual labor, to fix attention on books. Let them strive to overcome the difficulty by choosing subjects of deep interest, or by reading in company with those whom they love. Nothing can supply the place of books. They are cheering or soothing companions in solitude, illness, affliction. The wealth of both continents would not compensate for the good they impart. Let every man, if possible, gather some good books under his roof, and obtain access for himself and family to some social library. Almost any luxury should be sacrificed to this.

One of the very interesting features of our times is the multiplication of books, and their distribution through all conditions of society. At a small expense a man can now possess himself of the most precious treasures of English literature. Books, once confined to a few by their costliness, are now accessible to the multitude; and in this way a change of habits is going on in society, highly favorable to the culture of the people. Instead of depending on casual rumor and loose conversation for most of their knowledge and objects of thought; instead of forming their judgments in crowds, and receiving their chief excitement from the voice of neighbors, men are now learning to study and reflect alone, to follow out subjects continuously, to determine for themselves what shall engage their minds, and to call to their aid the knowledge, original views, and reasonings of men of all countries and ages; and the results must be, a deliberateness and independence of judgment, and a thoroughness and extent of information, unknown in former times. The diffusion of these silent teachers, books, through the whole community, is to work greater effects than artillery, machinery, and legislation. Its peaceful agency is to supersede stormy revolutions. The culture which it is to spread, whilst an unspeakable good to the individual, is also to become the stability of nations.

Another important means of self-culture is to free ourselves from the power of human opinion and example, except as far as these is sanctioned by our own deliberate judgment. We are all prone to keep the level of those we live with, to repeat their words, and dress our minds as well as bodies after their fashion; and hence the spiritless tameness of our characters and lives. Our greatest danger is not from the grossly wicked around us, but from the worldly, unreflecting multitude, who are borne along as a stream by foreign impulse, and bear us along with them. Even the influence of superior minds may harm us, by bowing us to servile acquiescence and damping our spiritual activity. The great use of intercourse with other minds is to stir up our own, to whet our appetite for truth, to carry our thoughts beyond their old tracks. We need connections with great thinkers to make us thinkers too. One of the chief arts of self-culture is to unite the child-like teachableness, which gratefully welcomes light from every human being who can give it, with manly resistance of opinions however current, of influences however generally revered, which do not approve themselves to our deliberate judgment. You ought, indeed, patiently and conscientiously to strengthen your reason by other men's intelligence, but you must not prostrate it before them. Especially if there springs up within you any view of God's word or universe, any sentiment or aspiration which seems to you of a higher order than what you meet abroad, give reverent heed to it; inquire into it earnestly, solemnly. Do not trust it blindly, for it may be an illusion; but it may be the Divinity moving within you, a new revelation, not supernatural, but still most precious, of truth or duty; and if, after inquiry, it so appear, then let no clamor, or scorn, or desertion turn you from it. Be true to your own highest convictions. Intimations from our own souls of something more perfect than others teach, if faithfully followed, give us a consciousness of spiritual force and progress never experienced by the vulgar of high life or low life, who march, as they are drilled, to the step of their times.

Some, I know, will wonder that I should think the mass of the people capable of such intimations and glimpses of truth as I have just supposed. These are commonly thought to be the prerogative of men of genius, who seem to be born to give law to the minds of the multitude. Undoubtedly nature has her nobility, and sends forth a few to be eminently "lights of the world." But it is also true that a portion of the same divine fire is given to all; for the many could not receive with a loving reverence the quickening influences of the few, were there not essentially the same spiritual life in both. The minds of the multitude are not masses of passive matter, created to receive impressions unresistingly from abroad. They are not wholly shaped by foreign instruction; but have a native force, a spring of thought in themselves. Even the child's mind outruns its lessons, and overflows in questionings which bring the wisest to a stand. Even the child starts the great problems, which philosophy has labored to solve for ages. But on this subject I cannot now enlarge. Let me only say that the power of original thought is particularly manifested in those who thirst for progress, who are bent on unfolding their whole nature. A man who wakes up to the consciousness of having been created for progress and perfection looks with new eyes on himself and on the world in which he lives. This great truth stirs the soul from its depths, breaks up old associations of ideas, and establishes new ones, just as a mighty agent of chemistry, brought into contact with natural substances, dissolves the old affinities which had bound their particles together, and arranges them anew. This truth particularly aids us to penetrate the mysteries of human life. By revealing to us the end of our being, it helps us to comprehend more and more the wonderful, the infinite system, to which we belong. A man in the common walks of life, who has faith in perfection, in the unfolding of the human spirit, as the great purpose of God, possesses more the secret of the universe, perceives more the harmonies or mutual adaptations of the world without and the world within him, is a wiser interpreter of Providence, and reads nobler lessons of duty in the events which pass before him, than the profoundest philosopher who wants this grand central truth. Thus illuminations, inward suggestions, are not confined to a favored few, but visit all who devote themselves to a generous self-culture.

Another means of self-culture may be found by every man in his condition or occupation, be it what it may. Had I time, I might go through all conditions of life, from the most conspicuous to the most obscure, and might show how each furnishes continual aids to improvement. But I will take one example, and that is, of a man living by manual labor. This may be made the means of self-culture. For instance, in almost all labor, a man exchanges his strength for an equivalent in the form of wages, purchase-money, or some other product. In other words, labor is a system of contracts, bargains, imposing mutual obligations. Now the man who, in working, no matter in what way, strives perpetually to fulfil his obligations thoroughly, to do his whole work faithfully, to be honest, not because honesty is the best policy, but for the sake of justice, and that he may render to every man his due, such a laborer is continually building up in himself one of the greatest principles of morality and religion. Every blow on the anvil, on the earth, or whatever material he works upon, contributes something to the perfection of his nature.

Nor is this all. Labor is a school of benevolence as well as justice. A man, to support himself, must serve others. He must do or produce something for their comfort or gratification. This is one of the beautiful ordinations of Providence, that, to get a living, a man must be useful. Now this usefulness ought to be an end in his labor as truly as to earn his living. He ought to think of the benefit of those he works for, as well as of his own; and in so doing, in desiring amidst his sweat and toil to serve others as well as himself, he is exercising and growing in benevolence, as truly as if he were distributing bounty with a large hand to the poor. Such a motive hallows and dignifies the commonest pursuit. It is strange that laboring men do not think more of the vast usefulness of their toils, and take a benevolent pleasure in them on this account. This beautiful city, with its houses, furniture, markets, public walks, and numberless accommodations, has grown up under the hands of artisans and other laborers; and ought they not to take a disinterested joy in their work? One would think that a carpenter or mason, on passing a house which he had reared, would say to himself, "This work of mine is giving comfort and enjoyment every day and hour to a family, and will continue to be a kindly shelter, a domestic gathering-place, an abode of affection, for a century or more after I sleep in the dust;" and ought not a generous satisfaction to spring up at the thought? It is by thus interweaving goodness with common labor that we give it strength, and make it a habit of the soul.

Again. Labor may be so performed as to be a high impulse to the mind. Be a man's vocation what it may, his rule should be to do its duties perfectly, to do the best he can, and thus to make perpetual progress in his art. In other words, perfection should be proposed; and this I urge not only for its usefulness to society, nor for the sincere pleasure which a man takes in seeing a work well done. This is an important means of self-culture. In this way the idea of perfection takes root in the mind, and spreads far beyond the man's trade. He gets a tendency towards completeness in whatever he undertakes. Slack, slovenly performance in any department of life is more apt to offend him. His standard of action rises, and everything is better done for his thoroughness in his common vocation.

There is one circumstance attending all conditions of life which may and ought to be turned to the use of self-culture. Every condition, be it what it may, has hardships, hazards, pains. We try to escape them; we pine for a sheltered lot, for a smooth path, for cheering friends, and unbroken success. But Providence ordains storms, disasters, hostilities, sufferings; and the great question, whether we shall live to any purpose or not, whether we shall grow strong in mind and heart, or be weak and pitiable, depends on nothing so much as on our use of these adverse circumstances. Outward evils are designed to school our passions, and to rouse our faculties and virtues into intenser action. Sometimes they seem to create new powers. Difficulty is the element, and resistance the true work of a man. Self-culture never goes on so fast as when embarrassed circumstances, the opposition of men or the elements, unexpected changes of the times, or other forms of suffering, instead of disheartening, throw us on our inward resources, turn us for strength to God, clear up to us the great purpose of life, and inspire calm resolution. No greatness or goodness is worth much unless tried in these fires. Hardships are not on this account to be sought for. They come fast enough of themselves, and we are in more danger of sinking under than of needing them. But when God sends them, they are noble means of self-culture, and as such let us meet and bear them cheerfully. Thus all parts of our condition may be pressed into the service of self-improvement.

I have time to consider but one more means of self-culture. We find it in our free government, in our political relations and duties. It is a great benefit of free institutions, that they do much to awaken and keep in action a nation's mind. We are told that the education of the multitude is necessary to the support of a republic; but it is equally true that a republic is a powerful means of educating the multitude. It is the people's university. In a free state, solemn responsibilities are imposed on every citizen; great subjects are to be discussed; great interests to be decided. The individual is called to determine measures affecting the well-being of millions and the destinies of posterity. He must consider not only the internal relations of his native land, but its connection with foreign states, and judge of a policy which touches the whole civilized world. He is called, by his participation in the national sovereignty, to cherish public spirit, a regard to the general weal. A man who purposes to discharge faithfully these obligations is carrying on a generous self-culture. The great public questions which divide opinion around him and provoke earnest discussion, of necessity invigorate his intellect, and accustom him to look beyond himself. He grows up to a robustness, force, enlargement of mind, unknown under despotic rule.

It may be said that I am describing what free institutions ought to do for the character of the individual, not their actual effects; and the objection, I must own, is too true. Our institutions do not cultivate us, as they might and should; and the chief cause of the failure is plain. It is the strength of party spirit; and so blighting is its influence, so fatal to self-culture, that I feel myself bound to warn every man against it who has any desire of improvement. I do not tell you it will destroy your country. It wages a worse war against yourselves. Truth, justice, candor, fair dealing, sound judgment, self-control, and kind affections, are its natural and perpetual prey.

I do not say that you must take no side in politics. The parties which prevail around you differ in character, principles, and spirit, though far less than the exaggeration of passion affirms; and, as far as conscience allows, a man should support that which he thinks best. In one respect, however, all parties agree. They all foster that pestilent spirit which I now condemn. In all of them party spirit rages. Associate men together for a common cause, be it good or bad, and array against them a body resolutely pledged to an opposite interest, and a new passion, quite distinct from the original sentiment which brought them together, a fierce, fiery zeal, consisting chiefly of aversion to those who differ from them, is roused within them into fearful activity. Human nature seems incapable of a stronger, more unrelenting passion. It is hard enough for an individual, when contending all alone for an interest or an opinion, to keep down his pride, wilfulness, love of victory, anger, and other personal feelings. But let him join a multitude in the same warfare, and, without singular self-control, he receives into his single breast the vehemence, obstinacy, and vindictiveness of all. The triumph of his party becomes immeasurably dearer to him than the principle, true or false, which was the original ground of division. The conflict becomes a struggle, not for principle but for power, for victory; and the desperateness, the wickedness of such struggles, is the great burden of history. In truth, it matters little what men divide about, whether it be a foot of land or precedence in a procession. Let them but begin to fight for it, and self-will, ill-will, the rage for victory, the dread of mortification and defeat, make the trifle as weighty as a matter of life and death. The Greek or Eastern empire was shaken to its foundation by parties which differed only about the merits of charioteers at the amphitheatre. Party spirit is singularly hostile to moral independence. A man, in proportion as he drinks into it, sees, hears, judges by the senses and understandings of his party. He surrenders the freedom of a man, the right of using and speaking his own mind, and echoes the applauses or maledictions with which the leaders or passionate partisans see fit that the country should ring. On all points, parties are to be distrusted; but on no one so much as on the character of opponents. These, if you may trust what you hear, are always men without principle and truth, devoured by selfishness, and thirsting for their own elevation, though on their country's ruin. When I was young, I was accustomed to hear pronounced with abhorrence, almost with execration, the names of men who are now hailed by their former foes as the champions of grand principles, and as worthy of the highest public trusts. This lesson of early experience, which later years have corroborated, will never be forgotten.

Of our present political divisions I have of course nothing to say. But, among the current topics of party, there are certain accusations and recriminations, grounded on differences of social condition, which seem to me so unfriendly to the improvement of individuals and the community that I ask the privilege of giving them a moment's notice. On one side we are told that the rich are disposed to trample on the poor; and, on the other, that the poor look with evil eye and hostile purpose on the possessions of the rich. These outcries seem to me alike devoid of truth and alike demoralizing. As for the rich, who constitute but a handful of our population, who possess not one peculiar privilege, and, what is more, who possess comparatively little of the property of the country, it is wonderful that they should be objects of alarm. The vast and ever-growing property of this country, where is it? Locked up in a few hands? hoarded in a few strong boxes? It is diffused like the atmosphere, and almost as variable, changing hands with the seasons, shifting from rich to poor, not by the violence but by the industry and skill of the latter class. The wealth of the rich is as a drop in the ocean; and it is a well-known fact, that those men among us who are noted for their opulence exert hardly any political power on the community. That the rich do their whole duty; that they adopt, as they should, the great object of the social state, which is the elevation of the people in intelligence, character, and condition, cannot be pretended; but that they feel for the physical sufferings of their brethren, that they stretch out liberal hands for the succor of the poor, and for the support of useful public institutions, cannot be denied. Among them are admirable specimens of humanity. There is no warrant for holding them up to suspicion as the people's foes.

Nor do I regard as less calumnious the outcry against the working classes, as if they were aiming at the subversion of property. When we think of the general condition and character of this part of our population; when we recollect that they were born and have lived amidst schools and churches, that they have been brought up to profitable industry, that they enjoy many of the accommodations of life, that most of them hold a measure of property and are hoping for more, that they possess unprecedented means of bettering their lot, that they are bound to comfortable homes by strong domestic affections, that they are able to give their children an education which places within their reach the prizes of the social state, that they are trained to the habits and familiarized to the advantages of a high civilization; when we recollect these things, can we imagine that they are so insanely blind to their interests, so deaf to the claims of justice and religion, so profligately thoughtless of the peace and safety of their families, as to be prepared to make a wreck of social order, for the sake of dividing among themselves the spoils of the rich, which would not support the community for a month? Undoubtedly there is insecurity in all stages of society, and so there must be until communities shall be regenerated by a higher culture, reaching and quickening all classes of the people; but there is not, I believe, a spot on earth where property is safer than here, because nowhere else is it so equally and righteously diffused. In aristocracies, where wealth exists in enormous masses, which have been entailed for ages by a partial legislation on a favored few, and where the multitude, after the sleep of ages, are waking up to intelligence, to self-respect, and to a knowledge of their rights, property is exposed to shocks which are not to be dreaded among ourselves. Here, indeed, as elsewhere, among the less prosperous members of the community, there are disappointed, desperate men, ripe for tumult and civil strife; but it is also true that the most striking and honorable distinction of this country is to be found in the intelligence, character, and condition of the great working class. To me it seems that the great danger to property here is not from the laborer, but from those who are making haste to be rich. For example, in this commonwealth no act has been thought by the alarmists or the conservatives so subversive of the rights of property as a recent law authorizing a company to construct a free bridge in the immediate neighborhood of another which had been chartered by a former legislature, and which had been erected in the expectation of an exclusive right. And with whom did this alleged assault on property originate? With levellers? with needy laborers? with men bent on the prostration of the rich? No; but with men of business, who are anxious to push a more lucrative trade. Again, what occurrence among us has been so suited to destroy confidence, and to stir up the people against the moneyed class, as the late criminal mismanagement of some of our banking institutions? And whence came this? from the rich, or the poor? From the agrarian, or the man of business? Who, let me ask, carry on the work of spoliation most extensively in society? Is not more property wrested from its owners by rash or dishonest failures than by professed highwaymen and thieves? Have not a few unprincipled speculators sometimes inflicted wider wrongs and sufferings than all the tenants of a State prison? Thus property is in more danger from those who are aspiring after wealth than from those who live by the sweat of their brow. I do not believe, however, that the institution is in serious danger from either. All the advances of society in industry, useful arts, commerce, knowledge, jurisprudence, fraternal union, and practical Christianity, are so many hedges around honestly acquired wealth, so many barriers against revolutionary violence and rapacity. Let us not torture ourselves with idle alarms, and, still more, let us not inflame ourselves against one another by mutual calumnies. Let not class array itself against class, where all have a common interest. One way of provoking men to crime is to suspect them of criminal designs. We do not secure our property against the poor by accusing them of schemes of universal robbery; nor render the rich better friends of the community by fixing on them the brand of hostility to the people. Of all parties, those founded on different social conditions are the most pernicious; and in no country on earth are they so groundless as in our own.

Among the best people, especially among the more religious, there are some who, through disgust with the violence and frauds of parties, withdraw themselves from all political action. Such, I conceive, do wrong. God has placed them in the relations, and imposed on them the duties, of citizens; and they are no more authorized to shrink from these duties than from those of sons, husbands, or fathers. They owe a great debt to their country, and must discharge it by giving support to what they deem the best men and the best measures. Nor let them say that they can do nothing. Every good man, if faithful to his convictions, benefits his country. All parties are kept in check by the spirit of the better portion of people whom they contain. Leaders are always compelled to ask what their party will bear, and to modify their measures, so as not to shock the men of principle within their ranks. A good man, not tamely subservient to the body with which he acts, but judging it impartially, criticising it freely, bearing testimony against its evils, and withholding his support from wrong, does good to those around him, and is cultivating generously his own mind.

I respectfully counsel those whom I address to take part in the politics of their country. These are the true discipline of a people, and do much for their education. I counsel you to labor for a clear understanding of the subjects which agitate the community, to make them your study, instead of wasting your leisure in vague, passionate talk about them. The time thrown away by the mass of the people on the rumors of the day might, if better spent, give them a good acquaintance with the constitution, laws, history, and interests of their country, and thus establish them in those great principles by which particular measures are to de determined. In proportion as the people thus improve themselves, they will cease to be the tools of designing politicians. Their intelligence, not their passions and jealousies, will be addressed by those who seek their votes. They will exert, not a nominal, but a real influence on the government and the destinies of the country, and at the same time will forward their own growth in truth and virtue.

I ought not to quit this subject of politics, considered as a means of self-culture, without speaking of newspapers; because these form the chief reading of the bulk of the people. They are the literature of multitudes. Unhappily, their importance is not understood; their bearing on the intellectual and moral cultivation of the community little thought of. A newspaper ought to be conducted by one of our most gifted men, and its income should be such as to enable him to secure the contributions of men as gifted as himself. But we must take newspapers as they are; and a man anxious for self-culture may turn them to account, if he will select the best within his reach. He should exclude from his house such as are venomous or scurrilous, as he would a pestilence. He should be swayed in his choice, not merely by the ability with which a paper is conducted, but still more by its spirit, by its justice, fairness, and steady adherence to great principles. Especially, if he would know the truth, let him hear both sides. Let him read the defence as well as the attack. Let him not give his ear to one party exclusively. We condemn ourselves when we listen to reproaches thrown on an individual and turn away from his exculpation; and is it just to read continual, unsparing invective against large masses of men, and refuse them the opportunity of justifying themselves?

A new class of daily papers has sprung up in our country, sometimes called cent papers, and designed for circulation among those who cannot afford costlier publications. My interest in the working class induced me some time ago to take one of these, and I was gratified to find it not wanting in useful matter. Two things, however, gave me pain. The advertising columns were devoted very much to patent medicines; and when I considered that a laboring man's whole fortune is his health, I could not but lament that so much was done to seduce him to the use of articles more fitted, I fear, to undermine than to restore his constitution. I was also shocked by accounts of trials in the police court. These were written in a style adapted to the most uncultivated minds, and intended to turn into matters of sport the most painful and humiliating events of life. Were the newspapers of the rich to attempt to extract amusement from the vices and miseries of the poor a cry would be raised against them, and very justly. But is it not something worse that the poorer classes themselves should seek occasions of laughter and merriment in the degradation, the crimes, the woes, the punishments of their brethren, of those who are doomed to bear like themselves the heaviest burdens of life, and who have sunk under the temptations of poverty? Better go to the hospital, and laugh over the wounds and writhings of the sick or the ravings of the insane, than amuse ourselves with brutal excesses and infernal passions, which not only expose the criminal to the crushing penalties of human laws, but incur the displeasure of Heaven, and, if not repented of, will be followed by the fearful retribution of the life to come.

One important topic remains. That great means of self-improvement, Christianity, is yet untouched, and its greatness forbids me now to approach it. I will only say, that if you study Christianity in its original records, and not in human creeds; if you consider its clear revelations of God, its life-giving promises of pardon and spiritual strength, its correspondence to man's reason, conscience, and best affections, and its adaptation to his wants, sorrows, anxieties, and fears; if you consider the strength of its proofs, the purity of its precepts, the divine greatness of the character of its author, and the immortality which it opens before us, you will feel yourselves bound to welcome it joyfully, gratefully, as affording aids and incitements to self-culture which would vainly be sought in all other means.

I have thus presented a few of the means of self-culture. The topics now discussed will, I hope, suggest others to those who have honored me with their attention, and create an interest which will extend beyond the present hour. I owe it, however, to truth to make one remark. I wish to raise no unreasonable hopes. I must say, then, that the means now recommended to you, though they will richly reward every man of every age who will faithfully use them, will yet not produce their full and happiest effect, except in cases where early education has prepared the mind for future improvement. They whose childhood has been neglected, though they may make progress in future life, can hardly repair the loss of their first years; and I say this, that we may all be excited to save our children from this loss, that we may prepare them, to the extent of our power, for an effectual use of all the means of self-culture which adult age may bring with it. With these views, I ask you to look with favor on the recent exertions of our legislature and of private citizens in behalf of our public schools, the chief hope of our country. The legislature has of late appointed a board of education, with a secretary, who is to devote his whole time to the improvement of public schools. An individual more fitted to this responsible office than the gentleman who now fills it [2] cannot, I believe, be found in our community; and if his labors shall be crowned with success, he will earn a title to the gratitude of the good people of this State unsurpassed by that of any other living citizen. Let me also recall to your minds a munificent individual,[3] who, by a generous donation, has encouraged the legislature to resolve on the establishment of one or more institutions called normal schools, the object of which is to prepare accomplished teachers of youth—a work on which the progress of education depends more than on any other measure. The efficient friends of education are the true benefactors of their country, and their names deserve to be handed down to that posterity for whose highest wants they are generously providing.

There is another mode of advancing education in our whole country, to which I ask your particular attention. You are aware of the vast extent and value of the public lands of the Union. By annual sales of these large amounts of money are

[2] Horace Mann. [3] Edmund Dwight.

brought into the national treasury, which are applied to the current expenses of the government. For this application there is no need. In truth, the country has received detriment from the excess of its revenues. Now, I ask, why shall not the public lands be consecrated (in whole or in part, as the case may require) to the education of the people? This measure would secure at once what the country most needs; that is, able, accomplished, quickening teachers of the whole rising generation. The present poor remuneration of instructors is a dark omen, and the only real obstacle which the cause of education has to contend with. We need for our schools gifted men and women, worthy, by their intelligence and their moral power, to be intrusted with a nation's youth; and, to gain these, we must pay them liberally, as well as afford other proofs of the consideration in which we hold them. In the present state of the country, when so many paths of wealth and promotion are opened, superior men cannot be won to an office so responsible and laborious as that of teaching, without stronger inducements than are now offered, except in some of our large cities. The office of instructor ought to rank and be recompensed as one of the most honorable in society; and I see not how this is to be done, at least in our day, without appropriating to it the public domain. This is the people's property, and the only part of their property which is likely to be soon devoted to the support of a high order of institutions for public education. This object, interesting to all classes of society, has peculiar claims on those whose means of improvement are restricted by narrow circumstances. The mass of the people should devote themselves to it as one man, should toil for it with one soul. Mechanics, farmers, laborers! let the country echo with your united cry, "The Public Lands for Education." Send to the public councils men who will plead this cause with power. No party triumphs, no trades-unions, no associations, can so contribute to elevate you as the measure now proposed. Nothing but a higher education can raise you in influence and true dignity. The resources of the public domain, wisely applied for successive generations to the culture of society and of the individual, would create a new people, would awaken through this community intellectual and moral energies, such as the records of no country display, and as would command the respect and emulation of the civilized world. In this grand object the working men of all parties, and in all divisions of the land, should join with an enthusiasm not to be withstood. They should separate it from all narrow and local strifes. They should not suffer it to be mixed up with the schemes of politicians. In it, they and their children have an infinite stake. May they be true to themselves, to posterity, to their country, to freedom, to the cause of mankind!

III. I am aware that the whole doctrine of this discourse will meet with opposition. There are not a few who will say to me: "What you tell us sounds well; but it is impracticable. Men who dream in their closets spin beautiful theories; but actual life scatters them, as the wind snaps the cobweb. You would have all men to be cultivated; but necessity wills that most men shall work; and which of the two is likely to prevail? A weak sentimentality may shrink from the truth; still it is true that most men were made, not for self-culture, but for toil."

I have put the objection into strong language, that we may all look it fairly in the face. For one I deny its validity. Reason, as well as sentiment, rises up against it. The presumption is certainly very strong, that the All-wise Father, who has given to every human being reason and conscience and affection, intended that these should be unfolded; and it is hard to believe that He who, by conferring this nature on all men, has made all his children, has destined the great majority to wear out a life of drudgery and unimproving toil, for the benefit of a few. God cannot have made spiritual beings to be dwarfed. In the body we see no organs created to shrivel by disuse; much less are the powers of the soul given to be locked up in perpetual lethargy.

Perhaps it will be replied that the purpose of the Creator is to be gathered, not from theory, but from facts; and that it is a plain fact, that the order and prosperity of society, which God must be supposed to intend, require from the multitude the action of their hands, and not the improvement of their minds. I reply that a social order demanding the sacrifice of the mind is very suspicious, that it cannot, indeed, be sanctioned by the Creator. Were I, on visiting a strange country, to see the vast majority of the people maimed, crippled, and bereft of sight, and were I told that social order required this mutilation,

I should say, Perish this order. Who would not think his understanding as well as best feelings insulted, by hearing this spoken of as the intention of God? Nor ought we to look with less aversion on a social system which can only be upheld by crippling and blinding the minds of the people.

But to come nearer to the point. Are labor and self-culture irreconcilable to each other? In the first place, we have seen that a man, in the midst of labor, may and ought to give himself to the most important improvements, that he may cultivate his sense of justice, his benevolence, and the desire of perfection. Toil is the school for these high principles; and we have here a strong presumption that, in other respects, it does not necessarily blight the soul. Next, we have seen that the most fruitful sources of truth and wisdom are not books, precious as they are, but experience and observation; and these belong to all conditions. It is another important consideration that almost all labor demands intellectual activity, and is best carried on by those who invigorate their minds; so that the two interests, toil and self-culture, are friends to each other. It is mind, after all, which does the work of the world, so that the more there is of mind, the more work will be accomplished. A man, in proportion as he is intelligent, makes a given force accomplish a greater task, makes skill take the place of muscles, and, with less labor, gives a better product. Make men intelligent, and they become inventive. They find shorter processes. Their knowledge of nature helps them to turn its laws to account, to understand the substances on which they work, and to seize on useful hints, which experience continually furnishes. It is among workmen that some of the most useful machines have been contrived. Spread education, and, as the history of this country shows, there will be no bounds to useful inventions. You think that a man without culture will do all the better what you call the drudgery of life. Go, then, to the Southern plantation. There the slave is brought up to be a mere drudge. He is robbed of the rights of a man, his whole spiritual nature is starved, that he may work, and do nothing but work; and in that slovenly agriculture, in that worn-out soil, in the rude state of the mechanic arts, you may find a comment on your doctrine, that, by degrading men, you make them more productive laborers.

But it is said, that any considerable education lifts men above their work, makes them look with disgust on their trades as mean and low, makes drudgery intolerable. I reply than a man becomes interested in labor just in proportion as the mind works with the hands. An enlightened farmer, who understands agricultural chemistry, the laws of vegetation, the structure of plants, the properties of manures, the influences of climate, who looks intelligently on his work, and brings his knowledge to bear on exigencies, is a much more cheerful, as well as more dignified laborer, than the peasant whose mind is akin to the clod on which he treads, and whose whole life is the same dull, unthinking, unimproving toil. But this is not all. Why is it, I ask, that we call manual labor low, that we associate with it the idea of meanness, and think that an intelligent people must scorn it? The great reason is, that, in most countries, so few intelligent people have been engaged in it. Once let cultivated men plough, and dig, and follow the commonest labors, and ploughing, digging, and trades will cease to be mean. It is the man who determines the dignity of the occupation, not the occupation which measures the dignity of the man. Physicians and surgeons perform operations less cleanly than fall to the lot of most mechanics. I have seen a distinguished chemist covered with dust like a laborer. Still these men were not degraded. Their intelligence gave dignity to their work, and so our laborers, once educated, will give dignity to their toils. Let me add, that I see little difference in point of dignity between the various vocations of men. When I see a clerk spending his days in adding figures, perhaps merely copying, or a teller of a bank counting money, or a merchant selling shoes and hides, I cannot see in these occupations greater respectableness than in making leather, shoes, or furniture. I do not see in them greater intellectual activity than in several trades. A man in the fields seems to have more chances of improvement in his work than a man behind the counter, or a man driving the quill. It is the sign of a narrow mind to imagine, as many seem to do, that there is a repugnance between the plain, coarse exterior of a laborer, and mental culture, especially the more refining culture. The laborer, under his dust and sweat, carries the grand elements of humanity, and he may put forth its highest powers. I doubt not there is as genuine enthusiasm in the contemplation of nature, and in the perusal of works of genius, under a homespun garb as under finery. We have heard of a distinguished author who never wrote so well as when he was full dressed for company. But profound thought and poetical inspiration have most generally visited men when, from narrow circumstances or negligent habits, the rent coat and shaggy face have made them quite unfit for polished *salons*. A man may see truth, and may be thrilled with beauty, in one costume or dwelling as well as another; and he should respect himself the more for the hardships under which his intellectual force has been developed.

But it will be asked, how can the laboring classes find time for self-culture? I answer, as I have already intimated, that an earnest purpose finds time or makes time. It seizes on spare moments, and turns large fragments of leisure to golden account. A man who follows his calling with industry and spirit, and uses his earnings economically, will always have some portion of the day at command; and it is astonishing how fruitful of improvement a short season becomes, when eagerly seized and faithfully used. It has often been observed that they who have most time at their disposal profit by it least. A single hour in the day, steadily given to the study of an interesting subject, brings unexpected accumulations of knowledge. The improvements made by well-disposed pupils in many of our country schools, which are open but three months in the year, and in our Sunday schools, which are kept but one or two hours in the week, show what can be brought to pass by slender means. The affections, it is said, sometimes crowd years into moments, and the intellect has something of the same power. Volumes have not only been read, but written, in flying journeys. I have known a man of vigorous intellect, who had enjoyed few advantages of early education, and whose mind was almost engrossed by the details of an extensive business, but who composed a book of much original thought, in steamboats and on horseback, while visiting distant customers. The succession of the seasons gives to many of the working class opportunities for intellectual improvement. The winter brings leisure to the husbandman, and winter evenings to many laborers in the city. Above all, in Christian countries, the seventh day is released from toil. The seventh part of the year, no small portion of existence, may be given by almost every one to intellectual and moral culture. Why is it that Sunday is not made a more effectual means of improvement? Undoubtedly the seventh day is to have a religious character; but religion connects itself with all the great subjects of human thought, and leads to and aids the study of all. God is in nature. God is in history. Instruction in the works of the Creator, so as to reveal His perfection in their harmony, beneficence, and grandeur; instruction in the histories of the church and the world, so as to show in all events His moral government, and to bring out the great moral lessons in which human life abounds; instruction in the lives of philanthropists, of saints, of men eminent for piety and virtue —all these branches of teaching enter into religion, and are appropriate to Sunday; and, through these, a vast amount of knowledge may be given to the people. Sunday ought not to remain the dull and fruitless season that it now is to multitudes. It may be clothed with a new interest and a new sanctity. It may give a new impulse to the nation's soul. I have thus shown that time may be found for improvement; and the fact is, that among our most improved people a considerable part consists of persons who pass the greatest portion of every day at the desk, in the counting-room, or in some other sphere, chained to tasks which have very little tendency to expand the mind. In the progress of society, with the increase of machinery, and with other aids which intelligence and philanthropy will multiply, we may expect that more and more time will be redeemed from manual labor for intellectual and social occupations.

But some will say: "Be it granted that the working classes may find some leisure; should they not be allowed to spend it in relaxation? Is it not cruel to summon them from toils of the hand to toils of the mind? They have earned pleasure by the day's toil, and ought to partake it." Yes, let them have pleasure. Far be it from me to dry up the fountains, to blight the spots of verdure, where they refresh themselves after life's labors. But I maintain that self-culture multiplies and increases their pleasures, that it creates new capacities of enjoyment, that it saves their leisure from being, what it too often is, dull and wearisome, that it saves them from rushing for excitement to indulgences destructive to body and soul. It is one of the great benefits of self-improvement, that it raises a people above the gratifications of the brute, and gives them pleasures worthy of men. In consequence of the present intellectual culture of our country, imperfect as it is, a vast amount of enjoyment is communicated to men, women, and children, of all conditions, by books—an enjoyment unknown to ruder times. At this moment a number of gifted writers are employed in multiplying entertaining works. Walter Scott, a name conspicuous among the brightest of his day, poured out his inexhaustible mind in fictions, at once so sportive and thrilling that they have taken their place among the delights of all civilized nations. How many millions have been chained to his pages! How many melancholy spirits has be steeped in forgetfulness of their cares and sorrows! What multitudes, wearied by their day's work, have owed some bright evening hours and balmier sleep to his magical creations? And not only do fictions give pleasure. In proportion as the mind is cultivated, it takes delight in history and biography, in descriptions of nature, in travels, in poetry, and even graver works. Is the laborer then defrauded of pleasure by improvement? There is another class of gratifications to which self-culture introduces the mass of the people. I refer to lectures, discussions, meetings of associations for benevolent and literary purposes, and to other like methods of passing the evening, which every year is multiplying among us. A popular address from an enlightened man, who has the tact to reach the minds of the people, is a high gratification, as well as a source of knowledge. The profound silence in our public halls, where these lectures are delivered to crowds, shows that cultivation is no foe to enjoyment. I have a strong hope, that by the progress of intelligence, taste, and morals among all portions of society, a class of public amusements will grow up among us, bearing some resemblance to the theatre, but purified from the gross evils which degrade our present stage, and which, I trust, will seal its ruin. Dramatic performances and recitations are means of bringing the mass of the people into a quicker sympathy with a writer of genius, to a profounder comprehension of his grand, beautiful, touching conceptions, than can be effected by the reading of the closet. No commentary throws such a light on a great poem or any impassioned work of literature as the voice of a reader or speaker who brings to the task a deep feeling of his author and rich and various powers of expression. A crowd, electrified by a sublime thought, or softened into a humanizing sorrow, under such a voice, partake a pleasure at once exquisite and refined; and I cannot but believe that this and other amusements, at which the delicacy of woman and the purity of the Christian can take no offence, are to grow up under a higher social culture. Let me only add, that, in proportion as culture spreads among a people, the cheapest and commonest of all pleasures, conversation, increases in delight. This, after all, is the great amusement of life, cheering us round our hearths, often cheering our work, stirring our hearts gently, acting on us like the balmy air or the bright light of heaven, so silently and continually, that we hardly think of its influence. This source of happiness is too often lost to men of all classes for want of knowledge, mental activity, and refinement of feeling; and do we defraud the laborer of his pleasure by recommending to him improvements which will place the daily, hourly blessings of conversation within his reach?

I have thus considered some of the common objections which start up when the culture of the mass of men is insisted on as the great end of society. For myself, these objections seem worthy little notice. The doctrine is too shocking to need refutation, that the great majority of human beings, endowed as they are with rational and immortal powers, are placed on earth simply to toil for their own animal subsistence, and to minister to the luxury and elevation of the few. It is monstrous, it approaches impiety, to suppose that God has placed insuperable barriers to the expansion of the free, illimitable soul. True, there are obstructions in the way of improvement. But in this country, the chief obstructions lie, not in our lot but in ourselves; not in outward hardships, but in our worldly and sensual propensities; and one proof of this is that a true self-culture is as little thought of on exchange as in the workshop, as little among the prosperous as among those of narrower conditions. The path to perfection is difficult to men in every lot; there is no royal road for rich or poor. But difficulties are meant to rouse, not discourage. The human spirit is to grow strong by conflict. And how much has it already overcome! Under what burdens of oppression has it made its way for ages! What mountains of difficulty has it cleared! And with all this experience, shall we say that the progress of the mass of men is to be despaired of; that the chains of bodily necessity are too strong and ponderous to be broken by the mind; that servile, unimproving drudgery is the unalterable condition of the multitude of the human race?

I conclude with recalling to you the happiest feature of our age, and that is, the progress of the mass of the people in intelligence, self-respect, and all the comforts of life. What a contrast does the present form with past times! Not many ages ago the nation was the property of one man, and all its interests were staked in perpetual games of war, for no end but to build up his family, or to bring new territories under his yoke. Society was divided into two classes, the high-born and the vulgar, separated from one another by a great gulf, as impassable as that between the saved and the lost. The people had no significance as individuals, but formed a mass, a machine, to be wielded at pleasure by their lords. In war, which was the great sport of the times, those brave knights, of whose prowess we hear, cased themselves and their horses in armor, so as to be almost invulnerable, whilst the common people on foot were left, without protection, to be hewn in pieces or trampled down by their betters. Who that compares the condition of Europe a few years ago with the present state of the world but must bless God for the change? The grand distinction of modern times is, the emerging of the people from brutal degradation, the gradual recognition of their rights, the gradual diffusion among them of the means of improvement and happiness, the creation of a new power in the state—the power of the people. And it is worthy remark, that this revolution is due in a great degree to religion, which, in the hands of the crafty and aspiring, had bowed the multitude to the dust, but which, in the fulness of time, began to fulfil its mission of freedom. It was religion which, by teaching men their near relation to God, awakened in them the consciousness of their importance as individuals. It was the struggle for religious rights which opened men's eyes to all their rights. It was resistance to religious usurpation which led men to withstand political oppression. It was religious discussion which roused the minds of all classes to free and vigorous thought. It was religion which armed the martyr and patriot in England against arbitrary power, which braced the spirits of our fathers against the perils of the ocean and wilderness, and sent them to found here the freest and most equal state on earth.

Let us thank God for what has been gained. But let us not think everything gained. Let the people feel that they have only started in the race. How much remains to be done! What a vast amount of ignorance, intemperance, coarseness, sensuality, may still be found in our community! What a vast amount of mind is palsied and lost! When we think that every house might be cheered by intelligence, disinterestedness, and refinement, and then remember in how many houses the higher powers and affections of human nature are buried as in tombs, what a darkness gathers over society! And how few of us are moved by this moral desolation! How few understand that to raise the depressed, by a wise culture, to the dignity of men, is the highest end of the social state? Shame on us, that the worth of a fellow-creature is so little felt.

I would that I could speak with an awakening voice to the people of their wants, their privileges, their responsibilities. I would say to them, You cannot, without guilt and disgrace, stop where you are. The past and the present call on you to advance. Let what you have gained be an impulse to something higher. Your nature is too great to be crushed. You were not created what you are, merely to toil, eat, drink, and sleep, like the inferior animals. If you will, you can rise. No power in society, no hardship in your condition can depress you, keep you down, in knowledge, power, virtue, influence, but by your own consent. Do not be lulled to sleep by the flatteries which you hear, as if your participation in the national sovereignty made you equal to the noblest of your race. You have many and great deficiencies to be remedied; and the remedy lies, not in the ballot-box, not in the exercise of your political powers, but in the faithful education of yourselves and your children. These truths you have often heard and slept over. Awake! Resolve earnestly on self-culture. Make yourselves worthy of your free institutions, and strengthen and perpetuate them by your intelligence and your virtues.

THE MUTABILITY OF LITERATURE

BY

WASHINGTON IRVING

WASHINGTON IRVING

1783—1859

The youngest of eleven children, Washington Irving was born in New York City in 1783. He received only a common school education, but soon developed a marked taste for literature, which was encouraged and confirmed by the success of some contributions to a paper edited by one of his older brothers. Ill-health suggested a trip to Europe. He remained two years, and the mental impressions and stimulus he received were such that this journey may properly be regarded as his university education. On his return, in 1807, Irving helped to launch a periodical called "Salmagundi," in frank imitation of the "Spectator," which was well received. In 1809 he published his "History of New York, by Diedrich Knickerbocker," the most delightful and ably sustained burlesque in American literature. This work at once made Irving the most noted of American men of letters, but his happiness was clouded by the death of the young lady whom he was engaged to marry. Although he recovered from the blow, he never married. Owing to the business reverses of a mercantile house in which Irving was interested, he determined to rely henceforth upon his literary efforts for a livelihood. In 1819 he published the "Sketch Book." Murray, the English publisher having at first refused it, only undertook the venture on the personal solicitation of Walter Scott. It proved a great success, both in England and America. "Bracebridge Hall" followed in 1822. These books contain some of his finest work, and are widely studied as models of English composition. After publishing "Tales of a Traveller" in 1824, Irving went to Spain for the purpose of translating some newly discovered papers referring to Columbus. Becoming interested in the subject, he wrote his admirable "History of Columbus," and this was followed by the "Conquest of Granada," "The Alhambra," and several other charming books on early Spanish history.

In 1832 Irving returned to the United States, after an absence of seven years, being everywhere received with genuine enthusiasm. He now purchased the beautiful cottage "Sunnyside" at Tarrytown-on-the-Hudson to pass here quietly, as he thought, his remaining years. In 1842, however, he returned once more to Europe, this time in the honored capacity of American Minister to Spain, an office which he filled with distinction for four years. Having served his country well, he now devoted himself to preparing his "Life of Washington." This work of five volumes he only completed at the cost of great physical suffering. He died in his Sunnyside home at Tarrytown, in 1859, at the age of seventy-six.

Irving's position in American literature is deservedly high. Not only was he the first of the group of writers who are the founders of American literature, but he was the first American writer to arouse the interest of Englishmen, or, as Thackeray's graceful phrase puts it, "the first ambassador whom the New World of Letters sent to the Old." Irving was not a versatile writer. He wrote no poetry. His essay on "The Mutability of Literature" is one of the most important of his papers in the essay style. His is master of the short story, and several of his efforts in this field rank among the finest in all literature. Diedrich Knickerbocker, Sleepy Hollow, Ichabod Crane, and especially Rip Van Winkle, have become household names. His style is clear, musical, full of delicate touches, and pervaded with an indescribable charm that emanated from the genial character of the man.

THE MUTABILITY OF LITERATURE

A Colloquy in Westminster Abbey

> I know that all beneath the moon decays,
> And what by mortals in this world is brought,
> In time's great period shall return to nought.
> I know that all the muse's heavenly lays,
> With toil of sprite which are so dearly bought,
> As idle sounds, of few or none are sought;
> That there is nothing lighter than mere praise.
> —*Drummond of Hawthornden.*

THERE are certain half-dreaming moods of mind, in which we naturally steal away from noise and glare, and seek some quiet haunt, where we may indulge our reveries and build our air-castles undisturbed. In such a mood I was loitering about the old gray cloisters of Westminster Abbey, enjoying that luxury of wandering thought which one is apt to dignify with the name of reflection; when suddenly an interruption of madcap boys from Westminster School, playing at football, broke in upon the monastic stillness of the place, making the vaulted passages and mouldering tombs echo with their merriment. I sought to take refuge from their noise by penetrating still deeper into the solitudes of the pile, and applied to one of the vergers for admission to the library. He conducted me through a portal rich with the crumbling sculpture of former ages, which opened upon a gloomy passage leading to the chapter-house and the chamber in which Doomsday Book is deposited. Just within the passage is a small door on the left. To this the verger applied a key; it was double-locked, and opened with some difficulty, as if seldom used. We now ascended a dark, narrow staircase, and, passing through a second door, entered the library.

I found myself in a lofty antique hall, the roof supported by massive joints of old English oak. It was soberly lighted by a row of Gothic windows at a considerable height from the floor, and which apparently opened upon the roofs of the cloisters. An ancient picture of some reverend dignitary of the Church in his robes hung over the fireplace. Around the hall and in a small gallery were the books, arranged in carved oaken cases. They consisted principally of old polemical writers, and were much more worn by time than use. In the centre of the library was a solitary table with two or three books on it, an inkstand without ink, and a few pens parched by long disuse. The place seemed fitted for quiet study and profound meditation. It was buried deep among the massive walls of the abbey, and shut up from the tumult of the world. I could only hear now and then the shouts of the schoolboys faintly swelling from the cloisters, and the sound of a bell tolling for prayers, echoing soberly along the roofs of the abbey. By degrees the shouts of merriment grew fainter and fainter, and at length died away; the bell ceased to toll, and a profound silence reigned through the dusky hall.

I had taken down a little thick quarto, curiously bound in parchment, with brass clasps, and seated myself at the table in a venerable elbow-chair. Instead of reading, however, I was beguiled by the solemn monastic air, and lifeless quiet of the place, into a train of musing. As I looked around upon the old volumes in their mouldering covers, thus ranged on the shelves, and apparently never disturbed in their repose, I could not but consider the library a kind of literary catacomb, where authors, like mummies, are piously entombed, and left to blacken and moulder in dusty oblivion.

How much, thought I, has each of these volumes, now thrust aside with such indifference, cost some aching head! how many weary days! how many sleepless nights! How have their authors buried themselves in the solitude of cells and cloisters; shut themselves up from the face of man, and the still more blessed face of nature; and devoted themselves to painful research and intense reflection! And all for what? to occupy an inch of dusty shelf—to have the title of their works read now and then in a future age, by some drowsy churchman or casual straggler like myself; and in another age to be lost, even to remembrance. Such is the amount of this boasted immortality. A mere temporary rumor, a local sound; like the tone of that bell which has just tolled among these towers, filling the ear for a moment—lingering transiently in echo—and then passing away like a thing that was not!

While I sat half murmuring, half meditating these unprofitable speculations, with my head resting on my hand, I was thrumming with the other hand upon the quarto, until I accidentally loosened the clasps; when, to my utter astonishment, the little book gave two or three yawns, like one awaking from a deep sleep; then a husky "hem"; and at length began to talk. At first its voice was very hoarse and broken, being much troubled by a cobweb which some studious spider had woven across it; and having probably contracted a cold from long exposure to the chills and damps of the abbey. In a short time, however, it became more distinct, and I soon found it an exceedingly fluent, conversable little tome. Its language, to be sure, was rather quaint and obsolete, and its pronunciation, what in the present day would be deemed barbarous; but I shall endeavor, as far as I am able, to render it in modern parlance.

It began with railings about the neglect of the world—about merit being suffered to languish in obscurity, and other such commonplace topics of literary repining, and complained bitterly that it had not been opened for more than two centuries. That the dean only looked now and then into the library, sometimes took down a volume or two, trifled with them for a few moments, and then returned them to their shelves. "What a plague do they mean," said the little quarto, which I began to perceive was somewhat choleric—"what a plague do they mean by keeping several thousand volumes of us shut up here, and watched by a set of old vergers, like so many beauties in a harem, merely to be looked at now and then by the dean? Books were written to give pleasure and to be enjoyed; and I would have a rule passed that the dean should pay each of us a visit at least once a year; or, if he is not equal to the task, let them once in a while turn loose the whole School of Westminster among us, that at any rate we may now and then have an airing."

"Softly, my worthy friend," replied I; "you are not aware how much better you are off than most books of your generation. By being stored away in this ancient library, you are like the treasured remains of those saints and monarchs which lie enshrined in the adjoining chapels; while the remains of your contemporary mortals, left to the ordinary course of nature, have long since returned to dust."

"Sir," said the little tome, ruffling his leaves and looking big, "I was written for all the world, not for the bookworms of an abbey. I was intended to circulate from hand to hand, like other great contemporary works; but here have I been clasped up for more than two centuries, and might have silently fallen a prey to these worms that are playing the very vengeance with my intestines, if you had not by chance given me an opportunity of uttering a few last words before I go to pieces."

"My good friend," rejoined I, "had you been left to the circulation of which you speak, you would long ere this have been no more. To judge from your physiognomy, you are now well stricken in years: very few of your contemporaries can be at present in existence; and those few owe their longevity to being immured like yourself in old libraries; which, suffer me to add, instead of likening to harems, you might more properly and gratefully have compared to those infirmaries attached to religious establishments, for the benefit of the old and decrepit, and where, by quiet fostering and no employment, they often endure to an amazingly good-for-nothing old age. You talk of your contemporaries as if in circulation—where do we meet with their works? What do we hear of Robert Grosseteste, of Lincoln? No one could have toiled harder than he for immortality. He is said to have written nearly two hundred volumes. He built, as it were, a pyramid of books to perpetuate his name; but, alas! the pyramid has long since fallen, and only a few fragments are scattered in various libraries, where they are scarcely disturbed even by the antiquarian. What do we hear of Giraldus Cambrensis, the historian, antiquary, philosopher, theologian, and poet? He declined two bishoprics, that he might shut himself up and write for posterity: but posterity never inquires after his labors. What of Henry of Huntingdon, who, besides a learned history of England, wrote a treatise on the contempt of the world, which the world has revenged by forgetting him? What is quoted of Joseph of Exeter, styled the miracle of his age in classical composition? Of his three great heroic poems one is lost forever, excepting a mere fragment; the others are known only to a few of the curious in literature; and as to his love-verses and epigrams, they have entirely disappeared. What is in current use of John Wallis, the Franciscan, who acquired the name of the 'Tree of Life'? Of William of Malmesbury; of Simeon of Durham; of Benedict of Peterborough; of John Hanvill of St. Albans; of ——"

"Prithee, friend," cried the quarto, in a testy tone, "how old do you think me? You are talking of authors that lived before my time, and wrote either in Latin or French, so that they in a manner expatriated themselves, and deserved to be forgotten;[1] but I, sir, was ushered into the world from the press of the renowned Wynkyn de Worde. I was written in my own native tongue, at a time when the language had become fixed; and indeed I was considered a model of pure and elegant English."

(I should observe that these remarks were couched in such intolerably antiquated terms, that I have had infinite difficulty in rendering them into modern phraseology.)

"I cry your mercy," said I, "for mistaking your age; but it matters little: almost all the writers of your time have likewise passed into forgetfulness; and De Worde's publications are mere literary rarities among book-collectors. The purity and stability of language, too, on which you found your claims to perpetuity, have been the fallacious dependence of authors of every age, even back to the times of the worthy Robert of Gloucester, who wrote his history in rhymes of mongrel Saxon.[2] Even now many talk of Spenser's 'Well of pure English undefiled' as if the language ever sprang from a well or fountain-head, and was not rather a mere confluence of various tongues, perpetually subject to changes and intermixtures. It is this which has made English literature so extremely mutable, and the reputation built upon it so fleeting. Unless thought can be committed to something more permanent and unchangeable

[1] "In Latin and French hath many soueraine wittes had great delyte to endite, and have many noble thinges fulfilde, but certes there ben some that speaken their poisye in French, of which speche the Frenchmen have as good a fantasye as we have in hearying of Frenchmen's Englishe."—*Chaucer*, "Testament of Love."

[2] Holinshed, in his "Chronicle," observes: "Afterwards, also, by deligent travell of Geffry Chaucer and of John Gowre, in the time of Richard the Second, and after them of John Scogan and John Lydgate, monke of Berrie, our said toong was brought to an excellent passe, notwithstanding that it never came unto the type of perfection until the time of Queen Elizabeth, wherein John Jewell, Bishop of Sarum, John Fox, and sundrie learned and excellent writers, have fully accomplished the ornature of the same, to their great praise and immortal commendation."

than such a medium, even thought must share the fate of everything else, and fall into decay. This should serve as a check upon the vanity and exultation of the most popular writer. He finds the language in which he has embarked his fame gradually altering, and subject to the dilapidations of time and the caprice of fashion. He looks back and beholds the early authors of his country, once the favorites of their day, supplanted by modern writers. A few short ages have covered them with obscurity, and their merits can only be relished by the quaint taste of the bookworm. And such, he anticipates, will be the fate of his own work, which, however it may be admired in its day, and held up as a model of purity, will in the course of years grow antiquated and obsolete; until it shall become almost as unintelligible in its native land as an Egyptian obelisk, or one of those Runic inscriptions said to exist in the deserts of Tartary. I declare," added I, with some emotion, " when I contemplate a modern library, filled with new works, in all the bravery of rich gilding and binding, I feel disposed to sit down and weep; like the good Xerxes, when he surveyed his army, pranked out in all the splendor of military array, and reflected that in one hundred years not one of them would be in existence!"

" Ah," said the little quarto, with a heavy sigh, " I see how it is; these modern scribblers have superseded all the good old authors. I suppose nothing is read nowadays but Sir Philip Sidney's 'Arcadia,' Sackville's stately plays, and 'Mirror for Magistrates,' or the fine-spun euphuisms of the 'unparalleled John Lyly.'"

" There you are again mistaken," said I; " the writers whom you suppose in vogue, because they happened to be so when you were last in circulation, have long since had their day. Sir Philip Sidney's 'Arcadia,' the immortality of which was so fondly predicted by his admirers,[3] and which, in truth, is full of noble thoughts, delicate images, and graceful turns of language, is now scarcely ever mentioned. Sackville has strutted into obscurity; and even Lyly, though his writings were once the delight of a court, and apparently perpetuated by a proverb,

[3] " Live ever sweete booke; the simple image of his gentle witt, and the golden-pillar of his noble courage; and ever notify unto the world that thy writer was the secretary of eloquence, the breath of the muses, the honey-bee of the daintyest flowers of witt and arte, the pith of morale and intellectual virtues, the arme of Bellona in the field, the tonge of Suada in the chamber, the sprite of Practise *in esse*, and the paragon of excellency in print."—*Harvey Pierce*, " Supererogation."

is now scarcely known even by name. A whole crowd of authors who wrote and wrangled at the time have likewise gone down, with all their writings and their controversies. Wave after wave of succeeding literature has rolled over them, until they are buried so deep that it is only now and then that some industrious diver after fragments of antiquity brings up a specimen for the gratification of the curious.

"For my part," I continued, "I consider this mutability of language a wise precaution of Providence for the benefit of the world at large, and of authors in particular. To reason from analogy, we daily behold the varied and beautiful tribes of vegetables springing up, flourishing, adorning the fields for a short time, and then fading into dust, to make way for their successors. Were not this the case, the fecundity of nature would be a grievance instead of a blessing. The earth would groan with rank and excessive vegetation, and its surface become a tangled wilderness. In like manner the works of genius and learning decline, and make way for subsequent productions. Language gradually varies, and with it fade away the writings of authors who have flourished their allotted time; otherwise, the creative powers of genius would overstock the world, and the mind would be completely bewildered in the endless mazes of literature. Formerly there were some restraints on this excessive multiplication. Works had to be transcribed by hand, which was a slow and laborious operation; they were written either on parchment, which was expensive, so that one work was often erased to make way for another; or on papyrus, which was fragile and extremely perishable. Authorship was a limited and unprofitable craft, pursued chiefly by monks in the leisure and solitude of their cloisters. The accumulation of manuscripts was slow and costly, and confined almost entirely to monasteries. To these circumstances it may, in some measure, be owing that we have not been inundated by the intellect of antiquity; that the fountains of thought have not been broken up, and modern genius drowned in the deluge. But the inventions of paper and the press have put an end to all these restraints. They have made everyone a writer, and enabled every mind to pour itself into print, and diffuse itself over the whole intellectual world. The consequences are alarming. The stream of literature has swollen into a torrent—augmented into a river—expanded into a sea. A few centuries since five or six hundred manuscripts constituted a great library; but what would you say to libraries such as actually exist containing three or four hundred thousand volumes; legions of authors at the same time busy; and the press going on with activity, to double and quadruple the number. Unless some unforeseen mortality should break out among the progeny of the Muse, now that she has become so prolific, I tremble for posterity. I fear the mere fluctuation of language will not be sufficient. Criticism may do much. It increases with the increase of literature, and resembles one of those salutary checks on population spoken of by economists. All possible encouragement, therefore, should be given to the growth of critics, good or bad. But I fear all will be in vain; let criticism do what it may, writers will write, printers will print, and the world will inevitably be overstocked with good books. It will soon be the employment of a lifetime merely to learn their names. Many a man of passable information, at the present day, reads scarcely anything but reviews; and before long a man of erudition will be little better than a mere walking catalogue."

"My very good sir," said the little quarto, yawning most drearily in my face, "excuse my interrupting you, but I perceive you are rather given to prose. I would ask the fate of an author who was making some noise just as I left the world. His reputation, however, was considered quite temporary. The learned shook their heads at him, for he was a poor half-educated varlet, that knew little of Latin, and nothing of Greek, and had been obliged to run the country for deer-stealing. I think his name was Shakespeare. I presume he soon sunk into oblivion."

"On the contrary," said I, "it is owing to that very man that the literature of his period has experienced a duration beyond the ordinary term of English literature. There rise authors now and then, who seem proof against the mutability of language, because they have rooted themselves in the unchanging principles of human nature. They are like gigantic trees that we sometimes see on the banks of a stream; which, by their vast and deep roots, penetrating through the mere surface, and laying hold on the very foundations of the earth, preserve the soil around them from being swept away by the ever-flowing current, and hold up many a neighboring plant, and, perhaps, worthless weed, to perpetuity. Such is the case with Shakespeare, whom we behold defying the encroachments of time, retaining in modern use the language and literature of his day, and giving duration to many an indifferent author, merely from having flourished in his vicinity. But even he, I grieve to say, is gradually assuming the tint of age, and his whole form is overrun by a profusion of commentators, who, like clambering vines and creepers, almost bury the noble plant that upholds them."

Here the little quarto began to heave his sides and chuckle, until at length he broke out in a plethoric fit of laughter that had wellnigh choked him, by reason of his excessive corpulency. "Mighty well!" cried he, as soon as he could recover breath; "mighty well! and so you would persuade me that the literature of an age is to be perpetuated by a vagabond deer-stealer! by a man without learning; by a poet, forsooth—a poet!" And here he wheezed forth another fit of laughter.

I confess that I felt somewhat nettled at this rudeness, which, however, I pardoned on account of his having flourished in a less polished age. I determined, nevertheless, not to give up my point.

"Yes," resumed I, positively, "a poet; for of all writers he has the best chance for immortality. Others may write from the head, but he writes from the heart, and the heart will always understand him. He is the faithful portrayer of nature, whose features are always the same, and always interesting. Prose-writers are voluminous and unwieldy; their pages are crowded with commonplaces, and their thoughts expanded into tediousness. But with the true poet everything is terse, touching, or brilliant. He gives the choicest thoughts in the choicest language. He illustrates them by everything that he sees most striking in nature and art. He enriches them by pictures of human life, such as it is passing before him. His writings, therefore, contain the spirit, the aroma, if I may use the phrase, of the age in which he lives. They are caskets which enclose within a small compass the wealth of the language—its family jewels, which are thus transmitted in a portable form to posterity. The setting may occasionally be antiquated, and require now and then to be renewed, as in the case of Chaucer; but the brilliancy and intrinsic value of the gems continue unaltered. Cast a look back over the long reach of literary history. What vast valleys of dulness, filled with monkish legends and academical controversies! what bogs of theological speculations! what dreary wastes of metaphysics! Here and there only do we behold the heaven-illuminated bards, elevated like beacons on their widely separate heights, to transmit the pure light of poetical intelligence from age to age." [4]

I was just about to launch forth into eulogiums upon the poets of the day, when the sudden opening of the door caused me to turn my head. It was the verger, who came to inform me that it was time to close the library. I sought to have a parting word with the quarto, but the worthy little tome was silent; the clasps were closed; and it looked perfectly unconscious of all that had passed. I have been to the library two or three times since, and have endeavored to draw it into further conversation, but in vain; and whether all this rambling colloquy actually took place, or whether it was another of those odd day-dreams to which I am subject, I have never to this moment been able to discover.

Thorow earth and waters deepe,
  The pen by skill doth passe;
And featly nyps the worldes abuse,
  And shoes us in a glasse
The vertu and the vice
  Of every wight alyve:
The honey-comb that bee doth make
  Is not so sweet in hyve,
As are the golden leves
  That drop from poet's head!
Which doth surmount our common talke
  As farre as dross doth lead.
—"Churchyard."

KEAN'S ACTING

—

BY

RICHARD HENRY DANA

RICHARD HENRY DANA

1787—1879

Richard Henry Dana, whose career must not be confounded with that of his son, Richard Henry Dana, Junior, the author of "Two Years before the Mast," was born at Cambridge, Massachusetts, in 1787. He spent three years at Harvard, and was admitted to the bar in 1811. The law, however, had no attraction for him, and he soon devoted himself to literary pursuits. In 1814 he assisted in founding the "North American Review" in Boston, and in 1818 became one of its editors. During this period he contributed to that magazine a series of critical papers, notably one reviewing the entire field of English poetry down to Wordsworth, which gave proof of his fine culture and literary ability. He published two psychological novels, "Tom Thornton" and "Paul Felton," now seldom read, and a volume of poems likewise too metaphysical to gain permanent popularity.

His lectures on Shakespeare, which were well received and greatly admired, are perhaps his best and most successful literary effort. His admirable essay on "Kean's Acting" shows his profound appreciation of Shakespeare, and gives an excellent idea of his literary acumen and artistic temperament. Few dramatic criticisms contain such subtle analyses of an actor's interpretation, few are more suggestive and instructive. In 1850 Dana published an edition of his collected works in two volumes. He seldom wrote for publication after this, and was but rarely seen in public, passing his summers at Manchester-by-the-Sea, and his winters at Boston. He died in 1879, at the advanced age of ninety-two.

Taken as a whole, Dana's work is somewhat disappointing, inasmuch as it failed in the fulfilment of the promises of his youth. His influence extended only to the limited circle of the cultured and refined. His literary style is classic and severe, perfectly polished, faultless in form, but somewhat cold and colorless. In his literary criticisms he is at his best. Here his style is admirably adapted to the subject, and his acute discernment and keen analytical powers find their proper field.

the character, whether right or wrong, creates in us an unmixed dislike of Richard, till the anguish of his mind makes him the object of pity; from which moment to the close, Kean is allowed to play the part better than anyone has before him.

In his highest wrought passion, when every limb and muscle are alive and quivering, and his gestures hurried and violent, nothing appears ranted or over-acted; because he makes us feel that, with all this, there is something still within him vainly struggling for utterance. The very breaking and harshness of his voice in these parts, though upon the whole it were better otherwise, help to this impression upon us, and make up in a good degree for the defect.

Though he is on the very verge of truth in his passionate parts, he does not pass into extravagance; but runs along the dizzy edge of the roaring and beating sea, with feet as sure as we walk our parlors. We feel that he is safe, for some preternatural spirit upholds him as it hurries him onward; and while all is uptorn and tossing in the whirl of the passions, we see that there is a power and order over the whole.

A man has feelings sometimes which can only be breathed out; there is no utterance for them in words. I had hardly written this when the terrible and indistinct, "Ha!" with which Kean makes Lear hail Cornwall and Regan, as they enter, in the fourth scene of the second act, came to my mind. That cry seemed at the time to take me up and sweep me along in its wild swell. No description in the world could give a tolerably clear notion of it; it must be formed, as well as it may be, from what has just been said of its effect.

Kean's playing is frequently giving instances of various, inarticulate sounds—the throttled struggle of rage, and the choking of grief—the broken laugh of extreme suffering, when the mind is ready to deliver itself over to an insane joy—the utterance of over-full love, which cannot, and would not speak in express words—and that of bewildering grief, which blanks all the faculties of man.

No other player whom I have heard has attempted these, except now and then; and should anyone have made the trial in the various ways in which Kean gives them, no doubt he would have failed. Kean thrills us with them as if they were wrung from him in his agony. They have no appearance of study or artifice. The truth is, that the labor of a mind of his genius constitutes its existence and delight. It is not like the toil of ordinary men at their task-work. What shows effort in them comes from him with the freedom and force of nature.

Some object to the frequent use of such sounds; and to others they are quite shocking. But those who permit themselves to consider that there are really violent passions in man's nature, and that they utter themselves a little differently from our ordinary feelings, understand and feel their language, as they speak to us in Kean. Probably no actor ever conceived passion with the intenseness and life that he does. It seems to enter into him and possess him, as evil spirits possessed men of old. It is curious to observe how some who have sat very contentedly year after year, and called the face-making which they have seen expression, and the stage-stride dignity, and the noisy declamation, and all the rhodomontade of acting, energy and passion, complain that Kean is apt to be extravagant; when in truth he seems to be little more than a simple personation of the feeling or passion to be expressed at the time.

It has been so common a saying that Lear is the most difficult of all characters to personate, that we had taken it for granted no man could play it so as to satisfy us. Perhaps it is the hardest to represent. Yet the part which has generally been supposed the most difficult, the insanity of Lear, is scarcely more so than the choleric old King. Inefficient rage is almost always ridiculous; and an old man, with a broken-down body and a mind falling in pieces from the violence of its uncontrolled passions, is in constant danger of exciting along with our pity a feeling of contempt. It is a chance matter to which we are moved. And this it is which makes the opening of Lear so difficult.

We may as well notice here the objection which some make to the abrupt violence with which Kean begins in Lear. If this is a fault, it is Shakespeare, and not Kean, who is to blame. For we have no doubt that he has conceived it according to his author. Perhaps, however, the mistake lies in this case, where it does in most others—with those who put themselves into the seat of judgment to pass upon greater men.

In most instances Shakespeare has given us the gradual growth of a passion with such little accompaniments as agree with it, and go to make up the whole man. In Lear, his object being to represent the beginning and course of insanity, he has properly enough gone but a little back of it, and introduced to us an old man of good feelings, but one who had lived without any true principle of conduct, and whose ungoverned passions had grown strong with age, and were ready, upon any disappointment, to make shipwreck of an intellect always weak. To bring this about he begins with an abruptness rather unusual; and the old King rushes in before us with all his passions at their height, and tearing him like fiends.

Kean gives this as soon as a fit occasion offers itself. Had he put more of melancholy and depression, and less of rage into the character, we should have been very much puzzled at his so suddenly going mad. It would have required the change to have been slower; and, besides, his insanity must have been of another kind. It must have been monotonous and complaining, instead of continually varying; at one time full of grief, at another playful, and then wild as the winds that roared about him, and fiery and sharp as the lightning that shot by him. The truth with which he conceived this was not finer than his execution of it. Not for an instant, in his utmost violence, did he suffer the imbecility of the old man's anger to touch upon the ludicrous: when nothing but the most just conception and feeling of character could have saved him from it.

It has been said that Lear was a study for anyone who would make himself acquainted with the workings of an insane mind. There is no doubt of it. Nor is it less true that the acting of Kean was a complete embodying of these workings. His eye, when his senses are first forsaking him, giving a questioning look at what he saw, as if all before him was undergoing a strange and bewildering change which confused his brain—the wandering, lost motions of his hands, which seemed feeling for something familiar to them, on which they might take hold and be assured of a safe reality—the under monotone of his voice, as if he was questioning his own being, and all which surrounded him—the continuous, but slight oscillating motion of the body—all these expressed with fearful truth the dreamy state of a mind fast unsettling, and making vain and weak efforts to find its way back to its wonted reason. There was a childish, feeble gladness in the eye, and a half piteous smile about the mouth at times, which one could scarce look upon without shedding tears. As the derangement increased upon him, his eye lost its notice of what surrounded him, wandering over everything as if he saw it not, and fastening upon the creatures of his crazed brain. The helpless and delighted fondness with which he clings to Edgar as an insane brother, is another instance of the justness of Kean's conceptions. Nor does he lose the air of insanity even in the fine moralizing parts, and where he inveighs against the corruptions of the world: There is a madness even in his reason.

The violent and immediate changes of the passions in Lear, so difficult to manage without offending us, are given by Kean with a spirit and with a fitness to nature which we had hardly imagined possible. These are equally well done both before and after he loses his reason. The most difficult scene, in this respect, is the last interview between Lear and his daughters, Goneril and Regan—(and how wonderfully does Kean carry it through!)—the scene which ends with the horrid shout and cry with which he runs out mad from their presence, as if his very brain had taken fire.

The last scene which we are allowed to have of Shakespeare's Lear, for the simply pathetic, was played by Kean with unmatched power. We sink down helpless under the oppressive grief. It lies like a dead weight upon our bosoms. We are denied even the relief of tears; and are thankful for the startling shudder that seizes us when he kneels to his daughter in the deploring weakness of his crazed grief.

It is lamentable that Kean should not be allowed to show his unequalled powers in the last scene of Lear, as Shakespeare has written it; and that this mighty work of genius should be profaned by the miserable, mawkish sort of Edgar's and Cordelia's loves: Nothing can surpass the impertinence of the man who made the change but the folly of those who sanctioned it.

When I began, I had no other intention than that of giving a few general impressions made upon me by Kean's acting; but, falling accidentally upon his Lear, I have been led into more particulars than I was aware of. It is only to take these as some of the instances of his powers in Lear, and then to think of him as not inferior in his other characters, and a slight notion may be formed of the effect of Kean's playing upon those who understand and like him. Neither this, nor all I could say, would reach his great and various powers.

Kean is never behind his author; but stands forward the living representative of the character he has drawn. When he is not playing in Shakespeare he fills up where his author is wanting, and when in Shakespeare, he gives not only what is set down, but whatever the situation and circumstances attendant upon the being he personates would naturally call forth. He seems, at the time, to have possessed himself of Shakespeare's imagination, and to have given it body and form. Read any scene of Shakespeare—for instance, the last of Lear that is played, and see how few words are there set down, and then remember how Kean fills it out with varied and multiplied expressions and circumstances, and the truth of this remark will be obvious at once. There are few men, I believe, let them have studied the plays of Shakespeare ever so attentively, who can see Kean in them without confessing that he has helped them almost as much to a true conception of the author as their own labors had done for them.

It is not easy to say in what character Kean plays best. He so fits himself to each in turn that if the effect he produces at one time is less than at another, it is because of some inferiority in stage-effect in the character. Othello is probably the greatest character for stage-effect; and Kean has an uninterrupted power over us in playing it. When he commands, we are awed; when his face is all sensitive with love, and love thrills in his soft tones, all that our imaginations had pictured to us is realized. His jealousy, his hate, his fixed purposes, are terrific and deadly; and the groans wrung from him in his grief have the pathos and anguish of Esau's when he stood before his old blind father, and sent up "an exceeding bitter cry."

Again, in Richard, how does he hurry forward to his object, sweeping away all between him and it! The world and its affairs are nothing to him till he gains his end. He is all life, and action, and haste—he fills every part of the stage, and seems to do all that is done.

I have before said that his voice is harsh and breaking in his high tones, in his rage, but that this defect is of little consequence in such places. Nor is it well suited to the more declamatory parts. This again is scarce worth considering; for how very little is there of mere declamation in good English plays! But it is one of the finest voices in the world for all the passions and feelings which can be uttered in the middle and lower tones. In Lear:

> "If you have poison for me I will drink it."

And again,

> "You do me wrong to take me o' the grave.
> Thou art a soul in bliss."

Why should I cite passages? Can any man open upon the scene in which these are contained, without Kean's piteous looks and tones being present to him? And does not the mere remembrance of them, as he reads, bring tears into his eyes? Yet, once more, in Othello:

> "Had it pleased heaven
> To try me with affliction," etc.

In the passage beginning with—

> "O now forever
> Farewell the tranquil mind,"——

there was "a mysterious confluence of sounds" passing off into infinite distance, and every thought and feeling within him seemed travelling with them.

How very graceful he is in Othello. It is not a practised, educated grace, but the "unbought grace" of his genius uttering itself in its beauty and grandeur in each movement of the outward man. When he says to Iago so touchingly, "Leave me, leave me, Iago," and turning from him, walks to the back of the stage, raising his hands, and bringing them down upon his head with clasped fingers, and stands thus with his back to us, there is a grace and imposing grandeur in his figure which we gaze on with admiration.

Talking of these things in Kean is something like reading the "Beauties of Shakespeare"; for he is as good in his subordinate as in his great parts. But he must be content to share with other men of genius, and think himself fortunate if one in a hundred sees his lesser beauties, and marks the truth and delicacy of his under playing. For instance; when he has no share in the action going on, he is not busy in putting himself into attitudes to draw attention, but stands or sits in a simple posture, like one with an engaged mind. His countenance is in a state of ordinary repose, with only a slight, general expression of the character of his thoughts; for this is all the face shows when the mind is taken up in silence with its own reflections. It does not assume marked or violent expressions, as in soliloquy. When a man gives utterance to his thoughts, though alone, the charmed rest of the body is broken; he speaks in his gestures too, and the countenance is put into a sympathizing action.

I was first struck with this in his Hamlet; for the deep and quiet interest so marked in Hamlet made the justness of Kean's playing, in this respect, the more obvious.

Since then, I have observed him attentively, and have found the same true acting in his other characters.

This right conception of situation and its general effect, seems to require almost as much genius as his conceptions of his characters. He deserves praise for it; for there is so much of the subtilty of nature in it, if I may so speak, that while a very few are able from his help to put themselves into the situation, and admire the justness of his acting in it, the rest, both those who like him upon the whole, as well as those who profess to see little that is good in him, will be very apt to let it pass by them without observing it.

Like most men, however, Kean receives a partial reward, at least, for his sacrifice of the praise of the many to what he thinks the truth. For when he passes from the state of natural repose, even into that of gentle motion and ordinary discourse, he is at once filled with a spirit and life which he makes everyone feel who is not armor-proof against him. This helps to the sparkling brightness and warmth of his playing; the grand secret of which, like that of colors in a picture, lies in a just contrast. We can all speculate concerning the general rules upon this; but when the man of genius gives us their results, how few are there who can trace them out with an observant eye, or look with a full pleasure upon the grand whole. Perhaps this very beauty in Kean has helped to an opinion, which, no doubt, is sometimes true, that he is too sharp and abrupt. For I well remember, while once looking at a picture in which the shadow of a mountain fell in strong outline upon a stream, I overheard some quite sensible people expressing their wonder that the artist should have made the water of two colors, seeing it was all one and the same thing. * * *

Instances of Kean's keeping of situations were very striking in the opening of the trial scene in the "Iron Chest," and in "Hamlet" when the father's ghost tells the story of his death.

The determined composure to which he is bent up in the first must be present with everyone who saw him. And, though from my immediate purpose, shall I pass by the startling and appalling change, when madness seized upon his brain with the deadly swiftness and power of a fanged monster? Wonderfully as this last part was played, we cannot well imagine how much the previous calm and the suddenness of the unlooked-for change from it added to the terror of the scene. The temple stood fixed on its foundations; the earthquakes shook it, and it was a heap. Is this one of Kean's violent contrasts?

While Kean listened in Hamlet to the father's story the entire man was absorbed in deep attention, mingled with a tempered awe. His posture was quite simple, with a slight inclination forward. The spirit was the spirit of his father whom he had loved and reverenced, and who was to that moment ever present in his thoughts. The first superstitious terror at meeting him had passed off. The account of his father's appearance given him by Horatio and the watch, and his having followed him some distance, had in a degree familiarized him to the sight, and he stood before us in the stillness of one who was to hear, then or never, what was to be told, but without that eager reaching forward which other players give, and which would be right, perhaps, in any character but that of Hamlet, who always connects with the present the past and what is to come, and mingles reflection with his immediate feelings, however deep.

As an instance of Kean's familiar, and, if I may be allowed the term, domestic acting, the first scene in the fourth act of his Sir Giles Overreach may be taken. His manner at meeting Lovell, and through the conversation with him, the way in which he turns his chair and leans upon it, were all as easy and natural as they could have been in real life had Sir Giles been actually existing, and engaged at that moment in conversation in Lovell's room.

It is in these things, scarcely less than in the more prominent parts of his playing, that Kean shows himself the great actor. He must always make a deep impression; but to suppose the world at large capable of a right estimate of his various powers would be forming a judgment against every-day proof. The gradual manner in which the character of his playing has opened upon me satisfies me that in acting, as in everything else, however great may be the first effect of genius upon us, we come slowly, and through study, to a perception of its minute beauties and fine characteristics; and that, after all, the greater part of men seldom get beyond the first vague and general impression.

As there must needs go a *modicum* of fault-finding along with commendation, it may be proper to remark that Kean plays his hands too much at times, and moves about the dress over his breast and neck too frequently in his hurried and impatient passages—that he does not always adhere with sufficient accuracy to the received readings of Shakespeare, and that the effect would be greater upon the whole were he to be more sparing of sudden changes from violent voice and gesticulation to a low conversation tone and subdued manner.

His frequent use of these in Sir Giles Overreach is with great effect, for Sir Giles is playing his part; so, too, in Lear, for Lear's passions are gusty and shifting; but, in the main, it is a kind of playing too marked and striking to bear frequent repetition, and had better sometimes be spared, where, considered alone, it might be properly enough used for the sake of bringing it in at some other place with greater effect.

It is well to speak of these defects, for though the little faults of genius, in themselves considered, but slightly affect those who can enter into its true character, yet such persons are made impatient at the thought that an opportunity is given those to carp who know not how to commend.

Though I have taken up a good deal of room, I must end without speaking of many things which occur to me. Some will be of the opinion that I have already said enough. Thinking of Kean as I do, I could not honestly have said less; for I hold it to be a low and wicked thing to keep back from merit of any kind its due—and, with Steele, that "there is something wonderful in the narrowness of those minds which can be pleased, and be barren of bounty to those who please them."

Although the self-important, out of self-concern, give praise sparingly, and the mean measure theirs by their likings or dislikings of a man, and the good even are often slow to allow the talents of the faulty their due, lest they bring the evil into repute, yet it is the wiser as well as the honester course not to take away from an excellence because it neighbors upon a fault, nor to disparage another with a view to our own name, nor to rest our character for discernment upon the promptings of an unkind heart. Where God has not feared to bestow great powers we may not fear giving them their due; nor need we be parsimonious of commendation, as if there were but a certain quantity for distribution, and our liberality would be to our loss; nor should we hold it safe to detract from another's merit, as if we could always keep the world blind; lest we live to see him whom we disparaged praised, and whom we hated loved.

Whatever be his failings, give every man a full and ready commendation for that in which he excels; it will do good to our own hearts, while it cheers his. Nor will it bring our judgment into question with the discerning; for strong enthusiasm for what is great does not argue such an unhappy want of discrimination as that measured and cold approval which is bestowed alike upon men of mediocrity, and upon those of gifted minds.

ESSAY ON AMERICAN POETRY

—

BY

WILLIAM CULLEN BRYANT

WILLIAM CULLEN BRYANT

1794—1878

William Cullen Bryant was born at Cummington, a small town in Massachusetts, in 1794. His father was a physician of considerable mental attainments, and Bryant's early training under private tutors was extensive and thorough. In 1810 he entered the sophomore class of Williams College, which he left a year later to devote himself to the study of law. From his earliest boyhood Bryant was a lover of nature, and at fourteen he had written some verses his father thought worth publishing. At eighteen he wrote "Thanatopsis," the noblest poem yet written in America, but owing to his innate modesty it remained hidden in his desk for several years till it was discovered by his father, who sent it to the "North American Review," in which it was published in 1817. The next year "To a Waterfowl" was published in the same magazine three years after it was written. Bryant also wrote at this time a review of a collection of American poetry which appeared later in a somewhat changed form as an "Essay on American Poetry." In this paper, which is interesting to-day both on account of its subject-matter and the date of its appearance, Bryant passed in review all the writers of verse on this side of the Atlantic who had ventured into print save, as he expressed himself, some "whose passage to that oblivion toward which, to the honor of our country they were hastening," he did not wish to interrupt.

In 1825 Bryant abandoned the practice of law, leaving Great Barrington for New York to devote himself entirely to literary pursuits. In 1826 he became connected with the "Evening Post," of which he continued to be the editor and principal proprietor till his death. While struggling to secure a foothold in New York, Bryant contributed to the magazines many of his finest poems. For "The Death of the Flowers" he received a remuneration of two dollars, and was "abundantly satisfied." In 1821, soon after reading "The Ages" before the Phi Beta Kappa Society at Harvard, Bryant published a small volume containing many of his best poems. Ten years later a second volume was published, containing about eighty additional poems, and others were added to subsequent editions. In 1863 appeared "Thirty Poems," consisting wholly of later work. In 1870 his translation of the Iliad appeared, followed two years later by his translation of the Odyssey. Most of Bryant's energies were, however, of necessity directed to his journalistic activity, especially during the stormy period of the slavery agitation of secession and reconstruction. His idea of the importance of an editor's mission was a lofty one, and he made the "Evening Post" a power during the half century that he was identified with it. He died in 1878.

Bryant's literary style, both in poetry and prose, is marked by great purity and elegance. His editorials, written invariably in the confusion of a newspaper office, were models of English prose. In our estimate of Bryant we must be guided by the quality of his work rather than its quantity. As a poet of nature he holds justly the foremost place among the poets of America.

ESSAY ON AMERICAN POETRY

OF the poetry of the United States[1] different opinions have been entertained, and prejudice on the one side and partiality on the other have equally prevented a just and rational estimate of its merits. Abroad our literature has fallen under unmerited contumely from those who were but slenderly acquainted with the subject on which they professed to decide; and at home it must be confessed that the swaggering and pompous pretensions of many have done not a little to provoke and excuse the ridicule of foreigners. Either of these extremes exerts an injurious influence on the cause of letters in our country. To encourage exertion and embolden merit to come forward, it is necessary that they should be acknowledged and rewarded. Few will have the confidence to solicit what is wantonly withheld, or the courage to tread a path which presents no prospect but the melancholy wrecks of those who have gone before them. National gratitude, national pride—every high and generous feeling that attaches us to the land of our birth, or that exalts our characters as individuals—ask of us that we should foster the infant literature of our country, and that genius and industry, employing their efforts to hasten its perfection, should receive from our hands that celebrity which reflects as much honor on the nation which confers it as on those to whom it is extended. On the other hand, it is not necessary for these purposes—it is even detrimental—to bestow on mediocrity the praise due to excellence, and still more so is the attempt to persuade ourselves and others into an admiration of the faults of favorite writers. We make but a contemptible figure in the eyes of the world, and set ourselves up as objects of pity to our posterity, when we affect to rank the poets of our own country with those mighty masters of song who have flourished in Greece, Italy, and Britain. Such

[1] [This essay was first published in the "North American Review" for July, 1818.—EDITOR.]

extravagant admiration may spring from a praiseworthy and patriotic motive, but it seems to us that it defeats its own object of encouraging our literature, by seducing those who would aspire to the favor of the public into an imitation of imperfect models, and leading them to rely too much on the partiality of their countrymen to overlook their deficiencies. Were our rewards to be bestowed only on what is intrinsically meritorious, merit alone would have any apology for appearing before the public. The poetical adventurer should be taught that it is only the productions of genius, taste, and diligence that can find favor at the bar of criticism; that his writings are not to be applauded merely because they are written by an American and are not decidedly bad; and that he must produce some more satisfactory evidence of his claim to celebrity than an extract from the parish register. To show him what we expect of him, it is as necessary to point out the faults of his predecessors as to commend their excellences. He must be taught as well what to avoid as what to imitate. This is the only way of diffusing and preserving a pure taste, both among those who read and those who write, and, in our opinion, the only way of affording merit a proper and effectual encouragement.

It must, however, be allowed that the poetry of the United States, though it has not reached any high degree of perfection, is yet, perhaps, better than it could have been expected to be, considering that our nation has scarcely seen two centuries since its founders erected their cabins on its soil, and that our citizens are just beginning to find leisure to attend to intellectual refinements, to indulge in intellectual luxury, and to afford the means of rewarding intellectual excellence. For the first century after the settlement of this country, the few quaint and unskilful specimens of poetry which yet remain to us are looked upon merely as objects of curiosity, are preserved only in the cabinet of the antiquary, and give little pleasure if read without reference to the age and people which produced them. After this period a purer taste began to prevail. The poems of the Rev. John Adams, written in the early part of the eighteenth century, which have been considered as no bad specimens of the poetry of his time, are tolerably free from the faults of the generation that preceded him, and show the dawnings of an ambition of correctness and elegance. The poetical writings of Joseph Green, Esq., who wrote about the middle of the same century, have been admired for their humor and the playful ease of their composition.

But previous to the contest which terminated in the independence of the United States we can hardly be said to have had any national poetry. Literary ambition was not then frequent amongst us—there was little motive for it, and few rewards. We were contented with considering ourselves as participating in the literary fame of that nation of which we were a part, and of which many of us were natives, and aspired to no separate distinction. And, indeed, we might well lay an equal claim, with those who remained on the British soil, to whatever glory the genius and learning, as well as the virtue and bravery, of other times reflected on the British name. These were qualities which ennobled our common ancestors; and, though their graves were not with us, and we were at a distance from the scenes and haunts which were hallowed by their deeds, their studies and their contemplations, yet we brought with us and preserved all the more valuable gifts which they left to their posterity and to mankind—their illumination, their piety, their spirit of liberty, reverence for their memory and example, and all the proud tokens of a generous descent.

Yet here was no theatre for the display of literary talent. The worshippers of fame could find no altars erected to that divinity in America, and he who would live by his pen must seek patronage in the parent country. Some men of taste and learning amongst us might occasionally amuse their leisure with poetical trifles, but a country struggling with the difficulties of colonization, and possessing no superfluous wealth, wanted any other class of men rather than poets. Accordingly, we find the specimens of American poetry before this period mostly desultory and occasional—rare and delicate exotics, cultivated only by the curious.

On our becoming an independent empire a different spirit began to manifest itself, and the general ambition to distinguish ourselves as a nation was not without its effect on our literature. It seems to us that it is from this time only that we can be said to have poets of our own, and from this period it is that we must date the origin of American poetry. About this time flourished Francis Hopkinson, whose humorous ballad, entitled "The Battle of the Kegs," is in most of our memories, and some of whose attempts, though deficient in vigor, are not inelegant. The keen and forcible invectives of Dr. Church, which are still recollected by his contemporaries, received an additional edge and sharpness from the exasperated feelings of the times. A writer in verse of inferior note was Philip Freneau, whose pen seems to have been chiefly employed on political subjects, and whose occasional productions, distinguished by a coarse strength of sarcasm, and abounding with allusions to passing events, which is perhaps their greatest merit, attracted in their time considerable notice, and, in the year 1786, were collected into a volume. But the influence of that principle which awoke and animated the exertions of all who participated in the political enthusiasm of that time was still more strongly exemplified in the Connecticut poets—Trumbull, Dwight, Barlow, Humphreys, and Hopkins—who began to write about this period. In all the productions of these authors there is a pervading spirit of nationality and patriotism, a desire to reflect credit on the country to which they belonged, which seems, as much as individual ambition, to have prompted their efforts, and which at times gives a certain glow and interest to their manner.

"McFingal," the most popular of the writings of the former of these poets, first appeared in the year 1782. This pleasant satire on the adherents of Britain in those times may be pronounced a tolerably successful imitation of the great work of Butler, though, like every other imitation of that author, it wants that varied and inexhaustible fertility of allusion which made all subjects of thought, the lightest and most abstruse parts of learning—everything in the physical and moral world, in art or nature—the playthings of his wit. The work of Trumbull cannot be much praised for the purity of its diction. Yet, perhaps great scrupulousness in this particular was not consistent with the plan of the author, and, to give the scenes of this poem their full effect, it might have been thought necessary to adopt the familiar dialect of the country and the times. We think his "Progress of Dulness" a more pleasing poem, more finished and more perfect in its kind, and, though written in the same manner, more free from the constraint and servility of imitation. The graver poems of Trumbull contain some vigorous and animated declamations.

Of Dr. Dwight we would speak with all the respect due to talents, to learning, to piety, and a long life of virtuous usefulness, but we must be excused from feeling any high admiration of his poetry. It seems to us modelled upon a manner altogether too artificial and mechanical. There is something strained, violent, and out of nature in all his attempts. His "Conquest of Canaan" will not secure immortality to its author. In this work he has been considered by some as by no means happy in the choice of his fable. However this may be, he has certainly failed to avail himself of the advantages it offered him; his epic wants the creations and colorings of an inventive and poetical fancy—the charm which, in the hands of genius, communicates an interest to the simplest incidents, and something of the illusion of reality to the most improbable fictions. The versification is remarkable for its unbroken monotony. Yet it contains splendid passages, which, separated from the body of the work, might be admired, but a few pages pall both on the ear and the imagination. It has been urged in its favor that the writer was young. The poetry of his maturer years does not, however, seem to possess greater beauties or fewer faults. The late Mr. Dennie at one time exerted his ingenuity to render this poem popular with his countrymen; in the year 1800 he published, in the "Farmers' Museum"—a paper printed at Walpole, of which he was the editor—a series of observations and criticisms on the "Conquest of Canaan," after the manner of Addison in those numbers of the "Spectator" which made Milton a favorite with the English people. But this attempt did not meet with success; the work would not sell, and loads of copies yet cumber the shelves of the booksellers. In the other poems of Dr. Dwight, which are generally open to the same criticisms, he sometimes endeavors to descend to a more familiar style, and entertains his reader with laborious attempts at wit; and here he is still unsuccessful. Parts of his "Greenfield Hill," and that most unfortunate of his productions, the "Triumph of Infidelity," will confirm the truth of this remark.

Barlow, when he began to write, was a poet of no inconsiderable promise. His "Hasty Pudding," one of his earliest productions, is a good specimen of mock-heroic poetry, and his "Vision of Columbus," at the time of its first appearance, attracted much attention, and was hailed as an earnest of better things. It is no small praise to say that, when appointed by the General Assembly of Churches in Connecticut to revise Watts's "Version of the Psalms," and to versify such as were omitted in that work, he performed the task in a manner which made a near approach to the simplicity and ease of that poet who, according to Dr. Johnson, "has done better than anybody else what nobody has done well." In his maturer years Barlow became ambitious of distinguishing himself and doing honor to his country by some more splendid and important exertions of his talents, and, for this purpose, projected a national epic, in which was sung the "Discovery of America," the successful struggle of the States in the defence of their liberties, and the exalted prospects which were opening before them. It is to be regretted that a design so honorable and so generously conceived should have failed. In 1807 appeared the "Columbiad," which was his poem of the "Vision of Columbus," much enlarged, and with such variations as the feelings and reflections of his riper age and judgment led him to make. The "Columbiad" is not, in our opinion, so pleasing a poem in its present form as in that in which it was originally written. The plan of the work is utterly destitute of interest, and that which was at first sufficiently wearisome has become doubly so by being drawn out to its present length. Nor are the additions of much value, on account of the taste in which they are composed. Barlow, in his later poetry, attempted to invigorate his style, but, instead of drawing strength and salubrity from the pure wells of ancient English, he corrupted and debased it with foreign infusions. The imposing but unchaste glitter which distinguished the manner of Darwin and his imitators appears likewise to have taken strong hold on his fancy, and he has not scrupled to bestow on his poem much of this meretricious decoration. But, notwithstanding the bad taste in which his principal work is composed, notwithstanding he cannot be said to write with much pathos or many of the native felicities of fancy, there is yet enough in the poetry of Mr. Barlow to prove that, had he fixed his eye on purer models, he might have excelled, not indeed in epic or narrative poetry nor in the delineation of passion and feeling, but in that calm, lofty, sustained style which suits best with topics of morality and philosophy, and for which the vigor and spirit of his natural manner, whenever he permits it to appear, show him to have been well qualified.

Humphreys was a poet of humbler pretensions. His writings, which were first collected in 1790, are composed in better taste than those of the two last, and if he has less genius, he has likewise fewer faults. Some of his lighter pieces are sufficiently pretty. He is most happy when he aims at nothing beyond an elegant mediocrity, and, to do him justice, this is generally the extent of his ambition. On the whole, he may be considered as sustaining a respectable rank among the poets of our country.

A writer of a different cast from those we have mentioned, and distinguished by a singular boldness of imagination as well as great humor, was Dr. Lemuel Hopkins, who, in 1786 and the year following, in conjunction with Trumbull, Barlow, and Humphreys, and other wits of that time, wrote the "Anarchiad," a satire on a plan similar to that of the "Rolliad," which appeared in the "New Haven Gazette" of those years, and of which the mildest parts are attributed to him. He was likewise author of the "Speech of Hesper," and some smaller poems, which have been praised for their wit. There is a coarseness, and want of polish in his style, and his imagination, daring and original, but unrestrained by a correct judgment, often wanders into absurdities and extravagances. Still if he had all the madness, he must be allowed to have possessed some of the inspiration of poetry.

One material error of taste pervades the graver productions of these authors, into which it would seem they were led by copying certain of the poets of England, who flourished near the period in which they began to write. It was their highest ambition to attain a certain lofty, measured, declamatory manner—an artificial elevation of style, from which it is impossible to rise or descend without abruptness and violence, and which allows just as much play and freedom to the faculties of the writer as a pair of stilts allows the body. The imagination is confined to one trodden circle, doomed to the chains of a perpetual mannerism, and condemned to tinkle the same eternal tune, with its fetters. Their versification, though not equally exceptionable in all, is formed upon the same stately model of balanced and wearisome regularity. Another fault, which arises naturally enough out of the peculiar style which we have imputed to these poets, is the want of pathos and feeling in their writings; the heart is rarely addressed, and never with much power or success. Amidst this coldness of manner, sameness of imagery, and monotony of versification, the reader lays down his book, dazzled and fatigued.

In 1800 appeared the poems of William Clifton, who fell, at the age of twenty-seven, a victim to that scourge of our climate which ceases not to waste when other diseases are sated—the pulmonary consumption. There is none of our American poetry on which we dwell with more pleasure, mingled, indeed, with regret at the untimely fate of the writer, than these charming remains. Amidst many of the immature effusions of his greener years, and unfinished productions which were never meant to meet the eye of the world, there are to be found specimens of poetry, not only more delicate, classical, and polished, but more varied in imagery, and possessing more of that flexibility of style, of the want of which in others we have complained, and more faithful to nature and the feelings, than it has often been our lot to meet with in the works of our native poets. In his later and more finished productions his diction is refined to an unusual degree of purity, and through this lucid medium the creations of his elegant fancy appear, with nothing to obscure their loveliness.

The posthumous works of St. John Honeywood, Esq., were published in the year 1801. These modest remains, the imperfect but vigorous productions of no common mind, have not been noticed as they deserved. They contain many polished and nervous lines.

We should not expect to be easily pardoned were we to pass by the writings of a poet who enjoyed, during his lifetime, so extensive a popularity as the late Mr. Paine.[2] The first glow of admiration, which the splendid errors of his man-

[2] [Robert Treat Paine, an American poet of great promise, whose collected works were published in 1812, is here referred to. He was the son of Robert Treat Paine, the statesman and signer of the Declaration of Independence.—EDITOR.]

ner excited in the public, is now over, and we can calmly estimate his merits and defects. He must be allowed to have possessed an active and fertile fancy. Even in the misty obscurity which often shrouds his conceptions, not only from the understanding of the reader, but, it would seem, from that of the writer himself, there sometimes break out glimpses of greatness and majesty. Yet with a force and exuberance of imagination which, if soberly directed, might have gained him the praise of magnificence, he is perpetually wandering in search of conceits and extravagances. He is ambitious of the epigrammatic style, and often bewilders himself with attempts to express pointedly what he does not conceive clearly. More instances of the false sublime might, perhaps, be selected from the writings of this poet than from those of any other of equal talents who lived in the same period. The brilliancy of Paine's poetry is like the brilliancy of frost-work—cold and fantastic. Who can point out the passage in his works in which he speaks to the heart in its own language? He was a fine but misguided genius.

With respect to the style of poetry prevailing at the present day in our country, we apprehend that it will be found, in too many instances, tinged with a sickly and affected imitation of the peculiar manner of some of the late popular poets of England. We speak not of a disposition to emulate whatever is beautiful and excellent in their writings, still less would we be understood as intending to censure that sort of imitation which, exploring all the treasures of English poetry, culls from all a diction that shall form a natural and becoming dress for the conceptions of the writer—this is a course of preparation which everyone ought to go through before he appears before the public—but we desire to set a mark on that servile habit of copying which adopts the vocabulary of some favorite author, and apes the fashion of his sentences, and cramps and forces the ideas into a shape which they would not naturally have taken, and of which the only recommendation is, not that it is most elegant or most striking, but that it bears some resemblance to the manner of him who is proposed as a model. This way of writing has an air of poverty and meanness; it seems to indicate a paucity of reading as well as a perversion of taste; it might almost lead us to suspect that the writer had but one or two examples of poetical composition in his hands and was afraid of expressing himself, except according to some formula which they might contain; and it ever has been, and ever will be, the resort of those who are sensible that their works need some factitious recommendation to give them even a temporary popularity.

We have now given a brief summary of what we conceive to be the characteristic merits and defects of our most celebrated American poets. Some names, of which we are not at present aware, equally deserving of notice with those whom we have mentioned, may have been omitted; some we have passed over because we would not willingly disturb their passage to that oblivion toward which, to the honor of our country, they are hastening; and some elegant productions of later date we have not commented on, because we were unwilling to tire our readers with a discussion which they may think already exhausted.

On the whole, there seems to be more good taste among those who read than those who write poetry in our country. With respect to the poets whom we have enumerated, and whose merits we have discussed, we think the judgment pronounced on their works by the public will be found, generally speaking, just. They hold that station in our literature to which they are entitled, and could heardly be admired more than they are without danger to the taste of the nation. We know of no instance in which great poetical merit has come forward, and, finding its claims unallowed, been obliged to retire to the shade from which it emerged. Whenever splendid talents of this description shall appear, we believe that there will be found a disposition to encourage and reward them. The fondness for literature is fast increasing, and, if this were not the case, the patrons of literature have multiplied, of course, and will continue to multiply with the mere growth of our population. The popular English works of the day are often reprinted in our country, they are dispersed all over the Union; they are found in everybody's hands, they are made the subject of everybody's conversation. What should hinder our native works, if equal in merit, from meeting an equally favorable reception?

APOLLO MUSAGETES.

(Leading the Muses.)

Photo-engraving from the statue in the Vatican Gallery at Rome.

The statue represents the god as crowned with laurel and wearing the long Ionian robe of a harper. It is a copy of an original work by Scopas, 420–350 B.C. This cop[illegible] was [illegible] set up [illegible] [illegible]ple of Apollo which the [illegible]mperor Augustus dedicated on the Palatine Hill, [illegible] B.C. [illegible] gardens of Cassius at Tivoli in 1774, and placed as one of the mos[illegible] [illegible]ciou[illegible] in th[illegible] of antique sculpture among the treasures of the Vatican.

SIR WALTER SCOTT

—

BY

WILLIAM HICKLING PRESCOTT

WILLIAM HICKLING PRESCOTT

1796—1859

William Hickling Prescott was born in Salem, Massachusetts, in 1796. His father was a prominent and wealthy lawyer who almost idolized his handsome and talented son. He entered Harvard College in 1811, intending to study law on his graduation, but during his junior year met with an accident to one of his eyes that changed all his life plans. Oculists both in this country and abroad were consulted, but in spite of expert treatment he became practically blind. Under these depressing circumstances he took up the study of literature with a view to making it his life work. He began a year of study, with the aid of a reader and an amanuensis, desiring in this way to perfect himself in style and in general culture. Then, in 1826, he decided to take up the "Reign of Ferdinand and Isabella" as his first subject of historical study and investigation. After three years and a half of preparation he began to write, but even then, so painstaking and thorough was his work that at the end of sixteen months only three hundred pages were completed. Ten years passed before the volumes were issued from the press. To the astonishment of author and publisher alike, copies could not be printed fast enough to meet the demand, and Prescott found himself suddenly famous. He next devoted six years to his "History of the Conquest of Mexico," which was brought out in 1843. Four years later "The Conquest of Peru" was published, and the "History of Philip II" begun. The first two volumes of the latter work came from the press in 1855, and a third volume was issued in 1858. Prescott, however, did not live to complete this volume. He died at his residence on Beacon Street in Boston in 1859.

Prescott has a twofold interest for the American student. Not only was he a great historian, but his writings have a distinct literary as well as historical value. Indeed, so brilliant is his literary method that some critics have questioned his historical accuracy, but later scholarship has borne him out in this respect, except, perhaps, in passages of "Mexico" and "Peru," where his Spanish authorities have since been found untrustworthy. Aside from his historical writings we have comparatively little from Prescott's pen. A number of articles were published in the "North American Review," chiefly historical and biographical, while a few are on purely literary topics. His essays on Italian poetry give proof of Prescott's literary culture and acumen as a critic, as does his admirable essay on "Sir Walter Scott." These, however, stand almost alone, and it is on his writings as an historian that Prescott's fame rests. That his reputation will be an enduring one there can be no doubt. His works still remain an authority and are as widely read as ever; they have lost none of their fascination, their vividness and power, in spite of the somewhat changed literary taste and the method of scientific investigation of our day.

Prescott's literary style, as Hallam declared, "appears to be nearly perfect." It is clear, vivid, full of movement, and abounds in dramatic passages of absorbing interest.

SIR WALTER SCOTT

THERE is no kind of writing which has truth and instruction for its main object so interesting and popular, on the whole, as biography. History, in its larger sense, has to deal with masses, which, while they divide the attention by the dazzling variety of objects, from their very generality are scarcely capable of touching the heart. The great objects on which it is employed have little relation to the daily occupations with which the reader is most intimate. A nation, like a corporation, seems to have no soul; and its checkered vicissitudes may be contemplated rather with curiosity for the lessons they convey than with personal sympathy. How different are the feelings excited by the fortunes of an individual—one of the mighty mass, who in the page of history is swept along the current, unnoticed and unknown! Instead of a mere abstraction, at once we see a being like ourselves, "fed with the same food, hurt with the same weapons, subject to the same diseases, healed by the same means, warmed and cooled by the same winter and summer" as we are. We place ourselves in his position, and see the passing current of events with the same eyes. We become a party to all his little schemes, share in his triumphs, or mourn with him in the disappointment of defeat. His friends become our friends. We learn to take an interest in their characters, from their relation to him. As they pass away from the stage, one after another, and as the clouds of misfortune, perhaps, or of disease, settle around the evening of his own day, we feel the same sadness that steals over us on a retrospect of earlier and happier hours. And, when at last we have followed him to the tomb, we close the volume, and feel that we have turned over another chapter in the history of life.

On the same principles, probably, we are more moved by the exhibition of those characters whose days have been passed in the ordinary routine of domestic and social life than by those most intimately connected with the great public events of their age. What, indeed, is the history of such men but that of the times? The life of Wellington, or of Bonaparte, is the story of the wars and revolutions of Europe. But that of Cowper, gliding away in the seclusion of rural solitude, reflects all those domestic joys, and, alas! more than the sorrows, which gather round every man's fireside and his heart. In this way the story of the humblest individual, faithfully recorded, becomes an object of lively interest. How much is that interest increased in the case of a man like Scott, who, from his own fireside, has sent forth a voice to cheer and delight millions of his fellow men; whose life, indeed, passed within the narrow circle of his own village, as it were, but who, nevertheless, has called up more shapes and fantasies within that magic circle, acted more extraordinary parts, and afforded more marvels for the imagination to feed on, than can be furnished by the most nimble-footed, nimble-tongued traveller, from Marco Polo down to Mrs. Trollope, and that literary Sindbad, Captain Hall!

Fortunate as Sir Walter Scott was in his life, it is not the least of his good fortunes that he left the task of recording it to one so competent as Mr. Lockhart;[1] who, to a familiarity with the person and habits of his illustrious subject, unites such entire sympathy with his pursuits, and such fine tact and discrimination in arranging the materials for their illustration We have seen it objected that the biographer has somewhat transcended his lawful limits in occasionally exposing what a nice tenderness for the reputation of Scott should have led him to conceal. But, on reflection, we are not inclined to adopt these views. It is, indeed, difficult to prescribe any precise rule by which the biographer should be guided in exhibiting the peculiarities, and still more the defects, of his subject. He should, doubtless, be slow to draw from obscurity those matters which are of a strictly personal and private nature, particularly when they have no material bearing on the character of the individual. But whatever the latter has done, said, or written to others, can rarely be made to come within this rule. A swell of panegyric, where everything is in broad sunshine, without the relief of a shadow to contrast it, is out of nature, and

[1] "Memoirs of the Life of Sir Walter Scott, Bart.," by J. G. Lockhart.

must bring discredit on the whole. Nor is it much better, when a sort of twilight mystification is spread over a man's actions, until, as in the case of all biographies of Cowper previous to that of Southey, we are completely bewildered respecting the real motives of conduct. If ever there was a character above the necessity of any management of this sort, it was Scott's; and we cannot but think that the frank exposition of the minor blemishes which sully it, by securing the confidence of the reader in the general fidelity of the portraiture, and thus disposing him to receive, without distrust, those favorable statements in his history which might seem incredible, as they certainly are unprecedented, is, on the whole, advantageous to his reputation. As regards the moral effect on the reader, we may apply Scott's own argument for not always recompensing suffering virtue, at the close of his fictions, with temporal prosperity, that such an arrangement would convey no moral to the heart whatever, since a glance at the great picture of life would show that virtue is not always thus rewarded.

In regard to the literary execution of Mr. Lockhart's work, the public voice has long since pronounced on it. A prying criticism may, indeed, discern a few of those contraband epithets, and slipshod sentences, more excusable in young "Peter's Letters to his Kinsfolk," where, indeed, they are thickly sown, than in the production of a grave Aristarch of British criticism. But this is small game where every reader of the least taste and sensibility must find so much to applaud. It is enough to say that, in passing from the letters of Scott, with which the work is besprinkled, to the text of the biographer, we find none of those chilling transitions which occur on the like occasions in more bungling productions; as, for example, in that recent one, in which the unfortunate Hannah More is done to death by her friend Roberts. On the contrary, we are sensible only to a new variety of beauty in the style of composition. The correspondence is illumined by all that is needed to make it intelligible to a stranger, and selected with such discernment as to produce the clearest impression of the character of its author. The mass of interesting details is conveyed in language richly colored with poetic sentiment, and at the same time without a tinge of that mysticism which, as Scott himself truly remarked, "will never do for a writer of fiction, no, nor of history, nor moral essays, nor sermons"; but which, nevertheless, finds more or less favor in our own community, at the present day, in each and all of these.

The work [2] from which the last remark of Sir Walter's was borrowed, is a series of notices originally published in "Fraser's Magazine," but now collected, with considerable additions, into a separate volume. Its author, Mr. Robert Pierce Gillies, is a gentleman of the Scotch bar, favorably known by translations from the German. The work conveys a lively report of several scenes and events which, before the appearance of Lockhart's book, were of more interest and importance than they can now be, lost as they are in the flood of light which is poured on us from that source. In the absence of the sixth and last volume, however, Mr. Gillies may help us to a few particulars respecting the closing years of Sir Walter's life that may have some novelty—we know not how much to be relied on—for the reader. In the present notice of a work so familiar to most persons we shall confine ourselves to some of those circumstances which contributed to form, or have an obvious connection with, his literary character.

Walter Scott was born at Edinburgh, August 15, 1771. The character of his father, a respectable member of that class of attorneys who in Scotland are called Writers to the Signet, is best conveyed to the reader by saying that he sat for the portrait of Mr. Saunders Fairford, in "Redgauntlet." His mother was a woman of taste and imagination, and had an obvious influence in guiding those of her son. His ancestors, by both father's and mother's side, were of "gentle blood"—a position which, placed between the highest and the lower ranks in society, was extremely favorable, as affording facilities for communication with both. A lameness in his infancy—a most fortunate lameness for the world, if, as Scott says, it spoiled a soldier—and a delicate constitution made it expedient to try the efficacy of country air and diet; and he was placed under the roof of his paternal grandfather at Sandy-Knowe, a few miles distant from the capital. Here his days were passed in the open fields, "with no other fellowship," as he says, "than that of the sheep and lambs"; and here, in the lap of nature—

"Meet nurse for a poetic child,"

[2] "Recollections of Sir Walter Scott," by R. P. Gillies.

his infant vision was greeted with those rude, romantic scenes which his own verses have since hallowed for the pilgrims from every clime. In the long evenings, his imagination, as he grew older, was warmed by traditionary legends of border heroism and adventure, repeated by the aged relative who had herself witnessed the last gleams of border chivalry. His memory was one of the first powers of his mind which exhibited an extraordinary development. One of the longest of these old ballads, in particular, stuck so close to it, and he repeated it with such stentorian vociferation, as to draw from the minister of a neighboring kirk the testy exclamation, "One may as well speak in the mouth of a cannon as where that child is."

On his removal to Edinburgh, in his eighth year, he was subjected to different influences. His worthy father was a severe martinet in all the forms of his profession, and it may be added, indeed, of his religion, which he contrived to make somewhat burdensome to his more volatile son. The tutor was still more strict in his religious sentiments, and the lightest literary *divertissement* in which either of them indulged was such as could be gleaned from the time-honored folios of Archbishop Spottiswoode, or worthy Robert Wodrow. Even here, however, Scott's young mind contrived to gather materials and impulses for future action. In his long arguments with Master Mitchell he became steeped in the history of the Covenanters and the persecuted Church of Scotland, while he was still more rooted in his own Jacobite notions, early instilled into his mind by the tales of his relatives of Sandy-Knowe, whose own family had been out in the "affair of forty-five." Amid the professional and polemical worthies of his father's library, Scott detected a copy of Shakespeare; and he relates with what *goût* he used to creep out of his bed, where he had been safely deposited for the night, and, by the light of the fire, *in puris naturalibus,* as it were, pore over the pages of the great magician, and study those mighty spells by which he gave to airy fantasies the forms and substance of humanity. Scott distinctly recollected the time and the spot where he first opened a volume of Percy's "Reliques of English Poetry"; a work which may have suggested to him the plan and the purpose of the "Border Minstrelsy." Every day's experience shows us how much more actively the business of education goes on out of school than in it. And Scott's history shows equally that genius, whatever obstacles may be thrown in its way in one direction, will find room for its expansion in another; as the young tree sends forth its shoots most prolific in that quarter where the sunshine is permitted to fall on it.

At the high school, in which he was placed by his father at an early period, he seems not to have been particularly distinguished in the regular course of studies. His voracious appetite for books, however, of a certain cast, as romances, chivalrous tales, and worm-eaten chronicles scarcely less chivalrous, and his wonderful memory for such reading as struck his fancy, soon made him regarded by his fellows as a phenomenon of black-letter scholarship, which in process of time achieved for him the cognomen of that redoubtable schoolman, Duns Scotus. He now also gave evidence of his powers of creation as well as of acquisition. He became noted for his own stories, generally bordering on the marvellous, with a plentiful seasoning of knight-errantry, which suited his bold and chivalrous temper. "Slink over beside me, Jamie," he would whisper to his schoolfellow Ballantyne, "and I'll tell you a story." Jamie was, indeed, destined to sit beside him during the greater part of his life.

The same tastes and talents continued to display themselves more strongly with increasing years. Having beaten pretty thoroughly the ground of romantic and legendary lore, at least so far as the English libraries to which he had access would permit, he next endeavored, while at the university, to which he had been transferred from the high school, to pursue the same subject in the Continental languages. Many were the strolls which he took in the neighborhood, especially to Arthur's Seat and Salisbury Crags, where, perched on some almost inaccessible eyrie, he might be seen conning over his Ariosto or Cervantes, or some other bard of romance, with some favorite companion of his studies, or pouring into the ears of the latter his own boyish legends, glowing with

"... achievements high,
And circumstance of chivalry."

A critical knowledge of these languages he seems not to have obtained; and, even in the French, made but an indifferent figure in conversation. An accurate acquaintance with the pronunciation and prosody of a foreign tongue is undoubtedly a desirable accomplishment. But it is, after all, a mere accomplishment, subordinate to the great purposes for which a language is to be learned. Scott did not, as is too often the case, mistake the shell for the kernel. He looked on language only as the key to unlock the foreign stores of wisdom, the pearls of inestimable price, wherever found, with which to enrich his native literature.

After a brief residence at the university he was regularly indented as an apprentice to his father, in 1786. One can hardly imagine a situation less congenial with the ardent, effervescing spirit of a poetic fancy; fettered down to a daily routine of drudgery, scarcely above that of a mere scrivener. It proved a useful school of discipline to him, however. It formed early habits of method, punctuality, and laborious industry; business habits, in short, most adverse to the poetic temperament, but indispensable to the accomplishment of the gigantic tasks which he afterward assumed. He has himself borne testimony to his general diligence in his new vocation, and tells us that on one occasion be transcribed no less than a hundred and twenty folio pages at a sitting.

In the midst of these mechanical duties, however, he did not lose sight of the favorite objects of his study and meditation. He made frequent excursions into the Lowland as well as Highland districts, in search of traditionary relics. These pilgrimages he frequently performed on foot. His constitution, now become hardy by severe training, made him careless of exposure, and his frank and warm-hearted manners—eminently favorable to his purposes, by thawing at once any feelings of frosty reserve, which might have encountered a stranger—made him equally welcome at the staid and decorous manse, and at the rough but hospitable board of the peasant. Here was indeed the study of the future novelist; the very school in which to meditate those models of character and situation which he was afterward, long afterward, to transfer, in such living colors, to the canvas. "He was makin' himsell a' the time," says one of his companions, "but he didna ken, maybe, what he was about, till years had past. At first he thought o' little, I dare say, but the queerness and the fun." The honest Writer to the

Signet does not seem to have thought it either so funny or so profitable; for on his son's return from one of these raids, as he styled them, the old gentleman peevishly inquired how he had been living so long. "Pretty much like the young ravens," answered Walter; "I only wished I had been as good a player on the flute as poor George Primrose in 'The Vicar of Wakefield.' If I had his art, I should like nothing better than to tramp like him from cottage to cottage over the world." "I doubt," said the grave Clerk to the Signet, "I greatly doubt, sir, you were born for nae better than a *gangrel scrapegut!*" Perhaps even the revelation, could it have been made to him, of his son's future literary glory, would scarcely have satisfied the worthy father, who, probably, would have regarded a seat on the bench of the Court of Sessions as much higher glory. At all events, this was not far from the judgment of Dominie Mitchell, who, in his notice of his illustrious pupil, "sincerely regrets that Sir Walter's precious time was so much devoted to the *dulce* rather than the *utile* of composition, and that his great talents should have been wasted on such subjects"!

It is impossible to glance at Scott's early life without perceiving how powerfully all its circumstances, whether accidental or contrived, conspired to train him for the peculiar position he was destined to occupy in the world of letters. There never was a character in whose infant germ, as it were, the mature and fully developed lineaments might be more distinctly traced. What he was in his riper age, so he was in his boyhood. We discern the same tastes, the same peculiar talents, the same social temper and affections, and, in a great degree, the same habits—in their embryo state, of course, but distinctly marked—and his biographer has shown no little skill in enabling us to trace their gradual, progressive expansion, from the hour of his birth up to the full prime and maturity of manhood.

In 1792, Scott, whose original destination of a Writer had been changed to that of an Advocate—from his father's conviction, as it would seem, of the superiority of his talents to the former station—was admitted to the Scottish bar. Here he continued in assiduous attendance during the regular terms, but more noted for his stories in the Outer House than his arguments in court. It may appear singular that a person so gifted, both as a writer and as a *raconteur,* should have had no greater success in his profession. But the case is not uncommon. Indeed, experience shows that the most eminent writers have not made the most successful speakers. It is not more strange than that a good writer of novels should not excel as a dramatic author. Perhaps a consideration of the subject would lead us to refer the phenomena in both cases to the same principle. At all events, Scott was an exemplification of both; and we leave the solution to those who have more leisure and ingenuity to unravel the mystery.

Scott's leisure, in the mean time, was well employed in storing his mind with German romance, with whose wild fictions, intrenching on the grotesque, indeed, he found at that time more sympathy than in later life. In 1796 he first appeared before the public as a translator of Bürger's well-known ballads, thrown off by him at a heat, and which found favor with the few into whose hands they passed. He subsequently adventured in Monk Lewis's crazy bark—"Tales of Wonder"—which soon went to pieces, leaving, however, among its surviving fragments the scattered contributions of Scott.

At last, in 1802, he gave to the world his first two volumes of the "Border Minstrelsy," printed by his old school-fellow, Ballantyne, and which, by the beauty of the typography, as well as literary execution, made a sort of epoch in Scottish literary history. There was no work of Scott's after-life which showed the result of so much preliminary labor. Before ten years old, he had collected several volumes of ballads and traditions, and we have seen how diligently he pursued the same vocation in later years. The publication was admitted to be far more faithful, as well as more skilfully collated, than its prototype, the "Reliques" of Bishop Percy; while his notes contained a mass of antiquarian information relative to border life, conveyed in a style of beauty unprecedented in topics of this kind, and enlivened with a higher interest than poetic fiction. Percy's "Reliques" had prepared the way for the kind reception of the "Minstrelsy," by the general relish—notwithstanding Dr. Johnson's protest—it had created for the simple pictures of a pastoral and heroic time. Burns had since familiarized the English ear with the Doric melodies of his native land; and now a greater than Burns appeared, whose first production, by a singular chance, came into the world in the very year in which the Ayrshire minstrel was withdrawn from it, as if nature had intended that the chain of poetic inspiration should not be broken. The delight of the public was further augmented on the appearance of the third volume of the "Minstrelsy," containing various imitations of the old ballad, which displayed all the rich fashion of the antique, purified from the mold and rust by which the beauties of such weather-beaten trophies are defaced.

The first edition of the "Minstrelsy," consisting of eight hundred copies, went off, as Lockhart tells us, in less than a year; and the poet, on the publication of a second, received £500 sterling from Longman—an enormous price for such a commodity, but the best bargain, probably, that the bookseller ever made, as the subsequent sale has since extended to twenty thousand copies.

Scott was not in great haste to follow up his success. It was three years later before he took the field as an independent author, in a poem which at once placed him among the great original writers of his country. The "Lay of the Last Minstrel," a complete expansion of the ancient ballad into an epic form, was published in 1805. It was opening a new creation in the realm of fancy. It seemed as if the author had transfused into his page the strong delineations of the Homeric pencil, the rude but generous gallantry of a primitive period, softened by the more airy and magical inventions of Italian romance,[3] and conveyed in tones of natural melody such as had not been heard since the strains of Burns. The book speedily found that unprecedented circulation which all his subsequent compositions attained. Other writers had addressed themselves to a more peculiar and limited feeling—to a narrower and generally a more select audience. But Scott was found to combine all the qualities of interest for every order. He drew from the pure springs which gush forth in every heart. His narrative chained every reader's attention by the stirring variety of its

[3] "Mettendo lo Turpin, lo metto anch' io,"

says Ariosto, playfully, when he tells a particularly tough story.

"I cannot tell how the truth may be,
I say the tale as 'twas said to me,"

says the author of the "Lay" on a similar occasion. The resemblance might be traced much further than mere forms of expression, to the Italian, who, like

". . . the Ariosto of the North,
Sung ladye-love, and war, romance, and knightly worth."

incidents, while the fine touches of sentiment with which it abounded, like wild flowers, springing up spontaneously around, were full of freshness and beauty, that made one wonder that others should not have stooped to gather them before.

The success of the "Lay" determined the course of its author's future life. Notwithstanding his punctual attention to his profession, his utmost profits for any one year of the ten he had been in practice had not exceeded £230; and of late they had sensibly declined. Latterly, indeed, he had coquetted somewhat too openly with the muse for his professional reputation. Themis has always been found a stern and jealous mistress, chary of dispensing her golden favors to those who are seduced into a flirtation with her more volatile sister.

Scott, however, soon found himself in a situation that made him independent of her favors. His income from the two offices to which he was promoted, of sheriff of Selkirk and clerk of the Court of Sessions, was so ample, combined with what fell to him by inheritance and marriage, that he was left at liberty freely to consult his own tastes. Amid the seductions of poetry, however, he never shrunk from his burdensome professional duties; and he submitted to all their drudgery with unflinching constancy, when the labors of his pen made the emoluments almost beneath consideration. He never relished the idea of being divorced from active life by the solitary occupations of a recluse. And his official functions, however severely they taxed his time, may be said to have, in some degree, compensated him by the new scenes of life which they were constantly disclosing —the very materials of those fictions on which his fame and his fortune were to be built.

Scott's situation was, on the whole, eminently propitious to literary pursuits. He was married, and passed the better portion of the year in the country, where the quiet pleasures of his fireside circle and a keen relish for rural sports relieved his mind and invigorated both health and spirits. In early life, it seems, he had been crossed in love; and, like Dante and Byron, to whom in this respect he is often compared, he has more than once, according to his biographer, shadowed forth in his verses the object of his unfortunate passion. He does not appear to have taken it so seriously, however, nor to have shown the morbid sensibility in relation to it discovered by both Byron and Dante, the former of whom perhaps found his *cara sposa* so much too cold, as the latter certainly did his too hot, for his own temperament, as to seek relief from the present in the poetical visions of the past.

Scott's next great poem was his "Marmion," transcending, in the judgment of many, all his other epics, and containing, in the judgment of all, passages of poetic fire which he never equalled; but which, nevertheless, was greeted on its entrance into the world by a *critique* in the leading journal of the day of the most caustic and unfriendly temper. The journal was the "Edinburgh," to which he had been a frequent contributor, and the reviewer was his intimate friend Jeffrey. The unkindest cut in the article was the imputation of a neglect of Scottish character and feeling. "There is scarcely one trait of true Scottish nationality or patriotism introduced into the whole poem; and Mr. Scott's only expression of admiration for the beautiful country to which he belongs is put, if we rightly remember, into the mouth of one of his southern favorites." This of Walter Scott! The critic had some misgivings, it would seem, as to the propriety of the part he was playing, or at least as to its effect on the mind of his friend, since he sent a copy of the yet unpublished article to the latter on the day he was engaged to dine with him, with a request for a speedy answer. Scott testified no visible marks of vexation, although his wife was not so discreet, telling Jeffrey rather bluntly she hoped Constable would pay him well for abusing his friend. The gossips of the day in Edinburgh exaggerated the story into her actually turning the reviewer out of doors. He well deserved it.

The affair, however, led to important consequences. Scott was not slow after this in finding the political principles of the "Edinburgh" so repugnant to his own (and they certainly were as opposite as the poles) that he first dropped the journal, and next labored with unwearied diligence to organize another, whose main purpose should be to counteract the heresies of the former. This was the origin of the London "Quarterly," more imputable to Scott's exertions than to those of any, indeed all, other persons. The result has been, doubtless, highly serviceable to the interests of both morals and letters. Not that the new review was conducted with more fairness or, in this sense, principle than its antagonist. A remark of Scott's own, in a letter to Ellis, shows with how much principle. "I have run up an attempt on 'The Curse of Kehama' for the 'Quarterly.' It affords cruel openings to the quizzers, and I suppose will get it roundly in the 'Edinburgh Review.' I would have made a very different hand of it, indeed, had the order of the day been *pour déchirer.*" But, although the fate of the individual was thus, to a certain extent, a matter of caprice or rather prejudgment in the critic, yet the great abstract questions in morals, politics, and literature, by being discussed on both sides, were presented in a fuller and of course fairer light to the public. Another beneficial result to letters was—and we shall gain credit, at least, for candor in confessing it—that it broke down somewhat of that divinity which hedged in the despotic *we* of the reviewer, so long as no rival arose to contest the sceptre. The claims to infallibility, so long and slavishly acquiesced in, fell to the ground when thus stoutly asserted by conflicting parties. It was pretty clear that the same thing could not be all black and all white at the same time. In short, it was the old story of pope and antipope; and the public began to find out that there might be hopes for the salvation of an author, though damned by the literary popedom. Time, indeed, by reversing many of its decisions, must at length have shown the same thing.

But to return. Scott showed how nearly he had been touched to the quick by two other acts not so discreet. These were the establishment of an Annual Register, and of the great publishing house of the Ballantynes, in which he became a silent partner. The last step involved him in grievous embarrassments, and stimulated him to exertions which required "a frame of adamant and soul of fire" to have endured. At the same time, we find him overwhelmed with poetical, biographical, historical, and critical compositions, together with editorial labors of appalling magnitude. In this multiplication of himself in a thousand forms, we see him always the same, vigorous and effective. "Poetry," he says, in one of his letters, "is a scourging crop, and ought not to be hastily repeated. Editing, therefore, may be considered as a green crop of turnips or peas, extremely useful to those whose circumstances do not admit of giving their farm a summer fallow." It might be regretted, however, that he should have wasted powers fitted for so much higher culture on the coarse products of a kitchen-garden, which might have been safely trusted to inferior hands.

In 1811 Scott gave to the world his exquisite poem, "The Lady of the Lake." One of his fair friends had remonstrated with him on thus risking again the laurel he had already won. He replied, with characteristic and indeed prophetic spirit: "If I fail, I will write prose all my life. But if I succeed—

"'Up wi' the bonnie blue bonnet,
The dirk and the feather an a'!'"

In his eulogy on Byron, Scott remarks: "There has been no reposing under the shade of his laurels, no living upon the resource of past reputation; none of that coddling and petty precaution which little authors call 'taking care of their fame.' Byron let his fame take care of itself." Scott could not have more accurately described his own character.

"The Lady of the Lake" was welcomed with an enthusiasm surpassing that which attended any other of his poems. It seemed like the sweet breathings of his native pibroch, stealing over glen and mountain, and calling up all the delicious associations of rural solitude, which beautifully contrasted with the din of battle and the shrill cry of the war-trumpet that stirred the soul in every page of his "Marmion." The publication of this work carried his fame as a poet to its most brilliant height. Its popularity may be inferred from the fact stated by Lockhart, that the post-horse duty rose to an extraordinary degree in Scotland, from the eagerness of travellers to visit the localities of the poem. A more substantial evidence was afforded in its amazing circulation, and consequently its profits. The press could scarcely keep pace with the public demand, and no less than fifty thousand copies of it have been sold since the date of its appearance. The successful author realized more than two thousand guineas from his production. Milton received ten pounds for the two editions which he lived to see of his "Paradise Lost." The Ayrshire bard had sighed for "a lass wi' a tocher." Scott had now found one in the muse, such as no Scottish nor any other poet had ever found before.

While the poetical fame of Scott was thus at its zenith, a new star rose above the horizon, whose eccentric course and dazzling radiance completely bewildered the spectator. In 1812 "Childe

Harold" appeared, and the attention seemed to be now called, for the first time, from the outward form of man and visible nature to the secret depths of the soul. The darkest recesses of human passion were laid open, and the note of sorrow was prolonged in tones of agonized sensibility, the more touching as coming from one who was placed on those dazzling heights of rank and fashion which, to the vulgar eye at least, seem to lie in unclouded sunshine. Those of the present generation who have heard only the same key thrummed *ad nauseam* by the feeble imitators of his lordship can form no idea of the effect produced when the chords were first swept by the master's fingers. It was found impossible for the ear once attuned to strains of such compass and ravishing harmony to return with the same relish to purer, it might be, but tamer melody; and the sweet voice of the Scottish minstrel lost much of its power to charm, let him charm never so wisely. While "Rokeby" was in preparation bets were laid on the rival candidates by the wits of the day. The sale of this poem, though great, showed a sensible decline in the popularity of its author. This became still more evident on the publication of "The Lord of the Isles"; and Scott admitted the conviction with his characteristic spirit and good nature. "'Well, James,' he said to his printer, 'I have given you a week; what are people saying about "The Lord of the Isles"?' I hesitated a little, after the fashion of Gil Blas, but he speedily brought the matter to a point. 'Come,' he said, 'speak out, my good fellow; what has put it into your head to be on so much ceremony with me all of a sudden? But, I see how it is, the result is given in one word—disappointment.' My silence admitted his inference to the fullest extent. His countenance certainly did look rather blank for a few seconds; in truth, he had been wholly unprepared for the event. At length he said, with perfect cheerfulness: 'Well, well, James, so be it; but you know we must not droop, for we can't afford to give over. Since one line has failed, we must stick to something else.'" This something else was a mine he had already hit upon, of invention and substantial wealth, such as Thomas the Rhymer, or Michael Scott, or any other adept in the black art, had never dreamed of.

Everybody knows the story of the composition of "Waverley"—the most interesting story in the annals of letters—and how, some ten years after its commencement, it was fished out of some old lumber in an attic, and completed in a few weeks for the press, in 1814. Its appearance marks a more distinct epoch in English literature than that of the poetry of its author. All previous attempts in the same school of fiction—a school of English growth—had been cramped by the limited information or talent of the writers. Smollett had produced his spirited sea-pieces, and Fielding his warm sketches of country life, both of them mixed up with so much Billingsgate as required a strong flavor of wit to make them tolerable. Richardson had covered acres of canvas with his faithful family pictures. Mrs. Radcliffe had dipped up to the elbows in horrors; while Miss Burney's fashionable gossip and Miss Edgeworth's Hogarth drawings of the prose—not the poetry—of life and character had each and all found favor in their respective ways. But a work now appeared in which the author swept over the whole range of character with entire freedom as well as fidelity, ennobling the whole by high historic associations, and in a style varying with his theme, but whose pure and classic flow was tinctured with just so much of poetic coloring as suited the purposes of romance. It was Shakespeare in prose.

The work was published, as we know, anonymously. Mr. Gillies states, however, that while in the press fragments of it were communicated to "Mr. Mackenzie, Dr. Brown, Mrs. Hamilton, and other *savants* or *savantes,* whose dicta on the merits of a new novel were considered unimpeachable." By their approbation "a strong body of friends was formed, and the curiosity of the public prepared the way for its reception." This may explain the rapidity with which the anonymous publication rose into a degree of favor which, though not less surely, perhaps, it might have been more slow in achieving. The author jealously preserved his *incognito,* and, in order to heighten the mystification, flung off almost simultaneously a variety of works, in prose and poetry, any one of which might have been the labor of months. The public for a moment was at fault. There seemed to be six Richmonds in the field. The world, therefore, was reduced to the dilemma of either supposing that half a dozen different hands could work in precisely the same style, or that one could do the work of half a dozen. With time, however, the veil wore thinner and thinner, until at length, and long before the ingenious argument of Mr. Adolphus, there was scarcely a critic so purblind as not to discern behind it the features of the mighty minstrel.

Constable had offered £700 for the new novel. "It was," says Lockhart, "ten times as much as Miss Edgeworth ever realized from any of her popular Irish tales." Scott declined the offer, which had been a good one for the bookseller had he made it as many thousand. But it passed the art of necromancy to divine this.

Scott, once entered on this new career, followed it up with an energy unrivalled in the history of literature. The public mind was not suffered to cool for a moment before its attention was called to another miracle of creation from the same hand. Even illness that would have broken the spirit of most men, as it prostrated the physical energies of Scott, opposed no impediment to the march of composition. When he could no longer write, he could dictate; and in this way, amid the agonies of a racking disease, he composed "The Bride of Lammermoor," the "Legend of Montrose," and a great part of "Ivanhoe." The first, indeed, is darkened with those deep shadows that might seem thrown over it by the sombre condition of its author. But what shall we say of the imperturbable dry humor of the gallant Captain Dugald Dalgetty of Drumthwacket, or of the gorgeous revelries of Ivanhoe—

> "Such sights as youthful poets dream,
> On summer eves by haunted stream"—

what shall we say of such brilliant day-dreams for a bed of torture? Never before had the spirit triumphed over such agonies of the flesh. "The best way," said Scott, in one of his talks with Gillies, "is, if possible, to triumph over disease by setting it at defiance, somewhat on the same principle as one avoids being stung by boldly grasping a nettle."

The prose fictions were addressed to a much larger audience than the poems could be. They had attractions for every age and every class. The profits, of course, were commensurate. Arithmetic has never been so severely taxed as in the computation of Scott's productions, and the proceeds resulting from them. In one year he received (or, more properly, was credited with—for it is somewhat doubtful how much he actually received) £15,000 for his novels, comprehending the first edition and the copyright. The discovery of this rich mine furnished its fortunate proprietor with the means of gratifying the fondest, and indeed most chimerical, desires. He had always coveted the situation of a lord of acres—a Scottish laird; where his passion for planting might find scope in the creation of whole forests—for everything with him was on a magnificent scale—and where he might indulge the kindly feelings of his nature in his benevolent offices to a numerous and dependent tenantry. The few acres of the original purchase now swelled into hundreds, and, for aught we know, thousands; for one tract alone we find incidentally noticed as costing £30,000. "It rounds off the property so handsomely," he says in one of his letters. There was always a corner to "round off." The mansion, in the mean time, from a simple cottage *orné,* was amplified into the dimensions almost, as well as the *bizarre* proportions, of some old feudal castle. The furniture and decorations were of the costliest kind; the wainscots of oak and cedar, the floors tessellated with marbles, or woods of different dyes, the ceilings fretted and carved with all the delicate tracery of a Gothic abbey, the storied windows blazoned with the richly colored insignia of heraldry, the walls garnished with time-honored trophies, or curious specimens of art, or volumes sumptuously bound—in short, with all that luxury could demand or ingenuity devise; while a copious reservoir of gas supplied every corner of the mansion with such fountains of light as must have puzzled the genius of the *lamp* to provide for the less fortunate Aladdin.

Scott's exchequer must have been seriously taxed in another form by the crowds of visitors whom he entertained under his hospitable roof. There was scarcely a person of note, or indeed not of note, who visited that country without paying his respects to the Lion of Scotland. Lockhart reckons up a full sixth of the British peerage who had been there within his recollection; and Captain Hall, in his amusing "Notes," remarks that it was not unusual for a dozen or more coach-loads to find their way into his grounds in the course of the day, most of whom found or forced an entrance into the mansion. Such was the heavy tax paid by his celebrity, and, we may add, his good nature. For, if the one had been a whit less than the other, he could never have tolerated such a nuisance.

The cost of his correspondence gives one no light idea of the demands made on his time, as well as purse, in another form. His postage for letters, independently of franks, by which a large portion of it was covered, amounted to a hundred and fifty pounds, it seems, in the course of the year. In this, indeed, should be included ten pounds for a pair of unfortunate "Cherokee Lovers," sent all the way from our own happy land, in order to be godfathered by Sir Walter on the London boards. Perhaps the smart-money he had to pay on this interesting occasion had its influence in mixing up rather more acid than was natural to him in his judgments of our countrymen. At all events the Yankees find little favor on the few occasions on which he has glanced at them in his correspondence. "I am not at all surprised," he says, in a letter to Miss Edgeworth, apparently chiming in with her own tune—"I am not at all surprised at what you say of the Yankees. They are a people possessed of very considerable energy, quickened and brought into eager action by an honorable love of their country, and pride in their institutions; but they are as yet rude in their ideas of social intercourse, and totally ignorant, speaking generally, of all the art of good-breeding, which consists chiefly in a postponement of one's own petty wishes or comforts to those of others. By rude questions and observations, an absolute disrespect to other people's feelings, and a ready indulgence of their own, they make one feverish in their company, though perhaps you may be ashamed to confess the reason. But this will wear off, and is already wearing away. Men when they have once got benches will soon fall into the use of cushions. They are advancing in the lists of our literature, and they will not be long deficient in the *petite morale,* especially as they have, like ourselves, the rage for travelling." On another occasion he does, indeed, admit having met with in the course of his life "four or five well-lettered Americans ardent in pursuit of knowledge, and free from the ignorance and forward presumption which distinguish many of their countrymen." This seems hard measure; but perhaps we should find it difficult among the many who have visited this country to recollect as great a number of Englishmen—and Scotchmen to boot—entitled to a higher degree of commendation. It can hardly be that the well-informed and well-bred men of both countries make a point of staying at home; so we suppose we must look for the solution of the matter in the existence of some disagreeable ingredient, common to the characters of both nations, sprouting as they do from a common stock, which remains latent at home, and is never fully disclosed till they get into a foreign climate. But as this problem seems pregnant with philosophical, physiological, and, for aught we know, psychological matter, we have not courage for it here, but recommend the solution to Miss Martineau, to whom it will afford a very good title for a new chapter in her next edition. The strictures we have quoted, however, to speak more seriously, are worth attending to, coming as they do from a shrewd observer, and one whose judgments, though here somewhat colored, no doubt, by political prejudice, are in the main distinguished by a sound and liberal philanthropy. But, were he ten times an enemy, we would say, "*Eas est ab hoste doceri.*"

With the splendid picture of the baronial residence at Abbotsford Mr. Lockhart closes all that at this present writing we have received of his delightful work in this country. And in the last sentence the melancholy sound of "the muffled drum" gives ominous warning of what we are to expect in the sixth and concluding volume. In the dearth of more authentic information, we will piece out our sketch with a few facts gleaned from the somewhat meagre bill of fare—meagre by comparison with the rich banquet of the true Amphitryon—afforded by the "Recollections" of Mr. Robert Pierce Gillies.

The unbounded popularity of the Waverley novels led to still more extravagant anticipations on the part both of the publishers and author. Some hints of a falling off, though but slightly, in the public favor, were unheeded by both parties; though, to say truth, the exact state of things was never disclosed to Scott, it being Ballantyne's notion that it would prove a damper, and that the true course was "to press on more sail as the wind lulled." In these sanguine calculations not only enormous sums, or, to speak correctly, bills, were given for what had been written, but the author's drafts, to the amount of many thousand pounds, were accepted by Constable in favor of works, the very embryos of which lay not only unformed but unimagined, in the womb of time. In return for this singular accommodation, Scott was induced to indorse the drafts of his publisher;

and in this way an amount of liabilities was incurred which, considering the character of the house, and its transactions, it is altogether inexplicable that a person in the independent position of Sir Walter Scott should have subjected himself to for a moment. He seems to have had entire confidence in the stability of the firm; a confidence to which it seems, from Mr. Gillies's account, not to have been entitled from the first moment of his connection with it. The great reputation of the house, however, the success and magnitude of some of its transactions, especially the publication of these novels, gave it a large credit, which enabled it to go forward with a great show of prosperity in ordinary times, and veiled the tottering state of things probably from Constable's own eyes. It is but the tale of yesterday. The case of Constable & Co. is, unhappily, a very familiar one to us. But, when the hurricane of 1825 came on, it swept away all those buildings that were not founded on a rock; and those of Messrs. Constable, among others, soon became literally mere castles in the air. In plain English, the firm stopped payment. The assets were very trifling in comparison with the debts. And Sir Walter Scott was found on their paper to the frightful amount of one hundred thousand pounds.

His conduct on the occasion was precisely what was to have been anticipated from one who had declared on a similar though much less appalling conjuncture, "I am always ready to make any sacrifices to do justice to my engagements, and would rather sell anything or everything than be less than a true man to the world." He put up his house and furniture in town at auction; delivered over his personal effects at Abbotsford, his plate, books, furniture, etc., to be held in trust for his creditors (the estate itself had been recently secured to his son, on occasion of his marriage), and bound himself to discharge a certain amount annually of the liabilities of the insolvent firm. He then, with his characteristic energy, set about the performance of his Herculean task. He took lodgings in a third-rate house in St. David's Street; saw but little company; abridged the hours usually devoted to his meals and his family; gave up his ordinary exercise; and, in short, adopted the severe habits of a regular Grub Street stipendiary.

"For many years," he said to Mr. Gillies, "I have been accustomed to hard work, because I found it a pleasure; now, with all due respect for Falstaff's principle, 'nothing on compulsion,' I certainly will not shrink from work because it has become necessary."

One of his first tasks was his "Life of Bonaparte," achieved in the space of thirteen months. For this he received fourteen thousand pounds, about eleven hundred per month; not a bad bargain, either, as it proved, for the publishers. The first two volumes of the nine which make up the English edition were a *rifacimento* of what he had before compiled for the "Annual Register." With every allowance for the inaccuracies and the excessive expansion incident to such a flashing rapidity of execution, the work, taking into view the broad range of its topics, its shrewd and sagacious reflections, and the free, bold, and picturesque coloring of its narration—and, above all, considering the brief time in which it was written—is indisputably one of the most remarkable monuments of genius and industry—perhaps the most remarkable ever recorded.

Scott's celebrity made everything that fell from him, however trifling—the dew-drops from the lion's mane—of value. But none of the many adventures he embarked in, or rather set afloat, proved so profitable as the republication of his novels, with his notes and illustrations. As he felt his own strength in the increasing success of his labors, he appears to have relaxed somewhat from them, and to have again resumed somewhat of his ancient habits, and in a mitigated degree his ancient hospitality. But still his exertions were too severe, and pressed heavily on the springs of health, already deprived by age of their former elasticity and vigor. At length, in 1831, he was overtaken by one of those terrible shocks of paralysis which seem to have been constitutional in his family, but which, with more precaution and under happier auspices, might doubtless have been postponed if not wholly averted. At this time he had, in the short space of little more than five years, by his sacrifices and efforts, discharged about two-thirds of the debt for which he was responsible; an astounding result, wholly unparalleled in the history of letters! There is something inexpressibly painful in this spectacle of a generous heart thus courageously contending with fortune, bearing up against the tide with unconquerable spirit, and finally overwhelmed by it just within reach of shore.

The rest of his story is one of humiliation and sorrow. He was induced to make a voyage to the Continent, to try the effect of a more genial climate. Under the sunny sky of Italy he seemed to gather new strength for a while. But his eye fell with indifference on the venerable monuments which in better days would have kindled all his enthusiasm. The invalid sighed for his own home at Abbotsford. The heat of the weather and the fatigue of rapid travel brought on another shock which reduced him to a state of deplorable imbecility. In this condition he returned to his own halls, where the sight of early friends and of the beautiful scenery—the creation, as it were, of his own hands—seemed to impart a gleam of melancholy satisfaction, which soon, however, sunk into insensibility. To his present situation might well be applied the exquisite verses which he indited on another melancholy occasion:

"Yet not the landscape to mine eye
  Bears those bright hues that once it bore;
Though evening, with her richest dye,
  Flames o'er the hills of Ettrick's shore.

"With listless look along the plain
  I see Tweed's silver current glide,
And coldly mark the holy fane
  Of Melrose rise in ruined pride.

"The quiet lake, the balmy air,
  The hill, the stream, the tower, the tree—
Are they still such as once they were,
  Or is the dreary change in me?"

Providence in its mercy did not suffer the shattered frame long to outlive the glorious spirit which had informed it. He breathed his last on September 21, 1832. His remains were deposited, as he had always desired, in the hoary abbey of Dryburgh; and the pilgrim from many a distant clime shall repair to the consecrated spot so long as the reverence for exalted genius and worth shall survive in the human heart.

This sketch, brief as we could make it, of the literary history of Sir Walter Scott, has extended so far as to leave but little space for—what Lockhart's volumes afford ample materials for—his personal character. Take it for all and all, it is not too much to say that this character is probably the most remarkable on record. There is no man that we now recall of historical celebrity who combined in so eminent a degree the highest qualities of the moral, the intellectual, and the physical. He united in his own character what hitherto had been found incompatible. Though a poet and living in an ideal world, he was an exact, methodical man of business; though achieving with the most wonderful fertility of genius, he was patient and laborious; a mousing antiquarian, yet with the most active interest in the present and whatever was going on around him; with a strong turn for a roving life and military adventure, he was yet chained to his desk more hours at some periods of his life than a monkish recluse; a man with a heart as capacious as his head; a Tory, brim full of Jacobitism, yet full of sympathy and unaffected familiarity with all classes, even the humblest; a successful author, without pedantry and without conceit; one, indeed, at the head of the republic of letters, and yet with a lower estimate of letters, as compared with other intellectual pursuits, than was ever hazarded before.

The first quality of his character, or rather that which forms the basis of it, as of all great characters, was his energy. We see it in his early youth triumphing over the impediments of nature, and in spite of lameness making him conspicuous in every sort of athletic exercise—clambering up dizzy precipices, wading through treacherous fords, and performing feats of pedestrianism that make one's joints ache to read of. As he advanced in life we see the same force of purpose turned to higher objects. A striking example occurs in his organization of the journals and the publishing-house in opposition to Constable. In what Herculean drudgery did not this latter business, in which he undertook to supply matter for the nimble press of Ballantyne, involve him! While, in addition to his own concerns, he had to drag along by his solitary momentum a score of heavier undertakings, that led Lockhart to compare him to a steam-engine with a train of coal-wagons hitched on to it. "Yes," said Scott, laughing, and making a crashing cut with his axe (for they were felling larches), "and there was a cursed lot of dung-carts, too."

We see the same powerful energies triumphing over disease at a later period, when, indeed, nothing but a resolution to get the better of it enabled him to do so. "Be assured," he remarked to Mr. Gillies, "that if pain could have prevented my application to literary labor not a page of 'Ivanhoe' would have been written. Now, if I had given way to mere feelings and ceased to work, it is a question whether the disorder might not have taken a deeper root and become incurable." But the most extraordinary instance of this trait is the readiness with which he assumed, and the spirit with which he carried through till his mental strength broke down under it, the gigantic task imposed on him by the failure of Constable.

It mattered little, indeed, what the nature of the task was, whether it were organizing an opposition to a political faction, or a troop of cavalry to resist invasion, or a medley of wild Highlanders and Edinburgh cockneys to make up a royal puppet-show—a loyal celebration—for "his Most Sacred Majesty" —he was the master-spirit that gave the cue to the whole *dramatis personæ*. This potent impulse showed itself in the thoroughness with which he prescribed not merely the general orders but the execution of the minutest details in his own person. Thus all around him was the creation, as it were, of his individual exertion. His lands waved with forests planted with his own hands, and in process of time cleared by his own hands. He did not lay the stones in mortar exactly for his whimsical castle, but he seems to have superintended the operation from the foundation to the battlements. The antique relics, the curious works of art, the hangings and furniture even with which his halls were decorated, were specially contrived or selected by him; and, to read his letters at this time to his friend Terry, one might fancy himself perusing the correspondence of an upholsterer, so exact and technical is he in his instructions. We say this not in disparagement of his great qualities. It is only the more extraordinary, for, while he stooped to such trifles, he was equally thorough in matters of the highest moment. It was a trait of character.

Another quality which, like the last, seems to have given the tone to his character, was his social or benevolent feelings. His heart was an unfailing fountain which, not merely the distresses, but the joys, of his fellow-creatures made to flow like water. In early life, and possibly sometimes in later, high spirits and a vigorous constitution led him occasionally to carry his social propensities into convivial excess. But he never was in danger of the habitual excess to which a vulgar mind—and sometimes, alas! one more finely tuned—abandons itself. Indeed, with all his conviviality, it was not the sensual relish, but the social, which acted on him. He was neither *gourmet* nor *gourmand;* but his social meetings were endeared to him by the free interchange of kindly feelings with his friends. La Bruyère says (and it is odd he should have found it out in Louis XIV's court), "The heart has more to do than the head with the pleasures, or rather promoting the pleasures, of society" *("Un homme est d'un meilleur commerce dans la société par le cœur que par l'esprit").* If report, the report of travellers, be true, we Americans, at least the New Englanders, are too much perplexed with the cares and crosses of life to afford many genuine specimens of this *bonhomie.* However this may be, we all, doubtless, know some such character, whose shining face, the index of a cordial heart radiant with beneficent pleasure, diffuses its own exhilarating glow wherever it appears. Rarely, indeed, is this precious quality found united with the most exalted intellect. Whether it be that Nature, chary of her gifts, does not care to shower too many of them on one head; or, that the public admiration has led the man of intellect to set too high a value on himself, or at least his own pursuits, to take an interest in the inferior concerns of others; or, that the fear of compromising his dignity puts him "on points" with those who approach him; or, whether, in truth, the very magnitude of his own reputation throws a freezing shadow over us little people in his neighborhood; whatever be the cause, it is too true that the highest powers of mind are very often deficient in the only one which can make the rest of much worth in society—the power of pleasing.

Scott was not one of these little great. His was not one of those dark-lantern visages which concentrate all their light on their own path and are black as midnight to all about them. He had a ready sympathy, a word of contagious kindness or cordial greeting for all. His manners, too, were of a kind to dispel the icy reserve and awe which his great name was calculated to inspire. His frank address was a sort of *open sesame* to every heart. He did not deal in sneers, the poisoned weapons which come not from the head, as the man who launches them is apt to think, but from an acid heart, or perhaps an acid stomach, a very common laboratory of such small artillery. Neither did Scott amuse the company with parliamentary harangues or metaphysical disquisitions. His conversation was of the narrative kind, not formal, but as casually suggested by some passing circumstance or topic, and thrown in by way of illustration. He did not repeat himself, however, but continued to give his anecdotes such variations, by rigging them out in a new "cocked hat and walking-cane," as he called it, that they never tired like the the thrice-told tale of a chronic *raconteur*. He allowed others, too, to take their turn, and thought with the Dean of St. Patrick's:

> "Carve to all but just enough,
> Let them neither starve nor stuff;
> And that you may have your due,
> Let your neighbors carve for you."

He relished a good joke, from whatever quarter it came, and was not over-dainty in his manner of testifying his satisfaction. "In the full tide of mirth he did indeed laugh the heart's laugh," says Mr. Adolphus. "Give me an honest laugher," said Scott himself, on another occasion, when a buckram man of fashion had been paying him a visit at Abbotsford. His manners, free from affectation or artifice of any sort, exhibited the spontaneous movements of a kind disposition, subject to those rules of good-breeding which Nature herself might have dictated. In this way he answered his own purposes admirably, as a painter of character, by putting every man in good humor with himself; in the same manner as a cunning portrait-painter amuses his sitters with such store of fun and anecdote as may throw them off their guard, and call out the happiest expressions of their countenances.

Scott, in his wide range of friends and companions, does not seem to have been over-fastidious. In the instance of John Ballantyne it has exposed him to some censure. Indeed, a more worthless fellow never hung on the skirts of a great man; for he did not take the trouble to throw a decent veil over the grossest excesses. But then he had been the schoolboy friend of Scott; had grown up with him in a sort of dependence—a relation which begets a kindly feeling in the party that confers the benefits at least. How strong it was in him may be inferred from his remark at his funeral. "I feel," said Scott, mournfully, as the solemnity was concluded—"I feel as if there would be less sunshine for me from this day forth." It must be admitted, however, that his intimacy with little Rigdumfunnidos, whatever apology it may find in Scott's heart, was not very creditable to his taste.

But the benevolent principle showed itself not merely in words, but in the more substantial form of actions. How many are the cases recorded of indigent merit which he drew from obscurity, and almost warmed into life by his own generous and most delicate patronage. Such were the cases, among others, of Leyden, Weber, Hogg. How often and how cheerfully did he supply such literary contributions as were solicited by his friends—and they taxed him pretty liberally—amid all the pressure of business, and at the height of his fame when his hours were golden hours indeed to him! In the more vulgar and easier forms of charity he did not stint his hand, though, instead of direct assistance, he preferred to enable others to assist themselves; in this way fortifying their good habits, and relieving them from the sense of personal degradation.

But the place where his benevolent impulses found their proper theatre for expansion was his own home; surrounded by a happy family, and dispensing all the hospitalities of a great feudal proprietor. "There are many good things in life," he says, in one of his letters, "whatever satirists and misanthropes may say to the contrary, but probably the best of all, next to a conscience void of offence (without which, by the by, they can hardly exist), are the quiet exercise and enjoyment of the social feelings in which we are at once happy ourselves and the cause of happiness to them who are dearest to us." Every page of the work almost shows us how intimately he blended himself with the pleasures and the pursuits of his own family, watched over the education of his children, shared in their rides, their rambles, and sports, losing no opportunity of kindling in their young minds a love of virtue and honorable principles of action. He delighted, too, to collect his tenantry around him, multiplying holidays, when young and old might come together under his roof-tree, when the jolly punch was liberally dispensed by himself and his wife among the elder people, and the Hogmanay cakes and pennies were distributed among the young ones; while his own children mingled in the endless reels and hornpipes on the earthen floor, and the laird himself, mixing in the groups of merry faces, had his "private joke for every old wife or 'gausie carle,' his arch compliment for the ear of every bonnie lass, and his hand and his blessing for the head of every little Eppie Daidle from Abbotstown or Broomylees." "Sir Walter," said one of his old retainers, "speaks to every man as if he were his blood-relation." No wonder that they should have returned this feeling with something warmer than blood-relations usually do. Mr. Gillies tells an anecdote of the "Ettrick Shepherd," showing how deep a root such feelings, notwithstanding his rather odd way of expressing them, sometimes had taken in his honest nature. "Mr. James Ballantyne walking home with him one evening from Scott's, where, by the by, Hogg had gone uninvited, happened to observe: 'I do not at all like this illness of Scott's. I have often seen him look jaded of late, and am afraid it is serious.' 'Haud your tongue, or I'll gar you measure your length on the pavement!' replied Hogg. 'You fause, down-hearted loon, that you are; ye daur to speak as if Scott were on his deathbed! It can not be, it must not be! I will not suffer you to speak that gait.' The sentiment was like that of Uncle Toby at the bedside of Le Fevre; and, at these words, the Shepherd's voice became suppressed with emotion."

But Scott's sympathies were not confined to his species; and, if he treated them like blood-relations, he treated his brute followers like personal friends. Everyone remembers old Maida, and faithful Camp, the "dear old friend," whose loss cost him a dinner. Mr. Gillies tells us that he went into his study on one occasion, when he was winding off his "Vision of Don Roderick." "'Look here,' said the poet, 'I have just begun to copy over the rhymes that you heard to-day, and applauded so much. Return to supper, if you can; only don't be late, as you perceive we keep early hours, and Wallace will not suffer me to rest after six in the morning. Come, good dog, and help the poet.' At this hint, Wallace seated himself upright on a chair next his master, who offered him a newspaper, which he directly seized, looking very wise, and holding it firmly and contentedly in his mouth. Scott looked at him with great satisfaction, for he was excessively fond of dogs. 'Very well,' said he, 'now we shall get on.' And so I left them abruptly, knowing that my 'absence would be the best company.'" This fellowship, indeed, extended much further than to his canine followers, of which, including hounds, terriers, mastiffs, and mongrels, he had certainly a goodly assortment. We find, also, Grimalkin installed in a responsible post in the library, and out of doors pet hens, pet donkeys, and—tell it not in Judea—a pet pig!

Scott's sensibilities, though easily moved, and widely diffused, were warm and sincere. None shared more cordially in the troubles of his friends; but on all such occasions, with a true manly feeling, he thought less of mere sympathy than of the most effectual way for mitigating their sorrows. After a touching allusion, in one of his epistles, to his dear friend Erskine's death, he concludes: "I must turn to, and see what can be done about getting some pension for his daughters." In another passage, which may remind one of some of the exquisite touches in Jeremy Taylor, he indulges in the following beautiful strain of philosophy: "The last three or four years have swept away more than half the friends with whom I lived in habits of great intimacy. So it must be with us:

> "'When ance life's day draws near the gloamin''—

and yet we proceed with our plantations and plans as if any tree but the sad cypress would accompany us to the grave, where our friends have gone before us. It is the way of the world, however, and must be so; otherwise life would be spent in unavailing mourning for those whom we have lost. It is better to enjoy the society of those who remain to us." His well-disciplined heart seems to have confessed the influence of this philosophy, in his most ordinary relations. "I can't help it," was a favorite maxim of his, "and therefore will not think about it; for that at least I *can* help."

Among his admirable qualities must not be omitted a certain worldly sagacity or shrewdness, which is expressed as strongly as any individual trait can be, in some of his portraits, especially in the excellent one of him by Leslie. Indeed, his countenance would seem to exhibit, ordinarily, much more of Dandie Dinmont's benevolent shrewdness than of the eye glancing from earth to heaven, which in fancy we assign to the poet, and which, in some moods, must have been his. This trait may be readily discerned in all his business transactions, which he managed with perfect knowledge of character, as well as of his own rights. No one knew better than he the market value of an article; and, though he underrated his literary wares, as to their mere literary rank, he set as high a money value on them, and made as sharp a bargain, as any of the trade could have done. In his business concerns, indeed, he managed rather too much; or, to speak more correctly, was too fond of mixing up mystery in his transactions, which, like most mysteries, proved of little service to their author. Scott's correspondence, especially with his son, affords obvious examples of shrewdness, in the advice he gives as to his deportment in the novel situations and society into which the young cornet was thrown. Occasionally, indeed, in the cautious hints about etiquette and social observances, we are reminded of that ancient "*arbiter elegantiarum,*" Lord Chesterfield; though, it must be confessed, there is throughout a high moral tone, which the noble lord did not very scrupulously affect.

Another feature in Scott's character was his loyalty; which, indeed, some people would extend into a more general deference to rank not royal. We do, indeed, meet with a tone of deference occasionally to the privileged orders (or rather privileged persons, as the King, his own chief, etc., for to the mass of stars and garters he showed no such respect), which falls rather unpleasantly on the ear of a republican. But, independently of the feelings which should rightfully have belonged to him as the subject of a monarchy, and without which he must have been a false-hearted subject, his own were heightened by a poetical coloring, that mingled in his mind even with much more vulgar relations of life. At the opening of the regalia in Holyrood House, when the honest burgomaster deposited the crown on the head of one of the young ladies present, the good man probably saw nothing more in the dingy diadem than we should have seen—a head-piece for a set of men no better than himself, and, if the old adage of a "dead lion" holds true, not quite so good. But to Scott's imagination other views were unfolded. "A thousand years their cloudy wings expanded" around him, and, in the dim visions of distant times, he beheld the venerable line of monarchs who had swayed the councils of his country in peace, and led her armies in battle. The "golden round" became in his eye the symbol of his nation's glory; and, as he heaved a heavy oath from his heart, he left the room in agitation, from which he did not speedily recover. There was not a spice of affectation in this—for who ever accused Scott of affectation?—but there was a good deal of poetry, the poetry of sentiment.

We have said that this feeling mingled in the more common concerns of his life. His cranium, indeed, to judge from his busts, must have exhibited a strong development of the organ of veneration. He regarded with reverence everything connected with antiquity. His establishment was on the feudal scale; his house was fashioned more after the feudal ages than his own; and even in the ultimate distribution of his fortune, although the circumstance of having made it himself relieved him from any legal necessity of contravening the suggestions of natural justice, he showed such attachment to the old aristocratic usage as to settle nearly the whole of it on his eldest son.

The influence of this poetic sentiment is discernible in his most trifling acts, in his tastes, his love of the arts, his social habits. His museum, house, and grounds were adorned with relics, curious not so much from their workmanship as their historic associations. It was the ancient fountain from Edinburgh, the Tolbooth lintels, the blunderbuss and spleughan of Rob Roy, the drinking-cup of Prince Charlie, or the like. It was the same in the arts. The tunes he loved were not the refined and complex melodies of Italy, but the simple notes of his native minstrelsy, from the bagpipe of John of Skye, or from the harp of his own lovely and accomplished daughter. So also in painting. It was not the masterly designs of the great Flemish and Italian schools that adorned his walls, but some portrait of Claverhouse, or of Queen Mary, or of "glorious old John." In architecture, we see the same spirit in the singular "romance of stone and lime," which may be said to have been his own device, down to the minutest details of its finishing. We see it again in the joyous celebrations of his feudal tenantry, the good old festivals, the Hogmanay, the Kirn, etc., long fallen into desuetude, when the old Highland piper sounded the same wild pibroch that had so often summoned the clans together, for war or for wassail, among the fastnesses of the mountains. To the same source, in fine, may be traced the feelings of superstition which seemed to hover round Scott's mind like some " strange, mysterious dream," giving a romantic coloring to his conversation and his writings, but rarely if ever influencing his actions. It was a poetic sentiment.

Scott was a Tory to the backbone. Had he come into the world half a century sooner he would, no doubt, have made a figure under the banner of the Pretender. He was at no great pains to disguise his political creed; witness his jolly drinking-song on the acquittal of Lord Melville. This was verse; but his prose is not much more qualified. " As for Whiggery in general," he says, in one of his letters, " I can only say that, as no man can be said to be utterly overset until his rump has been higher than his head, so I cannot read in history of any free State which has been brought to slavery until the rascal and uninstructed populace had had their short hour of anarchical government, which naturally leads to the stern repose of military despotism. . . . With these convictions, I am very jealous of Whiggery, under all modifications; and I must say my acquaintance with the total want of principle in some of its warmest professors does not tend to recommend it." With all this, however, his Toryism was not, practically, of that sort which blunts a man's sensibilities for those who are not of the same porcelain clay with himself. No man, Whig or Radical, ever had less of this pretension, or treated his inferiors with greater kindness, and indeed familiarity; a circumstance noticed by every visitor at his hospitable mansion, who saw him strolling round his grounds, taking his pinch of snuff out of the mull of some " gray-haired old hedger," or leaning on honest Tom Purdie's shoulder, and taking sweet counsel as to the right method of thinning a plantation. But, with all this familiarity, no man was better served by his domestics. It was the service of love; the only service that power cannot command, and money cannot buy.

Akin to the feelings of which we have been speaking was the truly chivalrous sense of honor which stamped his whole conduct. We do not mean that Hotspur honor which is roused only by the drum and fife—though he says of himself, " I like the sound of a drum as well as Uncle Toby ever did "—but that honor which is deep-seated in the heart of every true gentleman, shrinking with sensitive delicacy from the least stain or imputation of a stain on his faith. "If we lose everything else," writes he on a trying occasion to a friend who was not so nice in this particular, "we will at least keep our honor unblemished." It reminds one of the pithy epistle of a kindred chivalrous spirit, Francis I, to his mother from the unlucky field of Pavia: "*Tout est perdu, fors l'honneur.*" Scott's latter years furnished a noble commentary on the sincerity of his manly principles.

Little is said directly of his religious sentiments in the biography. They seem to have harmonized well with his political. He was a member of the English Church, a stanch champion of established forms, and a sturdy enemy to everything that savored of the sharp twang of Puritanism. On this ground, indeed, the youthful Samson used to wrestle manfully with worthy Dominie Mitchell, who, no doubt, furnished many a screed of doctrine for the Rev. Peter Poundtext, Master Nehemiah Holdenough, and other lights of the Covenant. Scott was no friend to cant under any form. But, whatever were his speculative opinions, in practice his heart overflowed with that charity which is the life-spring of our religion. And, whenever he takes occasion to allude to the subject directly, he testifies a deep reverence for the truths of revelation as well as for its divine Original.

Whatever estimate be formed of Scott's moral qualities, his intellectual were of a kind which well entitled him to the epithet conferred on Lope de Vega, "*monstruo de naturaleza,*" "a miracle of nature." His mind, indeed, did not seem to be subjected to the same laws which control the rest of his species. His memory, as is usual, was the first of his powers fully developed. While an urchin at school he could repeat whole cantos, he says, of Ossian and of Spenser. In riper years we are constantly meeting with similar feats of his achievement. Thus on one occasion he repeated the whole of a poem in some penny magazine incidentally alluded to, which he had not seen since he was a schoolboy. On another, when the Ettrick Shepherd was trying ineffectually to fish up from his own recollections some scraps of a ballad he had himself manufactured years before, Scott called to him, "Take your pencil, Jemmy, and I will tell it to you word for word"; and he accordingly did so. But it is needless to multiply examples of feats so startling as to look almost like the tricks of a conjurer.

What is most extraordinary is, that while he acquired with such facility that the bare perusal or the repetition of a thing once to him was sufficient, he yet retained it with the greatest pertinacity. Other men's memories are so much jostled in the rough and tumble of life that most of the facts get sifted out nearly as fast as they are put in; so that we are in the same pickle with those unlucky daughters of Danaus, of schoolboy memory, obliged to spend the greater part of the time in replenishing. But Scott's memory seemed to be hermetically sealed, suffering nothing once fairly in to leak out again. This was of immense service to him when he took up the business of authorship, as his whole multifarious stock of facts, whether from books or observation, became in truth his stock in trade, ready furnished to his hands. This may explain in part, though it is not less marvellous, the cause of his rapid execution of works, often replete with rare and curious information. The labor, the preparation, had been already completed. His whole life had been a business of preparation. When he ventured, as in the case of "Rokeby" and of "Quentin Durward," on ground with which he had not been familiar, we see how industriously he set about new acquisitions.

In most of the prodigies of memory which we have ever known the overgrowth of that faculty seems to have been attained at the expense of all the others. But in Scott the directly opposite power of the imagination—the inventive power—was equally strongly developed, and at the same early age. For we find him renowned for story-craft while at school. How many a delightful fiction, indeed, warm with the flush of ingenuous youth, did he not throw away on the ears of thoughtless childhood which, had they been duly registered, might now have amused children of a larger growth! We have seen Scott's genius in its prime and its decay. The frolic graces of childhood are alone wanting.

The facility with which he threw his ideas into language was also remarked very early. One of his first ballads, and a long one, was dashed off at the dinner-table. His "Lay" was written at the rate of a canto a week. "Waverley," or rather the last two volumes of it, cost the evenings of a summer month. Who that has ever read the account can forget the movements of that mysterious hand as descried by the two students from the window of a neighboring attic, throwing off sheet after sheet with untiring rapidity of the pages destined to immortality? Scott speaks pleasantly enough of this marvellous facility in a letter to his friend Morritt: "When once I set my pen to the paper it will walk fast enough. I am sometimes tempted to leave it alone, and see whether it will not write as well without the assistance of my head as with it. A hopeful prospect for the reader."

As to the time and place of composition, he appears to have been nearly indifferent. He possessed entire power of abstraction, and it mattered little whether he were nailed to his clerk's desk, under the drowsy eloquence of some long-winded barrister, or dashing his horse into the surf on Portobello sands, or rattling in a post-chaise, or amid the hum of guests in his overflowing halls at Abbotsford—it mattered not, the same well-adjusted little packet, "nicely corded and sealed," was sure to be ready at the regular time for the Edinburgh mail. His own account of his composition, to a friend who asked when he found time for it, is striking enough. "Oh," said Scott, "I lie simmering over things for an hour or so before I get up—and there's the time I am dressing to overhaul my half-sleeping half-waking *projet de chapitre*—and when I get the paper before me it commonly runs off pretty easily. Besides, I often take a doze in the plantations, and, while Tom marks out a dike or a drain, as I have directed, one's fancy may be running its ain riggs in some other world." Never, indeed, did this sort of simmering produce such a splendid bill of fare.

The quality of the material under such circumstances is, in truth, the great miracle of the whole. The execution of so much work as a mere feat of penmanship would undoubtedly be very extraordinary; but, as a mere scrivener's miracle, would be hardly worth recording. It is a sort of miracle that is every day performing under our own eyes, as it were, by Messrs. James, Bulwer & Co., who, in all the various staples of "comedy, history, pastoral, pastoral-comical, historical-pastoral," etc., etc., supply their own market and ours too with all that can be wanted. In Spain and in Italy, too, we may find abundance of *improvvisatori* and *improvvisatrici,* who perform miracles of the same sort in verse, too, in languages whose vowel terminations make it very easy for the thoughts to tumble into rhyme without any malice prepense. Governor Raffles, in his account of Java, tells us of a splendid avenue of trees before his house, which in the course of a year shot up to the height of forty feet. But who shall compare the brief, transitory splendors of a fungous vegetation with the mighty monarch of the forest, sending his roots deep into the heart of the earth, and his branches, amid storm and sunshine, to the heavens? And is not the latter the true emblem of Scott? For who can doubt that his prose creations, at least, will gather strength with time, living on through succeeding generations, even when the language in which they are written, like those of Greece and Rome, shall cease to be a living language?

The only writer deserving in these respects to be named with Scott is Lope de Vega, who in his own day held as high a rank in the republic of letters as our great contemporary. The beautiful dramas which he threw off for the entertainment of the capital, and whose success drove Cervantes from the stage, outstripped the abilities of an amanuensis to copy. His intimate friend Montalvan, one of the most popular and prolific authors of the time, tells us that he undertook with Lope once to supply the theatre with a comedy—in verse, and in three acts, as the Spanish dramas usually were—at a very short notice. In order to get through his half as soon as his partner, he rose by two in the morning, and at eleven had completed it; an extraordinary feat, certainly, since a play extended to between thirty and forty pages, of a hundred lines each. Walking into the garden he found his brother poet pruning an orange-tree. "Well, how do you get on?" said Montalvan. "Very well," answered Lope. "I rose betimes, at five; and, after I had got through, ate my breakfast; since which I have written a letter of fifty triplets, and watered the whole of the garden, which has tired me a good deal."

But a little arithmetic will best show the comparative fertility of Scott and Lope de Vega. It is so germane to the present matter that we shall make no apology for transcribing here some computations from a former article; and, as few of our readers, we suspect, have the air-tight memory of Sir Walter, we doubt not that enough of it has escaped them by this time to excuse us from equipping it with one of those "cocked hats and walking-sticks" with which he furbished up an old story:

"It is impossible to state the results of Lope de Vega's labors in any form that will not powerfully strike the imagination. Thus, he has left twenty-one million three hundred thousand verses in print, besides a mass of manuscript. He furnished the theatre, according to the statement of his intimate friend Montalvan, with eighteen hundred regular plays and four hundred *autos* or religious dramas —all acted. He composed, according to his own statement, more than one hundred comedies in the almost incredible space of twenty-four hours each; and a comedy averaged between two and three thousand verses, great part of them rhymed and interspersed with sonnets, and other more difficult forms of versification. He lived seventy-two years; and supposing him to have employed fifty of that period in composition, although he filled a variety of engrossing vocations during that time, he must have averaged a play a week, to say nothing of twenty-one volumes, quarto, of miscellaneous works, including five epics, written in his leisure moments, and all now in print!

"The only achievements we can recall in literary history bearing any resemblance to, though falling far short of this, are those of our illustrious contemporary, Sir Walter Scott. The complete edition of his works, recently advertised by Murray, with the addition of two volumes, of which Murray has not the copyright, probably contains ninety volumes, small octavo. [To these should further be added a large supply of matter for the 'Edinburgh Annual Register,' as well as other anonymous contributions.] Of these, forty-eight volumes of novels and twenty-one of history and biography were produced between 1814 and 1831, or in seventeen years. These would give an average of four volumes a year, or one for every three months during the whole of that period, to which must be added twenty-one volumes of poetry and prose previously published. The mere mechanical execution of so much work, both in his case and Lope de Vega's, would seem to be scarce possible in the limits assigned. Scott, too, was as variously occupied in other ways as his Spanish rival; and probably, from the social hospitality of his life, spent a much larger portion of his time in no literary occupation at all."

Of all the wonderful dramatic creations of Lope de Vega's genius what now remains? Two or three plays only keep possession of the stage, and few, very few, are still read with pleasure in the closet. They have never been collected into a uniform edition, and are now met with in scattered sheets only on the shelves of some mousing bookseller, or collected in miscellaneous parcels in the libraries of the curious.

Scott, with all his facility of execution, had none of that pitiable affectation sometimes found in men of genius, who think that the possession of this quality may dispense with regular, methodical habits of study. He was most economical of time.

He did not, like Voltaire, speak of it as "a terrible thing that so much time should be wasted in talking." He was too little of a pedant and far too benevolent not to feel that there are other objects worth living for than mere literary fame. But he grudged the waste of time on merely frivolous and heartless objects. "As for dressing when we are quite alone," he remarked one day to Mr. Gillies, whom he had taken home with him to a family dinner, "it is out of the question. Life is not long enough for such fiddle-faddle." In the early part of his life he worked late at night. But subsequently from a conviction of the superior healthiness of early rising, as well as the desire to secure, at all hazards, a portion of the day for literary labor, he rose at five the year round; no small effort, as anyone will admit who has seen the pain and difficulty which a regular bird of night finds in reconciling his eyes to daylight. He was scrupulously exact, moreover, in the distribution of his hours. In one of his letters to his friend Terry, the player, replete, as usual, with advice that seems to flow equally from the head and the heart, he says, in reference to the practice of dawdling away one's time: "A habit of the mind it is which is very apt to beset men of intellect and talent, especially when their time is not regularly filled up, but left to their own arrangement. But it is like the ivy round the oak, and ends by limiting, if it does not destroy, the power of manly and necessary exertion. I must love a man so well to whom I offer such a word of advice that I will not apologize for it, but expect to hear you are become as regular as a Dutch clock—hours, quarters, minutes, all marked and appropriated." With the same emphasis he inculcates the like habits on his son. If any man might dispense with them it was surely Scott. But he knew that without them the greatest powers of mind will run to waste and water but the desert.

Some of the literary opinions of Scott are singular, considering, too, the position he occupied in the world of letters. "I promise you," he says in an epistle to an old friend, "my oaks will outlast my laurels; and I pique myself more on my compositions for manure than on any other compositions to which I was ever accessary." This may seem *badinage*. But he repeatedly, both in writing and conversation, places literature, as a profession, below other intellectual professions, and especially the military. The Duke of Wellington, the representative of the last, seems to have drawn from him a very extraordinary degree of deference, which, we cannot but think, smacks a little of that strong relish for gunpowder which he avows in himself.

It is not very easy to see on what this low estimate of literature rested. As a profession, it has too little in common with more active ones to afford much ground for running a parallel. The soldier has to do with externals; and his contests and triumphs are over matter, in its various forms, whether of man or material nature. The poet deals with the bodiless forms of air, of fancy lighter than air. His business is contemplative; the other's is active, and depends for its success on strong moral energy and presence of mind. He must, indeed, have genius of the highest order to effect his own combinations, anticipate the movements of his enemy, and dart with eagle eye on his vulnerable point. But who shall say that this practical genius, if we may so term it, is to rank higher in the scale than the creative power of the poet, the spark from the mind of Divinity itself?

The orator might seem to afford better ground for comparison, since, though his theatre of action is abroad, he may be said to work with much the same tools as the writer. Yet, how much of his success depends on qualities other than intellectual! "Action," said the father of eloquence, "action, action, are the three most essential things to an orator." How much, indeed, depends on the look, the gesture, the magical tones of voice, modulated to the passions he has stirred; and how much on the contagious sympathies of the audience itself, which drown everything like critcism in the overwhelming tide of emotion! If anyone would know how much, let him, after patiently standing

> "till his feet throb,
> And his head thumps, to feed upon the breath
> Of patriots bursting with heroic rage,"

read the same speech in the columns of a morning newspaper, or in the well-concocted report of the orator himself. The productions of the writer are subjected to a fiercer ordeal. He has no excited sympathies of numbers to hurry his readers along over his blunders. He is scanned in the calm silence of the closet. Every flower of fancy seems here to wilt under the rude breath of criticism; every link in the chain of argument is subjected to the touch of prying scrutiny, and if there be the least flaw in it it is sure to be detected. There is no tribunal so stern as the secret tribunal of a man's own closet, far removed from all the sympathetic impulses of humanity. Surely there is no form in which intellect can be exhibited to the world so completely stripped of all adventitious aids as the form of written composition. But, says the practical man, let us estimate things by their utility. "You talk of the poems of Homer," said a mathematician, "but after all what do they prove?" A question which involves an answer somewhat too voluminous for the tail of an article. But, if the poems of Homer were, as Heeren asserts, the principal bond which held the Grecian States together, and gave them a national feeling, they "prove" more than all the arithmeticians of Greece—and there were many cunning ones in it—ever did. The results of military skill are, indeed obvious. The soldier by a single victory enlarges the limits of an empire; he may do more—he may achieve the liberties of a nation, or roll back the tide of barbarism ready to overwhelm them. Wellington was placed in such a position, and nobly did he do his work—or, rather, he was placed at the head of such a gigantic moral and physical apparatus as enabled him to do it. With his own unassisted strength of course he could have done nothing. But it is on his own solitary resources that the great writer is to rely. And yet who shall say that the triumphs of Wellington have been greater than those of Scott—whose works are familiar as household words to every fireside in his own land, from the castle to the cottage; have crossed oceans and deserts, and, with healing on their wings, found their way to the remotest regions; have helped to form the character, until his own mind may be said to be incorporated into those of hundreds of thousands of his fellow-men? Who is there that has not, at some time or other, felt the heaviness of his heart lightened, his pains mitigated, and his bright moments of life made still brighter by the magical touches of his genius? And shall we speak of his victories as less real, less serviceable to humanity, less truly glorious, than those of the greatest captain of his day? The triumphs of the warrior are bounded by the narrow theatre of his own age. But those of a Scott or a Shakespeare will be renewed, with greater and greater lustre, in ages yet unborn, when the victorious chieftain shall be forgotten, or shall live only in the song of the minstrel and the page of the chronicler.

But, after all, this sort of parallel is not very gracious nor very philosophical; and, to say truth, is somewhat foolish. We have been drawn into it by the not random, but very deliberate, and in our poor judgment very disparaging estimate by Scott of his own vocation; and, as we have taken the trouble to write it, our readers will excuse us from blotting it out. There is too little ground for the respective parties to stand on for a parallel. As to the pedantic *cui bono* standard, it is impossible to tell the final issues of a single act; how can we then hope to, those of a course of action? As for the honor of different vocations, there never was a truer sentence than the stale one of Pope—stale now because it is so true—

> "Act well your part, there all the honor lies."

And it is the just boast of our own country that in no civilized nation is the force of this philanthropic maxim so nobly illustrated as in ours—thanks to our glorious institutions.

A great cause, probably, of Scott's low estimate of letters was the facility with which he wrote himself. What costs us little we are apt to prize little. If diamonds were as common as pebbles, and gold dust as any other, who would stoop to gather them? It was the prostitution of his muse, by the by, for this same gold dust which brought a sharp rebuke on the poet from Lord Byron, in his "English Bards"—

> "For this we spurn Apollo's venal son";

a coarse cut, and the imputation about as true as most satire—that is, not true at all. This was indited in his Lordship's earlier days, when he most chivalrously disclaimed all purpose of bartering his rhymes for gold. He lived long enough, however, to weigh his literary wares in as nice a money-balance as any more vulgar manufacturer ever did. And, in truth, it would be ridiculous if the produce of the brain should not bring its price, in this form as well as any other; there is little danger, we imagine, of finding too much gold in the bowels of Parnassus.

Scott took a more sensible view of things. In a letter to

Ellis, written soon after the publication of the "Minstrelsy," he observes: "People may say this and that of the pleasure of fame, or of profit, as a motive of writing; I think the only pleasure is in the actual exertion and research, and I would no more write upon any other terms than I would hunt merely to dine upon hare-soup. At the same time, if credit and profit came unlooked for I would no more quarrel with them than with the soup." Even this declaration was somewhat more magnanimous than was warranted by his subsequent conduct. The truth is, he soon found out, especially after the Waverley vein had opened, that he had hit on a gold mine. The prodigious returns he got gave the whole thing the aspect of a speculation. Every new work was an adventure; and the proceeds naturally suggested the indulgence of the most extravagant schemes of expense, which, in their turn, stimulated him to fresh efforts. In this way the "profits" became, whatever they might have been once, a principal incentive to, as they were the recompense of, exertion. His productions were cash articles, and were estimated by him more on the Hudibrastic rule of "the real worth of a thing" than by any fanciful standard of fame. He bowed with deference to the judgment of the booksellers, and trimmed his sails dexterously as the *"aura popularis"* shifted. "If it is na weil bobbit," he writes to his printer, on turning out a less lucky novel, "we'll bobb it again." His muse was of that school who seek the greatest happiness of the greatest possible number. We can hardly imagine him invoking her, like Milton—

> "Still govern thou my song,
> Urania, and fit audience find, though few."

Still less can we imagine him, like the blind old bard, feeding his soul with visions of posthumous glory, and spinning out epics for five pounds apiece.

It is singular that Scott, although he set as high a money value on his productions as the most enthusiastic of the "trade" could have done, in a literary view, should have held them so cheap. "Whatever others may be," he said, "I have never been a partisan of my own poetry; as John Wilkes declared that, 'in the height of his success, he had himself never been a Wilkite.'" Considering the poet's popularity, this was but an indifferent compliment to the taste of his age. With all this disparagement of his own productions, however, Scott was not insensible to criticism. He says somewhere, indeed, that "if he had been conscious of a single vulnerable point in himself, he would not have taken up the business of writing." But on another occasion he writes, "I make it a rule never to read the attacks made upon me." And Captain Hall remarks: "He never reads the criticisms on his books; this I know, from the most unquestionable authority. Praise, he says, gives him no pleasure, and censure annoys him." Madame de Graffigny says, also, of Voltaire, that "he was altogether indifferent to praise, but the least word from his enemies drove him crazy." Yet both these authors banqueted on the sweets of panegyric as much as any who ever lived. They were in the condition of an epicure, whose palate has lost its relish for the dainty fare in which it has been so long revelling, without becoming less sensible to the annoyances of sharper and coarser flavors. It may afford some consolation to humble mediocrity, to the less fortunate votaries of the muse, that those who have reached the summit of Parnassus are not much more contented with their condition than those who are scrambling among the bushes at the bottom of the mountain. The fact seems to be, as Scott himself intimates more than once, that the joy is in the chase, whether in the prose or the poetry of life.

But it is high time to terminate our lucubrations, which, however imperfect and unsatisfactory, have already run to a length that must trespass on the patience of the reader. We rise from the perusal of these delightful volumes with the same sort of melancholy feeling with which we awake from a pleasant dream. The concluding volume, of which such ominous presage is given in the last sentence of the fifth, has not yet reached us; but we know enough to anticipate the sad catastrophe it is to unfold of the drama. In those which we have seen, however, we have beheld a succession of interesting characters come upon the scene—and pass away to their long home. "Bright eyes now closed in dust, gay voices forever silenced," seem to haunt us, too, as we write. The imagination reverts to Abbotsford—the romantic and once brilliant Abbotsford—the magical creation of his hands. We see its halls, radiant with the hospitality of his benevolent heart, thronged with pilgrims from every land, assembled to pay homage at the shrine of genius, echoing to the blithe music of those festal holidays when young and old met to renew the usages of the good old times.

> "These were its charms—but all these charms are fled."

Its courts are desolate, or trodden only by the foot of the stranger. The stranger sits under the shadows of the trees which his hand planted. The spell of the enchanter is dissolved. His wand is broken. And the mighty minstrel himself now sleeps in the bosom of the peaceful scenes, embellished by his taste and which his genius has made immortal.

THE LAST MOMENTS OF EMINENT MEN

—

BY

GEORGE BANCROFT

GEORGE BANCROFT

1800—1891

George Bancroft was born at Worcester, Massachusetts, in 1800, and was graduated from Harvard at the age of seventeen. With his graduation, however, his education was only begun. During the next five years he travelled extensively in Europe, and studied zealously at the Universities of Göttingen, Berlin, and Heidelberg, and at Paris, meeting many eminent scholars of the time whose friendship he enjoyed through life. His studies were chiefly devoted to the languages and to history. On his return he taught for a year in Harvard College, and later he held an appointment in a seminary in Massachusetts. About this time he had some thought of entering public life, and was elected to the legislature, but at the age of thirty-five he decided to devote his life to writing a history of his country.

The first volume of his history appeared in 1834. Four years later Bancroft was appointed Collector for the Port of Boston, but nothing was permitted to interfere seriously with the great work he had undertaken. In 1844 he was an unsuccessful candidate for Governor of Massachusetts, and in 1845 became Secretary of the Navy under President Polk. As a member of Polk's Cabinet he established the Naval Academy at Annapolis. The following year he was appointed Minister to Great Britain, remaining abroad three years. These duties interrupted only temporarily the progress of his great history. The third volume appeared in 1840; twelve years later Bancroft completed the fourth and fifth volumes. The remaining volumes appeared in steady succession at intervals of from two to four years down to 1874, when the tenth and last was published. The work, which had thus taken no less than forty years to complete, covered the history of the colonial and revolutionary periods only. In the preparation of this great work Bancroft ransacked every great public library in the country, besides examining newspaper files, documents, and local and family records innumerable. His high public position gave him ready access to numerous archives, both public and private, that would have been sealed to an investigator less known and respected. During his later years Bancroft wrote a " History of the Formation of the Constitution of the United States " in two volumes, which may be regarded as a continuation of his greater work. He died at Washington in 1891.

Bancroft's literary style, while lacking the brilliancy of Prescott's or Motley's, and the perfection of form of Parkman's, possesses none the less high merit of its own. It is clear and forcible, thoroughly dignified and convincing. That his works have not achieved a wider popularity is due more to their voluminousness than to any defect in the style of their composition. The essay on " The Last Moments of Eminent Men " shows Bancroft in one of his best moods. He wrote very little except on historical subjects; in fact it was his sole aim to write a worthy history of his country, and his later years were spent in revising what he had already written rather than in attempting new work. Bancroft's one great work is his " History," a lofty and enduring monument.

THE LAST MOMENTS OF EMINENT MEN

"LIFE," says Sir William Temple, "is like wine; he who would drink it pure must not drain it to the dregs." "I do not wish," Byron would say, "to live to become old." The expression of the ancient poet, "that to die young is a boon of Heaven to its favorites," was repeatedly quoted by him with approbation. The certainty of a speedy release he would call the only relief against burdens which could not be borne were they not of very limited duration.

But the general sentiment of mankind declares length of days to be desirable. After an active and successful career the repose of decline is serene and cheerful. By common consent gray hairs are a crown of glory; the only object of respect that can never excite envy. The hour of evening is not necessarily overcast; and the aged man, exchanging the pursuits of ambition for the quiet of observation, the strife of public discussion for the diffuse but instructive language of experience, passes to the grave amid grateful recollections and the tranquil enjoyment of satisfied desires.

The happy, it is agreed by all, are afraid to contemplate their end; the unhappy, it has been said, look forward to it as a release from suffering. "I think of death often," said a distinguished but dissatisfied man; "and I view it as a refuge. There is something calm and soothing to me in the thought; and the only time that I feel repugnance to it is on a fine day, in solitude, in a beautiful country, when all nature seems rejoicing in light and life."

This is the language of self-delusion. Numerous as may be the causes for disgust with life, its close is never contemplated with carelessness. Religion may elevate the soul to a sublime reliance on a future existence; nothing else can do it. The love of honor may brave danger; the passion of melancholy may indulge an aversion to continued being; philosophy may take its last rest with composure; the sense of shame may conduct to fortitude; yet they who would disregard the grave must turn their thoughts from the consideration of its terrors. It is an impulse of nature to strive to preserve our being; and the longing cannot be eradicated. The mind may shun the contemplation of horrors; it may fortify itself by refusing to observe the nearness or the extent of the impending evil; but the instinct of life is stubborn; and he who looks directly at its termination and professes indifference is a hypocrite or is self-deceived. He that calls boldly upon Death is sure to be dismayed on finding him near. The oldest are never so old, but they desire life for one day longer; the child looks to its parents as if to discern a glimpse of hope; even the infant, as it exhales its breath, springs from its pillow to meet its mother as if there were help where there is love.

There is a story told of one of the favorite marshals of Napoleon, who, in a battle in the south of Germany, was struck by a cannon-ball, and so severely wounded that there was no possibility of a respite. Summoning the surgeon, he ordered his wounds to be dressed; and, when aid was declared to be unavailing, the dying officer clamorously demanded that Napoleon should be sent for, as one who had power to stop the effusion of blood, and awe nature itself into submission. Life expired amid maledictions and threats heaped upon the innocent surgeon. This foolish frenzy may have appeared like blasphemy; it was but the uncontrolled outbreak of the instinct of self-preservation, in a rough and undisciplined mind.

Even in men of strong religious convictions the end is not always met with serenity; and the preacher and philosopher sometimes express an apprehension which cannot be pacified. The celebrated British moralist, Samuel Johnson, was the instructor of his age; his works are full of the austere lessons of reflecting wisdom. It might have been supposed that religion would have reconciled him to the decree of Providence; that philosophy would have taught him to acquiesce in a necessary issue; that science would have inspired him with confidence in the skill of his medical attendants. And yet it was not so. A sullen gloom overclouded his faculties; he could not summon resolution to tranquillize his emotions; and, in the absence of his attendants, he gashed himself with ghastly and debilitating wounds, as if the blind lacerations of his misguided arm could prolong the moments of an existence which the best physicians of London declared to be numbered.

"Is there anything on earth I can do for you?" said Taylor to Wolcott, known as Peter Pindar, as he lay on his death-bed. "Give me back my youth," were the last words of the satirical buffoon.

If Johnson could hope for relief from self-inflicted wounds, if the poet could prefer to his friend the useless prayer for a restoration of youth, we may readily believe what historians relate to us of the end of Louis XI of France, a monarch who was not destitute of eminent qualities as well as repulsive vices; possessing courage, a knowledge of men and of business, an indomitable will, a disposition favorable to the administration of justice among his subjects; viewing impunity in wrong as exclusively a royal prerogative. Remorse, fear, a consciousness of being detected, disgust with life and horror of death—these were the sentiments which troubled the sick-couch of the absolute king. The first of his line who bore the epithet of "the most Christian," he was so abandoned to egotism that he allowed the veins of children to be opened, and greedily drank their blood; believing, with physicians of that day, that it would renovate his youth, or at least check the decay of nature. The cruelty was useless. At last, feeling the approach of death to be certain, he sent for an anchorite from Calabria, since revered as St. Francis de Paula; and, when the hermit arrived, the monarch of France entreated him to spare his life. He threw himself at the feet of the man who was believed to derive healing virtues from the sanctity of his character; he begged the intercession of his prayers; he wept, he supplicated, he hoped that the voice of a Calabrian monk would reverse the order of nature, and successfully plead for his respite.

We find the love of life still more strongly acknowledged by an English poet, who, after describing our being as the dream of a shadow, "a weak-built isthmus between two eternities, so frail that it can sustain neither wind nor wave," yet avows his preference of a few days', nay, of a few hours' longer residence upon earth, to all the fame which poetry can achieve.

> "Fain would I see that prodigal,
> Who his to-morrow would bestow,
> For all old Homer's life, e'er since he died, till now."

We do not believe the poet sincere, for one passion may prevail over another, and in many a breast the love of fame is at times, if not always, the strongest. But if those who pass their lives in a struggle for glory may desire the attainment of their object at any price, the competitors for political power are apt to cling fast to the scene of their rivalry. Lord Castlereagh could indeed commit suicide; but it was not from disgust; his mind dwelt on the precarious condition of his own elevation, and the unsuccessful policy in which he had involved his country. He did not love death; he did not contemplate it with indifference; he failed to observe its terrors, because his attention was absorbed by apprehensions which pressed themselves upon him with unrelenting force.

The ship of the Marquis of Badajoz, Viceroy of Peru, was set on fire by Captain Stayner. The marchioness, and her daughter, who was betrothed to the Duke of Medina-Celi, swooned in the flames, and could not be rescued. The marquis resigned himself also to die, rather than survive with the memory of such horrors. It was not that he was careless of life; the natural feelings remained unchanged; the love of grandeur, the pride of opulence and dominion; but he preferred death, because that was out of sight, and would rescue him from the presence of absorbing and intolerable sorrows.

Madame de Sévigné, in her charming letters, gives the true sensations of the ambitious man when suddenly called to leave the scenes of his efforts and his triumphs. Rumor, with its wonted credulity, ascribed to Louvois, the powerful minister of Louis XIV, the crime of suicide. His death was sudden, but not by his own arm; he fell a victim, if not to disease, to the revenge of a woman. In a night the most energetic, reckless statesman in Europe, passionately fond of place, extending his influence to every cabinet, and embracing in his views the destiny of continents, was called away. How much business was arrested in progress! how many projects defeated! how many secrets buried in the silence of the grave! Who should disentangle the interests which his policy had rendered complicate? Who should terminate the wars which he had begun? Who should follow up the blows which he had aimed? Well might he have exclaimed to the angel of death: "Ah, grant me a short reprieve; spare me till I can check the Duke of Savoy; checkmate the Prince of Orange!"—"No! no! You shall not have a single, single minute." Death is as inexorable to the prayer of ambition as to the entreaty of despair. The ruins of the Palatinate, the wrongs of the Huguenots, were to be avenged; and Louvois, like Louis XI and like the rest of mankind, was to learn that the passion for life, whether expressed in the language of superstition, of abject despondency, or of the desire of continued power, could not prolong existence for a moment.

But, though the love of life may be declared a universal instinct, it does not follow that death is usually met with abjectness. It belongs to virtue and to manliness to accept the inevitable decree with firmness. It is often sought voluntarily, but even then the latent passion is discernible. A sense of shame, a desire of plunder, a hope of emolument—these, not less than a sense of duty, are motives sufficient to influence men to defy all danger; yet the feeling tor self-preservation does not cease to exert its power. The common hireling soldier contracts to expose himself to the deadly fire of a hostile army whenever his employers may command it; he does it, in a controversy of which he knows not the merits, for a party to which he is essentially indifferent, for purposes which, perhaps, if his mind were enlightened, he would labor to counteract. The life of the soldier is a life of contrast; of labor and idleness; it is a course of routine, easy to be endured, and leading only at intervals to exposure. The love of ease, the certainty of obtaining the means of existence, the remoteness of peril, conspire to tempt adventurers, and the armies of Europe have never suffered from any other limit than the wants of the treasury. But the same soldier would fly precipitately from any hazard which he had not bargained to encounter. The merchant will visit the deadliest climates in pursuit of gain; he will pass over regions where the air is known to be corrupt, and disease to have anchored itself in the hot, heavy atmosphere. And this he will attempt repeatedly, and with firmness, in defiance of the crowds of corpses which he may see carried by wagon-loads to the graveyards. But the same merchant would be struck by panic and desert his own residence in a more favored clime, should it be invaded by epidemic disease. He who would fearlessly meet the worst forms of a storm at sea, and take his chance of escaping the fever as he passed through New Orleans, would shun New York in the season of the cholera, and shrink from any danger which was novel and unexpected. The widows of India ascend the funeral-pile with a fortitude which man could never display, and emulously yield up their lives to a barbarous usage which, if men had been called upon to endure it, would never have been perpetuated. Yet is it to be supposed that these unhappy victims are indifferent to the charms of existence, or blind to the terrors of its extinction? Calmly as they may lay themselves upon the pyre, they would beg for mercy were their execution to be demanded in any other way; they would confess their fear were it not that love and honor and custom confirm their doom.

No class of men in the regular discharge of duty incur danger more frequently than the honest physician. There is no type of malignant maladies with which he fails to become acquainted, no hospital so crowded with contagion that he dares not walk freely through its wards. His vocation is among the sick and the dying; he is the familiar friend of those who are sinking under infectious disease; and he never shrinks from the horror of observing it under all its aspects. He must do so with equanimity; as he inhales the poisoned atmosphere he must coolly reflect on the medicines which may mitigate the sufferings that he cannot remedy. Nay, after death has ensued, he must search with the dissecting-knife for its hidden cause, if so by multiplying his own perils he may discover some alleviation for the afflictions of others. And why is this? Because the physician is indifferent to death? Because he is steeled and hardened against the fear of it? Because he despises or pretends to despise it? By no means. It is his especial business to value life, to cherish the least spark of animated existence. And the habit of caring for the lives of his fellow-men is far from leading him to an habitual indifference to his own. The physician shuns every danger but such as the glory of his profession commands him to defy.

Thus we are led to explain the anomaly of suicide, and reconcile the apparent contradiction of a terror of death, which is yet voluntarily encountered. It may seem a paradox; but the dread of dying has itself sometimes prompted suicide, and the man who seeks to destroy himself at the very moment of perpetrating his crime betrays the passion for life. Menace him with death under a different form from that which he has chosen, and, like other men, he will get out of its way. He will defend himself against the assassin, though he might be ready to cut his own throat; he will, if at sea, and the ship were sinking in a storm, labor with his whole strength to save it from going down, even if he had formed the design to leap into the ocean in the first moment of a calm. Place him in the van of an army, it is by no means certain that he will not prove a coward; tell him the cholera is about to rage, and he will deluge himself with preventive remedies; send him to a house visited with yellow fever, and he will steep himself in vinegar and carry with him an atmosphere of camphor. It is only under the one form, which the mind in some insane excitement may have chosen, that he preserves the desire to leave the world.

It will not be difficult, then, to set a right value on the declaration of those who profess to regard death not with indifference merely, but with contempt. It is pure affectation, or the indulgence of a vulgar levity; and must excite either compassion or disgust, according as it is marked by the spirit of fiendish scoffing or of human vanity and self-deception. A French moralist tells us of a valet who danced merrily on the scaffold, where he was to be broken on the wheel. A New England woman, belonging to a family which esteemed itself one of the first, was convicted of aiding her paramour to kill her husband. She was a complete sensualist, one to whom life was everything, and the loss of it the total shipwreck of everything. On her way to the place of execution she was accompanied by a clergyman of no very great ability; and all along the road, with the gallows in plain sight, she amused herself in teasing the good man, whose wits were no match for her raillery. He had been buying a new chaise, quite an event in the life of a humble country pastor, and when he spoke of the next world she would amuse herself in praising his purchase. If he deplored her fate and her prospects, she would grieve at his exposure to the inclement weather, and laughed and chatted as if she had been driving to a wedding and not to her own funeral. And why was this? Because death was not feared? No; but because death was feared, and feared intensely. The Eastern women, who are burned alive with their deceased husbands, often utter shrieks that would pierce the hearers to the soul; and, to prevent a compassion which would endanger the reign of superstition, the priests, with drums and cymbals, drown the terrific cries of their victims. So it is with those who go to the court of the King of Terrors with merriment on their lips. They dread his presence, and they seek to drown the noise of his approaching footsteps by the sound of their own ribaldry. If the scaffold often rings with a jest, it is because the mind shrinks from the solemnity of the impending change.

Perhaps the most common device for averting contemplation from death itself is, in directing it to the manner of dying. *Vanitas vanitatum!* Vanity does not give up its hold on the last hour. Men wish to die with distinction, to be buried in state; and the last thoughts are employed on the decorum of the moment, or in the anticipation of funeral splendors. It was no uncommon thing among the Romans for a rich man to appoint an heir on condition that his obsequies should be celebrated with costly pomp. "When I am dead," said an Indian chief, who fell into his last sleep at Washington—"when I am dead let the big guns be fired over me." The words were thought worthy of being engraved on his tomb; but they are no more than a plain expression of a very common passion; the same which leads the humblest to desire that at least a stone may be placed at the head of his grave, and demands the erection of splendid mausoleums and costly tombs for the mistaken men—

> "Who by the proofs of death pretend to live."

Among the ancients, an opulent man, while yet in health, would order his own sarcophagus; and nowadays the wealthy sometimes build their own tombs, for the sake of securing a satisfactory monument. A vain man, who had done this at a great expense, showed his motive so plainly that his neighbors laughed with the sexton of the parish, who wished that the builder might not be kept long out of the interest of his money.

But it is not merely in the decorations of the grave that vanity is displayed. Saladin, in his last illness, instead of his usual standard, ordered his shroud to be uplifted in front of his tent; and the herald, who hung out this winding-sheet as a flag, was commanded to exclaim aloud: "Behold! this is all which Saladin, the vanquisher of the East, carries away of all his conquests." He was wrong there. He came naked into the world, and he left it naked. Grave-clothes were a superfluous luxury, and, to the person receiving them, as barren of comfort as his sceptre or his scimitar. Saladin was vain. He sought in dying to contrast the power he had enjoyed with the feebleness of his condition; to pass from the world in a striking antithesis; to make his death-scene an epigram. All was vanity.

A century ago it was the fashion for culprits to appear on the scaffold in the dress of dandies. Some centuries before it was the privilege of noblemen, if they merited hanging, to escape the gallows and perish on the block. The Syrian priests had foretold to the Emperor Heliogabalus that he would be reduced to the necessity of committing suicide; believing them true prophets, he kept in readiness silken cords and a sword of gold. Admirable privilege of the nobility, to be beheaded instead of hanged! Enviable prerogative of imperial dignity, to be strangled with a knot of silk or to be assassinated with a golden sword!

> "'Odious! in woollen! 'twould a saint provoke'
> (Were the last words that poor Narcissa spoke).
> 'No, let a charming chintz and Brussels lace
> Wrap my cold limbs and shade my lifeless face;
> One would not sure be frightful when one's dead,
> And—Betty—give this cheek a little red.'"

The example chosen by the poet extended to appearances after death; for the presence of the same weakness in the hour of mortality we must look to the precincts of courts, where folly used to reign by prescriptive right; where caprice gives law and pleasures consume life. There you may witness the harlot's euthanasia. The French court was at Choisy when Madame de Pompadour felt the pangs of a fatal malady. It had been the established etiquette that none but princes and persons of royal blood should breathe their last in Versailles. Proclaim to the gay circles of Paris that a thing new and unheard-of is to be permitted! Announce to the world that the rules of palace propriety and Bourbon decorum are to be broken! that the chambers where vice had fearlessly lived and laughed, but never been permitted to expire, were to admit the novel spectacle of the King's favorite mistress struggling with death!

The marchioness questioned the physicians firmly; she perceived their hesitation; she saw the hand that beckoned her away; and she determined, says the historian, to depart in the pomp of a queen. Louis XV, himself not capable of a strong emotion, was yet willing to concede to his dying friend the consolation which she coveted, the opportunity to reign till her parting gasp. The courtiers thronged round the death-bed of a woman who distributed favors with the last exhalations of her breath; and the King hurried to name to public offices the persons whom her faltering accents recommended. Her sickroom became a scene of state; the princes and grandees still entered to pay their homage to the woman whose power did not yield to mortal disease, and were surprised to find her richly attired. The traces of death in her countenance were concealed by rouge. She reclined on a splendid couch; questions of public policy were discussed by ministers in her presence; she gloried in holding to the end the reins of the kingdom in her hands. Even a sycophant clergy showed respect to the expiring favorite, and felt no shame at sanctioning with their frequent visits the vices of a woman who had entered the palace only as an adulteress. Having complied with the rites of the Roman Church, she next sought the approbation of the philosophers. She lisped no word of penitence; she shed no tears of regret. The curate left her as she was in the agony. "Wait a moment," said she; "we will leave the house together."

The dying mistress was worshipped while she breathed; hardly was she dead when the scene changed: two domestics carried out her body on a hand-barrow from the palace to her private home. The King stood at the window looking at the clouds as her remains were carried by. "The marchioness," said he, "will have bad weather on her journey."

The flickering lamp blazes with unusual brightness just as it goes out. "The fit gives vigor, as it destroys." He who has but a moment remaining is released from the common motives for dissimulation; and Time, that lays his hand on everything else, destroying beauty, undermining health, and wasting the powers of life, spares the ruling passion, which is connected with the soul itself. That passion

> ". . . sticks to our last sand.
> Consistent in our follies and our sins,
> Here honest Nature ends as she begins."

Napoleon expired during the raging of a whirlwind, and his last words showed that his thoughts were in the battle-field. The meritorious author of the "Memoir of Cabot," a work which in accuracy and in extensive research is very far superior to most late treatises on maritime discovery, tells us that the discoverer of our continent, in an hallucination before his death, believed himself again on the ocean, once more steering in quest of adventure over waves which knew him as the steed knows its rider. How many a gentle eye has been dimmed with tears as it read the fabled fate of Fergus MacIvor! Not inferior to the admirable hero of the romance was the Marquis of Montrose, who had fought for the Stuarts and fell into the hands of the Presbyterians. His head and his limbs were ordered to be severed from his body, and to be hanged on the Tolbooth in Edinburgh and in other public towns of the kingdom. He listened to the sentence with the pride of loyalty and the fierce anger of a generous defiance. "I wish," he exclaimed, "I had flesh enough to be sent to every city in Christendom, as a testimony to the cause for which I suffer."

But let us take an example of sublimer virtue, such as we find in a statesman who lived without a stain from youth to maturity, and displayed an unwavering consistency to the last; a hero in civil life, who was in some degree our own. It becomes America to take part in rescuing from undeserved censure the names and the memory of victims to the unconquerable love of republican liberty.

> "Vane, young in years, in counsel old: to know
> Both spiritual power and civil, what each means,
> What severs each, thou'st learned, which few have done.
> The bounds of either sword to thee we owe;
> Therefore on thy firm hand Religion leans
> In peace, and reckons thee her eldest son."

He that would discern the difference between magnanimous genius and a shallow wit may compare this splendid eulogy of

Milton with the superficial levity in the commentary of Warton. It is a fashion to call Sir Henry Vane a fanatic. And what is fanaticism? True, he was a rigid Calvinist. True, he has written an obscure book on the mystery of godliness, of which all that we understand is excellent, and we may therefore infer that the vein of the rest is good. But does this prove him a fanatic? If to be the uncompromising defender of civil and religious liberty be fanaticism; if to forgive injuries be fanaticism; if to believe that the mercy of God extends to all his creatures, and may reach even the angels of darkness, be fanaticism; if to have earnestly supported in the Long Parliament the freedom of conscience; if to have repeatedly, boldly, and zealously interposed to check the persecution of Roman Catholics; if to have labored that the sect which he least approved should enjoy their property in security and be safe from all penal enactments for nonconformity; if in his public life to have pursued a career of firm, conscientious, disinterested consistency, never wavering, never trimming, never changing—if all this be fanaticism, then was Sir Harry Vane a fanatic. Not otherwise. The people of Massachusetts declined to continue him in office; and when his power in England was great, he requited the colony with the benefits of his favoring influence. He resisted the arbitrariness of Charles I, but would not sit as one of his judges. He opposed the tyranny of Cromwell. When that extraordinary man entered the House of Commons to break up the Parliament which was about to pass laws that would have endangered his supremacy, Vane rebuked him for his purpose of treason. When the musketeers invaded the hall of debate, and others were silent, Vane exclaimed to the most despotic man in Europe: "This is not honest. It is against morality and common honesty." Well might Cromwell, since his designs were criminal, reply: "Sir Henry Vane! Sir Henry Vane! The Lord deliver me from Sir Henry Vane!"

Though Vane suffered from the usurpation of the Protector, he lived to see the Restoration. On the return of the Stuarts, like Lafayette among the Bourbons, he remained the stanch enemy of tyranny. The austere patriot whom Cromwell had feared struck terror into the hearts of a faithless and licentious court. It was resolved to destroy him. In a different age or country the poisoned cup, or the knife of the assassin, might have been used; in that season of corrupt influence a judicial murder was resolved upon. His death was a deliberate crime, contrary to the royal promise; contrary to the express vote of "the healing Parliament"; contrary to law, to equity, to the evidence. But it suited the designs of a monarch who feared to be watched by a statesman of incorruptible elevation of character. The night before his execution he enjoyed the society of his family as if he had been reposing in his own mansion. The next morning he was beheaded. The least concession would have saved him. If he had only consented to deny the supremacy of Parliament the King would have restrained the malignity of his hatred. "Ten thousand deaths for me," exclaimed Vane, "ere I will stain the purity of my conscience." Historians report that life was dear to him; he submitted to his and with the firmness of a patriot, the serenity of a Christian.

> "'I give and I devise' (old Euclio said,
> And sighed) 'my lands and tenements to Ned.'
> 'Your money, sir?' 'My money, sir! what, all?
> 'Why, if I must' (then wept), 'I give it Paul.'
> 'The manor, sir?' 'The manor! hold,' he cried,
> 'Not that—I can not part with that'—and died."

Lorenzo de' Medici, upon his death-bed, sent for Savonarola to receive his confession and grant him absolution. The severe anchorite questioned the dying sinner with unsparing rigor. "Do you believe entirely in the mercy of God?" "Yes, I feel it in my heart." "Are you truly ready to restore all the possessions and estates which you have unjustly acquired?" The dying duke hesitated; he counted up in his mind the sums which he had hoarded; delusion whispered that nearly all had been so honestly gained that the sternest censor would strike but little from his opulence. The pains of hell were threatened if he denied, and he gathered courage to reply that he was ready to make restitution. Once more the unyielding priest resumed his inquisition. "Will you resign the sovereignty of Florence, and restore the democracy of the republic?" Lorenzo, like Macbeth, had acquired a crown; but, unlike Macbeth, he saw sons of his own about to become his successors. He gloried in the hope of being the father of princes, the founder of a line of hereditary sovereigns. Should he crush this brilliant expectation and tremble at the wild words of a visionary? Should he who had reigned as a monarch stoop to die as a merchant? No! though hell itself were opening beneath his bed. "Not that! I cannot part with that." Savonarola left his bedside with indignation, and Lorenzo died without shrift.

> "And you, brave Cobham, to the latest breath,
> Shall feel your ruling passion strong in death,
> Such in those moments, as in all the past—
> 'Oh, save my country, Heaven!' shall be your last."

Like this was the exclamation of the patriot Quincy, whose virtues have been fitly commemorated by the pious reverence of his son. The celebrated Admiral Blake breathed his last as he came in sight of England, happy in at least descrying the land of which he had advanced the glory by his brilliant victories. Quincy died as he approached the coast of Massachusetts. He loved his family; but at that moment he gave his whole soul to the cause of freedom. "Oh, that I might live" —it was his dying wish—"to render to my country one last service!"

The coward falls panic-stricken; the superstitious man dies with visions of terror floating before his fancy. It has even happened that a man has been in such dread of eternal woe as to cut his throat in his despair. The phenomenon seems strange; but the fact is unquestionable. The giddy that are near a precipice, totter toward the brink which they would shun. Everybody remembers the atheism and bald sensuality of the septuagenarian Alexander VI; and the name of his natural son, Cæsar Borgia, is a proverb, as a synonym for the most vicious selfishness. Let one tale, of which Macchiavelli attests the truth, set forth the deep baseness of a cowardly nature. Borgia had, by the most solemn oaths, induced the Duke of Gravina, Oliverotto, Vitellozzo Vitelli, and another, to meet him in Sinigaglia, for the purpose of forming a treaty, and then issued the order for the massacre of Oliverotto and Vitelli. Can it be believed? Vitelli, as he expired, begged of the infamous Borgia, his assassin, to obtain of Alexander a dispensation for his omissions, a release from purgatory.

The death-bed of Cromwell himself was not free from superstition. When near his end, he asked if the elect could never fall. "Never," replied Godwin the preacher. "Then I am safe," said the man whose last years had been stained by cruelty and tyranny; "for I am sure I was once in a state of grace."

Ximenes languished from disappointment at the loss of power and the want of royal favor. A smile from Louis would have cheered the death-bed of Racine.

In a brave mind the love of honor endures to the last. "Don't give up the ship!" cried Lawrence, as his life-blood was flowing in torrents. Abimelech groaned that he fell ignobly by the hand of a woman. We have ever admired the gallant death of Sir Richard Grenville, who, in a single ship, encountered a numerous fleet; and, when mortally wounded, husbanded his strength till he could summon his victors to bear testimony to his courage and his patriotism. "Here die I, Richard Grenville, with a joyous and quiet mind, for that I have ended my life as a true soldier ought to do, fighting for his country, queen, religion, and honor."

The public has been instructed through the press in the details of the treason of Benedict Arnold, by an inquirer, who has compassed earth and sea in search of historic truth, and has merited the applause of his country, not less for candor and judgment, than for diligence and ability. The victim of the intrigue was André. The mind of the young soldier revolted at the service of treachery in which he had become involved, and, holding a stain upon honor to be worse than the forfeiture of life, he shuddered at the sight of the gallows, but not at the thought of dying. He felt the same sentiment which made death welcome to Nelson and to Wolfe, to whom it came with glory and victory for its companions; but for André the keen sense of honor added bitterness to the cup of affliction by exciting fear lest the world should take the manner of his execution as evidence of merited opprobrium.

Finally: he who has a good conscience and a well-balanced mind meets death with calmness, resignation, and hope. Saint Louis died among the ruins of Carthage—a Christian king, laboring in vain to expel the religion of Mohammed from the spot where Dido had planted the gods of Syria. "My friends," said he, "I have finished my course. Do not mourn for me. It is natural that I, as your chief and leader, should go before you. You must follow me. Keep yourselves in readiness for the journey." Then, giving his son his blessing and the best advice, he received the sacrament, closed his eyes, and died as he was repeating from the Psalms: "I will come into thy house; I will worship in thy holy temple."

The curate of St. Sulpice asked the confessor who had shrived Montesquieu on his death-bed if the penitent had given satisfaction. "Yes," replied Father Roust, "like a man of genius." The curate was displeased; unwilling to leave the dying man a moment of tranquillity, he addressed him, "Sir, are you truly conscious of the greatness of God?" "Yes," said the departing philosopher, "and of the littleness of man."

How calm were the last moments of Cuvier! Benevolence of feeling and self-possession diffused serenity round the hour of his passing away. Confident that the hand of death was upon him, he yet submitted to the application of remedies, that he might gratify his more hopeful friends. They had recourse to leeches; and with delightful simplicity the great naturalist observed, it was he who had discovered that leeches possess red blood. The discovery, which he made in his youth, had been communicated to the public in the memoir that first gained him celebrity. The thoughts of the dying naturalist recurred to the scenes of his early life, to the coast of Normandy, where, in the solitude of conscious genius, he had roamed by the side of the ocean, and achieved fame by observing the wonders of animal life which are nourished in its depths. He remembered his years of poverty, the sullen rejection which his first claims for advancement had received, and all the vicissitudes through which he had been led to the highest distinctions in science. The son of the Würtemberg soldier, of too feeble a frame to embrace the profession of his father, had found his way to the secrets of nature. The man who, in his own province, had been refused the means of becoming the village pastor of an ignorant peasantry, had succeeded in charming the most polished circles of Paris by the clearness of his descriptions, and commanding the attention of the deputies of France by the grace and fluency of his elocution. And now he was calmly predicting his departure; his respiration became rapid, and his head fell as if he were in meditation. Thus his soul passed to its Creator without a struggle. "Those who entered afterward would have thought that the noble old man, seated in his arm-chair by the fireplace, was asleep, and would have walked softly across the room for fear of disturbing him." Heaven had but "recalled its own."

The death of Haller himself was equally tranquil. When its hour approached, he watched the ebbing of life and continued to observe the beating of his pulse till sensation was gone.

A tranquil death becomes the man of science, or the scholar. He should cultivate letters to the last moment of life; he should resign public honors as calmly as one would take off a domino on returning from a mask. He should listen to the signal for his departure, not with exultation, and not with indifference. Respecting the dread solemnity of the change, and reposing in hope on the bosom of death, he should pass without boldness and without fear, from the struggles of inquiry to the certainty of knowledge, from a world of doubt to a world of truth.

COMPENSATION

—

BY

RALPH WALDO EMERSON

RALPH WALDO EMERSON

1803—1882

Ralph Waldo Emerson, who was born in Boston in 1803, was descended from a family of ministers, "eight generations of culture," as Holmes once expressed it. He was educated at the Boston Latin School and at Harvard, where he graduated in 1821 without attracting much attention at the time. He then taught school for a while, studied divinity and became a minister himself in turn, preaching to the congregation of the Second Unitarian Church of Boston with great acceptance. In 1832, however, he resigned because he felt unable to agree with his congregation on an important point of doctrine. The next year he went abroad, meeting, among other celebrated men, Carlyle, with whom he formed a friendship that deeply influenced them both, and which is one of the most famous friendships of great literary men. Returning home, he settled in Concord in the "Old Manse," which had been for a time the residence of Hawthorne. He now began to support himself and his family by lecturing. In 1836 he wrote his immortal "Concord Hymn," and published his first essay, "Nature," of which, however, less than five hundred copies were sold in ten years. In 1837 Emerson delivered his famous address before the Phi Beta Kappa Society of Harvard on "The American Scholar," in which he made a strong plea for the emancipation of American thought. "We will walk on our own feet; we will work with our own hands; we will speak our own minds." This striving after originality is characteristic of Emerson. "Think for yourself," he says again and again. "Believe your own thought." "The highest merit we ascribe to Moses, Plato, and Milton is that they set at naught books and traditions, and spoke, not what men, but what *they*, thought."

In 1841 the first volume of the "Essays" appeared, followed by the second in 1844. In these two volumes are included the most notable and representative of all his writings. In any one of these essays may be found the germ of the whole of Emerson's philosophy, and any one of them may be taken as fully representative of his style. The titles do not, except in the most general way, give an indication of their contents. In each of these essays, whether it be the one on "History," on "Self-Reliance," on "Compensation," on "Love," on "Friendship," or on "The Over-Soul," we shall find the same intellectual merits and shortcomings, the same literary beauties and defects. In 1847 Emerson again visited Europe, where he delivered a series of lectures afterwards published in the volume entitled "Representative Men." Gradually the lofty character of his genius came to be recognized, and when he published his "Conduct of Life" twenty-five hundred copies were sold in two days. Toward the close of life his mind became clouded, but he continued his work to the very end, dying in Concord in 1882 at the age of seventy-nine.

Emerson's high place in American literature is undisputed. He is the foremost thinker this country has produced. As a French critic remarked, "In this North America, which is pictured to us as so materialistic, I find the most ideal writer of our times." Emerson was noted also as a poet, though as a poet he is lacking in perfection of form. It is as an essayist and philosopher that he is pre-eminent. His literary style is distinctly characteristic of the man. His sentences are short and epigrammatic, Saxon words usually predominating. Some of his passages are difficult of interpretation, but in Emerson, as in Shakespeare and in all writers of the highest genius, there will always remain greater depths to be revealed, and loftier beauties to be discovered with each reading.

COMPENSATION

EVER since I was a boy I have wished to write a discourse on compensation: for, it seemed to me when very young, that, on this subject, life was ahead of theology, and the people knew more than the preachers taught. The documents too, from which the doctrine is to be drawn, charmed my fancy by their endless variety, and lay always before me, even in sleep; for they are the tools in our hands, the bread in our basket, the transactions of the street, the farm, and the dwelling-house, the greetings, the relations, the debts and credits, the influence of character, the nature and endowment of all men. It seemed to me also that in it might be shown men a ray of divinity, the present action of the soul of this world, clean from all vestige of tradition, and so the heart of man might be bathed by an inundation of eternal love, conversing with that which he knows was always and always must be, because it really is now. It appeared, moreover, that if this doctrine could be stated in terms with any resemblance to those bright intuitions in which this truth is sometimes revealed to us, it would be a star in many dark hours and crooked passages in our journey that would not suffer us to lose our way.

I was lately confirmed in these desires by hearing a sermon at church. The preacher, a man esteemed for his orthodoxy, unfolded in the ordinary manner the doctrine of the last judgment. He assumed that judgment is not executed in this world; that the wicked are successful; that the good are miserable; and then urged from reason and from Scripture a compensation to be made to both parties in the next life. No offence appeared to be taken by the congregation at this doctrine. As far as I could observe, when the meeting broke up, they separated without remark on the sermon.

Yet what was the import of this teaching? What did the

preacher mean by saying that the good are miserable in the present life? Was it that houses and lands, offices, wine, horses, dress, luxury, are had by unprincipled men, whilst the saints are poor and despised; and that a compensation is to be made to these last hereafter, by giving them the like gratifications another day—bank-stock and doubloons, venison and champagne? This must be the compensation intended; for, what else? Is it that they are to have leave to pray and praise? to love and serve men? Why, that they can do now. The legitimate inference the disciple would draw, was; "We are to have such a good time as the sinners have now;"—or, to push it to its extreme import—"You sin now; we shall sin by and by; we would sin now, if we could; not being successful, we expect our revenge to-morrow."

The fallacy lay in the immense concession that the bad are successful; that justice is not done now. The blindness of the preacher consisted in deferring to the base estimate of the market of what constitutes a manly success, instead of confronting and convicting the world from the truth; announcing the presence of the soul; the omnipotence of the will: and so establishing the standard of good and ill, of success and falsehood, and summoning the dead to its present tribunal.

I find a similar base tone in the popular religious works of the day, and the same doctrines assumed by the literary men when occasionally they treat the related topics. I think that our popular theology has gained in decorum, and not in principle, over the superstitions it has displaced. But men are better than this theology. Their daily life gives it the lie. Every ingenuous and aspiring soul leaves the doctrine behind him in his own experience; and all men feel sometimes the falsehood which they cannot demonstrate. For men are wiser than they know. That which they hear in schools and pulpits without afterthought, if said in conversation, would probably be questioned in silence. If a man dogmatize in a mixed company on providence and the divine laws, he is answered by a silence which conveys well enough to an observer the dissatisfaction of the hearer, but his incapacity to make his own statement.

I shall attempt in this and the following chapter to record some facts that indicate the path of the law of compensation;

happy beyond my expectation, if I shall truly draw the smallest arc of this circle.

Polarity, or action and reaction, we meet in every part of nature; in darkness and light; in heat and cold; in the ebb and flow of waters; in male and female; in the inspiration and expiration of plants and animals; in the systole and diastole of the heart; in the undulations of fluids, and of sound; in the centrifugal and centripetal gravity; in electricity, galvanism, and chemical affinity. Superinduce magnetism at one end of a needle; the opposite magnetism takes place at the other end. If the south attracts, the north repels. To empty here, you must condense there. An inevitable dualism bisects nature, so that each thing is a half, and suggests another thing to make it whole; as spirit, matter; man, woman; subjective, objective; in, out; upper, under; motion, rest; yea, nay.

Whilst the world is thus dual, so is every one of its parts. The entire system of things gets represented in every particle. There is somewhat that resembles the ebb and flow of the sea, day and night, man and woman, in a single needle of the pine, in a kernel of corn, in each individual of every animal tribe. The reaction so grand in the elements, is repeated within these small boundaries. For example, in the animal kingdom, the physiologist has observed that no creatures are favorites, but a certain compensation balances every gift and every defect. A surplusage given to one part is paid out of a reduction from another part of the same creature. If the head and neck are enlarged, the trunk and extremities are cut short.

The theory of the mechanic forces is another example. What we gain in power is lost in time; and the converse. The periodic or compensating errors of the planets, is another instance. The influences of climate and soil in political history are another. The cold climate invigorates. The barren soil does not breed fevers, crocodiles, tigers, or scorpions.

The same dualism underlies the nature and condition of man. Every excess causes a defect; every defect an excess. Every sweet hath its sour; every evil its good. Every faculty which is a receiver of pleasure, has an equal penalty put on its abuse. It is to answer for its moderation with its life. For every grain of wit there is a grain of folly. For everything you have missed, you have gained something else; and for everything you gain, you lose something. If riches increase, they are increased that use them. If the gatherer gathers too much, nature takes out of the man what she puts into his chest; swells the estate, but kills the owner. Nature hates monopolies and exceptions. The waves of the sea do not more speedily seek a level from their loftiest tossing, than the varieties of condition tend to equalize themselves. There is always some levelling circumstance that puts down the overbearing, the strong, the rich, the fortunate, substantially on the same ground with all others. Is a man too strong and fierce for society, and by temper and position a bad citizen —a morose ruffian with a dash of the pirate in him—nature sends him a troop of pretty sons and daughters who are getting along in the dame's classes at the village school, and love and fear for them smooth his grim scowl to courtesy. Thus she contrives to intenerate the granite and felspar, takes the boar out and puts the lamb in, and keeps her balance true.

The farmer imagines power and place are fine things. But the President has paid dear for his White House. It has commonly cost him all his peace and the best of his manly attributes. To preserve for a short time so conspicuous an appearance before the world, he is content to eat dust before the real masters who stand erect behind the throne. Or, do men desire the more substantial and permanent grandeur of genius? Neither has this an immunity. He who by force of will or of thought is great, and overlooks thousands, has the responsibility of overlooking. With every influx of light, comes new danger. Has he light? he must bear witness to the light, and always outrun that sympathy which gives him such keen satisfaction, by his fidelity to new revelations of the incessant soul. He must hate father and mother, wife and child. Has he all that the world loves and admires and covets? —he must cast behind him their admiration, and afflict them by faithfulness to his truth, and become a by-word and a hissing.

This law writes the laws of cities and nations. It will not be balked of its end in the smallest iota. It is in vain to build or plot or combine against it. Things refuse to be mismanaged long. *Res nolunt diu male administrari.* Though no checks to a new evil appear, the checks exist and will appear.

If the government is cruel, the governor's life is not safe. If you tax too high, the revenue will yield nothing. If you make the criminal code sanguinary, juries will not convict. Nothing arbitrary, nothing artificial can endure. The true life and satisfactions of man seem to elude the utmost rigors or felicities of condition, and to establish themselves with great indifferency under all varieties of circumstance. Under all governments the influence of character remains the same—in Turkey and in New England about alike. Under the primeval despots of Egypt, history honestly confesses that man must have been as free as culture could make him.

These appearances indicate the fact that the universe is represented in every one of its particles. Everything in nature contains all the powers of nature. Everything is made of one hidden stuff; as the naturalist sees one type under every metamorphosis, and regards a horse as a running man, a fish as a swimming man, a bird as a flying man, a tree as a rooted man. Each new form repeats not only the main character of the type, but part for part all the details, all the aims, furtherances, hinderances, energies, and whole system of every other. Every occupation, trade, art, transaction, is a compend of the world, and a correlative of every other. Each one is an entire emblem of human life; of its good and ill, its trials, its enemies, its course and its end. And each one must somehow accommodate the whole man, and recite all his destiny.

The world globes itself in a drop of dew. The microscope cannot find the animalcule which is less perfect for being little. Eyes, ears, taste, smell, motion, resistance, appetite, and organs of reproduction that take hold on eternity—all find room to consist in the small creature. So do we put our life into every act. The true doctrine of omnipresence is that God reappears with all his parts in every moss and cobweb. The value of the universe contrives to throw itself into every point. If the good is there, so is the evil; if the affinity, so the repulsion; if the force, so the limitation.

Thus is the universe alive. All things are moral. That soul which within us is a sentiment, outside of us is a law. We feel its inspirations; out there in history we can see its fatal strength. It is almighty. All nature feels its grasp. "It is in the world and the world was made by it." It is eternal, but its enacts itself in time and space. Justice is not postponed. A perfect equity adjusts its balance in all parts of life. *Οἱ κύβοι Διος ἀεὶ εὐπίπτουσι.* The dice of God are always loaded. The world looks like a multiplication-table or a mathematical equation, which, turn it how you will, balances itself. Take what figure you will, its exact value, nor more nor less, still returns to you. Every secret is told, every crime is punished, every virtue rewarded, every wrong redressed, in silence and certainty. What we call retribution is the universal necessity by which the whole appears wherever a part appears. If you see smoke, there must be a fire. If you see a hand or a limb, you know that the trunk to which it belongs, is there behind.

Every act rewards itself, or, in other words, integrates itself, in a twofold manner; first, in the thing, or, in real nature; and secondly, in the circumstance, or, in apparent nature. Men call the circumstance the retribution. The causal retribution is in the thing, and is seen by the soul. The retribution in the circumstance is seen by the understanding; it is inseparable from the thing, but is often spread over a long time, and so does not become distinct until after many years. The specific stripes may follow late after the offence, but they follow because they accompany it. Crime and punishment grow out of one stem. Punishment is a fruit that unsuspected ripens within the flower of the pleasure which concealed it. Cause and effect, means and end, seed and fruit, cannot be severed; for the effect already blooms in the cause, the end preëxists in the means, the fruit in the seed.

Whilst thus the world will be whole, and refuses to be disparted, we seek to act partially; to sunder; to appropriate; for example—to gratify the senses, we sever the pleasure of the senses from the needs of the character. The ingenuity of man has been dedicated always to the solution of one problem—how to detach the sensual sweet, the sensual strong, the sensual bright, etc., from the moral sweet, the moral deep, the moral fair; that is, again, to contrive to cut clean off this upper surface so thin as to leave it bottomless; to get a one end, without an other end. The soul says, Eat; the body would feast. The soul says, The man and woman shall be one flesh and one soul; the body would join the flesh only. The soul says, Have dominion over all things to the ends of virtue; the body would have the power over things to its own ends.

The soul strives amain to live and work through all things. It would be the only fact. All things shall be added unto it —power, pleasure, knowledge, beauty. The particular man aims to be somebody; to set up for himself; to truck and higgle for a private good; and, in particulars, to ride, that he may ride; to dress, that he may be dressed; to eat, that he may eat; and to govern that he may be seen. Men seek to be great; they would have offices, wealth, power, and fame. They think that to be great is to get only one side of nature —the sweet, without the other side—the bitter.

Steadily is this dividing and detaching counteracted. Up to this day, it must be owned, no projector has had the smallest success. The parted water reunites behind our hand. Pleasure is taken out of pleasant things, profit out of profitable things, power out of strong things, the moment we seek to separate them from the whole. We can no more halve things and get the sensual good, by itself, than we can get an inside that shall have no outside, or a light without a shadow. "Drive out nature with a fork, she comes running back."

Life invests itself with inevitable conditions, which the unwise seek to dodge, which one and another brags that he does not know; brags that they do not touch him—but the brag is on his lips, the conditions are in his soul. If he escapes them in one part, they attack him in another more vital part. If he has escaped them in form, and in the appearance, it is that he has resisted his life, and fled from himself, and the retribution is so much death. So signal is the failure of all attempts to make this separation of the good from the tax, that the experiment would not be tried—since to try it is to be mad—but for the circumstance, that when the disease began in the will, of rebellion and separation, the intellect is at once infected, so that the man ceases to see God whole in each object, but is able to see the sensual allurement of an object, and not see the sensual hurt; he sees the mermaid's head, but not the dragon's tail; and thinks he can cut off that which he would have, from that which he would not have. "How secret art thou who dwellest in the highest heavens in silence, O thou only great God, sprinkling with an unwearied providence certain penal blindnesses upon such as have unbridled desires!"[1]

The human soul is true to these facts in the painting of fable, of history, of law, of proverbs, of conversation. It finds a tongue in literature unawares. Thus the Greeks called Jupiter, Supreme Mind; but having traditionally ascribed to him many base actions, they involuntarily made amends to reason, by tying up the hands of so bad a god. He is made as helpless as a king of England. Prometheus knows one secret, which Jove must bargain for; Minerva, another. He cannot get his own thunders; Minerva keeps the key of them.

> "Of all the gods I only know the keys
> That ope the solid doors within whose vaults
> His thunders sleep."

A plain confession of the in-working of the All, and of its moral aim. The Indian mythology ends in the same ethics; and indeed it would seem impossible for any fable to be invented and get any currency which was not moral. Aurora forgot to ask youth for her lover, and though Tithonus is immortal, he is old. Achilles is not quite invulnerable; for Thetis held him by the heel when she dipped him in the Styx, and the sacred waters did not wash that part. Siegfried, in the Nibelungen, is not quite immortal, for a leaf fell on his back whilst he was bathing in the dragon's blood, and that spot which it covered is mortal. And so it always is. There is a crack in everything God has made. Always, it would seem, there is this vindictive circumstance stealing in at unawares, even into the wild poesy in which the human fancy attempted to make bold holiday, and to shake itself free of the old laws—this back-stroke, this kick of the gun, certifying that the law is fatal; that in nature, nothing can be given, all things are sold.

This is that ancient doctrine of Nemesis, who keeps watch in the universe, and lets no offence go unchastised. The Furies, they said, are attendants on Justice, and if the sun in heaven should transgress his path, they would punish him. The poets related that stone walls, and iron swords, and leathern thongs had an occult sympathy with the wrongs of

[1] St. Augustine: "Confessions," Bk. I.

their owners; that the belt which Ajax gave Hector dragged the Trojan hero over the field at the wheels of the car of Achilles; and the sword which Hector gave Ajax was that on whose point Ajax fell. They recorded that when the Thasians erected a statue to Theogenes, a victor in the games, one of his rivals went to it by night, and endeavored to throw it down by repeated blows, until at last he moved it from its pedestal and was crushed to death beneath its fall.

This voice of fable has in it somewhat divine. It came from thought above the will of the writer. That is the best part of each writer, which has nothing private in it. That is the best part of each, which he does not know, that which flowed out of his constitution, and not from his too active invention; that which in the study of a single artist you might not easily find, but in the study of many, you would abstract as the spirit of them all. Phidias it is not, but the work of man in that early Hellenic world, that I would know. The name and circumstance of Phidias, however convenient for history, embarrasses when we come to the highest criticism. We are to see that which man was tending to do in a given period, and was hindered, or, if you will, modified in doing, by the interfering volitions of Phidias, of Dante, of Shakespeare, the organ whereby man at the moment wrought.

Still more striking is the expression of this fact in the proverbs of all nations, which are always the literature of reason, or the statements of an absolute truth, without qualification. Proverbs, like the sacred books of each nation, are the sanctuary of the intuitions. That which the droning world, chained to appearances, will not allow the realist to say in his own words, it will suffer him to say in proverbs without contradiction. And this law of laws which the pulpit, the senate, and the college deny, is hourly preached in all markets and all languages by flights of proverbs, whose teaching is as true and as omnipresent as that of birds and flies.

All things are double, one against another. Tit for tat; an eye for an eye; a tooth for a tooth; blood for blood; measure for measure; love for love. Give and it shall be given you. He that watereth shall be watered himself. What will you have? quoth God; pay for it and take it. Nothing venture, nothing have. Thou shalt be paid exactly for what thou hast done, no more, no less. Who doth not work shall not eat. Harm watch, harm catch. Curses always recoil on the head of him who imprecates them. If you put a chain around the neck of a slave, the other end fastens itself around your own. Bad counsel confounds the adviser. The devil is an ass.

It is thus written, because it is thus in life. Our action is overmastered and characterized above our will by the law of nature. We aim at a petty end quite aside from the public good, but our act arranges itself by irresistible magnetism in a line with the poles of the world.

A man cannot speak but he judges himself. With his will, or against his will, he draws his portrait to the eye of his companions by every word. Every opinion reacts on him who utters it. It is a thread-ball thrown at a mark, but the other end remains in the thrower's bag. Or, rather, it is a harpoon thrown at the whale, unwinding, as it flies, a coil of cord in the boat, and if the harpoon is not good, or not well thrown, it will go nigh to cut the steersman in twain, or to sink the boat.

You cannot do wrong without suffering wrong. "No man had ever a point of pride that was not injurious to him," said Burke. The exclusive in fashionable life does not see that he excludes himself from enjoyment, in the attempt to appropriate it. The exclusionist in religion does not see that he shuts the door of heaven on himself, in striving to shut out others. Treat men as pawns and ninepins, and you shall suffer as well as they. If you leave out their heart, you shall lose your own. The senses would make things of all persons; of women, of children, of the poor. The vulgar proverb, "I will get it from his purse or get it from his skin," is sound philosophy.

All infractions of love and equity in our social relations are speedily punished. They are punished by fear. Whilst I stand in simple relations to my fellow-man, I have no displeasure in meeting him. We meet as water meets water, or a current of air meets another, with perfect diffusion and interpenetration of nature. But as soon as there is any departure from simplicity, and attempt at halfness, or good for me that is not good for him, my neighbor feels the wrong; he shrinks from me as far as I have shrunk from him; his eyes no longer seek mine; there is war between us; there is hate in him and fear in me.

All the old abuses in society, the great and universal and the petty and particular, all unjust accumulations of property and power, are avenged in the same manner. Fear is an instructor of great sagacity, and the herald of all revolutions. One thing he always teaches, that there is rottenness where he appears. He is a carrion crow, and though you see not well what he hovers for, there is death somewhere. Our property is timid, our laws are timid, our cultivated classes are timid. Fear for ages has boded and mowed and gibbered over government and property. That obscene bird is not there for nothing. He indicates great wrongs which must be revised.

Of the like nature is that expectation of change which instantly follows the suspension of our voluntary activity. The terror of cloudless noon, the emerald of Polycrates, the awe of prosperity, the instinct which leads every generous soul to impose on itself tasks of a noble asceticism and vicarious virtue, are the tremblings of the balance of justice through the heart and mind of man.

Experienced men of the world know very well that it is always best to pay scot and lot as they go along, and that a man often pays dear for a small frugality. The borrower runs in his own debt. Has a man gained anything who has received a hundred favors and rendered none? Has he gained by borrowing, through indolence or cunning, his neighbor's wares, or horses, or money? There arises on the deed the instant acknowledgment of benefit on the one part, and of debt on the other; that is, of superiority and inferiority. The transaction remains in the memory of himself and his neighbor; and every new transaction alters, according to its nature, their relation to each other. He may soon come to see that he had better have broken his own bones than to have ridden in his neighbor's coach, and that "the highest price he can pay for a thing is to ask for it."

A wise man will extend this lesson to all parts of life, and know that it is always the part of prudence to face every claimant, and pay every just demand on your time, your talents, or your heart. Always pay; for, first or last, you must pay your entire debt. Persons and events may stand for a time between you and justice, but it is only a postponement. You must pay at last your own debt. If you are wise, you will dread a prosperity which only loads you with more. Benefit is the end of nature. But for every benefit which you receive, a tax is levied. He is great who confers the most benefits. He is base—and that is the only base thing in the universe—to receive favors and render none. In the order of nature we cannot render benefits to those from whom we receive them, or only seldom. But the benefit we receive must be rendered again, line for line, deed for deed, cent for cent, to somebody. Beware of too much good staying in your hand. It will fast corrupt and worm worms. Pay it away quickly in some sort.

Labor is watched over by the same pitiless laws. Cheapest, say the prudent, is the dearest labor. What we buy in a broom, a mat, a wagon, a knife, is some application of good sense to a common want. It is best to pay in your land a skilful gardener, or to buy good sense applied to gardening; in your sailor, good sense applied to navigation; in the house, good sense applied to cooking, sewing, serving; in your agent, good sense applied to accounts and affairs. So do you multiply your presence, or spread yourself throughout your estate. But because of the dual constitution of all things, in labor as in life there can be no cheating. The thief steals from himself. The swindler swindles himself. For the real price of labor is knowledge and virtue, whereof wealth and credit are signs. These signs, like paper money, may be counterfeited or stolen, but that which they represent, namely, knowledge and virtue, cannot be counterfeited or stolen. These ends of labor cannot be answered but by real exertions of the mind, and in obedience to pure motives. The cheat, the defaulter, the gambler cannot extort the benefit, cannot extort the knowledge of material and moral nature which his honest care and pains yield to the operative. The law of nature is, Do the thing, and you shall have the power: but they who do not the thing have not the power.

Human labor, through all its forms, from the sharpening of a stake to the construction of a city or an epic, is one immense illustration of the perfect compensation of the universe.

Everywhere and always this law is sublime. The absolute balance of give and take, the doctrine that everything has its price; and if that price is not paid, not that thing but something else is obtained, and that it is impossible to get anything without its price—this doctrine is not less sublime in the columns of a ledger than in the budgets of states, in the laws of light and darkness, in all the action and reaction of nature. I cannot doubt that the high laws which each man sees ever implicated in those processes with which he is conversant, the stern ethics which sparkle on his chisel-edge, which are measured out by his plumb and foot-rule, which stand as manifest in the footing of the shop-bill as in the history of a state—do recommend to him his trade, and though seldom named, exalt his business to his imagination.

The league between virtue and nature engages all things to assume a hostile front to vice. The beautiful laws and substances of the world persecute and whip the traitor. He finds that things are arranged for truth and benefit, but there is no den in the wide world to hide a rogue. There is no such thing as concealment. Commit a crime, and the earth is made of glass. Commit a crime, and it seems as if a coat of snow fell on the ground, such as reveals in the woods the track of every partridge and fox and squirrel and mole. You cannot recall the spoken word, you cannot wipe out the foot-track, you cannot draw up the ladder, so as to leave no inlet or clue. Always some damning circumstance transpires. The laws and substances of nature, water, snow, wind, gravitation, become penalties to the thief.

On the other hand, the law holds with equal sureness for all right action. Love, and you shall be loved. All love is mathematically just, as much as the two sides of an algebraic equation. The good man has absolute good, which like fire turns everything to its own nature, so that you cannot do him any harm; but as the royal armies sent against Napoleon, when he approached, cast down their colors and from enemies became friends, so do disasters of all kinds, as sickness, offence, poverty, prove benefactors.

> "Winds blow and waters roll
> Strength to the brave, and power and deity,
> Yet in themselves are nothing."

The good are befriended even by weakness and defect. As no man had ever a point of pride that was not injurious to him, so no man had ever a defect that was not somewhere made useful to him. The stag in the fable admired his horns and blamed his feet, but when the hunter came, his feet saved him, and afterwards, caught in the thicket, his horns destroyed him. Every man in his lifetime needs to thank his faults. As no man thoroughly understands a truth until first he has contended against it, so no man has a thorough acquaintance with the hinderances or talents of men, until he has suffered from the one, and seen the triumph of the other over his own want of the same. Has he a defect of temper that unfits him to live in society? Thereby he is driven to entertain himself alone, and acquire habits of self-help; and thus, like the wounded oyster, he mends his shell with pearl.

Our strength grows out of our weakness. Not until we are pricked and stung and sorely shot at, awakens the indignation which arms itself with secret forces. A great man is always willing to be little. Whilst he sits on the cushion of advantages, he goes to sleep. When he is pushed, tormented, defeated, he has a chance to learn something; he has been put on his wits, on his manhood; he has gained facts; learns his ignorance; is cured of the insanity of conceit; has got moderation and real skill. The wise man always throws himself on the side of his assailants. It is more his interest than it is theirs to find his weak point. The wound cicatrizes and falls off from him, like a dead skin, and when they would triumph, lo! he has passed on invulnerable. Blame is safer than praise. I hate to be defended in a newspaper. As long as all that is said, is said against me, I feel a certain assurance of success. But as soon as honeyed words of praise are spoken for me, I feel as one that lies unprotected before his enemies. In general, every evil to which we do not succumb, is a benefactor. As the Sandwich Islander believes that the strength and valor of the enemy he kills, passes into himself, so we gain the strength of the temptation we resist.

The same guards which protect us from disaster, defect, and enmity, defend us, if we will, from selfishness and fraud. Bolts and bars are not the best of our institutions, nor is shrewdness in trade a mark of wisdom. Men suffer all their life long, under the foolish superstition that they can be cheated. But it is as impossible for a man to be cheated by anyone but himself, as for a thing to be, and not to be, at the same time. There is a third silent party to all our bargains. The nature and soul of things takes on itself the guaranty of the fulfilment of every contract, so that honest service cannot come to loss. If you serve an ungrateful master, serve him the more. Put God in your debt. Every stroke shall be repaid. The longer the payment is withholden, the better for you; for compound interest on compound interest is the rate and usage of this exchequer.

The history of persecution is a history of endeavors to cheat nature, to make water run up hill, to twist a rope of sand. It makes no difference whether the actors be many or one, a tyrant or a mob. A mob is a society of bodies voluntarily bereaving themselves of reason and traversing its work. The mob is man voluntarily descending to the nature of the beast. Its fit hour of activity is night. Its actions are insane like its whole constitution. It persecutes a principle: it would whip a right; it would tar and feather justice, by inflicting fire and outrage upon the houses and persons of those who have these. It resembles the prank of boys who run with fire-engines to put out the ruddy aurora streaming to the stars. The inviolate spirit turns their spite against the wrong-doers. The martyr cannot be dishonored. Every lash inflicted is a tongue of fame; every prison a more illustrious abode; every burned book or house enlightens the world; every suppressed or expunged word reverberates through the earth from side to side. The minds of men are at last aroused; reason looks out and justifies her own, and malice finds all her work vain. It is the whipper who is whipped, and the tyrant who is undone.

Thus do all things preach the indifferency of circumstances. The man is all. Everything has two sides, a good and an evil. Every advantage has its tax. I learn to be content. But the doctrine of compensation is not the doctrine of indifferency. The thoughtless say, on hearing these representations, What boots it to do well? there is one event to good and evil; if I gain any good, I must pay for it; if I lose my good, I gain some other; all actions are indifferent.

There is a deeper fact in the soul than compensation, to wit, its own nature. The soul is not a compensation, but a life. The soul *is*. Under all this running sea of circumstance, whose waters ebb and flow with perfect balance, lies the aboriginal abyss of real being. Existence, or God, is not a relation, or a part, but the whole. Being is the vast affirmative, excluding negation, self-balanced, and swallowing up all relations, parts and times, within itself. Nature, truth, virtue are the influx from thence. Vice is the absence or departure of the same. Nothing, falsehood, may indeed stand as the great night or shade, on which, as a background, the living universe paints itself forth; but no fact is begotten by it; it cannot work; for it is not. It cannot work any good; it cannot work any harm. It is harm inasmuch as it is worse not to be than to be.

We feel defrauded of the retribution due to evil acts, because the criminal adheres to his vice and contumacy, and does not come to a crisis or judgment anywhere in visible nature. There is no stunning confutation of his nonsense before men and angels. Has he therefore outwitted the law? Inasmuch as he carries the malignity and the lie with him, he so far deceases from nature. In some manner there will be a demonstration of the wrong to the understanding also; but should we not see it, this deadly deduction makes square the eternal account.

Neither can it be said, on the other hand, that the gain of rectitude must be bought by any loss. There is no penalty to virtue; no penalty to wisdom; they are proper additions of being. In a virtuous action, I properly *am;* in a virtuous act, I add to the world; I plant into deserts conquered from chaos and nothing, and see the darkness receding on the limits of the horizon. There can be no excess to love; none to knowledge; none to beauty, when these attributes are considered in the purest sense. The soul refuses all limits. It affirms in man always an optimism, never a pessimism.

His life is a progress, and not a station. His instinct is trust. Our instinct uses "more" and "less" in application to man, always of the presence of the soul, and not of its absence; the brave man is greater than the coward; the true, the benevolent, the wise, is more a man and not less, than the fool and knave. There is, therefore, no tax on the good of virtue; for, that is the incoming of God himself, or absolute existence, without any comparative. All external good has its tax, and if it came without desert or sweat, has no root in me and the next wind will blow it away. But all the good of nature is the soul's, and may be had, if paid for in nature's lawful coin, that is, by labor which the heart and the head will allow. I no longer wish to meet a good I do not earn, for example, to find a pot of buried gold, knowing that it brings with it new responsibility. I do not wish more external goods —neither possessions, nor honors, nor powers, nor persons. The gain is apparent: the tax is certain. But there is no tax on the knowledge that the compensation exists, and that it is not desirable to dig up treasure. Herein I rejoice with a serene eternal peace. I contract the boundaries of possible mischief. I learn the wisdom of St. Bernard, "Nothing can work me damage except myself; the harm that I sustain, I carry about with me, and never am a real sufferer but by my own fault."

In the nature of the soul is the compensation for the inequalities of condition. The radical tragedy of nature seems to be the distinction of more and less. How can less not feel the pain; how not feel indignation or malevolence towards more? Look at those who have less faculty, and one feels sad, and knows not well what to make of it. Almost he shuns their eye; almost he fears they will upbraid God. What should they do? It seems a great injustice. But face the facts, and see them nearly, and these mountainous inequalities vanish. Love reduces them all, as the sun melts the iceberg in the sea. The heart and soul of all men being one, this bitterness of *his* and *mine* ceases. His is mine. I am my brother, and my brother is me. If I feel overshadowed and outdone by great neighbors, I can yet love; I can still receive; and he that loveth, maketh his own the grandeur he loves. Thereby I make the discovery that my brother is my guardian, acting for me with the friendliest designs, and the estate I so admired and envied, is my own. It is the eternal nature of the soul to appropriate and make all things its own. Jesus and Shakespeare are fragments of the soul, and by love I conquer and incorporate them in my own conscious domain. His virtue—is not that mine? His wit—if it cannot be made mine, it is not wit.

Such, also, is the natural history of calamity. The changes which break up at short intervals the prosperity of men, are advertisements of a nature whose law is growth. Evermore it is the order of nature to grow, and every soul is by this intrinsic necessity quitting its whole system of things, its friends, and home, and laws, and faith, as the shell-fish crawls out of its beautiful but stony case, because it no longer admits of its growth, and slowly forms a new house. In proportion to the vigor of the individual, these revolutions are frequent, until in some happier mind they are incessant, and all worldly relations hang very loosely about him, becoming, as it were, a transparent fluid membrane through which the form is alway seen, and not as in most men an indurated heterogeneous fabric of many dates, and of no settled character, in which the man is imprisoned. Then there can be enlargement, and the man of to-day scarcely recognizes the man of yesterday. And such should be the outward biography of man in time, a putting off of dead circumstances day by day, as he renews his raiment day by day. But to us, in our lapsed estate, resting not advancing, resisting not co-operating with the divine expansion, this growth comes by shocks.

We cannot part with our friends. We cannot let our angels go. We do not see that they only go out, that archangels may come in. We are idolaters of the old. We do not believe in the riches of the soul, in its proper eternity and omnipresence. We do not believe there is any force in to-day to rival or re-create that beautiful yesterday. We linger in the ruins of the old tent, where once we had bread and shelter and organs, nor believe that the spirit can feed, cover, and nerve us again. We cannot again find aught so dear, so sweet, so graceful. But we sit and weep in vain. The voice of the Almighty saith, "Up and onward forevermore!" We cannot stay amid the ruins. Neither will we rely on the new; and so we walk ever with reverted eyes, like those monsters who look backwards.

And yet the compensations of calamity are made apparent to the understanding also, after long intervals of time. A fever, a mutilation, a cruel disappointment, a loss of wealth, a loss of friends seems at the moment unpaid loss, and unpayable. But the sure years reveal the deep remedial force that underlies all facts. The death of a dear friend, wife, brother, lover, which seemed nothing but privation, somewhat later assumes the aspect of a guide or genius; for it commonly operates revolutions in our way of life, terminates an epoch of infancy or of youth which was waiting to be closed, breaks up a wonted occupation, or a household, or style of living, and allows the formation of new ones more friendly to the growth of character. It permits or constrains the formation of new acquaintances, and the reception of new influences that prove of the first importance to the next years; and the man or woman who would have remained a sunny garden flower, with no room for its roots and too much sunshine for its head, by the falling of the walls and the neglect of the gardener, is made the banian of the forest, yielding shade and fruit to wide neighborhoods of men.

"Thou sayest an undisputed thing
In such a solemn way!"
(Holmes to the Katydid)
And then keepst on, the self same things
In different forms to say
HTB

THE PROCESSION OF LIFE

—

BY

NATHANIEL HAWTHORNE

NATHANIEL HAWTHORNE

1804—1864

Nathaniel Hawthorne was born at Salem, Massachusetts, in 1804, and came of a seafaring family. Owing to the death of his father, much of his boyhood was passed with an uncle among the woods and lakes of Maine, a circumstance that, no doubt, intensified his love of nature and of solitude. After graduating from Bowdoin College, where his classmates included Longfellow and Franklin Pierce, he settled in 1825 in Salem. Here he remained for twelve years, reading, writing and burning his manuscripts, and becoming, in his own familiar phrase, "the obscurest man of letters in America." In 1837 he published the first series of "Twice-Told Tales." Through the influence of Bancroft he received an appointment in the Boston Custom House in 1837. In 1841 Hawthorne became a member of the Brook Farm community, an experience which furnished material for his "Blithedale Romance," published eleven years later. In 1843 he married Miss Peabody, and now began what proved a most happy wedded life in the "Old Manse" at Concord. "Mosses from an Old Manse" came from the press in 1846, and the same year Hawthorne removed to Salem, where he held another government appointment for four years. In 1850 "The Scarlet Letter" appeared, and made its author at once the most famous writer in America. An edition of five thousand copies was sold in ten days. "The House of the Seven Gables" was published the following year, and "The Blithedale Romance" was brought out in 1852.

In 1853 Hawthorne was appointed consul at Liverpool by President Pierce. He served in this capacity with honor and distinction for four years, and after his resignation spent three years in study and travel in France, Italy, and England. The English, and the French and Italian notebooks, published after his death, contain the record of many delightful impressions received during his travels abroad. In 1860 Hawthorne published his last complete romance "The Marble Faun." He then returned to Concord, where, after a lingering illness, he passed away in 1864. After his death a number of fragments of his works were published, including three incomplete romances and the "Note Books."

Hawthorne in many respects is entitled to the first rank in American literature. Although he called his books romances, they prove on closer study to be infinitely more. Few writers have described more accurately and studied more profoundly the influences of the moral and spiritual forces in human life. Considered as narratives of the outward incidents of human life, or as depicting the innermost workings of the human conscience, his tales are of rare excellence. In his shorter sketches written in the essay style, such as "The Procession of Human Life," in which he treats the theme of the universal brotherhood of man, Hawthorne also shows the profound and philosophic bent of his intellect. His style is perhaps the most polished of all American prose writers. He revised and even burned his manuscripts repeatedly, satisfied only with the nearest approach to literary perfection that lay in his power. It is thus that his work in every field he attempted exhibits the highest degree of artistic excellence.

THE PROCESSION OF LIFE

LIFE figures itself to me as a festal or funeral procession. All of us have our places and are to move onward under the direction of the chief marshal. The grand difficulty results from the invariably mistaken principles on which the deputy marshals seek to arrange this immense concourse of people, so much more numerous than those that train their interminable length through streets and highways in times of political excitement. Their scheme is ancient far beyond the memory of man, or even the record of history, and has hitherto been very little modified by the innate sense of something wrong and the dim perception of better methods that have disquieted all the ages through which the procession has taken its march. Its members are classified by the merest external circumstances, and thus are more certain to be thrown out of their true positions than if no principle of arrangement were attempted. In one part of the procession we see men of landed estate or moneyed capital gravely keeping each other company for the preposterous reason that they chance to have a similar standing in the tax-gatherer's book. Trades and professions march together with scarcely a more real bond of union. In this manner, it cannot be denied, people are disentangled from the mass and separated into various classes according to certain apparent relations; all have some artificial badge which the world, and themselves among the first, learn to consider as a genuine characteristic. Fixing our attention on such outside shows of similarity or difference, we lose sight of those realities by which nature, fortune, fate, or providence has constituted for every man a brotherhood, wherein it is one great office of human wisdom to classify him. When the mind has once accustomed itself to a proper arrangement of the procession of life or a true classification of society, even though merely speculative, there is thenceforth a satisfaction which pretty well suffices for itself, without the aid of any actual reformation in the order of march.

For instance, assuming to myself the power of marshalling the aforesaid procession, I direct a trumpeter to send forth a blast loud enough to be heard from hence to China, and a herald with world-pervading voice to make proclamation for a certain class of mortals to take their places. What shall be their principle of union? After all, an external one, in comparison with many that might be found, yet far more real than those which the world has selected for a similar purpose. Let all who are afflicted with like physical diseases form themselves into ranks.

Our first attempt at classification is not very successful. It may gratify the pride of aristocracy to reflect that disease, more than any other circumstance of human life, pays due observance to the distinctions which rank and wealth and poverty and lowliness have established among mankind. Some maladies are rich and precious, and only to be acquired by the right of inheritance or purchased with gold. Of this kind is the gout, which serves as a bond of brotherhood to the purple-visaged gentry who obey the herald's voice and painfully hobble from all civilized regions of the globe to take their post in the grand procession. In mercy to their toes let us hope that the march may not be long. The dyspeptics, too, are people of good standing in the world. For them the earliest salmon is caught in our Eastern rivers, and the shy woodcock stains the dry leaves with his blood in his remotest haunts, and the turtle comes from the far Pacific islands to be gobbled up in soup. They can afford to flavor all their dishes with indolence, which, in spite of the general opinion, is a sauce more exquisitely piquant than appetite won by exercise. Apoplexy is another highly respectable disease. We will rank together all who have the symptom of dizziness in the brain, and as fast as any drop by the way supply their places with new members of the board of aldermen.

On the other hand, here come whole tribes of people whose physical lives are but a deteriorated variety of life, and themselves a meaner species of mankind, so sad an effect has been wrought by the tainted breath of cities, scanty and unwholesome food, destructive modes of labor and the lack of those moral supports that might partially have counteracted such bad influences. Behold here a train of house-painters all afflicted with a peculiar sort of colic. Next in place we will marshal those workmen in cutlery who have breathed a fatal disorder into their lungs with the impalpable dust of steel. Tailors and shoemakers, being sedentary men, will chiefly congregate in one part of the procession and march under similar banners of disease, but among them we may observe here and there a sickly student who has left his health between the leaves of classic volumes, and clerks, likewise, who have caught their deaths on high official stools, and men of genius, too, who have written sheet after sheet with pens dipped in their hearts' blood. These are a wretched, quaking, short-breathed set. But what is this crowd of pale-cheeked, slender girls, who disturb the ear with the multiplicity of their short, dry coughs! They are seamstresses who have plied the daily and nightly needle in the service of master-tailors and close-fisted contractors, until now it is almost time for each to hem the borders of her own shroud. Consumption points their place in the procession. With their sad sisterhood are intermingled many youthful maidens who have sickened in aristocratic mansions, and for whose aid science has unavailingly searched its volumes and whom breathless love has watched. In our ranks the rich maiden and the poor seamstress may walk arm in arm. We might find innumerable other instances where the bond of mutual disease—not to speak of nation-sweeping pestilence—embraces high and low and makes the king a brother of the clown. But it is not hard to own that disease is the natural aristocrat. Let him keep his state and have his established orders of rank and wear his royal mantle of the color of a fever-flush, and let the noble and wealthy boast their own physical infirmities and display their symptoms as the badges of high station. All things considered, these are as proper subjects of human pride as any relations of human rank that men can fix upon.

Sound again, thou deep-breathed trumpeter!—and, herald, with thy voice of might, shout forth another summons that shall reach the old baronial castles of Europe and the rudest cabin of our Western wilderness! What class is next to take its place in the procession of mortal life? Let it be those whom the gifts of intellect have united in a noble brotherhood.

Ay, this is a reality before which the conventional distinctions of society melt away like a vapor when we would grasp it with the hand. Were Byron now alive, and Burns, the first would come from his ancestral abbey, flinging aside, although unwillingly, the inherited honors of a thousand years to take the arm of the mighty peasant who grew immortal while he stooped behind his plough. These are gone, but the hall, the farmer's fireside, the hut—perhaps the palace—the counting-room, the workshop, the village, the city, life's high places and low ones, may all produce their poets whom a common temperament pervades like an electric sympathy. Peer or ploughman will muster them pair by pair and shoulder to shoulder. Even society in its most artificial state consents to this arrangement. These factory-girls from Lowell shall mate themselves with the pride of drawing-rooms and literary circles—the bluebells in fashion's nosegay, the Sapphos and Montagues and Nortons of the age.

Other modes of intellect bring together as strange companies. Silk-gowned professor of languages, give your arm to this sturdy blacksmith and deem yourself honored by the conjunction, though you behold him grimy from the anvil. All varieties of human speech are like his mother-tongue to this rare man.[1] Indiscriminately let those take their places, of whatever rank they come, who possess the kingly gifts to lead armies or to sway a people—nature's generals, her lawgivers, her kings, and with them, also, the deep philosophers who think the thought in one generation that is to revolutionize society in the next. With the hereditary legislator in whom eloquence is a far descended attainment—a rich echo repeated by powerful voices, from Cicero downward—we will match some wondrous backwoodsman who has caught a wild power of language from the breeze among his native forest boughs. But we may safely leave brethren and sisterhood to settle their own congenialities. Our ordinary distinctions become so trifling, so impalpable, so ridiculously visionary, in comparison with a classification founded on truth, that all talk about the matter is immediately a commonplace.

Yet, the longer I reflect, the less am I satisfied with the idea of forming a separate class of mankind on the basis of high intellectual power. At best, it is but a higher development of innate gifts common to all. Perhaps, moreover, he whose genius appears deepest and truest excels his fellows in nothing save the knack of expression; he throws out, occasionally, a lucky hint

[1] [Hawthorne refers here to Elihu Burritt, the "Learned Blacksmith." Burritt studied mathematics and languages while working at his forge, and thus became familiar with Latin, Greek, Hebrew, Arabic, and nearly all modern European tongues.—EDITOR.]

at truths of which every human soul is profoundly though unutterably, conscious. Therefore, though we suffer the brotherhood of intellect to march onward together, it may be doubted whether their peculiar relation will not begin to vanish as soon as the procession shall have passed beyond the circle of this present world. But we do not classify for eternity.

And next let the trumpet pour forth a funeral wail and the herald's voice give breath in one vast cry to all the groans and grievous utterances that are audible throughout the earth. We appeal now to the sacred bond of sorrow, and summon the great multitude who labor under similar afflictions to take their places in the march. How many a heart that would have been insensible to any other call has responded to the doleful accents of that voice! It has gone far and wide and high and low, and left scarcely a mortal roof unvisited. Indeed, the principle is only too universal for our purpose, and, unless we limit it, will quite break up our classification of mankind and convert the whole procession into a funeral train. We will, therefore, be at some pains to discriminate.

Here comes a lonely rich man: he has built a noble fabric for his dwelling-house, with a front of stately architecture, and marble floors, and doors of precious woods. The whole structure is as beautiful as a dream and as substantial as the native rock, but the visionary shapes of a long posterity for whose home this mansion was intended have faded into nothingness since the death of the founder's only son. The rich man gives a glance at his sable garb in one of the splendid mirrors of his drawing-room, and descending a flight of lofty steps, instinctively offers his arm to yonder poverty-stricken widow in the rusty black bonnet and with a check-apron over her patched gown. The sailor-boy who was her sole earthly stay was washed overboard in a late tempest. This couple from the palace and the alms-house are but the types of thousands more who represent the dark tragedy of life and seldom quarrel for the upper parts. Grief is such a leveller with its own dignity and its own humility that the noble and the peasant, the beggar and the monarch, will waive their pretensions to external rank without the officiousness of interference on our part. If pride—the influence of the world's false distinctions—remain in the heart, then sorrow lacks the earnestness which makes it holy and reverend. It loses its reality and becomes a miserable shadow. On this ground we have an opportunity to assign over multitudes who would willingly claim places here to other parts of the procession. If the mourner have anything dearer than his grief, he must seek his true position elsewhere. There are so many unsubstantial sorrows which the necessity of our mortal state begets on idleness that an observer, casting aside sentiment, is sometimes led to question whether there be any real woe except absolute physical suffering and the loss of closest friends. A crowd who exhibit what they deem to be broken hearts—and among them many lovelorn maids and bachelors, and men of disappointed ambition in arts or politics, and the poor who were once rich or who have sought to be rich in vain—the great majority of these may ask admittance in some other fraternity. There is no room here. Perhaps we may institute a separate class where such unfortunates will naturally fall into the procession. Meanwhile, let them stand aside and patiently await their time.

If our trumpeter can borrow a note from the doomsday trumpet-blast, let him sound it now. The dread alarm should make the earth quake to its centre, for the herald is about to address mankind with a summons to which even the purest mortal may be sensible of some faint responding echo in his breast. In many bosoms it will awaken a still small voice more terrible than its own reverberating uproar.

The hideous appeal has swept around the globe. Come, all ye guilty ones, and rank yourselves in accordance with the brotherhood of crime. This, indeed, is an awful summons. I almost tremble to look at the strange partnerships that begin to be formed—reluctantly, but by the invincible necessity of like to like—in this part of the procession. A forger from the state-prison seizes the arm of the distinguished financier. How indignantly does the latter plead his fair reputation upon 'Change, and insist that his operations by their magnificence of scope were removed into quite another sphere of morality than those of his pitiful companion! But let him cut the connection if he can. Here comes a murderer with his clanking chains, and pairs himself—horrible to tell—with as pure and upright a man in all observable respects as ever partook of the consecrated bread and wine. He is one of those—perchance the most hopeless of all sinners—who practise such an exemplary system of outward duties that even a deadly crime may be hidden from their own sight and remembrance under this unreal frostwork. Yet he now finds his place. Why do that pair of flaunting girls with the pert, affected laugh and the sly leer at the bystanders intrude themselves into the same rank with yonder decorous matron and that somewhat prudish maiden? Surely these poor creatures born to vice as their sole and natural inheritance can be no fit associates for women who have been guarded round about by all the proprieties of domestic life, and who could not err unless they first created the opportunity! Oh, no! It must be merely the impertinence of those unblushing hussies, and we can only wonder how such respectable ladies should have responded to a summons that was not meant for them.

We shall make short work of this miserable class, each member of which is entitled to grasp any other member's hand by that vile degradation wherein guilty error has buried all alike. The foul fiend to whom it properly belongs must relieve us of our loathsome task. Let the bond-servants of sin pass on. But neither man nor woman in whom good predominates will smile or sneer, nor bid the "Rogue's March" be played, in derision of their array. Feeling within their breasts a shuddering sympathy which at least gives token of the sin that might have been, they will thank God for any place in the grand procession of human existence save among those most wretched ones. Many, however, will be astonished at the fatal impulse that drags them thitherward. Nothing is more remarkable than the various deceptions by which guilt conceals itself from the perpetrator's conscience, and oftenest, perhaps, by the splendor of its garments. Statesmen, rulers, generals, and all men who act over an extensive sphere, are most liable to be deluded in this way; they commit wrong, devastation and murder on so grand a scale that it impresses them as speculative rather than actual, but in our procession we find them linked in detestable conjunction with the meanest criminals whose deeds have the vulgarity of petty details. Here the effect of circumstance and accident is done away, and a man finds his rank according to the spirit of his crime, in whatever shape it may have been developed.

We have called the evil; now let us call the good. The trumpet's brazen throat should pour heavenly music over the earth and the herald's voice go forth with the sweetness of an angel's accents, as if to summon each upright man to his reward. But how is this? Does none answer to the call? Not one; for the just, the pure, the true, and all who might most worthily obey it shrink sadly back as most conscious of error and imperfection. Then let the summons be to those whose pervading principle is love. This classification will embrace all the truly good, and none in whose souls there exists not something that may expand itself into a heaven both of well-doing and felicity.

The first that presents himself is a man of wealth who has bequeathed the bulk of his property to a hospital; his ghost, methinks, would have a better right here than his living body. But here they come, the genuine benefactors of their race. Some have wandered about the earth with pictures of bliss in their imagination and with hearts that shrank sensitively from the idea of pain and woe, yet have studied all varieties of misery that human nature can endure. The prison, the insane asylum, the squalid chamber of the almshouse, the manufactory where the demon of machinery annihilates the human soul, and the cotton-field where God's image becomes a beast of burden—to these, and every other scene where man wrongs or neglects his brother, the apostles of humanity have penetrated. This missionary black with India's burning sunshine shall give his arm to a pale-faced brother who has made himself familiar with the infected alleys and loathsome haunts of vice in one of our own cities. The generous founder of a college shall be the partner of a maiden lady of narrow substance, one of whose good deeds it has been to gather a little school of orphan children. If the mighty merchant whose benefactions are reckoned by thousands of dollars deem himself worthy, let him join the procession with her whose love has proved itself by watching at the sick-bed, and all those lowly offices which bring her into actual contact with disease and wretchedness. And with those whose impulses have guided them to benevolent actions we will rank others, to whom providence has assigned a different tendency and different powers. Men who have spent their lives in generous and holy contemplation for the human race, those who, by a certain heavenliness of spirit, have purified the atmosphere around them, and thus supplied a medium in which good and high things may be projected and performed—give to these a lofty place among the benefactors of mankind, although no deed such as the world calls deeds may be recorded of them. There are some individuals of whom we cannot conceive it proper that they should apply their hands to any earthly instrument or work out any definite act, and others—perhaps not less high —to whom it is an essential attribute to labor in body as well as spirit for the welfare of their brethren. Thus, if we find a spiritual sage whose unseen inestimable influence has exalted the moral standard of mankind, we will choose for his companion some poor laborer who has wrought for love in the potato-field of a neighbor poorer than himself.

We have summoned this various multitude—and, to the credit of our nature, it is a large one—on the principle of love. It is singular, nevertheless, to remark the shyness that exists among many members of the present class, all of whom we might expect to recognize one another by the freemasonry of mutual goodness, and to embrace like brethren, giving God thanks for such various specimens of human excellence. But it is far otherwise. Each sect surrounds its own righteousness with a hedge of thorns. It is difficult for the good Christian to acknowledge the good pagan, almost impossible for the good orthodox to grasp the hand of the good Unitarian, leaving to their Creator to settle the matters in dispute and giving their mutual efforts strongly and trustingly to whatever right thing is too evident to be mistaken. Then, again, though the heart be large, yet the mind is often of such moderate dimensions as to be exclusively filled up with one idea. When a good man has long devoted himself to a particular kind of beneficence, to one species of reform, he is apt to become narrowed into the limits of the path wherein he treads, and to fancy that there is no other good to be done on earth but that self-same good to which he has put his hand and in the very mode that best suits his own conceptions. All else is worthless: his scheme must be wrought out by the united strength of the whole world's stock of love, or the world is no longer worthy of a position in the universe. Moreover, powerful truth, being the rich grape-juice expressed from the vineyard of the ages, has an intoxicating quality when imbibed by any save a powerful intellect, and often, as it were, impels the quaffer to quarrel in his cups. For such reasons, strange to say, it is harder to contrive a friendly arrangement of these brethren of love and righteousness in the procession of life than to unite even the wicked, who, indeed, are chained together by their crimes. The fact is too preposterous for tears, too lugubrious for laughter.

But let good men push and elbow one another as they may during their earthly march, all will be peace among them when the honorable array of their procession shall tread on heavenly ground. There they will doubtless find that they have been working each for the other's cause, and that every well-delivered stroke which with an honest purpose any mortal struck, even for a narrow object, was indeed stricken for the universal cause of good. Their own view may be bounded by country, creed, profession, the diversities of individual character, but above them all is the breadth of providence. How many who have deemed themselves antagonists will smile hereafter when they look back upon the world's wide harvest-field, and perceive that in unconscious brotherhood they were helping to bind the self-same sheaf!

But come! The sun is hastening westward, while the march of human life, that never paused before, is delayed by our attempt to rearrange its order. It is desirable to find some comprehensive principle that shall render our task easier by bringing thousands into the ranks where hitherto we have brought one. Therefore let the trumpet, if possible, split its brazen throat with a louder note than ever, and the herald summon all mortals who, from whatever cause, have lost, or never found, their proper places in the world.

Obedient to this call, a great multitude come together, most of them with a listless gait betokening weariness of soul, yet with a gleam of satisfaction in their faces at a prospect of at length reaching those positions which hitherto they have vainly sought. But here will be another disappointment, for we can attempt no more than merely to associate in one fraternity all who are afflicted with the same vague trouble. Some great mistake in life is the chief condition of admittance into this class. Here are members of the learned professions whom providence endowed with special gifts for the plough, the forge, and the wheelbarrow, or for the routine of unintellectual business. We will assign them as partners in the march those lowly laborers and handicraftsmen who have pined as with a dying thirst after the unattainable fountains of knowledge. The latter have lost less than their companions, yet more, because they deem it infinite. Perchance the two species of unfortunates may comfort one another. Here are Quakers with the instinct of battle in them, and men of war who should have worn the broad brim. Authors shall be ranked here whom some freak of nature, making game of her poor children, had imbued with the confidence of genius, and strong desire of fame, but has favored with no corresponding power, and others whose lofty gifts were unaccompanied with the faculty of expression, or any of that earthly machinery by which ethereal endowments must be manifested to mankind. All these, therefore, are melancholy laughing-stocks. Next, here are honest and well-intentioned persons who, by a want of tact, by inaccurate perceptions, by a distorting imagination, have been kept continually at cross-purposes with the world, and bewildered upon the path of life. Let us see if they can confine themselves within the line of our procession. In this class, likewise, we must assign places to those who have encountered that worst of ill-success, a higher fortune than their abilities could vindicate—writers, actors, painters, the pets of a day, but whose laurels wither, unrenewed amid their hoary hair, politicians whom some malicious contingency of affairs has thrust into conspicuous station, where, while the world stands gazing at them, the dreary consciousness of imbecility makes them curse their birth-hour. To such men we give for a companion him whose rare talents, which perhaps require a revolution for their exercise, are buried in the tomb of sluggish circumstances.

Not far from these we must find room for one whose success has been of the wrong kind—the man who should have lingered in the cloisters of a university digging new treasures out of the Herculaneum of antique lore, diffusing depth and accuracy of literature throughout his country, and thus making for himself a great and quiet fame. But the outward tendencies around him have proved too powerful for his inward nature, and have drawn him into the arena of political tumult, there to contend at disadvantage, whether front to front, or side by side, with the brawny giants of actual life. He becomes, it may be, a name for brawling parties to bandy to and fro, a legislator of the Union, a Governor of his native State, an ambassador to the courts of kings or queens, and the world may deem him a man of happy stars. But not so the wise, and not so himself, when he looks through his experience and sighs to miss that fitness, the one invaluable touch which makes all things true and real, so much achieved yet how abortive is his life! Whom shall we choose for his companion? Some weak-framed blacksmith, perhaps, whose delicacy of muscle might have suited a tailor's shop-board better than the anvil.

Shall we bid the trumpet sound again? It is hardly worth the while. There remain a few idle men of fortune, tavern and grog-shop loungers, lazzaroni, old bachelors, decaying maidens and people of crooked intellect or temper, all of whom may find their like, or some tolerable approach to it, in the plentiful diversity of our latter class. There, too, as his ultimate destiny, must we rank the dreamer who all his life long has cherished the idea that he was peculiarly apt for something, but never could determine what it was, and there the most unfortunate of men, whose purpose it has been to enjoy life's pleasures, but to avoid a manful struggle with its toil and sorrow. The remainder, if any, may connect themselves with whatever rank of the procession they shall find best adapted to their tastes and consciences. The worst possible fate would be to remain behind shivering in the solitude of time while all the world is on the move toward eternity.

Our attempt to classify society is now complete. The result may be anything but perfect, yet better—to give it the very lowest phrase—than the antique rule of the herald's office or the modern one of the tax-gatherer, whereby the accidents and superficial attributes with which the real nature of individuals has least to do are acted upon as the deepest characteristics of mankind. Our task is done! Now let the grand procession move!

Yet, pause awhile; we had forgotten the chief marshal.

Hark! That world-wide swell of solemn music with the clang of a mighty bell breaking forth through its regulated uproar announces his approach. He comes, a severe, sedate, immovable, dark rider, waving his truncheon of universal sway as he passes along the lengthened line on the pale horse of the Revelations. It is Death. Who else could assume the guidance of a procession that comprehends all humanity? And if some among these many millions should deem themselves classed amiss, yet let them take to their hearts the comfortable truth that Death levels us all into one great brotherhood, and that another state of being will surely rectify the wrong of this. Then breathe thy wail upon the earth's wailing wind, thou band of melancholy music made up of every sigh that the human heart unsatisfied has uttered! There is yet triumph in thy tones.

And now we move, beggars in their rags and kings trailing the regal purple in the dust, the warrior's gleaming helmet, the priest in his sable robe, the hoary grandsire who has run life's circle and come back to childhood, the ruddy school-boy with his golden curls frisking along the march, the artisan's stuff jacket, the noble's star-decorated coat, the whole presenting a motley spectacle, yet with a dusky grandeur brooding over it. Onward, onward, into that dimness where the lights of time which have blazed along the procession are flickering in their sockets! And whither? We know not, and Death, hitherto our leader, deserts us by the wayside, as the tramp of our innumerable footsteps passes beyond his sphere. He knows not more than we our destined goal, but God, who made us, knows, and will not leave us on our toilsome and doubtful march, either to wander in infinite uncertainty or perish by the way.

DEFENCE OF POETRY

—

BY

HENRY WADSWORTH LONGFELLOW

HENRY WADSWORTH LONGFELLOW

1807—1882

Henry Wadsworth Longfellow was born in Portland, Maine, in 1807. His father was a prominent lawyer, and had served in Congress, but was not wealthy. At the age of twelve he entered Bowdoin College, where he graduated in 1825. One of the trustees of the college had been greatly pleased with some of Longfellow's work, and shortly after graduation he was appointed to the professorship of modern languages, then just established. A suggestion of three years' study in Europe as a preparation for the position accompanied the appointment. This offer was accepted joyfully, and his stay abroad proved of the greatest advantage both to himself and his pupils. He began his duties in 1829.

In 1835 he published his first book, "Outre Mer," sketches of travel abroad, not unlike the sketches of Irving. The same year he was appointed professor of modern languages at Harvard, and again went abroad in preparation for his new duties. During this journey he met with his first great sorrow, in the death of his wife. In "The Footsteps of Angels," and in several other poems, he honors her memory. In 1839 appeared the prose romance, "Hyperion," and the first collection of his poems, "The Voices of the Night." Some of the poems published in this collection, such as "The Psalm of Life" and "The Reaper and the Flowers," have since become household words in America. "Ballads and Other Poems," containing some of his finest lyrics and ballads, followed two years later.

The next year Longfellow married for the second time, and acquired the Cragie House, in Cambridge, for his home. "The Belfry of Bruges" appeared in 1846, "Evangeline" in 1847, "The Golden Legend" in 1851, "The Song of Hiawatha" in 1855, "The Courtship of Miles Standish" in 1858, and many others. He resigned his professorship in Harvard in 1854 in order to devote his best energies to literary work. In 1861 his beautiful wife perished before his eyes, a tragedy that clouded the remainder of his life, and gave a tinge of sadness to much of his later poetry. He continued, however, to write with the same industry and success as before, and a new volume from his pen was brought out almost every year. At the time of his death, which occurred in Cambridge in 1882, he left two volumes in manuscript, which were published as a posthumous work.

Longfellow takes high rank among the great poets of English literature. Although rarely profound, Longfellow struck a note that awakened responsive echoes in all hearts. His fame rests chiefly on his lyrics, and he is likely to remain one of America's most popular poets. His prose works, while of minor importance, are marked by the same grace and delicacy of style, and are pervaded by the same noble spirit as his poetry. Both in his sketches of travel and in his literary essays we are impressed by his scholarly and felicitous treatment of the topic in question, and charmed by the even flow of his style, always mellow and sympathetic.

DEFENCE OF POETRY

GENTLE Sir Philip Sidney, thou knewest what belonged to a scholar; thou knewest what pains, what toil, what travel, conduct to perfection; well couldest thou give every virtue his encouragement, every art his due, every writer his desert, 'cause none more virtuous, witty, or learned than thyself."[1] This eulogium was bestowed upon one of the most learned and illustrious men that adorned the last half of the sixteenth century. Literary history is full of his praises. He is spoken of as the ripe scholar, the able statesman—" the soldier's, scholar's, courtier's eye, tongue, sword "—the man " whose whole life was poetry put into action." He and the Chevalier Bayard were the connecting links between the ages of chivalry and our own.

Sir Philip Sidney was born at Penshurst, in West Kent, on November 29, 1554, and died on October 16, 1586, from the wound of a musket-shot received under the walls of Zutphen, a town in Guelderland, on the banks of the Issel. When he was retiring from the field of battle an incident occurred which well illustrates his chivalrous spirit, and that goodness of heart which gained him the appellation of the " Gentle Sir Philip Sidney." The circumstance has been made the subject of an historical painting by West. It is thus related by Lord Brooke:

" The horse he rode upon was rather furiously choleric than bravely proud, and so forced him to forsake the field, but not his back, as the noblest and fittest bier to carry a martial commander to his grave. In which sad progress, passing along by the rest of the army where his uncle the general was, and being thirsty with excess of bleeding, he called for drink, which was presently brought him; but, as he was putting the bottle to his mouth, he saw a poor soldier carried along, who had eaten his last at the same feast, ghastly casting up his eyes at the bottle. Which Sir Philip perceiving, took it from his head, before he drank, and

[1] Nash's " Pierce Penniless."

delivered it to the poor man, with these words, 'Thy necessity is yet greater than mine.'"

The most celebrated productions of Sidney's pen are the "Arcadia" and the "Defence of Poesy." The former was written during the author's retirement at Wilton, the residence of his sister, the Countess of Pembroke. Though so much celebrated in its day,[2] it is now little known, and still less read. Its very subject prevents it from being popular at present; for now the pastoral reed seems entirely thrown aside. The muses no longer haunt the groves of Arcadia. The shepherd's song—the sound of oaten pipe, and the scenes of pastoral loves and jealousies, are no becoming themes for the spirit of the age. Few at present take for their motto, "*flumina amo silvasque inglorius,*" and, consequently, few read the "Arcadia."

The "Defence of Poesy" is a work of rare merit. It is a golden little volume, which the scholar may lay beneath his pillow, as Chrysostom did the works of Aristophanes. We do not, however, mean to analyze it in this place; but recommend to our readers to purchase this "sweet food of sweetly uttered knowledge." It will be read with delight by all who have a taste for the true beauties of poetry; and may go far to remove the prejudices of those who have not. To this latter class we address the concluding remarks of the author:

"So that since the ever-praiseworthy poesy is full of virtue, breeding delightfulness, and void of no gift that ought to be in the noble name of learning; since the blames laid against it are either false or feeble; since the cause why it is not esteemed in England is the fault of poet-apes, not poets; since, lastly, our tongue is most fit to honor poesy, and to be honored by poesy; I conjure you all that have had the evil luck to read this ink-wasting toy of mine, even in the name of the nine muses, no more to scorn the sacred mysteries of poesy; no more to laugh at the name of poets, as though they were next inheritors to fools; no more to jest at the reverend title of 'a rhymer'; but to believe, with Aristotle, that they were the ancient treas-

[2] Many of our readers will recollect the high-wrought eulogium of Harvey Pierce, when he consigned the work to immortality: "Live ever sweete, sweete booke: the simple image of his gentle witt; and the golden pillar of his noble courage; and ever notify unto the world that thy writer was the secretary of eloquence, the breath of the muses, the honey-bee of the daintyest flowers of witt and arte; the pith of morale and intellectual virtues, the arme of Bellona in the field, the tongue of Suada in the chamber, the sprite of Practice in esse, and the paragon of excellency in print."

urers of the Grecians' divinity; to believe, with Bembus, that they were the first bringers in of all civility; to believe, with Scaliger, that no philosopher's precepts can sooner make you an honest man, than the reading of Vergil; to believe, with Clauserus, the translator of Cornutus, that it pleased the heavenly deity by Hesiod and Homer, under the veil of fables, to give us all knowledge, logic, rhetoric, philosophy, natural and moral, and '*quid non?*' to believe, with me, that there are many mysteries contained in poetry, which of purpose were written darkly, lest by profane wits it should be abused; to believe, with Landin, that they are so beloved of the gods, that whatsoever they write proceeds of a divine fury; lastly, to believe themselves, when they tell you they will make you immortal by their verses.

"Thus doing, your names shall flourish in the printers' shops; thus doing, you shall be of kin to many a poetical preface; thus doing, you shall be most fair, most rich, most wise, most all; you shall dwell upon superlatives; thus doing, though you be '*libertino patre natus,*' you shall suddenly grow '*Herculea proles*'—

'*Si quid mea carmina possunt*':

thus doing, your soul shall be placed with Dante's Beatrix, or Vergil's Anchises.

"But if (fie of such a but!) you be born so near the dull-making cataract of Nilus that you cannot hear the planet-like music of poetry; if you have so earth-creeping a mind that it cannot lift itself up to look to the sky of poetry, or rather, by a certain rustical disdain, will become such a mome as to be a Momus of poetry; then, though I will not wish unto you the ass's ears of Midas, nor to be driven by a poet's verses, as Bubonax was, to hang himself; nor to be rhymed to death, as is said to be done in Ireland; yet thus much curse I must send you in the behalf of all poets; that while you live, you live in love, and never get favor, for lacking skill of a sonnet; and when you die, your memory die from the earth for want of an epitaph."

As no "Apologie for Poetrie" has appeared among us, we hope that Sir Philip Sidney's "Defence" will be widely read and long remembered. O that in our country it might be the harbinger of as bright an intellectual day as it was in his own!

With us, the spirit of the age is clamorous for utility—for visible, tangible utility—for bare, brawny, muscular utility. We would be roused to action by the voice of the populace, and the sounds of the crowded mart, and not "lulled asleep in shady idleness with poet's pastimes." We are swallowed up in schemes for gain, and engrossed with contrivances for bodily enjoyments, as if this particle of dust were immortal—as if the soul needed no aliment, and the mind no raiment. We glory in the extent of our territory, in our rapidly increasing population, in our agricultural privileges, and our commercial advantages. We boast of the magnificence and beauty of our natural scenery—of the various climates of our sky—the summers of our northern regions—the salubrious winters of the south, and of the various products of our soil, from the pines of our northern highlands to the palm-tree and aloes of our southern frontier. We boast of the increase and extent of our physical strength, the sound of populous cities, breaking the silence and solitude of our western Territories—plantations conquered from the forest, and gardens springing up in the wilderness. Yet the true glory of a nation consists not in the extent of its territory, the pomp of its forests, the majesty of its rivers, the height of its mountains, and the beauty of its sky, but in the extent of its mental power—the majesty of its intellect—the height, and depth, and purity of its moral nature. It consists not in what nature has given to the body, but in what nature and education have given to the mind—not in the world around us, but in the world within us—not in the circumstances of fortune, but in the attributes of the soul—not in the corruptible, transitory, and perishable forms of matter, but in the incorruptible, the permanent, the imperishable mind. True greatness is the greatness of the mind—the true glory of a nation is moral and intellectual preëminence.

But still the main current of education runs in the wide and not well-defined channel of immediate and practical utility. The main point is how to make the greatest progress in worldly prosperity—how to advance most rapidly in the career of gain. This, perhaps, is necessarily the case to a certain extent in a country where every man is taught to rely upon his own exertions for a livelihood, and is the artificer of his own fortune and estate. But it ought not to be exclusively so. We ought not, in the pursuit of wealth and worldly honor, to forget those embellishments of the mind and the heart which sweeten social intercourse and improve the condition of society. And yet, in the language of Dr. Paley, " Many of us are brought up with this world set before us, and nothing else. Whatever promotes this world's prosperity is praised; whatever hurts and obstructs this world's prosperity is blamed; and there all praise and censure end. We see mankind about us in motion and action, but all these motions and actions directed to worldly objects. We hear their conversation, but it is all the same way. And this is what we see and hear from the first: The views which are continually placed before our eyes regard this life alone and its interests. Can it then be wondered at that an early worldly-mindedness is bred in our hearts so strong as to shut out heavenly-mindedness entirely?" And this, though not in so many words, yet in fact and in its practical tendency, is the popular doctrine of utility.

Now, under correction be it said, we are much led astray by this word utility. There is hardly a word in our language whose meaning is so vague, and so often misunderstood and misapplied. We too often limit its application to those acquisitions and pursuits which are of immediate and visible profit to ourselves and the community; regarding as comparatively or utterly useless many others which, though more remote in their effects and more imperceptible in their operation, are, notwithstanding, higher in their aim, wider in their influence, more certain in their results, and more intimately connected with the common weal. We are too apt to think that nothing can be useful but what is done with a noise, at noonday, and at the corners of the streets; as if action and utility were synonymous, and it were not as useless to act without thinking as it is to think without acting. But the truth is, the word utility has a wider signification than this. It embraces in its proper definition whatever contributes to our happiness; and thus includes many of those arts and sciences, many of those secret studies and solitary avocations which are generally regarded either as useless or as absolutely injurious to society. Not he alone does service to the state whose wisdom guides her councils at home, nor he whose voice asserts her dignity abroad. A thousand little rills, springing up in the retired walks of life, go to swell the rushing tide of national glory and prosperity; and whoever in the solitude of his chamber, and by even a single effort of his mind, has added to the intellectual preëminence of his country, has not lived in vain, nor to himself alone. Does not the pen of the historian perpetuate the fame of the hero and the statesman? Do not their names live in the song of the bard? Do not the pencil and the chisel touch the soul while they delight the eye? Does not the spirit of the patriot and the sage, looking from the painted canvas, or eloquent from the marble lip, fill our hearts with veneration for all that is great in intellect and godlike in virtue?

If this be true, then are the ornamental arts of life not merely ornamental, but at the same time highly useful; and poetry and the fine arts become the instruction as well as the amusement of mankind. They will not till our lands, nor freight our ships, nor fill our granaries and our coffers; but they will enrich the heart, freight the understanding, and make up the garnered fulness of the mind. And this we hold to be the true view of the subject.

Among the barbarous nations, which in the early centuries of our era overran the south of Europe, the most contumelious epithet which could be applied to a man was to call him a Roman. All the corruption and degeneracy of the Western Empire were associated, in the minds of the Gothic tribes, with a love of letters and the fine arts. So far did this belief influence their practice that they would not suffer their children to be instructed in the learning of the south. "Instruction in the sciences," said they, "tends to corrupt, enervate, and depress the mind; and he who has been accustomed to tremble under the rod of a pedagogue will never look on a sword or a spear with an undaunted eye."[3] We apprehend that there are some, and indeed not a few in our active community, who hold the appellation of scholar and man of letters in as little repute as did our Gothic ancestors that of Roman; associating with it about the same ideas of effeminacy and inefficiency. They think that the learning of books is not wisdom; that study unfits a man for action; that poetry and nonsense are convertible terms; that literature begets an effeminate and craven spirit; in a word, that the dust and cobwebs of a library are a kind of armor which

[3] "Procop. de bello Gothor." apud Robertson, "History of Charles V," vol. i., p. 234.

will not stand long against the hard knocks of the "bone and muscle of the state" and the "huge two-fisted sway" of the stump orator. Whenever intellect is called into action, they would have the mind display a rough and natural energy—strength, straightforward strength, untutored in the rules of art, and unadorned by elegant and courtly erudition. They want the stirring voice of Demosthenes, accustomed to the roar of the tempest and the dashing of the sea upon its hollow-sounding shore, rather than the winning eloquence of Phalereus, coming into the sun and dust of the battle, not from the martial tent of the soldier, but from the philosophic shades of Theophrastus.

But against no branch of scholarship is the cry so loud as against poetry, "the quintessence, or rather the luxury of all learning." Its enemies pretend that it is injurious both to the mind and the heart; that it incapacitates us for the severer discipline of professional study; and that, by exciting the feelings and misdirecting the imagination, it unfits us for the common duties of life and the intercourse of this matter-of-fact world. And yet such men have lived, as Homer, and Dante, and Milton—poets and scholars whose minds were bathed in song, and yet not weakened; men who severally carried forward the spirit of their age, who soared upward on the wings of poetry, and yet were not unfitted to penetrate the deepest recesses of the human soul and search out the hidden treasures of wisdom and the secret springs of thought, feeling, and action. None fought more bravely at Marathon, Salamis, and Platæa than did the poet Æschylus. Richard Cœur-de-Lion was a poet; but his boast was in his very song:

> "Bon guerrier à l'estendart
> Trouvaretz le Roi Richard."

Ercilla and Garcilaso were poets; but the great epic of Spain was written in the soldier's tent and on the field of battle, and the descendant of the Incas was slain in the assault of a castle in the south of France. Cervantes lost an arm at the battle of Lepanto, and Sir Philip Sidney was the breathing reality of the poet's dream, a living and glorious proof that poetry neither enervates the mind nor unfits us for the practical duties of life.

Nor is it less true that the legitimate tendency of poetry is to exalt rather than to debase—to purify rather than to corrupt. Read the inspired pages of the Hebrew prophets; the eloquent aspirations of the Psalmist! Where did ever the spirit of devotion bear up the soul more steadily and loftily than in the language of their poetry? And where has poetry been more exalted, more spirit-stirring, more admirable, or more beautiful, than when thus soaring upward on the wings of sublime devotion, the darkness and shadows of earth beneath it, and from above the brightness of an opened heaven pouring around it? It is true the poetic talent may be, for it has been, most lamentably perverted. But when poetry is thus perverted—when it thus forgets its native sky to grovel in what is base, sensual, and depraved—though it may not have lost all its original brightness, nor appear less than "the excess of glory obscured," yet its birthright has been sold, its strength has been blasted, and its spirit wears "deep scars of thunder."

It does not, then, appear to be the necessary nor the natural tendency of poetry to enervate the mind, corrupt the heart, or incapacitate us for performing the private and public duties of life. On the contrary, it may be made, and should be made, an instrument for improving the condition of society, and advancing the great purpose of human happiness. Man must have his hours of meditation as well as of action. The unities of time are not so well preserved in the great drama but that moments will occur when the stage must be left vacant, and even the busiest actors pass behind the scenes. There will be eddies in the stream of life, though the main current sweeps steadily onward, till "it pours in full cataract over the grave." There are times when both mind and body are worn down by the severity of daily toil; when the grasshopper is a burden, and, thirsty with the heat of labor, the spirit longs for the waters of Shiloah that go softly. At such seasons both mind and body should unbend themselves; they should be set free from the yoke of their customary service, and thought take some other direction than that of the beaten, dusty thoroughfare of business. And there are times, too, when the divinity stirs within us; when the soul abstracts herself from the world, and the slow and regular motions of earthly business do not keep pace with the heaven-directed mind. Then earth lets go her hold; the soul feels herself more akin to heaven; and soaring upward, the denizen of her native sky, she "begins to reason like herself, and to discourse in a strain above mortality." Call, if you will, such thoughts and feelings the dreams of the imagination; yet they are no unprofitable dreams. Such moments of silence and meditation are often those of the greatest utility to ourselves and others. Yes, we would dream awhile, that the spirit is not always the bondman of the flesh; that there is something immortal in us, something which, amid the din of life, urges us to aspire after the attributes of a more spiritual nature. Let the cares and business of the world sometimes sleep, for this sleep is the awakening of the soul.

To fill up these interludes of life with a song, that shall soothe our worldly passions and inspire us with a love of heaven and virtue, seems to be the peculiar province of poetry. On this moral influence of the poetic art, there is a beautifully written passage in the "Defence of Poesy":

"The philosopher showeth you the way, he informeth you of the particularities, as well of the tediousness of the way and of the pleasant lodging you shall have when your journey is ended, as of the many by-turnings that may divert you from your way; but this is to no man, but to him that will read him, and read him with attentive, studious painfulness; which constant desire whosoever hath in him hath already passed half the hardness of the way, and therefore is beholden to the philosopher but for the other half. Nay, truly, learned men have learnedly thought that, where once reason hath so much overmastered passion as that the mind hath a free desire to do well, the inward light each mind hath in itself is as good as a philosopher's book; since in nature we know it is well to do well, and what is well and what is evil, although not in the words of art which philosophers bestow upon us; for out of natural conceit the philosophers drew it; but to be moved to do that which we know, or to be moved with desire to know, '*hoc opus, hic labor est.*'

"Now, therein, of all sciences (I speak still of human, and according to the human conceit) is our poet the monarch. For he doth not only show the way, but giveth so sweet a prospect into the way as will entice any man to enter into it; nay, he doth, as if your journey should lie through a fair vineyard, at the very first give you a cluster of grapes, that full of that taste you may long to pass farther. He beginneth not with obscure definitions, which must blur the margin with interpretations, and load the memory with doubtfulness, but he cometh to you with words set in delightful proportion, either accompanied with, or prepared for, the well-enchanting skill of music; and with a tale, forsooth, he cometh unto you, with a tale which holdeth children from play, and old men from the chimney-corner; and, pretending no more, doth intend the winning of the mind from wickedness to virtue."

In fine, we think that all the popular objections against poetry may be not only satisfactorily but triumphantly answered. They are all founded upon its abuse, and not upon its natural and legitimate tendencies. Indeed, popular judgment has seldom fallen into a greater error than that of supposing that poetry must necessarily, and from its very nature, convey false and therefore injurious impressions. The error lies in not discriminating between what is true to nature and what is true to fact. From the very nature of things, neither poetry nor any one of the imitative arts can in itself be false. They can be false no further than, by the imperfection of human skill, they convey to our minds imperfect and garbled views of what they represent. Hence a painting or poetical description may be true to nature, and yet false in point of fact. The canvas before you may represent a scene in which every individual feature of the landscape shall be true to nature--the tree, the waterfall, the distant mountain—every object there shall be an exact copy of an original that has a real existence, and yet the scene itself may be absolutely false in point of fact. Such a scene, with the features of the landscape combined precisely in the way represented, may exist nowhere but in the imagination of the artist. The statue of the Venus de' Medici is the perfection of female beauty; and every individual feature had its living original. Still, the statue itself had no living archetype. It is true to nature, but it is not true to fact. So with the stage. The scene represented, the characters introduced, the plot of the piece, and the action of the performers may all be conformable to nature, and yet not be conformable to any preëxisting reality. The characters there personified may never have existed; the events represented may never have transpired. And so, too, with poetry. The scenes and events it describes, the characters and passions it portrays, may all be natural though not real. Thus, in a certain sense, fiction itself may be true—true to the nature of things, and consequently true in the impressions it conveys. And hence the reason why fiction has always been made so subservient to the cause of truth.

Allowing, then, that poetry is nothing but fiction, that all it describes is false in point of fact, still its elements have a real existence, and the impressions we receive can be erroneous so far only as the views presented to the mind are garbled and false to nature. And this is a fault incident to the artist, and not inherent in the art itself. So that we may fairly conclude, from these considerations, that the natural tendency of poetry is to give us correct moral impressions, and thereby advance the cause of truth and the improvement of society.

There is another very important view of the subject arising out of the origin and nature of poetry, and its intimate connection with individual character and the character of society.

The origin of poetry loses itself in the shades of a remote and fabulous age, of which we have only vague and uncertain traditions. Its fountain, like that of the river of the desert, springs up in a distant and unknown region, the theme of visionary story and the subject of curious speculation. Doubtless, however, it originated amid the scenes of pastoral life and in the quiet and repose of a golden age. There is something in the soft melancholy of the groves which pervades the heart and kindles the imagination. Their retirement is favorable to the musings of the poetic mind. The trees that waved their leafy branches to the summer wind or heaved and groaned beneath the passing storm, the shadow moving on the grass, the bubbling brook, the insect skimming on its surface, the receding valley and the distant mountain—these would be some of the elements of pastoral song. Its subject would naturally be the complaint of a shepherd and the charms of some gentle shepherdess—

> "A happy soul, that all the way
> To heaven hath a summer's day."

It is natural, too, that the imagination, familiar with the outward world, and connecting the idea of the changing seasons and the spontaneous fruits of the earth with the agency of some unknown power that regulated and produced them, should suggest the thought of presiding deities, propitious in the smiling sky and adverse in the storm. The fountain that gushed up as if to meet the thirsty lip was made the dwelling of a nymph; the grove that lent its shelter and repose from the heat of noon became the abode of dryads; a god presided over shepherds and their flocks, and a goddess shook the yellow harvest from her lap. These deities were propitiated by songs and festive rites. And thus poetry added new charms to the simplicity and repose of bucolic life, and the poet mingled in his verse the delights of rural ease and the praise of the rural deities which bestowed them.

Such was poetry in those happy ages, when, camps and courts unknown, life was itself an eclogue. But in later days it sang the achievements of Grecian and Roman heroes, and pealed in the war-song of the Gothic Skald. These early essays were rude and unpolished. As nations advanced in civilization and refinement poetry advanced with them. In each successive age it became the image of their thoughts and feelings, of their manners, customs, and characters; for poetry is but the warm expression of the thoughts and feelings of a people, and we speak of it as being national when the character of a nation shines visibly and distinctly through it.

Thus, for example, Castilian poetry is characterized by sounding expressions, and that pomp and majesty so peculiar to Spanish manners and character. On the other hand, English poetry possesses in a high degree the charms of rural and moral feeling; it flows onward like a woodland stream, in which we see the reflection of the sylvan landscape and of the heaven above us.

It is from this intimate connection of poetry with the manners, customs, and characters of nations, that one of its highest uses is drawn. The impressions produced by poetry upon national character, at any period, are again reproduced, and give a more pronounced and individual character to the poetry of a subsequent period. And hence it is that the poetry of a nation sometimes throws so strong a light upon the page of its history, and renders luminous those obscure passages which often baffle the long-searching eye of studious erudition. In this view, poetry assumes new importance with all who search for historic truth. Besides, the view of the various fluctuations of the human mind, as exhibited, not in history, but in the poetry of successive epochs, is more interesting, and less liable to convey erroneous impressions, than any record of mere events. The great advantage drawn from the study of history is not to treasure up in the mind a multitude of disconnected facts, but from these facts to derive some conclusions, tending to illustrate the movements of the general mind, the progress of society, the manners, customs, and institutions, the moral and intellectual character of mankind in different nations, at different times, and under the operation of different circumstances. Historic facts are chiefly valuable as exhibiting intellectual phenomena. And, so far as poetry exhibits these phenomena more perfectly and distinctly than history does, so far is it superior to history. The history of a nation is the external symbol of its character; from it we reason back to the spirit of the age that fashioned its shadowy outline. But poetry is the spirit of the age itself—embodied in the forms of language, and speaking in a voice that is audible to the external as well as the internal sense. The one makes known the impulses of the popular mind, through certain events resulting from them; the other displays the more immediate presence of that mind, visible in its action, and presaging those events. The one is like the marks left by the thunder-storm—the blasted tree—the purified atmosphere; the other like the flash from the bosom of the cloud, or the voice of the tempest, announcing its approach. The one is the track of the ocean on its shore; the other the continual movement and murmur of the sea.

Besides, there are epochs which have no contemporaneous history; but have left in their popular poetry pretty ample materials for estimating the character of the times. The events, indeed, therein recorded may be exaggerated facts, or vague traditions, or inventions entirely apocryphal; yet they faithfully represent the spirit of the ages which produced them; they contain direct allusions and incidental circumstances, too insignificant in themselves to have been fictitious, and yet on that very account the most important parts of the poem in an historical point of view. Such, for example, are the "Nibelungen Lied" in Germany; the "Poema del Cid" in Spain; and the "Songs of the Troubadours" in France. Hence poetry comes in for a large share in that high eulogy which, in the true spirit of the scholar, a celebrated German critic has bestowed upon letters: "If we consider literature in its widest sense, as the voice which gives expression to human intellect—as the aggregate mass of symbols, in which the spirit of an age or the character of a nation is shadowed forth, then indeed a great and various literature is, without doubt, the most valuable possession of which any nation can boast." [4]

From all these considerations, we are forced to the conclusion that poetry is a subject of far greater importance in itself, and in its bearing upon the condition of society, than the majority of mankind would be willing to allow. We heartily regret that this opinion is not a more prevailing one in our land. We give too little encouragement to works of imagination and taste. The vocation of the poet does not stand high enough in our esteem; we are too cold in admiration, too timid in praise. The poetic lute and the high-sounding lyre are much too often and too generally looked upon as the baubles of effeminate minds, or bells and rattles to please the ears of children. The prospect, however, brightens. But a short time ago not a poet "moved the wing, or opened the mouth, or peeped"; and now we have a host of them—three or four good ones, and three or four hundred poor ones. This, however, we will not stop to cavil about at present. To those of them who may honor us by reading our article we would whisper this request—that they should be more original, and withal more national. It seems every way important that now, while we are forming our literature, we should make it as original, characteristic, and national as possible. To effect this, it is not necessary that the war-whoop should ring in every line, and every page be rife with scalps, tomahawks, and wampum. Shade of Tecumseh forbid! The whole secret lies in Sidney's maxim—"Look in thy heart and write." For—

> "Cantars non pot gaire valer.
> Si d'inz del cor no mov lo chang." [5]

Of this anon. We will first make a few remarks upon the word national, as applied to the literature of a country; for when we speak of a national poetry we do not employ the term in that vague and indefinite way in which many writers use it.

A national literature, then, in the widest signification of the words, embraces every mental effort made by the inhabitants of

[4] Schlegel, "Lectures on the History of Literature," vol. i., lec. vii.

[5] "The poet's song is little worth, If it moveth not from within the heart."

a country, through the medium of the press. Every book written by a citizen of a country belongs to its national literature. But the term has also a more peculiar and appropriate definition; for, when we say that the literature of a country is national, we mean that it bears upon it the stamp of national character. We refer to those distinguishing features which literature receives from the spirit of a nation—from its scenery and climate, its historic recollections, its government, its various institutions—from all those national peculiarities which are the result of no positive institutions; and, in a word, from the thousand external circumstances, which either directly or indirectly exert an influence upon the literature of a nation, and give it a marked and individual character, distinct from that of the literature of other nations.

In order to be more definite and more easily understood in these remarks, we will here offer a few illustrations of the influence of external causes upon the character of the mind, the peculiar habits of thought and feeling, and consequently the general complexion of literary performances. From the causes enumerated above, we select natural scenery and climate as being among the most obvious in their influence upon the prevailing tenor of poetic composition. Everyone who is acquainted with the works of the English poets must have noted that a moral feeling and a certain rural quiet and repose are among their most prominent characteristics. The features of their native landscape are transferred to the printed page, and as we read we hear the warble of the skylark—the "hollow murmuring wind, or silver rain." The shadow of the woodland scene lends a pensive shadow to the ideal world of poetry:

> "Why lure me from these pale retreats?
> Why rob me of these pensive sweets?
> Can Music's voice, can Beauty's eye,
> Can Painting's glowing hand supply,
> A charm so suited to my mind,
> As blows this hollow gust of wind,
> As drops this little weeping rill,
> Soft tinkling down the moss-grown hill,
> While through the west, where sinks the crimson day,
> Meek Twilight slowly sails, and waves her banners gray?" [6]

[6] Mason's "Ode to a Friend."

In the same richly poetic vein are the following lines from Collins's "Ode to Evening":

> "Or if chill blustering winds, or driving rain,
> Prevent my willing feet, be mine the hut,
> That from the mountain's side,
> Views wilds and swelling floods,
>
> "And hamlets brown, and dim-discovered spires,
> And hears their simple bell, and marks o'er all
> The dewy fingers draw
> The gradual dusky veil."

In connection with the concluding lines of these two extracts, and as an illustration of the influence of climate on the character of poetry, it is worthy of remark that the English poets excel those of the south of Europe in their descriptions of morning and evening. They dwell with long delight and frequent repetition upon the brightening glory of the hour, when "the northern wagoner has set his sevenfold teme behind the stedfast starre"; and upon the milder beauty of departing day, when "the bright-haired sun sits in yon western tent." What, for example, can be more descriptive of the vernal freshness of a morning in May than the often quoted song in "Cymbeline"?—

> "Hark! hark! the lark at heaven's gate sings,
> And Phœbus 'gins arise
> His steeds to water at those springs
> On chaliced flowers that *lies;*
> And winking Mary-buds begin
> To ope their golden eyes;
> With everything that pretty bin;
> My lady sweet, arise;
> Arise, arise!"

How full of poetic feeling and imagery is the following description of the dawn of day, taken from Fletcher's "Faithful Shepherdess"!—

> "See, the day begins to break,
> And the light shoots like a streak
> Of subtle fire, the wind blows cold,
> While the morning doth unfold;
> Now the birds begin to rouse,
> And the squirrel from the boughs

Leaps, to get him nuts and fruit;
The early lark that erst was mute,
Carols to the rising day
Many a note and many a lay."

Still more remarkable than either of these extracts, as a graphic description of morning, is the following from Beattie's "Minstrel":

"But who the melodies of morn can tell?
The wild brook babbling down the mountain's side;
The lowing herd; the sheepfold's simple bell;
The pipe of early shepherd dim descried
In the lonely valley; echoing far and wide,
The clamorous horn along the cliffs above;
The hollow murmur of the ocean-tide;
The hum of bees, and linnet's lay of love,
And the full choir that wakes the universal grove.

"The cottage curs at early pilgrim bark;
Crowned with her pail, the tripping milkmaid sings;
The whistling ploughman stalks afield; and hark!
Down the rough slope the ponderous wagon rings;
Through rustling corn the hare astonished springs;
Slow tolls the village clock the drowsy hour;
The partridge bursts away on whirring wings;
Deep mourns the turtle in sequestered bower;
And shrill lark carols clear from her aërial tower."

Extracts of this kind we might multiply almost without number. The same may be said of similar ones, descriptive of the gradual approach of evening and the close of day. But we have already quoted enough for our present purpose. Now, to what peculiarities of natural scenery and climate may we trace these manifold and beautiful descriptions, which in their truth, delicacy, and poetic coloring surpass all the pictures of the kind in Tasso, Guarini, Boscan, Garcilaso, and, in a word, all the most celebrated poets of the south of Europe? Doubtless, to the rural beauty which pervades the English landscape, and to the long morning and evening twilight of a northern climate.

Still, with all this taste for the charms of rural description and sylvan song, pastoral poetry has never been much cultivated nor much admired in England. The "Arcadia" of Sir Philip Sidney, it is true, enjoyed a temporary celebrity, but this was, doubtless, owing in a great measure to the rank of its author;

and though the pastorals of Pope are still read and praised, their reputation belongs in part to their author's youth at the time of their composition. Nor is this remarkable. For though the love of rural ease is characteristic of the English, yet the rigors of their climate render their habits of pastoral life anything but delightful. In the mind of an Englishman, the snowy fleece is more intimately associated with the weaver's shuttle than with the shepherd's crook. Horace Walpole has a humorous passage in one of his letters on the affectation of pastoral habits in England. " In short," says he, " every summer one lives in a state of mutiny and murmur, and I have found the reason; it is because we will affect to have a summer, and we have no title to any such thing. Our poets learned their trade of the Romans, and so adopted the terms of their masters. They talk of shady groves, purling streams, and cooling breezes, and we get sore throats and agues by attempting to realize these visions. Master Damon writes a song, and invites Miss Chloe to enjoy the cool of the evening, and the deuce a bit have we of any such thing as a cool evening. Zephyr is a northeast wind, that makes Damon button up to the chin, and pinches Chloe's nose till it is red and blue; and they cry, ' This is a bad summer '; as if we ever had any other. The best sun we have is made of Newcastle coal, and I am determined never to reckon upon any other." On the contrary, the poetry of the Italians, the Spaniards, and the Portuguese is redolent of the charms of pastoral indolence and enjoyment; for they inhabit countries in which pastoral life is a reality and not a fiction, where the winter's sun will almost make you seek the shade, and the summer nights are mild and beautiful in the open air. The babbling brook and cooling breeze are luxuries in a southern clime, where you

> " See the sun set, sure he'll rise to-morrow,
> Not through a misty morning twinkling, weak as
> A drunken man's dead eye, in maudlin sorrow,
> But with all heaven t' himself."

A love of indolence and a warm imagination are characteristic of the inhabitants of the South. These are natural effects of a soft, voluptuous climate. It is there a luxury to let the body lie at ease, stretched by a fountain in the lazy stillness of a summer noon, and suffer the dreamy fancy to lose itself in idle reverie and give a form to the wind and a spirit to the shadow and the leaf. Hence the prevalence of personification and the exaggerations of figurative language, so characteristic of the poetry of southern nations. As an illustration, take the following beautiful sonnet from the Spanish. It is addressed to a mountain brook:

"Laugh of the mountain! lyre of bird and tree!
Mirror of morn, and garniture of fields!
The soul of April, that so gently yields
The rose and jasmine bloom, leaps wild in thee!

"Although, where'er thy devious current strays,
The lap of earth with gold and silver teems,
To me thy clear proceeding brighter seems
Than golden sands, that charm each shepherd's gaze.

"How without guile thy bosom, all transparent
As the pure crystal, lets the curious eye
Thy secrets scan, thy smooth round pebbles count!
How, without malice murmuring, glides thy current!
O sweet simplicity of days gone by!
Thou shunnest the haunts of man, to dwell in limpid fount!" [7]

We will pursue these considerations no longer, for fear of digressing too far. What we have already said will illustrate, perhaps superficially, but sufficiently for our present purpose, the influence of natural scenery and climate upon the character of poetical composition. It will at least show that in speaking of this influence we did not speak at random and without a distinct meaning. Similar and much more copious illustrations of the influence of various other external circumstances on national literature might here be given. But it is not our intention to go into details. They will naturally suggest themselves to the mind of every reflecting reader.

We repeat, then, that we wish our native poets would give a more national character to their writings. In order to effect

[7] "Risa del monte, de las aves lira!
pompa del prado, espejo de la aurora!
alma de Abril, espíritu de Flora
por quien la rosa y el jazmin espira!

"Aunque tu curso en cuantos pasos gira
tanta jurisdiccion argenta y dora,
tu claro proceder mas me enamora
que lo que en tí todo pastor admira.

"Cuan sin engaño tus entrañas puras
dejan por transparente vidriera
las guijuelas al número patentes!

"Cuan sin malicia cándida murmuras!
O sencillez de aquella edad primera,
huyes del hombre y vives en las fuentes."

this they have only to write more naturally, to write from their own feelings and impressions, from the influence of what they see around them, and not from any preconceived notions of what poetry ought to be, caught by reading many books and imitating many models. This is peculiarly true in descriptions of natural scenery. In these let us have no more skylarks and nightingales. For us they only warble in books. A painter might as well introduce an elephant or a rhinoceros into a New England landscape. We would not restrict our poets in the choice of their subjects or the scenes of their story; but, when they sing under an American sky and describe a native landscape, let the description be graphic, as if it had been seen and not imagined. We wish, too, to see the figures and imagery of poetry a little more characteristic, as if drawn from nature and not from books. Of this we have constantly recurring examples in the language of our North American Indians. Our readers will all recollect the last words of Pushmataha, the Choctaw chief, who died at Washington in the year 1824: "I shall die, but you will return to your brethren. As you go along the paths you will see the flowers and hear the birds; but Pushmataha will see them and hear them no more. When you come to your home they will ask you, 'Where is Pushmataha?' and you will say to them, 'He is no more.' They will hear the tidings like the sound of the fall of a mighty oak in the stillness of the wood." More attention on the part of our writers to these particulars would give a new and delightful expression to the face of our poetry. But the difficulty is, that instead of coming forward as bold, original thinkers, they have imbibed the degenerate spirit of modern English poetry. They have hitherto been imitators either of decidedly bad, or of at best very indifferent models. It has been the fashion to write strong lines—to aim at point and antithesis. This has made writers turgid and extravagant. Instead of ideas they give us merely the signs of ideas. They erect a great bridge of words, pompous and imposing, where there is hardly a drop of thought to trickle beneath. Is not he who thus apostrophizes the clouds, "Ye posters of the wakeless air!" quite as extravagant as the Spanish poet who calls a star a "burning doubloon of the celestial bank"? (*"Doblon ardiente del celeste banco!"*)

This spirit of imitation has spread far and wide. But a few

years ago what an aping of Lord Byron exhibited itself throughout the country! It was not an imitation of the brighter characteristics of his intellect, but a mimicry of his sullen misanthropy and irreligious gloom. We do not wish to make a bugbear of Lord Byron's name, nor figuratively to disturb his bones; still we cannot but express our belief that no writer has done half so much to corrupt the literary taste as well as the moral principle of our country as the author of "Childe Harold."[8] Minds that could not understand his beauties could imitate his great and glaring defects. Souls that could not fathom his depths could grasp the straw and bubbles that floated upon the agitated surface, until at length every city, town, and village had its little Byron, its self-tormenting scoffer at morality, its gloomy misanthropist in song. Happily, this noxious influence has been in some measure checked and counteracted by the writings of Wordsworth, whose pure and gentle philosophy has been gradually gaining the ascendancy over the bold and visionary speculations of an unhealthy imagination. The sobriety, and if we may use the expression, the republican simplicity of his poetry, are in unison with our moral and political doctrines. But even Wordsworth, with all his simplicity of diction and exquisite moral feeling, is a very unsafe model for imitation; and it is worth while to observe how invariably those who have imitated him have fallen into tedious mannerism. As the human mind is so constituted that all men receive to a greater or less degree a complexion from those with whom they are conversant, the writer who means to school himself to poetic composition—we mean so far as regards style and diction—should be very careful what authors he studies. He should leave the present age and go back to the olden time. He should make, not the writings of an individual, but the whole body of English classical

[8] We here subjoin Lord Byron's own opinion of the poetical taste of the present age. It is from a letter in the second volume of Moore's "Life of Byron": "With regard to poetry in general, I am convinced, the more I think of it, that he and all of us—Scott, Southey, Wordsworth, Moore, Campbell, I—are all in the wrong, one as much as another; that we are upon a wrong revolutionary poetical system, or systems, and from which none but Rogers and Crabbe are free; and that the present and next generations will finally be of this opinion. I am the more confirmed in this by having lately gone over some of our classics, particularly Pope, whom I tried in this way: I took Moore's poems and my own and some others, and went over them side by side with Pope's, and I was really astonished (I ought not to have been so) and mortified at the ineffable distance in point of sense, learning, effect, and even imagination, passion, and invention between the Queen Anne's man and us of the Lower Empire. Depend upon it, it is all Horace then, and Claudian now, among us; and if I had to begin again, I would mould myself accordingly."

literature his study. There is a strength of expression, a clearness, and force and raciness of thought in the elder English poets which we may look for in vain among those who flourish in these days of verbiage. Truly, the degeneracy of modern poetry is no school-boy declamation! The stream, whose fabled fountain gushes from the Grecian mount, flowed brightly through those ages, when the souls of men stood forth in the rugged freedom of nature and gave a wild and romantic character to the ideal landscape. But in these practical days, whose spirit has so unsparingly levelled to the even surface of utility the bold irregularities of human genius, and lopped off the luxuriance of poetic feeling which once lent its grateful shade to the haunts of song, that stream has spread itself into stagnant pools which exhale an unhealthy atmosphere, while the party-colored bubbles that glitter on its surface show the corruption from which they spring.

Another circumstance which tends to give an effeminate and unmanly character to our literature is the precocity of our writers. Premature exhibitions of talent are an unstable foundation to build a national literature upon. Roger Ascham, the school-master of princes, and for the sake of antithesis, we suppose, called the Prince of School-masters, has well said of precocious minds: "They be like trees that showe forth faire blossoms and broad leaves in spring-time, but bring out small and not long-lasting fruit in harvest-time; and that only such as fall and rott before they be ripe, and so never or seldome come to any good at all." It is natural that the young should be enticed by the wreaths of literary fame, whose hues are so passing beautiful even to the more sober-sighted, and whose flowers breathe around them such exquisite perfumes. Many are deceived into a misconception of their talents by the indiscreet and indiscriminate praise of friends. They think themselves destined to redeem the glory of their age and country; to shine as "bright particular stars"; but in reality their genius

> "Is like the glow-worm's light the apes so wondered at,
> Which, when they gathered sticks and laid upon't,
> And blew—and blew—turned tail and went out presently."

We have set forth the portrait of modern poetry in rather gloomy colors; for we really think that the greater part of what is published in this book-writing age ought in justice to suffer the fate of the children of Thetis, whose immortality was tried by fire. We hope, however, that ere long some one of our most gifted bards will throw his fetters off, and, relying in himself alone, fathom the recesses of his own mind, and bring up rich pearls from the secret depths of thought.

We will conclude these suggestions to our native poets by quoting Ben Jonson's "Ode to Himself," which we address to each of them individually:

"When do'st thou careless lie
Buried in ease and sloth?
Knowledge, that sleeps, doth die;
And this securitie—
It is the common moth
That eats on wits, and arts, and quite destroys them both.

"Are all th' Aonian springs
Dri'd up? Thespia waste?
Doth Clarius' harp want strings,
That not a nymph now sings!
Or droop they as disgrac't,
To see their seats and bowers by chatt'ring pies defac't?

"If hence thy silence be,
As 'tis too just a cause,
Let this thought quicken thee,
Minds that are great and free
Should not on fortune pause;
'Tis crowne enough to virtue still, her owne applause.

"What though the greedy frie
Be taken with false baytes
Of worded balladrie,
And thinke it poesie?
They die with their conceits,
And only piteous scorne upon their folly waites."

JOHN BUNYAN

—

BY

JOHN GREENLEAF WHITTIER

JOHN GREENLEAF WHITTIER

1807—1892

Unlike Emerson, Longfellow, Lowell, and Holmes, who fell heirs to the culture and learning of generations of scholarship, John Greenleaf Whittier began life with few intellectual advantages. Born on a farm near Haverhill, Massachusetts, in 1807, his boyhood was passed in toil unrelieved by any opportunities for mental development. A copy of Burns's poems which chanced to fall into his hands gave the Quaker farm-boy the first inspiration to write poetry himself. For a few weeks each winter he was permitted to attend the district school, until William Lloyd Garrison, who had published some of his boyish verses, persuaded his parents to send him to Haverhill Academy. Two terms at this institution completed his education at school, nor was he privileged in after life to visit Europe, an experience which to many of his contemporaries had been the rich equivalent of a university course.

At the age of twenty Whittier left the farm to take up journalism as his profession. For twelve years, from 1828 to 1840, he was an editor of daily journals in various towns, at Haverhill, at Hartford, then at Boston, and at Philadelphia. During this period he became more and more identified with the abolition movement, and published numerous stirring poems on this subject. His anti-slavery verses, however, have proved to be the least enduring of his writings. In 1831 he published his first book, a miscellany of prose and verse called "Legends of New England." In 1840, the farm in Haverhill having been sold, Whittier purchased a house in Amesbury, where he lived for the remainder of his life. Much of his time was spent in anti-slavery agitation, speaking fearlessly, writing passionately, and attending many conventions. He also edited the "National Era," and was one of the founders of the "Atlantic Monthly." Aside from his anti-slavery poems Whittier published "Lays of my Home" in 1843, "Songs of Labor" in 1850, and "Home Ballads" in 1860. These books contain some of the finest lyrics and most stirring ballads in American literature, including as they do "Angels of Buena Vista," "Maud Muller," "Ichabod," "Barefoot Boy," and "Skipper Ireson's Ride." In 1863 "In War Time" appeared, containing among other poems "Barbara Freitchie." Three years later Whittier published "Snow-Bound," and achieved his first great popular success. The sales of this book placed him for the first time, at the age of fifty-nine, in comfortable circumstances. "The Tent on the Beach" and "Among the Hills," published in quick succession, were received with almost equal favor, but "Snow-Bound" was, and still remains, Whittier's greatest work, an idyll of New England life comparable, in regard to literary worth and popularity, to Goldsmith's "Deserted Village" and Burns's "Cottar's Saturday Night." During his later years Whittier published several volumes of poetry which, while they increased his popularity, added nothing to his fame. He died in 1892, perhaps the most popular of American poets after Longfellow.

It is as a poet that Whittier will be longest and best remembered, but he is also the author of much charming prose. Besides a number of tales and sketches from his pen, concerned chiefly with New England scenes and legends, we have various literary criticisms and reviews, such as his article on "John Bunyan," which show that the poet possessed skill of no mean order as an essayist. His prose style, as we are led to expect from his personal character, is simple, unaffected, and direct.

JOHN BUNYAN

"Wouldst see
A man i' the clouds, and hear him speak to thee?"

WHO has not read "Pilgrim's Progress"? Who has not, in childhood, followed the wandering Christian on his way to the Celestial City? Who has not laid at night his young head on the pillow, to paint on the walls of darkness pictures of the Wicket Gate and the Archers, the Hill of Difficulty, the Lions and Giants, Doubting Castle and Vanity Fair, the sunny Delectable Mountains and the Shepherds, the Black River and the wonderful glory beyond it; and at last fallen asleep, to dream over the strange story, to hear the sweet welcomings of the sisters at the House Beautiful, and the song of birds from the window of that "upper chamber which opened towards the sunrising?" And who, looking back to the green spots in his childish experiences, does not bless the good tinker of Elstow?

And who, that has reperused the story of the pilgrim at a maturer age, and felt the plummet of its truth sounding in the deep places of the soul, has not reason to bless the author for some timely warning or grateful encouragement? Where is the scholar, the poet, the man of taste and feeling, who does not, with Cowper,

"Even in transitory life's late day,
Revere the man whose pilgrim marks the road,
And guides the progress of the soul to God"?

We have just been reading, with no slight degree of interest, that simple but wonderful piece of autobiography, entitled "Grace Abounding to the Chief of Sinners," from the pen of the author of "Pilgrim's Progress." It is the record of a journey more terrible than that of the ideal pilgrim; "truth stranger than fiction;" the painful upward struggling of a spirit from the blackness of despair and blasphemy, into the high, pure air of hope and faith. More earnest words were never written. It is the entire unveiling of a human heart; the tearing off of the fig-leaf covering of its sin. The voice which speaks to us from these old pages seems not so much that of a denizen of the world in which we live, as of a soul at the last solemn confessional. Shorn of all ornament, simple and direct as the contrition and prayer of childhood, when for the first time the spectre of sin stands by its bedside, the style is that of a man dead to self-gratification, careless of the world's opinion, and only desirous to convey to others, in all truthfulness and sincerity, the lesson of his inward trials, temptations, sins, weaknesses, and dangers; and to give glory to Him who had mercifully led him through all, and enabled him, like his own pilgrim, to leave behind the Valley of the Shadow of Death, the snares of the Enchanted Ground, and the terrors of Doubting Castle, and to reach the land of Beulah, where the air was sweet and pleasant, and the birds sang and the flowers sprang up around him, and the Shining Ones walked in the brightness of the not distant Heaven. In the introductory pages he says: "I could have dipped into a style higher than this in which I have discoursed, and could have adorned all things more than here I have seemed to do; but I dared not. God did not play in tempting me; neither did I play when I sunk, as it were, into a bottomless pit, when the pangs of hell took hold on me; wherefore, I may not play in relating of them, but be plain and simple, and lay down the thing as it was."

This book, as well as "Pilgrim's Progress," was written in Bedford prison, and was designed especially for the comfort and edification of his "children, whom God had counted him worthy to beget in faith by his ministry." In his introduction he tells them, that, although taken from them, and tied up, "sticking, as it were, between the teeth of the lions of the wilderness," he once again, as before, from the top of Shemer and Hermon, so now, from the lion's den and the mountain of leopards, would look after them with fatherly care and desires for their everlasting welfare. "If," said he, "you have sinned against light; if you are tempted to blaspheme; if you are drowned in despair; if you think God fights you; or if Heaven is hidden from your eyes, remember it was so with your father. But out of all the Lord delivered me."

He gives no dates; he affords scarcely a clew to his localities; of the man, as he worked, and ate, and drank, and lodged, of his neighbors and contemporaries, of all he saw and heard of the world about him, we have only an occasional glimpse, here and there, in his narrative. It is the story of his inward life only that he relates. What had time and place to do with one who trembled always with the awful consciousness of an immortal nature, and about whom fell alternately the shadows of hell and the splendors of heaven? We gather, indeed, from his record, that he was not an idle on-looker in the time of England's great struggle for freedom, but a soldier of the Parliament, in his young years, among the praying sworders and psalm-singing pikemen, the Greathearts and Holdfasts whom he has immortalized in his allegory; but the only allusion which he makes to this portion of his experience is by way of illustration of the goodness of God in preserving him on occasions of peril.

He was born in Elstow, in Bedfordshire, in 1628; and, to use his own words, "his father's house was of that rank which is the meanest and most despised of all the families of the land." His father was a tinker, and his son followed the same calling, which necessarily brought him into association with the lowest and most depraved classes of English society. The estimation in which the tinker and his occupation were held, in the seventeenth century, may be learned from the quaint and humorous description of Sir Thomas Overbury. "The tinker," saith he, "is a movable, for he has no abiding in one place; he seems to be devout, for his life is a continual pilgrimage, and sometimes, in humility, goes barefoot, therein making necessity a virtue; he is a gallant, for he carries all his wealth upon his back; or a philosopher, for he bears all his substance with him. He is always furnished with a song, to which his hammer, keeping tune, proves that he was the first founder of the kettle-drum; where the best ale is, there stands his music most upon crotchets. The companion of his travel is some foul, sun-burnt quean, that, since the terrible statute, has recanted gipsyism, and is turned pedlaress. So marches he all over England, with his bag and baggage; his conversation is irreprovable, for he is always mending. He observes truly the statutes, and therefore had rather steal than beg. He is so strong an enemy of idleness, that in mending one hole he would rather make three than want work;

and when he hath done, he throws the wallet of his faults behind him. His tongue is very voluble, which, with canting, proves him a linguist. He is entertained in every place, yet enters no farther than the door, to avoid suspicion. To conclude, if he escape Tyburn and Banbury, he dies a beggar."

Truly, but a poor beginning for a pious life was the youth of John Bunyan. As might have been expected, he was a wild, reckless, swearing boy, as his father doubtless was before him. "It was my delight," says he, "to be taken captive by the devil. I had few equals, both for cursing and swearing, lying and blaspheming." Yet, in his ignorance and darkness, his powerful imagination early lent terror to the reproaches of conscience. He was scared, even in childhood, with dreams of hell and apparitions of devils. Troubled with fears of eternal fire, and the malignant demons who fed it in the regions of despair, he says that he often wished either that there was no hell, or that he had been born a devil himself, that he might be a tormentor rather than one of the tormented.

At an early age he appears to have married. His wife was as poor as himself, for he tells us that they had not so much as a dish or spoon between them; but she brought with her two books on religious subjects, the reading of which seems to have had no slight degree of influence on his mind. He went to church regularly, adored the priest and all things pertaining to his office, being, as he says, "overrun with superstition." On one occasion a sermon was preached against the breach of the Sabbath by sports or labor, which struck him at the moment as especially designed for himself; but by the time he had finished his dinner, he was prepared to "shake it out of his mind, and return to his sports and gaming."

"But the same day," he continues, "as I was in the midst of a game of 'cat,' and having struck it one blow from the hole, just as I was about to strike it a second time, a voice did suddenly dart from Heaven into my soul, which said, 'Wilt thou leave thy sins and go to Heaven, or have thy sins and go to hell?' At this, I was put to an exceeding maze; wherefore, leaving my 'cat' upon the ground, I looked up to Heaven, and it was, as if I had, with the eyes of my understanding, seen the Lord Jesus look down upon me, as being very hotly displeased with me, and as if he did severely threaten me with some grievous punishment for those and other ungodly practices.

"I had no sooner thus conceived in my mind, but suddenly this conclusion fastened on my spirit (for the former hint did set my sins again before my face), that I had been a great and grievous sinner, and that it was now too late for me to look after Heaven; for Christ would not forgive me nor pardon my transgressions. Then, while I was thinking of it, and fearing lest it should be so, I felt my heart sink in despair, concluding it was too late; and therefore I resolved in my mind to go on in sin; for thought I, if the case be thus, my state is surely miserable; miserable if I leave my sins, and but miserable if I follow them; I can but be damned; and if I must be so, I had as good be damned for many sins as be damned for few."

The reader of "Pilgrim's Progress" cannot fail here to call to mind the wicked suggestions of the Giant to Christian, in the dungeon of Doubting Castle.

"I returned," he says, "desperately to my sport again; and I well remember, that presently this kind of despair did so possess my soul, that I was persuaded I could never attain to other comfort than what I should get in sin; for Heaven was gone already, so that on that I must not think; wherefore, I found within me great desire to take my fill of sin, that I might taste the sweetness of it; and I made as much haste as I could to fill my belly with its delicates, lest I should die before I had my desires; for that I feared greatly. In these things, I protest before God, I lie not, neither do I frame this sort of speech; these were really, strongly, and with all my heart, my desires; the good Lord, whose mercy is unsearchable, forgive my transgressions."

One day, while standing in the street, cursing and blaspheming, he met with a reproof which startled him. The woman of the house in front of which the wicked young tinker was standing, herself, as he remarks, "a very loose, ungodly wretch," protested that his horrible profanity made her tremble; that he was the ungodliest fellow for swearing she had ever heard, and able to spoil all the youth of the town who came in his company. Struck by this wholly unexpected rebuke, he at once abandoned the practice of swearing; although previously he tells us that "he had never known how to speak, unless he put an oath before and another behind."

The good name which he gained by this change was now a

temptation to him. "My neighbors," he says, "were amazed at my great conversion from prodigious profaneness to something like a moral life and sober man. Now, therefore, they began to praise, to commend, and to speak well of me, both to my face and behind my back. Now I was, as they said, become godly; now I was become a right honest man. But oh! when I understood those were their words and opinions of me, it pleased me mighty well; for though as yet I was nothing but a poor painted hypocrite, yet I loved to be talked of as one that was truly godly. I was proud of my godliness, and, indeed, I did all I did either to be seen of or well spoken of by men; and thus I continued for about a twelvemonth or more."

The tyranny of his imagination at this period is seen in the following relation of his abandonment of one of his favorite sports.

"Now you must know, that before this I had taken much delight in ringing, but my conscience beginning to be tender, I thought such practice was but vain, and therefore forced myself to leave it; yet my mind hankered; wherefore, I would go to the steeple-house and look on, though I durst not ring; but I thought this did not become religion neither; yet I forced myself, and would look on still. But quickly after, I began to think, 'How if one of the bells should fall?' Then I chose to stand under a main beam, that lay overthwart the steeple, from side to side, thinking here I might stand sure; but then I thought again, should the bell fall with a swing, it might first hit the wall, and then, rebounding upon me, might kill me for all this beam. This made me stand in the steeple door; and now, thought I, I am safe enough; for if a bell should then fall, I can slip out behind these thick walls, and so be preserved notwithstanding.

"So after this I would yet go to see them ring, but would not go any farther than the steeple door. But then it came in my head, 'How if the steeple itself should fall?' And this thought (it may, for aught I know, when I stood and looked on) did continually so shake my mind, that I durst not stand at the steeple door any longer, but was forced to flee, for fear the steeple should fall upon my head."

About this time, while wandering through Bedford in pursuit of employment, he chanced to see three or four poor old women sitting at a door, in the evening sun, and, drawing near them, heard them converse upon the things of God; of His work in their hearts; of their natural depravity; of the temptations of the Adversary; and of the joy of believing, and of the peace of reconciliation. The words of the aged women found a response in the soul of the listener. "He felt his heart shake," to use his own words; he saw that he lacked the true tokens of a Christian. He now forsook the company of the profane and licentious, and sought that of a poor man who had the reputation of piety, but, to his grief, he found him "a devilish ranter, given up to all manner of uncleanness; he would laugh at all exhortations to sobriety, and deny that there was a God, an angel, or a spirit."

"Neither," he continues, "was this man only a temptation to me, but, my calling lying in the country, I happened to come into several people's company, who, though strict in religion formerly, yet were also drawn away by these ranters. These would also talk with me of their ways, and condemn me as illegal and dark; pretending that they only had attained to perfection, that could do what they would, and not sin. Oh! these temptations were suitable to my flesh, I being but a young man, and my nature in its prime; but God, who had, as I hope, designed me for better things, kept me in the fear of his name, and did not suffer me to accept such cursed principles."

At this time he was sadly troubled to ascertain whether or not he had that faith which the Scriptures spake of. Travelling one day from Elstow to Bedford, after a recent rain, which had left pools of water in the path, he felt a strong desire to settle the question, by commanding the pools to become dry, and the dry places to become pools. Going under the hedge, to pray for ability to work the miracle, he was struck with the thought, that if he failed he should know, indeed, that he was a castaway, and give himself up to despair. He dared not attempt the experiment, and went on his way, to use his own forcible language, "tossed up and down between the devil and his own ignorance."

Soon after, he had one of those visions which foreshadowed the wonderful dream of his "Pilgrim's Progress." He saw some holy people of Bedford on the sunny side of a high mountain, refreshing themselves in the pleasant air and sunlight, while he was shivering in cold and darkness, amidst snows and never-melting ices, like the victims of the Scandinavian hell. A wall

16

compassed the mountain, separating him from the blessed, with one small gap or doorway, through which, with great pain and effort, he was at last enabled to work his way into the sunshine, and sit down with the saints, in the light and warmth thereof.

But now a new trouble assailed him. Like Milton's metaphysical spirits, who sat apart,

> "And reasoned of foreknowledge, will, and fate,"

he grappled with one of those great questions which have always perplexed and baffled human inquiry, and upon which much has been written to little purpose. He was tortured with anxiety to know whether, according to the Westminster formula, he was elected to salvation or damnation. His old adversary vexed his soul with evil suggestions, and even quoted Scripture to enforce them. "It may be you are not elected," said the Tempter, and the poor tinker thought the supposition altogether too probable. "Why, then," said Satan, "you had as good leave off, and strive no farther; for if, indeed, you should not be elected and chosen of God, there is no hope of your being saved; for it is neither in him that willeth nor in him that runneth, but in God who showeth mercy." At length when, as he says, he was about giving up the ghost of all his hopes, this passage fell with weight upon his spirit: "Look at the generations of old, and see; did ever any trust in God, and were confounded?" Comforted by these words, he opened his Bible to note them, but the most diligent search and inquiry of his neighbors failed to discover them. At length, his eye fell upon them in the apocryphal book of Ecclesiasticus. This, he says, somewhat doubted him at first, as the book was not canonical; but in the end he took courage and comfort from the passage. "I bless God," he says, "for that word; it was good for me. That word doth still oftentimes shine before my face."

A long and weary struggle was now before him. "I cannot," he says, "express with what longings and breathings of my soul I cried unto Christ to call me. Gold! could it have been gotten by gold, what would I have given for it. Had I a whole world, it had all gone ten thousand times over for this, that my soul might have been in a converted state. How lovely now was everyone in my eyes, that I thought to be converted men and women. They shone, they walked like a people who carried the broad seal of Heaven with them."

With what force and intensity of language does he portray in the following passage the reality and earnestness of his agonizing experience:

"While I was thus afflicted with the fears of my own damnation, there were two things would make me wonder: the one was, when I saw old people hunting after the things of this life, as if they should live here always; the other was, when I found professors much distressed and cast down, when they met with outward losses; as of husband, wife, or child. Lord, thought I, what seeking after carnal things by some, and what grief in others for the loss of them! If they so much labor after and shed so many tears for the things of this present life, how am I to be bemoaned, pitied, and prayed for! My soul is dying, my soul is damning. Were my soul but in a good condition, and were I but sure of it, ah! how rich should I esteem myself, though blessed but with bread and water! I should count these but small afflictions, and should bear them as little burdens. 'A wounded spirit who can bear!'"

He looked with envy, as he wandered through the country, upon the birds in the trees, the hares in the preserves, and the fishes in the streams. They were happy in their brief existence, and their death was but a sleep. He felt himself alienated from God, a discord in the harmonies of the universe. The very rooks which fluttered around the old church spire seemed more worthy of the Creator's love and care than himself. A vision of the infernal fire, like that glimpse of hell which was afforded to Christian by the Shepherds, was continually before him, with its "rumbling noise, and the cry of some tormented, and the scent of brimstone." Whithersoever he went, the glare of it scorched him, and its dreadful sound was in his ears. His vivid but disturbed imagination lent new terrors to the awful figures by which the sacred writers conveyed the idea of future retribution to the Oriental mind. Bunyan's World of Wo, if it lacked the colossal architecture and solemn vastness of Milton's Pandemonium, was more clearly defined; its agonies were within the pale of human comprehension; its victims were men and women, with the same keen sense of corporeal suffering which they possessed in life; and who, to use his own terrible description, had "all the loathed variety of hell to grapple with; fire unquenchable, a lake of choking brimstone, eternal chains, darkness more black than night, the everlasting gnawing of the worm, the sight of devils, and the yells and outcries of the damned."

His mind at this period was evidently shaken in some degree from its balance. He was troubled with strange wicked thoughts, confused by doubts and blasphemous suggestions, for which he could only account by supposing himself possessed of the devil. He wanted to curse and swear, and had to clap his hands on his mouth to prevent it. In prayer, he felt, as he supposed, Satan behind him, pulling his clothes, and telling him to have done, and break off; suggesting that he had better pray to him, and calling up before his mind's eye the figures of a bull, a tree, or some other object, instead of the awful idea of God.

He notes here, as cause of thankfulness, that, even in this dark and clouded state, he was enabled to see the "vile and abominable things fomented by the Quakers," to be errors. Gradually, the shadow wherein he had so long

> "Walked beneath the day's broad glare,
> A darkened man,"

passed from him, and for a season he was afforded an "evidence of his salvation from Heaven, with many golden seals thereon hanging in his sight." But, ere long, other temptations assailed him. A strange suggestion haunted him, to sell or part with his Saviour. His own account of this hallucination is too painfully vivid to awaken any other feeling than that of sympathy and sadness.

"I could neither eat my food, stoop for a pin, chop a stick, or cast mine eye to look on this or that, but still the temptation would come, Sell Christ for this, or sell Christ for that; sell him, sell him.

"Sometimes it would run in my thoughts, not so little as a hundred times together, Sell him, sell him; against which, I may say, for whole hours together, I have been forced to stand as continually leaning and forcing my spirit against it, lest haply, before I were aware, some wicked thought might arise in my heart, that might consent thereto; and sometimes the Tempter would make me believe I had consented to it; but then I should be as tortured upon a rack, for whole days together.

"This temptation did put me to such scares, lest I should at sometimes, I say, consent thereto, and be overcome therewith, that, by the very force of my mind, my very body would be put into action or motion, by way of pushing or thrusting with my hands or elbows; still answering, as fast as the destroyer said, Sell him, I will not, I will not, I will not; no, not for thousands, thousands, thousands of worlds; thus reckoning, lest I should set too low a value on him, even until I scarce well knew where I was, or how to be composed again.

"But to be brief: one morning, as I did lie in my bed, I was, as at other times, most fiercely assaulted with this temptation, to sell and part with Christ; the wicked suggestion still running in my mind, Sell him, sell him, sell him, sell him, sell him, as fast as a man could speak; against which, also, in my mind, as at other times, I answered, No, no, not for thousands, thousands, thousands, at least twenty times together; but at last, after much striving, I felt this thought pass through my heart, *Let him go if he will;* and I thought also, that I felt my heart freely consent thereto. Oh! the diligence of Satan! Oh! the desperateness of man's heart!

"Now was the battle won, and down fell I, as a bird that is shot from the top of a tree, into great guilt, and fearful despair. Thus getting out of my bed, I went moping into the field; but God knows, with as heavy a heart as mortal man, I think, could bear; where, for the space of two hours, I was like a man bereft of life; and, as now, past all recovery, and bound over to eternal punishment.

"And withal, that Scripture did seize upon my soul: 'Or profane person, as Esau, who, for one morsel of meat, sold his birthright; for ye know, how that afterward, when he would have inherited the blessing, he was rejected; for he found no place for repentance, though he sought it carefully with tears.'"

For two years and a half, as he informs us, that awful Scripture sounded in his ears like the knell of a lost soul. He believed that he had committed the unpardonable sin. His mental anguish was united with bodily illness and suffering. His nervous system became fearfully deranged; his limbs trembled; and he supposed this visible tremulousness and agitation to be the mark of Cain. Troubled with pain and distressing sensations in his chest, he began to fear that his breastbone would split open, and that he should perish like Judas Iscariot. He feared that the tiles of the houses would fall upon him as he walked the streets. He was like his own Man in the Cage at the House of the Interpreter, shut out from the promises, and looking forward to certain judgment. "Methought," he says, "the very sun that shineth in heaven did grudge to give me light." And still the dreadful words, "He found no place for repentance, though he sought it carefully with tears," sounded in the depths of his soul. They were, he says, like fetters of brass to his legs, and their continual clanking followed him for months. Regarding himself elected and predestined for damnation, he thought that all things worked for his damage and eternal overthrow, while all things wrought for the best, and to do good to the elect and called of God unto salvation. God and all His universe had, he thought, conspired against him; the green earth, the bright waters, the sky itself, were written over with his irrevocable curse.

Well was it said by Bunyan's contemporary, the excellent Cudworth, in his eloquent sermon before the Long Parliament, that "we are nowhere commanded to pry into the secrets of God, but the wholesome advice given us is this: 'To make our calling and election sure.' We have no warrant from Scripture to peep into the hidden rolls of eternity, to spell out our names among the stars." "Must we say that God sometimes, to exercise His uncontrollable dominion, delights rather in plunging wretched souls down into infernal night and everlasting darkness? What, then, shall we make the God of the whole world? Nothing but a cruel and dreadful *Errinys,* with curled fiery snakes about His head, and firebrands in His hand; thus governing the world! Surely, this will make us either secretly think there is no God in the world, if He must needs be such, or else to wish heartily there were none." It was thus at times with Bunyan. He was tempted, in this season of despair, to believe that there was no resurrection and no judgment.

One day he tells us a sudden rushing sound, as of wind or the wings of angels, came to him through the window, wonderfully sweet and pleasant; and it was as if a voice spoke to him from heaven words of encouragement and hope, which, to use his language, commanded, for the time, " a silence in his heart to all those tumultuous thoughts that did use, like masterless hell-hounds, to roar and bellow and make a hideous noise within him." About this time, also, some comforting passages of Scripture were called to mind; but he remarks, that whenever he strove to apply them to his case, Satan would thrust the curse of Esau in his face, and wrest the good word from him. The blessed promise, " Him that cometh to me, I will in no wise cast out," was the chief instrumentality in restoring his lost peace. He says of it: " If ever Satan and I did strive for any word of God in all my life, it was for this good word of Christ; he at one end, and I at the other; oh, what work we made! It was for this in John, I say, that we did so tug and strive; he pulled, and I pulled, but, God be praised! I overcame him; I got sweetness from it. Oh! many a pull hath my heart had with Satan for this blessed sixth chapter of John!"

Who does not here call to mind the struggle between Christian and Apollyon in the valley! That was no fancy sketch; it was the narrative of the author's own grapple with the Spirit of Evil. Like his ideal Christian, he " conquered through Him that loved him." Love wrought the victory: the Scripture of Forgiveness overcame that of Hatred.

He never afterwards relapsed into that state of religious melancholy from which he so hardly escaped. He speaks of his deliverance, as the waking out of a troublesome dream. His painful experience was not lost upon him; for it gave him, ever after, a tender sympathy for the weak, the sinful, the ignorant, and desponding. In some measure, he had been " touched with the feeling of their infirmities." He could feel for those in the bonds of sin and despair, as bound with them. Hence his power as a preacher; hence the wonderful adaptation of his great allegory to all the variety of spiritual conditions. Like Fearing, he had lain a month in the Slough of Despond, and had played, like him, the long melancholy bass of spiritual heaviness. With Feeble-mind, he had fallen into the hands of Slay-good, of the nature of Man-eaters; and had limped along his difficult way upon the crutches of Ready-to-halt. Who better than himself could describe the condition of Despondency, and his daughter Muchafraid, in the dungeon of Doubting Castle? Had he not also fallen among thieves, like Little-faith?

His account of his entering upon the solemn duties of a preacher of the gospel is at once curious and instructive. He deals honestly with himself, exposing all his various moods, weaknesses, doubts, and temptations. "I preached," he says, "what I felt; for the terrors of the law and the guilt of transgression lay heavy on my conscience. I have been as one sent to them from the dead. I went, myself in chains, to preach to them in chains; and carried that fire in my conscience which I persuaded them to beware of." At times, when he stood up to preach, blasphemies and evil doubts rushed into his mind, and he felt a strong desire to utter them aloud to his congregation; and at other seasons, when he was about to apply to the sinner some searching and fearful text of Scripture, he was tempted to withhold it, on the ground that it condemned himself also; but, withstanding the suggestion of the Tempter, to use his own simile, he bowed himself like Samson to condemn sin wherever he found it, though he brought guilt and condemnation upon himself thereby, choosing rather to die with the Philistines than to deny the truth.

Foreseeing the consequences of exposing himself to the operation of the penal laws by holding conventicles and preaching, he was deeply afflicted at the thought of the suffering and destitution to which his wife and children might be exposed by his death or imprisonment. Nothing can be more touching than his simple and earnest words on this point. They show how warm and deep were his human affections, and what a tender and loving heart he laid as a sacrifice on the altar of duty:

"I found myself a man compassed with infirmities; the parting with my wife and poor children, hath often been to me in this place, as the pulling the flesh from the bones; and also it brought to my mind the many hardships, miseries, and wants, that my poor family was like to meet with, should I be taken from them, especially my poor blind child, who lay nearer my heart than all beside. Oh! the thoughts of the hardships I thought my poor blind one might go under, would break my heart to pieces.

"Poor child! thought I, what sorrow art thou like to have for thy portion in this world! thou must be beaten, must beg, suffer hunger, cold, nakedness, and a thousand calamities, though I cannot now endure the wind should blow upon thee. But yet, thought I, I must venture you all with God, though it goeth to the quick to leave you: Oh! I saw I was as a man who was pulling down his house upon the heads of his wife and children; yet I thought on those 'two milch kine that were to carry the ark of God into another country, and to leave their calves behind them.'

"But that which helped me in this temptation was divers considerations: the first was, the consideration of those two Scriptures, 'Leave thy fatherless children, I will preserve them alive; and let thy widows trust in me:' and again, 'The Lord said, verily it shall go well with thy remnant; verily I will cause the enemy to entreat them well in the time of evil.'"

He was arrested in 1660, charged with "devilishly and perniciously abstaining from church," and of being "a common upholder of conventicles." At the quarter sessions, where his trial seems to have been conducted somewhat like that of Faithful at Vanity Fair, he was sentenced to perpetual banishment. This sentence, however, was never executed, but he was remanded to Bedford jail, where he lay a prisoner for twelve years.

Here, shut out from the world, with no other books than the Bible and Fox's "Martyrs," he penned that great work which has attained a wider and more stable popularity than any other book in the English tongue. It is alike the favorite of the nursery and the study. Many experienced Christians hold it only second to the Bible; the infidel himself would not willingly let it die. Men of all sects read it with delight, as in the main a truthful representation of the Christian pilgrimage, without indeed assenting to all the doctrines which the author puts in the mouth of his fighting sermonizer, Greatheart, or which may be deduced from some other portions of his allegory. A recollection of his fearful sufferings, from misapprehension of a single text in the Scriptures, relative to the question of election, we may suppose gave a milder tone to the theology of his Pilgrim than was altogether consistent with the Calvinism of the seventeenth century. "Religion," says Macaulay, "has scarcely ever worn a form so calm and soothing as in Bunyan's allegory." In composing it, he seems never to have altogether lost sight of the fact, that, in his life and death struggle with Satan for the blessed promise recorded by the Apostle of Love, the adversary was generally found on the Genevan side of the argument.

Little did the short-sighted persecutors of Bunyan dream,

when they closed upon him the door of Bedford jail, that God would overrule their poor spite and envy, to his own glory and the world-wide renown of their victim. In the solitude of his prison, the ideal forms of beauty and sublimity, which had long flitted before him vaguely, like the vision of the Temanite, took shape and coloring; and he was endowed with power to reduce them to order, and arrange them in harmonious groupings. His powerful imagination, no longer self-tormenting, but under the direction of reason and grace, expanded his narrow cell into a vast theatre, lighted up for the display of its wonders. To this creative faculty of his mind might have been aptly applied the language which George Wither, a contemporary prisoner, addressed to his muse:

> "The dull loneness, the black shade
> Which these hanging vaults have made,
> The rude portals that give light
> More to terror than delight;
> This my chamber of neglect,
> Walled about with disrespect—
> From all these, and this dull air,
> A fit object for despair,
> She hath taught me by her might,
> To draw comfort and delight."

That stony cell of his was to him like the rock of Padan-aram to the wandering patriarch. He saw angels ascending and descending. The House Beautiful rose up before him, and its holy sisterhood welcomed him. He looked, with his Pilgrim, from the Chamber of Peace. The Valley of Humiliation lay stretched out beneath his eye, and he heard "the curious melodious note of the country birds, who sing all the day long in the springtime, when the flowers appear, and the sun shines warm, and make the woods and groves and solitary places glad." Side by side with the good Christiana and the loving Mercy, he walked through the green and lowly valley, "fruitful as any the crow flies over," through "meadows beautiful with lilies;" the song of the poor but fresh-faced shepherd boy, who lived a merry life, and wore the herb heart's-ease in his bosom, sounded through his cell:

> "He that is down need fear no fall;
> He that is low no pride."

The broad and pleasant "river of the Water of Life" glided peacefully before him, fringed "on either side with green trees, with all manner of fruit," and leaves of healing, with "meadows beautified with lilies, and green all the year long;" he saw the Delectable Mountains, glorious with sunshine, overhung with gardens and orchards and vineyards; and beyond all, the Land of Beulah, with its eternal sunshine, its song of birds, its music of fountains, its purple clustered vines, and groves through which walked the Shining Ones, silver-winged and beautiful.

What were bars and bolts and prison walls to him, whose eyes were anointed to see, and whose ears opened to hear, the glory and the rejoicing of the City of God, when the pilgrims were conducted to its golden gates, from the black and bitter river, with the sounding trumpeters, the transfigured harpers with their crowns of gold, the sweet voices of angels, the welcoming peal of bells in the holy city, and the songs of the redeemed ones? In reading the concluding pages of the first part of "Pilgrim's Progress," we feel as if the mysterious glory of the Beatific Vision was unveiled before us. We are dazzled with the excess of light. We are entranced with the mighty melody; overwhelmed by the great anthem of rejoicing spirits. It can only be adequately described in the language of Milton in respect to the apocalypse, as "a seven-fold chorus of hallelujahs and harping symphonies."

Few who read Bunyan nowadays think of him as one of the brave old English confessors, whose steady and firm endurance of persecution baffled, and in the end overcame, the tyranny of the established church in the reign of Charles II. What Milton and Penn and Locke wrote in defence of liberty, Bunyan lived out and acted. He made no concessions to wordly rank. Dissolute lords and proud bishops he counted less than the humblest and poorest of his disciples at Bedford. When first arrested and thrown into prison, he supposed he should be called to suffer death for his faithful testimony to the truth; and his great fear was, that he should not meet his fate with the requisite firmness, and so dishonor the cause of his Master. And when dark clouds came over him, and he sought in vain for a sufficient evidence that in the event of his death it would be well with him, he girded up his soul with the reflection, that, as he suffered for the word and way of God, he was engaged not to shrink one hair's breadth from it. "I will leap," he says, "off the ladder blindfold into eternity, sink or swim, come heaven, come hell. Lord Jesus, if thou wilt catch me, do; if not, I will venture in thy name!"

The English revolution of the seventeenth century, while it humbled the false and oppressive aristocracy of rank and title, was prodigal in the development of the real nobility of the mind and heart. Its history is bright with the footprints of men whose very names still stir the hearts of freemen, the world over, like a trumpet peal. Say what we may of its fanaticism, laugh as we may at its extravagant enjoyment of newly acquired religious and civil liberty, who shall now venture to deny that it was the golden age of England? Who that regards freedom above slavery, will now sympathize with the outcry and lamentation of those interested in the continuance of sects and schism, but who, at the same time, as Milton shrewdly intimates, dreaded more the rending of their pontifical sleeves than the rending of the church? Who shall now sneer at Puritanism, with the "Defence of Unlicensed Printing" before him? Who scoff at Quakerism over the journal of George Fox? Who shall join with debauched lordlings and fat-witted prelates in ridicule of Anabaptist levellers and dippers, after rising from the perusal of "Pilgrim's Progress?" "There were giants in those days." And foremost amidst that band of liberty-loving and God-fearing men,

> "The slandered Calvinists of Charles's time,
> Who fought, and won it, freedom's holy fight,"

stands the subject of our sketch, the tinker of Elstow. Of his high merit as an author there is no longer any question. The "Edinburgh Review" expressed the common sentiment of the literary world, when it declared that the two great creative minds of the seventeenth century were those which produced "Paradise Lost" and the "Pilgrim's Progress."

THE PHILOSOPHY OF COMPOSITION

—

BY

EDGAR ALLAN POE

EDGAR ALLAN POE

1809—1849

The father of Edgar Allan Poe came of a good Maryland family; his mother was a young English actress. After their marriage, which resulted in his father being disinherited, both gained a somewhat uncertain livelihood on the stage, and it was on one of their tours that their son, Edgar, was born, at Boston in 1809. Three years later he was left an orphan, but was ultimately adopted by a wealthy Richmond family named Allan. He received his early education in England, at Stoke-Newington, near London, and we have a vivid account of his childish impressions of this period in the semi-autobiographical tale "William Wilson." On his return to America he was sent to a private school near Richmond, and later to the University of Virginia. After two years of study, interrupted somewhat by a wild and unrestrained life, his foster-father decided he should leave college. Soon afterwards he ran away, and tried to gain his livelihood by the pen. His first literary effort was "Tamerlane, and Other Poems," published at Boston in 1827. He met, however, with no encouragement in this attempt, and consequently joined the army. After a year of this life his guardian procured his discharge, and he returned to Richmond. A second volume of poems was published in 1829, but met with no more favorable reception than the first. In 1830 he entered the military academy at West Point, the appointment having been secured for him by Mr. Allan, but he was dismissed for neglect of duties in less than a year.

In 1831 Poe settled in Baltimore, and began a journalistic and literary career that continued till his death. His first notable success was a prize story, "The Manuscript found in a Bottle," which secured for him a position as editor of the "Southern Literary Messenger," at Richmond. His criticisms and tales now gained for him a wide reputation, but his restless spirit soon prompted him to resign his editorship, and in 1837 he removed to New York, where he supported himself by contributing to the "New York Quarterly Review" and other periodicals. From 1839-40 he was editor of "The Gentleman's Magazine," at Philadelphia. Afterwards he edited "Graham's Magazine" for a year. In 1845 he went to New York, where he was associated for a while with Charles F. Briggs in editing the "Broadway Journal." In 1840 he brought out "Tales of the Grotesque and Arabesque," and, in 1845, he issued "The Raven, and Other Poems." At no time during this period was Poe in comfortable circumstances, and his desire for strong drink grew upon him steadily. In 1847 his child wife died, and he entered upon the darkest and most tragic stage of his life. He died two years later at the Washington Hospital in Baltimore, at the age of forty.

Poe's position in American literature is unique. Undoubtedly possessed of genius of a high order, his work is as remarkable for the narrowness of its range as for its perfection within the self-prescribed limits. His poems are not numerous, but include some of the most weird and fantastic poems in all literature. His tales, too, are comparatively few in number, but many of them are original and effective. As a literary critic Poe enjoyed considerable reputation in his day, and many of his literary essays are examples of an admirable prose style, as, for instance, "The Philosophy of Composition," written in 1846, in which he discusses his own masterpiece, "The Raven." Poe's writings show no trace of humor, and little or no human sympathy. But in his keen sense of the weird and the grotesque, in his subtle appreciation of word values, in his portrayal of gloom, mystery, mental and physical decay, and death, and in his power of expressing the emotions of terror, inconsolable grief and desire, Poe has no superior.

THE PHILOSOPHY OF COMPOSITION

CHARLES DICKENS, in a note now lying before me, alluding to an examination I once made of the mechanism of " Barnaby Rudge," says—" By the way, are you aware that Godwin wrote his ' Caleb Williams ' backwards? He first involved his hero in a web of difficulties, forming the second volume, and then, for the first, cast about him for some mode of accounting for what had been done."

I cannot think this the precise mode of procedure on the part of Godwin—and indeed what he himself acknowledges is not altogether in accordance with Mr. Dickens's idea—but the author of " Caleb Williams " was too good an artist not to perceive the advantage derivable from at least a somewhat similar process. Nothing is more clear than that every plot, worth the name, must be elaborated to its *dénouement* before anything be attempted with the pen. It is only with the *dénouement* constantly in view that we can give a plot its indispensable air of consequence, or causation, by making the incidents, and especially the tone at all points, tend to the development of the intention.

There is a radical error, I think, in the usual mode of constructing a story. Either history affords a thesis—or one is suggested by an incident of the day—or, at best, the author sets himself to work in the combination of striking events to form merely the basis of his narrative—designing, generally, to fill in with description, dialogue, or authorial comment, whatever crevices of fact or action may, from page to page, render themselves apparent.

I prefer commencing with the consideration of an effect. Keeping originality always in view—for he is false to himself who ventures to dispense with so obvious and so easily attainable a source of interest—I say to myself, in the first place, " Of the innumerable effects or impressions of which the heart, the intellect, or (more generally) the soul is susceptible, what one shall I, on the present occasion, select?" Having chosen a novel first, and secondly, a vivid effect, I consider whether it can be best wrought by incident or tone—whether by ordinary incidents and peculiar tone, or the converse, or by peculiarity both of incident and tone—afterwards looking about me (or rather within) for such combinations of event or tone as shall best aid me in the construction of the effect.

I have often thought how interesting a magazine paper might be written by any author who would—that is to say, who could—detail, step by step, the processes by which any one of his compositions attained its ultimate point of completion. Why such a paper has never been given to the world I am much at a loss to say—but perhaps the authorial vanity has had more to do with the omission than any one other cause. Most writers—poets in especial—prefer having it understood that they compose by a species of fine frenzy—an ecstatic intuition—and would positively shudder at letting the public take a peep behind the scenes, at the elaborate and vacillating crudities of thought—at the true purposes seized only at the last moment—at the innumerable glimpses of idea that arrived not at the maturity of full view—at the fully matured fancies discarded in despair as unmanageable—at the cautious selections and rejections—at the painful erasures and interpolations—in a word, at the wheels and pinions—the tackle for scene-shifting—the step-ladders and demon-traps—the cock's feathers, the red paint and the black patches, which, in ninety-nine cases out of the hundred, constitute the properties of the literary *histrio*.

I am aware, on the other hand, that the case is by no means common in which an author is at all in condition to retrace the steps by which his conclusions have been attained. In general, suggestions, having arisen pell-mell, are pursued and forgotten in a similar manner.

For my own part, I have neither sympathy with the repugnance alluded to, nor, at any time, the least difficulty in recalling to mind the progressive steps of any of my compositions; and, since the interest of an analysis, or reconstruction, such as I have considered a *desideratum*, is quite independent of any real or fancied interest in the thing analyzed, it will not be regarded as a breach of decorum on my part to show the *modus operandi* by which some one of my own works was put together. I select

"The Raven" as most generally known. It is my design to render it manifest that no one point in its composition is referable either to accident or intuition—that the work proceeded step by step to its completion with the precision and rigid consequence of a mathematical problem.

Let us dismiss, as irrelevant to the poem, *per se,* the circumstance—or say the necessity—which, in the first place, gave rise to the intention of composing a poem that should suit at once the popular and the critical taste.

We commence, then, with this intention.

The initial consideration was that of extent. If any literary work is too long to be read at one sitting, we must be content to dispense with the immensely important effect derivable from unity of impression—for, if two sittings be required, the affairs of the world interfere, and everything like totality is at once destroyed. But since, *cæteris paribus,* no poet can afford to dispense with anything that may advance his design, it but remains to be seen whether there is, in extent, any advantage to counterbalance the loss of unity which attends it. Here I say no at once. What we term a long poem is, in fact, merely a succession of brief ones—that is to say, of brief poetical effects. It is needless to demonstrate that a poem is such only inasmuch as it intensely excites, by elevating the soul; and all intense excitements are, through a psychical necessity, brief. For this reason at least one-half of the "Paradise Lost" is essentially prose—a succession of poetical excitements interpersed, inevitably, with corresponding depressions—the whole being deprived, through the extremeness of its length, of the vastly important artistic element, totality, or unity of effect.

It appears evident, then, that there is a distinct limit, as regards length, to all works of literary art—the limit of a single sitting—and that, although in certain classes of pure composition, such as "Robinson Crusoe" (demanding no unity), this limit may be advantageously overpassed, it can never properly be overpassed in a poem. Within this limit the extent of a poem may be made to bear mathematical relation to its merit—in other words, to the excitement or elevation—again, in other words, to the degree of the true poetical effect which it is capable of inducing; for it is clear that the brevity must be in direct ratio of the intensity of the intended effect—this, with one proviso—that a certain degree of duration is absolutely requisite for the production of any effect at all.

Holding in view these considerations, as well as that degree of excitement which I deemed not above the popular, while not below the critical taste, I reached at once what I conceived the proper length for my intended poem—a length of about one hundred lines. It is, in fact, a hundred and eight.

My next thought concerned the choice of an impression, or effect, to be conveyed: and here I may as well observe that, throughout the construction, I kept steadily in view the design of rendering the work universally appreciable. I should be carried too far out of my immediate topic were I to demonstrate a point upon which I have repeatedly insisted, and which, with the poetical, stands not in the slightest need of demonstration—the point, I mean, that beauty is the sole legitimate province of the poem. A few words, however, in elucidation of my real meaning, which some of my friends have evinced a disposition to misrepresent. That pleasure which is at once the most intense, the most elevating, and the most pure, is, I believe, found in the contemplation of the beautiful. When, indeed, men speak of beauty, they mean, precisely, not a quality, as is supposed, but an effect—they refer, in short, just to that intense and pure elevation of soul—not of intellect, or of heart—upon which I have commented, and which is experienced in consequence of contemplating "the beautiful." Now I designate beauty as the province of the poem, merely because it is an obvious rule of art that effects should be made to spring from direct causes—that objects should be attained through means best adapted for their attainment—no one as yet having been weak enough to deny that the peculiar elevation alluded to is most readily attained in the poem. Now, the object truth, or the satisfaction of the intellect, and the object passion, or the excitement of the heart, are, although attainable to a certain extent in poetry, far more readily attainable in prose. Truth, in fact, demands a precision, and passion a homeliness (the truly passionate will comprehend me) which are absolutely antagonistic to that beauty which, I maintain, is the excitement, or pleasurable elevation, of the soul. It by no means follows from anything here said that passion, or even truth, may not be introduced, and even profitably introduced, into a poem—for they may serve in elucidation, or aid the general effect, as do discords in music, by contrast—but the true artist will always contrive, first, to tone them into proper subservience to the predominant aim, and, secondly, to enveil them, as far as possible, in that beauty which is the atmosphere and the essence of the poem.

Regarding, then, beauty as my province, my next question referred to the tone of its highest manifestation—and all experience has shown that this tone is one of sadness. Beauty of whatever kind, in its supreme development, invariably excites the sensitive soul to tears. Melancholy is thus the most legitimate of all the poetical tones.

The length, the province, and the tone, being thus determined, I betook myself to ordinary induction, with the view of obtaining some artistic piquancy which might serve me as a key-note in the construction of the poem—some pivot upon which the whole structure might turn. In carefully thinking over all the usual artistic effects—or more properly points, in the theatrical sense—I did not fail to perceive immediately that no one had been so universally employed as that of the refrain. The universality of its employment sufficed to assure me of its intrinsic value, and spared me the necessity of submitting it to analysis. I considered it, however, with regard to its susceptibility of improvement, and soon saw it to be in a primitive condition. As commonly used, the refrain, or burden, not only is limited to lyric verse, but depends for its impression upon the force of monotone—both in sound and thought. The pleasure is deduced solely from the sense of identity—of repetition. I resolved to diversify, and so heighten the effect, by adhering in general to the monotone of sound, while I continually varied that of thought: that is to say, I determined to produce continuously novel effects, by the variation of the application—of the refrain—the refrain itself remaining, for the most part, unvaried.

These points being settled, I next bethought me of the nature of my refrain. Since its application was to be repeatedly varied, it was clear that the refrain itself must be brief, for there would have been an insurmountable difficulty in frequent variations of application in any sentence of length. In proportion to the brevity of the sentence would, of course, be the facility of the variation. This led me at once to a single word as the best refrain.

The question now arose as to the character of the word. Having made up my mind to a refrain, the division of the poem into stanzas was, of course, a corollary, the refrain forming the close of each stanza. That such a close, to have force, must be sonorous and susceptible of protracted emphasis, admitted no doubt, and these considerations inevitably led me to the long "o" as the most sonorous vowel in connection with "r" as the most producible consonant.

The sound of the refrain being thus determined, it became necessary to select a word embodying this sound, and at the same time in the fullest possible keeping with that melancholy which I had predetermined as the tone of the poem. In such a search it would have been absolutely impossible to overlook the word "Nevermore." In fact, it was the very first which presented itself.

The next *desideratum* was a pretext for the continuous use of the one word "nevermore." In observing the difficulty which I at once found in inventing a sufficiently plausible reason for its continuous repetition, I did not fail to perceive that this difficulty arose solely from the preassumption that the word was to be so continuously or monotonously spoken by a human being—I did not fail to perceive, in short, that the difficulty lay in the reconciliation of this monotony with the exercise of reason on the part of the creature repeating the word. Here, then, immediately arose the idea of a non-reasoning creature capable of speech, and very naturally, a parrot, in the first instance, suggested itself but was superseded forthwith by a raven as equally capable of speech, and infinitely more in keeping with the intended tone.

I had now gone so far as the conception of a raven, the bird of ill-omen, monotonously repeating the one word "Nevermore" at the conclusion of each stanza in the poem of melancholy tone, and in length about one hundred lines. Now, never losing sight of the object—supremeness or perfection at all points, I asked myself—"Of all melancholy topics what, according to the universal understanding of mankind, is the most melancholy?" Death, was the obvious reply. "And when," I said, "is this most melancholy of topics most poetical?"

From what I have already explained at some length the answer here also is obvious—"when it most closely allies itself to beauty: the death, then, of a beautiful woman is unquestionably the most poetical topic in the world, and equally is it beyond doubt that the lips best suited for such topic are those of a bereaved lover."

I had now to combine the two ideas of a lover lamenting his deceased mistress and a raven continuously repeating the word "Nevermore." I had to combine these, bearing in mind my design of varying at every turn the application of the word repeated, but the only intelligible mode of such combination is that of imagining the raven employing the word in answer to the queries of the lover. And here it was that I saw at once the opportunity afforded for the effect on which I had been depending, that is to say, the effect of the variation of application. I saw that I could make the first query propounded by the lover—the first query to which the raven should reply "Nevermore"—that I could make this first query a commonplace one, the second less so, the third still less, and so on, until at length the lover, startled from his original *nonchalance* by the melancholy character of the word itself, by its frequent repetition, and by a consideration of the ominous reputation of the fowl that uttered it, is at length excited to superstition, and wildly propounds queries of a far different character—queries whose solution he has passionately at heart—propounds them half in superstition and half in that species of despair which delights in self-torture—propounds them not altogether because he believes in the prophetic or demoniac character of the bird (which reason assures him is merely repeating a lesson learned by rote), but because he experiences a frenzied pleasure in so modelling his questions as to receive from the expected "Nevermore" the most delicious because the most intolerable of sorrows. Perceiving the opportunity thus afforded me, or, more strictly, thus forced upon me in the progress of construction, I first established in my mind the climax or concluding query—that query to which "Nevermore" should be in the last place an answer—that query in reply to which this word "Nevermore" should involve the utmost conceivable amount of sorrow and despair.

Here, then, the poem may be said to have had its beginning, at the end where all works of art should begin, for it was here at this point of my preconsiderations that I first put pen to paper in the composition of the stanza:—

"'Prophet!' said I, 'thing of evil! prophet still if bird or devil!
By that Heaven that bends above us—by that God we both adore,
Tell this soul with sorrow laden if, within the distant Aidenn,
It shall clasp a sainted maiden whom the angels name Lenore—
Clasp a rare and radiant maiden whom the angels name Lenore.'
Quoth the Raven—'Nevermore.'"

I composed this stanza, at this point, first, that, by establishing the climax, I might the better vary and graduate, as regards seriousness and importance, the preceding queries of the lover, and secondly, that I might definitely settle the rhythm, the metre, and the length and general arrangement of the stanza, as well as graduate the stanzas which were to precede, so that none of them might surpass this in rhythmical effect. Had I been able in the subsequent composition to construct more vigorous stanzas I should without scruple have purposely enfeebled them so as not to interfere with the climacteric effect.

And here I may as well say a few words of the versification. My first object (as usual) was originality. The extent to which this has been neglected in versification is one of the most unaccountable things in the world. Admitting that there is little possibility of variety in mere rhythm, it is still clear that the possible varieties of metre and stanza are absolutely infinite, and yet, for centuries, no man, in verse, has ever done, or ever seemed to think of doing, an original thing. The fact is that originality (unless in minds of very unusual force) is by no means a matter, as some suppose, if impulse or intuition. In general, to be found, it must be elaborately sought, and although a positive merit of the highest class, demands in its attainment less of invention than negation.

Of course, I pretend to no originality in either the rhythm or metre of the "Raven." The former is trochaic—the latter is octametre acatalectic, alternating with heptametre catalectic repeated in the refrain of the fifth verse(and terminating with tetrametre catalectic. Less pedantically—the feet employed throughout (trochees) consist of a long syllable followed by a short; the first line of the stanza consists of eight of these feet, the second of seven and a half (in effect two-thirds), the third of eight, the fourth of seven and a half, the fifth the same, the sixth three and a half. Now, each of these lines taken individually has been employed before, and what originality the "Raven" has, is in their combination into stanza, nothing even remotely approaching this combination has ever been attempted. The effect of this originality of combination is aided by other unusual and some altogether novel effects, arising from an extension of the application of the principles of rhyme and alliteration.

The next point to be considered was the mode of bringing together the lover and the raven—and the first branch of this consideration was the *locale*. For this the most natural suggestion might seem to be a forest, or the fields—but it has always appeared to me that a close circumscription of space is absolutely necessary to the effect of insulated incident—it has the force of a frame to a picture. It has an indisputable moral power in keeping concentrated the attention, and, of course, must not be confounded with mere unity of place.

I determined, then, to place the lover in his chamber—in a chamber rendered sacred to him by memories of her who had frequented it. The room is represented as richly furnished—this in mere pursuance of the ideas I have already explained on the subject of beauty, as the sole true poetical thesis.

The *locale* being thus determined, I had now to introduce the bird—and the thought of introducing him through the window was inevitable. The idea of making the lover suppose, in the first instance, that the flapping of the wings of the bird against the shutter is a "tapping" at the door, originated in a wish to increase, by prolonging the reader's curiosity, and in a desire to admit the incidental effect arising from the lover's throwing open the door, finding all dark, and thence adopting the half-fancy that it was the spirit of his mistress that knocked.

I made the night tempestuous, first to account for the raven's seeking admission, and secondly, for the effect of contrast with the (physical) serenity within the chamber.

I made the bird alight on the bust of Pallas, also for the effect of contrast between the marble and the plumage—it being understood that the bust was absolutely suggested by the bird—the bust of Pallas being chosen, first, as most in keeping with the scholarship of the lover, and, secondly, for the sonorousness of the word, Pallas, itself.

About the middle of the poem, also, I have availed myself of the force of contrast, with a view of deepening the ultimate impression. For example, an air of the fantastic—approaching as nearly to the ludicrous as was admissible—is given to the raven's entrance. He comes in " with many a flirt and flutter."

> " Not the least obeisance made he—not a moment stopped or stayed he,
> But, with mien of lord or lady, perched above my chamber door."

In the two stanzas which follow, the design is more obviously carried out:

> " Then this ebon bird, beguiling my sad fancy into smiling
> By the grave and stern decorum of the countenance it wore,
> 'Though thy crest be shorn and shaven, thou,' I said, 'art sure no craven,
> Ghastly grim and ancient Raven wandering from the nightly shore—
> Tell me what thy lordly name is on the night's Plutonian shore?'
> Quoth the Raven, 'Nevermore.'
>
> " Much I marvelled this ungainly fowl to hear discourse so plainly,
> Though its answer little meaning—little relevancy bore;
> For we cannot help agreeing that no living human being
> Ever yet was blessed with seeing bird above his chamber door—
> Bird or beast upon the sculptured bust above his chamber door,
> With such name as 'Nevermore.' "

The effect of the *dénouement* being thus provided for, I immediately drop the fantastic for a tone of the most profound seriousness—this tone commencing in the stanza directly following the one last quoted, with the line—

> " But the Raven, sitting lonely on that placid bust, spoke only," etc.

From this epoch the lover no longer jests—no longer sees anything even of the fantastic in the raven's demeanor. He speaks of him as a " grim, ungainly, ghastly, gaunt, and ominous bird of yore," and feels the " fiery eyes " burning into his " bosom's core." This revolution of thought, or fancy, on the lover's part, is intended to induce a similar one on the part of the reader—to bring the mind into a proper frame for the *dénouement*—which is now brought about as rapidly and as directly as possible.

With the *dénouement* proper—with the raven's reply, "Nevermore," to the lover's final demand if he shall meet his mistress in another world—the poem, in its obvious phase, that of a simple narrative, may be said to have its completion. So far, everything is within the limits of the accountable—of the real. A raven, having learned by rote the single word " Nevermore," and having escaped from the custody of its owner, is driven at midnight, through the violence of a storm, to seek admission at a window from which a light still gleams—the chamber-window of a student, occupied half in poring over a volume, half in dreaming of a beloved mistress deceased. The casement being thrown open at the fluttering of the bird's wings, the bird itself perches on the most convenient seat out of the immediate reach of the student, who, amused by the incident and the oddity of the visitor's demeanor, demands of it, in jest and without looking for a reply, its name. The raven addressed, answers with its customary word, " Nevermore "—a word which finds immediate echo in the melancholy heart of the student, who, giving utterance aloud to certain thoughts suggested by the occasion, is again startled by the fowl's repetition of " Nevermore." The student now guesses the state of the case, but is impelled, as I have before explained, by the human thirst for self-torture, and in part by superstition, to propound such queries to the bird as will bring him, the lover, the most of the luxury of sorrow, through the anticipated answer " Nevermore." With the indulgence, to the extreme, of this self-torture, the narration, in what I have termed its first or obvious phase, has a natural termination, and so far there has been no overstepping of the limits of the real.

But in subjects so handled, however skilfully, or with however vivid an array of incident, there is always a certain hardness or nakedness which repels the artistical eye. Two things are invariably required—first, some amount of complexity, or more properly, adaptation; and, secondly, some amount of suggestiveness—some under-current, however indefinite, of meaning. It is this latter, in especial, which imparts to a work of art so much of that richness (to borrow from colloquy a forcible term) which we are too fond of confounding with the ideal. It is the excess of the suggested meaning—it is the rendering this the upper instead of the under-current of the theme—which turns into prose (and that of the very flattest kind) the so-called poetry of the so-called transcendentalists.

Holding these opinions, I added the two concluding stanzas of the poem—their suggestiveness being thus made to pervade all the narrative which has preceded them. The under-current of meaning is rendered first apparent in the lines:

"'Take thy beak from out my heart, and take thy form from off my door!'
Quoth the Raven, 'Nevermore!'"

It will be observed that the words "from out my heart" involve the first metaphorical expression in the poem. They, with the answer, "Nevermore," dispose the mind to seek a moral in all that has been previously narrated. The reader begins now to regard the raven as emblematical—but it is not until the very last line of the very last stanza that the intention of making him emblematical of mournful and never-ending remembrance is permitted distinctly to be seen:

"And the Raven, never flitting, still is sitting, still is sitting,
On the pallid bust of Pallas just above my chamber door;
And his eyes have all the seeming of a demon's that is dreaming,
And the lamplight o'er him streaming throws his shadow on the floor;
And my soul from out that shadow that lies floating on the floor
Shall be lifted—nevermore."

THE PROFESSOR'S PAPER

—

BY

OLIVER WENDELL HOLMES

OLIVER WENDELL HOLMES

1809—1894

Born at Cambridge, Massachusetts, in 1809, Oliver Wendell Holmes received his early education in the private schools of that classic town. At the age of fifteen he was sent to Phillips Academy, Andover, and then to Harvard College, where he graduated in 1829. He was the poet of his class, and wrote frequently for social events and public occasions. This habit became a second nature to him through life, and is responsible, if we may believe a statistical biographer, for nearly one-half of all his poems. In 1831 his spirited lyric "Old Ironsides" laid the foundation of a national reputation. In 1836 Holmes received his degree of doctor of medicine, and the same year he published his first volume of poems, containing among others "The Last Leaf," one of the best from his pen. Two years later he published his Boylston prize essays on medical subjects, and was chosen professor of anatomy and physiology in Dartmouth College. In 1847 he was called to fill a similar position in Harvard College, which he held with distinction for thirty-five years.

In 1857 a new literary magazine was started in Boston which Dr. Holmes named the "Atlantic Monthly." James Russell Lowell accepted the position of editor only on the condition "that Dr. Holmes should be the first contributor to be engaged." Under such circumstances began the series of papers entitled "The Autocrat of the Breakfast Table." This work was immediately recognized as one of the most notable that had yet appeared in American literature. The author's plan, peculiar to himself, enabled him to write with greater ease and discursiveness than would be permissible in the formal essay. He could, moreover, add greater variety, humor, and human interest by means of the dramatic setting employed. So great was its success that "The Autocrat" was followed at varying intervals by other works written in the same style: "The Professor at the Breakfast Table" (1859), "The Poet at the Breakfast Table" (1872), and "Over the Tea-Cups" (1890). In these charming productions Dr. Holmes introduced some of his finest poems, notably "The Deacon's Masterpiece," and "The Chambered Nautilus," in which he strikes the highest poetic note he ever reached. Here also we find interspersed occasional masterpieces in prose, such as "The Professor's Paper," in which all of his powers come into play, as it were, in miniature, and still at their very best. In addition to these brilliant papers, on which, together with his poems, his literary reputation chiefly rests, Dr. Holmes wrote three psychological novels, of which "Elsie Venner" is the best. During his later years he wrote biographies of Motley and Emerson, numerous medical essays, and added occasionally to successive new editions of his poems. In 1887 he undertook a brief journey to England. where he was received with great honor. Dr. Holmes was the last to leave us of all the greater New England writers, his death occurring in 1894, at the age of eighty-five.

While not so profound as some of his contemporaries, the works of Holmes abounds in geniality and wit that are inimitable. He was one of the most versatile of men, achieving success as a physician, lecturer, novelist, poet, and essayist, and in the last-mentioned capacity his work has an individuality and charm surpassed only by Montaigne and Addison. His prose style is clear, sparkling with wit, abounding in clever anecdotes, sometimes discursive, yet never losing sight of the main purpose. The prose of Holmes is always fascinating, and truly representative of the genial "Autocrat" himself.

THE PROFESSOR'S PAPER[1]

MY friend, the Professor, began talking with me one day in a dreary sort of way.[2] I couldn't get at the difficulty for a good while, but at last it turned out that somebody had been calling him an old man. He didn't mind his students calling him *the* old man, he said. That was a technical expression, and he thought that he remembered hearing it applied to himself when he was about twenty-five. It may be considered as a familiar and sometimes endearing appellation. An Irishwoman calls her husband "the old man," and he returns the caressing expression by speaking of her as "the old woman." But now, said he, just suppose a case like one of these. A young stranger is overheard talking of you as a very nice old gentleman. A friendly and genial critic speaks of your green old age as illustrating the truth of some axiom you had uttered with reference to that period of life. What *I* call an old man is a person with a smooth, shining crown and a fringe of scattered white hairs, seen in the streets on sunshiny days, stooping as he walks, bearing a cane, moving cautiously and slowly; telling old stories, smiling at present follies, living in a narrow world of dry habits; one that remains waking when others have dropped asleep, and keeps a little night-lamp-flame of life burning year after year, if the lamp is not upset, and there is only a careful hand held round it to prevent the puffs of wind from blowing the flame out. That's what I call an old man.

Now, said the Professor, you don't mean to tell me that I

[1] This particular record is noteworthy principally for containing a paper by my friend, the Professor, with a poem or two annexed or intercalated. I would suggest to young persons that they should pass over it for the present, and read, instead of it, that story about the young man who was in love with the young lady, and in great trouble for something like nine pages, but happily married on the tenth page or thereabouts, which, I take it for granted, will be contained in the periodical where this is found, unless it differ from all other publications of the kind. Perhaps, if such young people will lay the number aside, and take it up ten years, or a little more, from the present time, they may find something in it for their advantage. They can't possibly understand it all now.

[2] This is one of the essays included in "The Autocrat of the Breakfast Table."

have got to that yet? Why, bless you, I am several years short of the time when—[I knew what was coming, and could hardly keep from laughing; twenty years ago he used to quote it as one of those absurd speeches men of genius will make, and now he is going to argue from it]—several years short of the time when Balzac says that men are—most—you know—dangerous to—the hearts of—in short, most to be dreaded by duennas that have charge of susceptible females. What age is that? said I, statistically. Fifty-two years, answered the Professor. Balzac ought to know, said I, if it is true that Goethe said of him that each of his stories must have been dug out of a woman's heart. But fifty-two is a high figure.

Stand in the light of the window, Professor, said I. The Professor took up the desired position. You have white hairs, I said. Had 'em any time these twenty years, said the Professor. And the crow's-foot, *pesanserinus*, rather. The Professor smiled, as I wanted him to, and the folds radiated like the ridges of a half-opened fan, from the outer corner of the eyes to the temples. And the calipers, said I. What are the calipers? he asked, curiously. Why, the parenthesis, said I. Parenthesis? said the Professor; what's that? Why, look in the glass when you are disposed to laugh, and see if your mouth isn't framed in a couple of crescent lines—so, my boy ( ). It's all nonsense, said the Professor; just look at my biceps;—and he began pulling off his coat to show me his arm. Be careful, said I; you can't bear exposure to the air, at your time of life, as you could once. I will box with you, said the Professor, row with you, walk with you, ride with you, swim with you, or sit at table with you, for fifty dollars a side. Pluck survives stamina, I answered.

The Professor went off a little out of humor. A few weeks afterwards he came in, looking very good-natured, and brought me a paper, which I have here, and from which I shall read you some portions, if you don't object. He had been thinking the matter over, he said—had read Cicero "De Senectute," and made up his mind to meet old age half-way. These were some of his reflections that he had written down; so here you have

THE PROFESSOR'S PAPER

There is no doubt when old age begins. The human body is a furnace which keeps in blast three-score years and ten, more or less. It burns about three hundred pounds of carbon a year (besides other fuel), when in fair working order, according to a great chemist's estimate. When the fire slackens life declines; when it goes out, we are dead.

It has been shown by some noted French experimenters that the amount of combustion increases up to about the thirtieth year, remains stationary to about forty-five, and then diminishes. This last is the point where old age starts from. The great fact of physical life is the perpetual commerce with the elements, and the fire is the measure of it.

About this time of life, if food is plenty where you live—for that, you know, regulates matrimony—you may be expecting to find yourself a grandfather some fine morning; a kind of domestic felicity that gives one a cool shiver of delight to think of, as among the not remotely possible events.

I don't mind much those slipshod lines Dr. Johnson wrote to Thrale, telling her about life's declining from thirty-five; the furnace is in full blast for ten years longer, as I have said. The Romans came very near the mark; their age of enlistment reached from seventeen to forty-six years.

What is the use of fighting against the seasons, or the tides, or the movements of the planetary bodies, or this ebb in the wave of life that flows through us? We are old fellows from the moment the fire begins to go out. Let us always behave like gentlemen when we are introduced to new acquaintances.

Incipit Allegoria Senectutis

Old Age, this is Mr. Professor; Mr. Professor, this is Old Age.

Old Age: Mr. Professor, I hope to see you well. I have known you for some time, though I think you did not know me. Shall we walk down the street together?

Professor (drawing back a little): We can talk more quietly, perhaps, in my study. Will you tell me how it is you seem to be acquainted with everybody you are introduced to, though he evidently considers you an entire stranger?

Old Age: I make it a rule never to force myself upon a person's recognition until I have known him at least five years.

Professor: Do you mean to say that you have known me so long as that?

Old Age: I do. I left my card on you longer ago than that, but I am afraid you never read it; yet I see you have it with you.

Professor: Where?

Old Age: There, between your eyebrows—three straight lines running up and down; all the probate courts know that token—"Old Age, his mark." Put your forefinger on the inner end of one eyebrow, and your middle finger on the inner end of the other eyebrow; now separate the fingers, and you will smooth out my sign-manual; that's the way you used to look before I left my card on you.

Professor: What message do people generally send back when you first call on them?

Old Age: Not at home. Then I leave a card and go. Next year I call; get the same answer; leave another card. So for five or six—sometimes ten years or more. At last, if they don't let me in, I break in through the front door or the windows.

We talked together in this way some time. Then Old Age said again: Come, let us walk down the street together—and offered me a cane, an eyeglass, a tippet, and a pair of over-shoes. No, much obliged to you, said I. I don't want those things, and I had a little rather talk with you here, privately, in my study. So I dressed myself up in a jaunty way and walked out alone—got a fall, caught a cold, was laid up with a lumbago, and had time to think over this whole matter.

Explicit Allegoria Senectutis

We have settled when old age begins. Like all nature's processes, it is gentle and gradual in its approaches, strewed with illusions, and all its little griefs soothed by natural sedatives. But the iron hand is not less irresistible because it wears the velvet glove. The button-wood throws off its bark in large flakes, which one may find lying at its foot, pushed out, and at last pushed off, by that tranquil movement from beneath, which is too slow to be seen, but too powerful to be arrested. One finds them always, but one rarely sees them fall. So it is our youth drops from us—scales off, sapless and lifeless, and lays bare the tender and immature fresh growth of old age. Looked at collectively, the changes of old age appear as a series of personal insults and indignities, terminating at last in death, which Sir Thomas Browne has called "the very disgrace and ignominy of our natures."

My lady's cheek can boast no more
The cranberry white and pink it wore;
And where her shining locks divide,
The parting line is all too wide——

No, no—this will never do. Talk about men, if you will, but spare the poor women.

We have a brief description of seven stages of life by a remarkably good observer. It is very presumptuous to attempt to add to it, yet I have been struck with the fact that life admits of a natural analysis into no less than fifteen distinct periods. Taking the five primary divisions, infancy, childhood, youth, manhood, old age, each of these has its own three periods of immaturity, complete development, and decline. I recognize an old baby at once—with its "pipe and mug" (a stick of candy and a porringer)—so does everybody; and an old child shedding its milk-teeth is only a little prototype of the old man shedding his permanent ones. Fifty or thereabouts is only the childhood, as it were, of old age; the graybeard youngster must be weaned from his late suppers now. So you will see that you have to make fifteen stages at any rate, and that it would not be hard to make twenty-five; five primary, each with five secondary divisions.

The infancy and childhood of commencing old age have the same ingenuous simplicity and delightful unconsciousness about them that the first stage of the earlier periods of life shows. The great delusion of mankind is in supposing that to be individual and exceptional which is universal and according to law. A person is always startled when he hears himself seriously called an old man for the first time.

Nature gets us out of youth into manhood, as sailors are hurried on board of vessels—in a state of intoxication. We are hustled into maturity reeling with our passions and imaginations, and we have drifted far away from port before we awake out of our illusions. But to carry us out of maturity into old age, without our knowing where we are going, she drugs us with strong opiates, and so we stagger along with wide open eyes that see nothing until snow enough has fallen on our heads to rouse our comatose brains out of their stupid trances.

There is one mark of age that strikes me more than any of the physical ones; I mean the formation of habits. An old man who shrinks into himself falls into ways that become as positive and as much beyond the reach of outside influences as if they were governed by clock-work. The animal functions, as the physiologists call them, in distinction from the organic, tend, in the process of deterioration to which age and neglect united gradually lead them, to assume the periodical or rhythmical type of movement. Every man's heart (this organ belongs, you know, to the organic system) has a regular mode of action; but I know a great many men whose brains, and all their voluntary existence flowing from their brains, have a systole and diastole as regular as that of the heart itself. Habit is the approximation of the animal system to the organic. It is a confession of failure in the highest function of being, which involves a perpetual self-determination, in full view of all existing circumstances. But habit, you see, is an action in present circumstances from past motives. It is substituting a *vis a tergo* for the evolution of living force.

When a man, instead of burning up three hundred pounds of carbon a year, has got down to two hundred and fifty, it is plain enough he must economize force somewhere. Now habit is a labor-saving invention which enables a man to get along with less fuel—that is all; for fuel is force, you know, just as much in the page I am writing for you as in the locomotive or the legs that carry it to you. Carbon is the same thing, whether you call it wood, or coal, or bread and cheese. A reverend gentleman demurred to this statement, as if, because combustion is asserted to be the *sine qua non* of thought, therefore thought is alleged to be a purely chemical process. Facts of chemistry are one thing, I told him, and facts of consciousness another. It can be proved to him, by a very simple analysis of some of his spare elements, that every Sunday, when he does his duty faithfully, he uses up more phosphorus out of his brain and nerves than on ordinary days. But then he had his choice whether to do his duty, or to neglect it, and save his phosphorus and other combustibles.

It follows from all this that the formation of habits ought naturally to be, as it is, the special characteristic of age. As for the muscular powers, they pass their maximum long before the time when the true decline of life begins, if we may judge by the experience of the ring. A man is "stale," I think, in their language, soon after thirty—often, no doubt, much earlier, as gentlemen of the pugilistic profession are exceedingly apt to keep their vital fire burning with the blower up.

So far without Tully. But in the mean time I have been reading the treatise "De Senectute." It is not long, but a leisurely performance. The old gentleman was sixty-three years of age when he addressed it to his friend T. Pomponius Atticus, Esq., a person of distinction, some two or three years older. We read it when we are schoolboys, forget all about it for thirty years, and then take it up again by a natural instinct—provided always that we read Latin as we drink water, without stopping to taste it, as all of us who ever learned it at school or college ought to do.

Cato is the chief speaker in the dialogue. A good deal of it is what would be called in vulgar phrase "slow." It unpacks and unfolds incidental illustrations which a modern writer would look at the back of, and toss each to its pigeon-hole. I think ancient classics and ancient people are alike in the tendency to this kind of expansion.

An old doctor came to me once (this is literal fact) with some contrivance or other for people with broken kneepans. As the patient would be confined for a good while, he might find it dull work to sit with his hands in his lap. Reading, the ingenious inventor suggested, would be an agreeable mode of passing the time. He mentioned, in his written account of his contrivance, various works that might amuse the weary hour. I remember only three—"Don Quixote," "Tom Jones," and Watts's "On the Mind."

It is not generally understood that Cicero's essay was delivered as a lyceum lecture (*concio popularis*) at the temple of

Mercury. The journals (*papyri*) of the day ("Tempora Quotidiana," "Tribunas Quirinalis," "Præco Romanus," and the rest) gave abstracts of it, one of which I have translated and modernized, as being a substitute for the analysis I intended to make.

"IV. Kal. Mart. . . .

"The lecture at the temple of Mercury, last evening, was well attended by the *élite* of our great city. Two hundred thousand sestertia were thought to have been represented in the house. The doors were besieged by a mob of shabby fellows (*illotum vulgus*), who were at length quieted after two or three had been somewhat roughly handled (*gladio jugulati*). The speaker was the well-known Mark Tully, Esq.; the subject, Old Age. Mr. T. has a lean and scraggy person, with a very unpleasant excrescence upon his nasal feature, from which his nickname of chick-pea (Cicero) is said by some to be derived. As a lecturer is public property, we may remark that his outer garment (*toga*) was of cheap stuff and somewhat worn, and that his general style and appearance of dress and manner (*habitus, vestitusque*) were somewhat provincial.

"The lecture consisted of an imaginary dialogue between Cato and Lælius. We found the first portion rather heavy, and retired a few moments for refreshments (*pocula quædam vini*). All want to reach old age, says Cato, and grumble when they get it; therefore they are donkeys. The lecturer will allow us to say that he is the donkey; we know we shall grumble at old age, but we want to live through youth and manhood, in spite of the troubles we shall groan over. There was considerable prosing as to what old age can do and can't. True, but not new. Certainly, old folks can't jump—break the necks of their thigh-bones (*femorum cervices*) if they do—can't crack nuts with their teeth; can't climb a greased pole (*malum inunctum scandere non possunt*); but they can tell old stories and give you good advice; if they know what you have made up your mind to do when you ask them. All this is well enough, but won't set the Tiber on fire (*Tiberim accendere nequaquam potest*).

"There were some clever things enough (*dicta haud inepta*), a few of which are worth reporting. Old people are accused of being forgetful; but they never forget where they have put their money. Nobody is so old he doesn't think he can live a year. The lecturer quoted an ancient maxim, 'Grow old early, if you would be old long,' but disputed it. Authority, he thought, was the chief privilege of age. It is not great to have money, but fine to govern those that have it. Old age begins at forty-six years, according to the common opinion. It is not every kind of old age or of wine that grows sour with time. Some excellent remarks were made on immortality, but mainly borrowed from and credited to Plato. Several pleasing anecdotes were told—Old Milo, champion of the heavy-weights in his day, looked at his arms and whimpered, 'They are dead.' Not so dead as you, you old fool, says Cato; you never were good for anything but for your shoulders and flanks. Pisistratus asked Solon what made him dare to be so obstinate. Old age, said Solon.

"The lecture was on the whole acceptable, and a credit to our culture and civilization. The reporter goes on to state that there will be no lecture next week, on account of the expected combat between the bear and the barbarian. Betting (*sponsio*) two to one (*duo ad unum*) on the bear."

After all, the most encouraging things I find in the treatise, "De Senectute," are the stories of men who have found new occupations when growing old, or kept up their common pursuits in the extreme period of life. Cato learned Greek when he was old, and speaks of wishing to learn the fiddle, or some such instrument (*fidibus*), after the example of Socrates. Solon learned something new, every day, in his old age, as he gloried to proclaim. Cyrus pointed out with pride and pleasure the trees he had planted with his own hand. [I remember a pillar on the Duke of Northumberland's estate at Alnwick, with an inscription in similar words, if not the same. That, like other country pleasures, never wears out. None is too rich, none too poor, none too young, none too old to enjoy it.] There is a New England story I have heard more to the point, however, than any of Cicero's. A young farmer was urged to set out some apple-trees. No, said he, they are too long growing, and I don't want to plant for other people. The young farmer's father was spoken to about it; but he, with better reason, alleged that apple-trees were slow and life was fleeting. At last some one mentioned it to the old grandfather of the young farmer. He had nothing else to do, so he stuck in some trees. He lived long enough to drink barrels of cider made from the apples that grew on those trees.

As for myself, after visiting a friend lately—[Do remember all the time that this is the Professor's paper]—I satisfied myself that I had better concede the fact that—my contemporaries are not so young as they have been—and that—awkward as it is—science and history agree in telling me that I can claim the immunities and must own the humiliations of the early stage of senility. Ah! but we have all gone down the hill together. The dandies of my time have split their waistbands and taken to high-low shoes. The beauties of my recollections—where are they? They have run the gantlet of the years as well as I. First the years pelted them with red roses till their cheeks were all on fire. By and by they began throwing white roses, and that morning flush passed away. As last one of the years threw a snow-ball, and after that no year let the poor girls pass without throwing snow-balls. And then came rougher missiles—ice and stones; and from time to time an arrow whistled, and down went one of the poor girls. So there are but few left; and we don't call those few *girls*, but——

Ah, me! here am I groaning just as the old Greek sighed ***Aî aî*** ! and the old Roman *Eheu!* I have no doubt we should die of shame and grief at the indignities offered us by age, if it were not that we see so many others as badly or worse off than ourselves. We always compare ourselves with our contemporaries.

[I was interrupted in my reading just here. Before I began at the next breakfast, I read them these verses; I hope you will like them, and get a useful lesson from them.]

THE LAST BLOSSOM

Though young no more, we still would dream
  Of beauty's dear deluding wiles;
The leagues of life to graybeards seem
  Shorter than boyhood's lingering miles.

Who knows a woman's wild caprice?
  It played with Goethe's silvered hair,
And many a Holy Father's "niece"
  Has softly smoothed the papal chair.

When sixty bids us sigh in vain
  To melt the heart of sweet sixteen,
We think upon those ladies twain
  Who loved so well the tough old dean.

We see the patriarch's wintry face,
  The maid of Egypt's dusky glow,
And dream that youth and age embrace,
  As April violets fill with snow.

Tranced in her lord's Olympian smile
  His lotus-loving Memphian lies—
The musky daughter of the Nile
  With plaited hair and almond eyes.

Might we but share one wild caress
  Ere life's autumnal blossoms fall,
And earth's brown, clinging lips impress
  The long cold kiss that waits us all!

My bosom heaves, remembering yet
  The morning of that blissful day
When Rose, the flower of spring, I met,
  And gave my raptured soul away.

Flung from her eyes of purest blue,
  A lasso, with its leaping chain
Light as a loop of larkspurs, flew
  O'er sense and spirit, heart and brain.

Thou com'st to cheer my waning age,
  Sweet vision, waited for so long!
Dove that wouldst seek the poet's cage
  Lured by the magic breath of song!

She blushes! Ah, reluctant maid,
  Love's *drapeau rouge* the truth has told!
O'er girlhood's yielding barricade
  Floats the great Leveller's crimson fold!

Come to my arms!—love heeds not years;
  No frost the bud of passion knows.
Ha! what is this my frenzy hears?
  A voice behind me uttered, Rose!

Sweet was her smile—but not for me:
  Alas, when woman looks too kind,
Just turn your foolish head and see—
  Some youth is walking close behind!

As to giving up because the almanac or the family Bible says that it is about time to do it, I have no intention of doing any such thing. I grant you that I burn less carbon than some years ago. I see people of my standing really good for nothing, decrepit, effete *la lèvre inferieure déjà pendante,* with what little life they have left mainly concentrated in their epigastrium. But as the disease of old age is epidemic, endemic, and sporadic, and everybody that lives long enough is sure to catch it, I am going to say, for the encouragement of such as need it, how I treat the malady in my own case.

First. As I feel, that, when I have anything to do, there is less time for it than when I was younger, I find that I give my attention more thoroughly, and use my time more economically than ever before; so that I can learn anything twice as easily as in my earlier days. I am not, therefore, afraid to attack a new study. I took up a difficult language a very few years ago with good success, and think of mathematics and metaphysics by and by.

Secondly. I have opened my eyes to a good many neglected privileges and pleasures within my reach, and requiring only a little courage to enjoy them. You may well suppose it pleased me to find that old Cato was thinking of learning to play the fiddle, when I had deliberately taken it up in my old age, and satisfied myself that I could get much comfort, if not much music, out of it.

Thirdly. I have found that some of those active exercises, which are commonly thought to belong to young folks only, may be enjoyed at a much later period.

A young friend has lately written an admirable article in one of the journals, entitled "Saints and their Bodies." Approving of his general doctrines, and grateful for his records of personal experience, I cannot refuse to add my own experimental confirmation of his eulogy of one particular form of active exercise and amusement, namely, boating. For the past nine years I have rowed about, during a good part of the summer, on fresh or salt water. My present fleet on the river Charles consists of three row-boats. 1. A small flat-bottomed skiff of the shape of a flat-iron, kept mainly to lend to boys. 2. A fancy "dory" for two pairs of sculls, in which I sometimes go out with my young folks. 3. My own particular water-sulky, a "skeleton" or "shell" race-boat, twenty-two feet long, with huge outriggers, which boat I pull with ten-foot sculls—alone, of course, as it holds but one, and tips him out, if he doesn't mind what he is about. In this I glide along the Back Bay, down the stream, up the Charles to Cambridge and Watertown, up the Mystic, round the wharves, in the wake of steamboats, which have a swell after them delightful to rock upon; I linger under the bridges—those "caterpillar bridges" as my brother Professor so happily called them; rub against the black sides of old wood-schooners; cool down under the overhanging stern of some tall Indiaman; stretch across to the Navy-Yard, where the sentinel warns me off from the Ohio—just as if I should hurt her by lying in her shadow; then strike out into the harbor, where the water gets clear and the air smells of the ocean—till all at once I remember, that, if a west wind blows up of a sudden, I shall drift along past the islands, out of sight of the dear old State-house—plate, tumbler, knife, and fork all waiting at home, but no chair drawn up to the table—all the dear people waiting, waiting, waiting, while the boat is sliding, sliding, sliding into the great desert, where there is no tree and no fountain. As I don't want my wreck to be washed up on one of the beaches in company with devils'-aprons, bladder-weeds, dead horse-shoes, and bleached crab-shells, I turn about and flap my long, narrow wings for home. When the tide is running out swiftly I have a splendid fight to get through the bridges, but always make it a rule to beat—though I have been jammed up into pretty tight places at times, and was caught once between a vessel swinging round and the pier, until our bones (the boat's that is) cracked as if we had been in the jaws of Behemoth. Then back to my moorings at the foot of the Common, off with the rowing dress, dash under the green translucent wave, return to the garb of civilization, walk through my Garden, take a look at my elms on the Common, and, reaching my habitat, in consideration of my advanced period of life, indulge in the elysian abandonment of a huge recumbent chair.

When I have established a pair of well-pronounced feathering-calluses on my thumbs, when I am in training so that I can do my fifteen miles at a stretch without coming to grief in any way, when I can perform my mile in eight minutes or a little less, then I feel as if I had old Time's head in chancery, and could give it to him at my leisure.

I do not deny the attraction of walking. I have bored this ancient city through and through in my daily travels, until I know it as an old inhabitant of a Cheshire knows his cheese. Why, it was I who, in the course of these rambles, discovered that remarkable avenue called Myrtle Street, stretching in one long line from east of the Reservoir to a precipitous and rudely paved cliff which looks down on the grim abode of science, and beyond it to the far hills; a promenade so delicious in its repose, so cheerfully varied with glimpses down the northern slope into busy Cambridge Street with its iron river of the horse railroad, and wheeled barges gliding back and forward over it—so delightfully closing at its western extremity in sunny courts and passages where I know peace, and beauty, and virtue, and serene old age must be perpetual tenants—so alluring to all who desire to take their daily stroll, in the words of Dr. Watts—

"Alike unknowing and unknown"—

that nothing but a sense of duty would have prompted me to reveal the secret of its existence. I concede, therefore, that walking is an immeasurably fine invention, of which old age ought constantly to avail itself.

Saddle-leather is in some respects even preferable to sole-leather. The principal objection to it is of a financial character. But you may be sure that Bacon and Sydenham did not recommend it for nothing. One's *hepar*, or, in vulgar language, liver—a ponderous organ, weighing some three or four pounds—goes up and down like the dasher of a churn in the midst of the other vital arrangements, at every step of a trotting horse. The brains also are shaken up like coppers in a money-box. Riding is good, for those that are born with a silver-mounted bridle in their hand, and can ride as much and as often as they like, without thinking all the time they hear that steady grinding sound as the horse's jaws triturate with calm lateral movement the bank-bills and promises to pay upon which it is notorious that the profligate animal in question feeds day and night.

Instead, however, of considering these kinds of exercise in this empirical way, I will devote a brief space to an examination of them in a more scientific form.

The pleasure of exercise is due first to a purely physical impression, and secondly to a sense of power in action. The first source of pleasure varies of course with our condition and the state of the surrounding circumstances; the second with the amount and kind of power, and the extent and kind of action. In all forms of active exercise there are three powers simultaneously in action—the will, the muscles, and the intellect. Each of these predominates in different kinds of exercise. In walking, the will and muscles are so accustomed to work together and perform their task with so little expenditure of force, that the intellect is left comparatively free. The mental pleasure in walking, as such, is in the sense of power over all our moving machinery. But in riding, I have the additional pleasure of governing another will, and my muscles extend to the tips of the animal's ears and to his four hoofs, instead of stopping at my hands and feet. Now in this extension of my volition and my physical frame into another animal, my tyrannical instincts and my desire for heroic strength are at once gratified. When the horse ceases to have a will of his own and his muscles require no special attention on your part, then you may live on horseback as Wesley did, and write sermons or take naps, as you like. But you will observe, that, in riding on horseback, you always have a feeling, that, after all, it is not you that do the work, but the animal, and this prevents the satisfaction from being complete.

Now let us look at the conditions of rowing. I won't suppose you to be disgracing yourself in one of those miserable tubs, tugging in which is to rowing the true boat what riding a cow is to bestriding an Arab. You know the Esquimau *kayak* (if that is the name of it), don't you? Look at that model of one over my door. Sharp, rather? On the contrary, it is a lubber to the one you and I must have; a Dutch fish-wife to Psyche, contrasted with what I will tell you about. Our boat, then, is something of the shape of a pickerel, as you look down upon his back, he lying in the sunshine just where the sharp edge of the water cuts in among the lily-pads. It is a kind of a giant pod, as one may say—tight everywhere, except in a little place in the middle, where you sit. Its length is from seven to ten yards, and as it is only from sixteen to thirty inches wide in its widest part, you understand why you want those "outriggers," or projecting iron frames with the rowlocks in which the oars play. My rowlocks are five feet apart; double or more than double the greatest width of the boat.

Here you are, then, afloat with a body a rod and a half long, with arms, or wings as you may choose to call them, stretching more than twenty feet from tip to tip; every volition of yours extending as perfectly into them as if your spinal cord ran down the centre strip of your boat, and the nerves of your arms tingled as far as the broad blades of your oars—oars of spruce, balanced, leathered, and ringed under your own special direction. This, in sober earnest, is the nearest approach to flying that man has ever made or perhaps ever will make. As the hawk sails without flapping his pinions, so you drift with the tide when you will, in the most luxurious form of locomotion indulged to an embodied spirit. But if your blood wants rousing, turn round that stake in the river, which you see a mile from here; and when you come in in sixteen minutes (if you do, for we are old boys, and not champion scullers, you remember) then say if you begin to feel a little warmed up or not! You can row easily and gently all day, and you can row yourself blind and black in the face in ten minutes, just as you like. It has been long agreed that there is no way in which a man can accomplish so much labor with his muscles as in rowing. It is in the boat, then, that man finds the largest extension of his volitional and muscular existence; and yet he may tax both of them so slightly, in that most delicious of exercises, that he shall mentally write his sermon, or his poem, or recall the remarks he has made in company and put them in form for the public, as well as in his easy-chair.

I dare not publicly name the rare joys, the infinite delights, that intoxicate me on some sweet June morning, when the river and bay are smooth as a sheet of beryl-green silk, and I run along ripping it up with my knife-edged shell of a boat, the rent closing after me like those wounds of angels which Milton tells of, but the seam still shining for many a long rood behind me. To lie still over the Flats, where the waters are shallow, and see the crabs crawling and the sculpins gliding busily and silently beneath the boat, to rustle in through the long harsh grass that leads up some tranquil creek, to take shelter from the sunbeams under one of the thousand-footed bridges, and look down its interminable colonnades, crusted with green and oozy growths, studded with minute barnacles, and belted with rings of dark mussels, while overhead streams and thunders that other river whose every wave is a human soul flowing to eternity as the river below flows to the ocean; lying there moored unseen, in loneliness so profound that the columns of Tadmor in the desert could not seem more remote from life, the cool breeze on one's forehead, the stream whispering against the half-sunken pillars—why should I tell of these things, that I should live to see my beloved haunts invaded and the waves blackened with boats as with a swarm of water-beetles? What a city of idiots we must be not to have covered the glorious bay with gondolas and wherries, as we have just learned to cover the ice in winter with skaters!

I am satisfied that such a set of black-coated, stiff-jointed, soft-muscled, paste-complexioned youth as we can boast in our Atlantic cities never before sprang from loins of Anglo-Saxon lineage. Of the females that are the mates of these males I do not here speak. I preached my sermon from the lay-pulpit on this matter a good while ago. Of course, if you heard it, you know my belief is that the total climatic influences here are getting up a number of new patterns of humanity, some of which are not an improvement on the old model. Clipper-built, sharp in the bows, long in the spars, slender to look at, and fast to go, the ship, which is the great organ of our national life of relation, is but a reproduction of the typical form which the elements impress upon its builder. All this we cannot help; but we can make the best of these influences, such as they are. We have a few good boatmen, no good horsemen that I hear of, nothing remarkable, I believe, in cricketing, and as for any great athletic feat performed by a gentleman in these latitudes, society would drop a man who should run round the Common in five minutes. Some of our amateur fencers, single-stick players, and boxers, we have no reason to be ashamed of. Boxing is rough play, but not too rough for a hearty young fellow. Anything is better than this white-blooded degeneration to which we all tend.

I dropped into a gentlemen's sparring exhibition only last evening. It did my heart good to see that there were a few young and youngish youths left who could take care of their own heads in case of emergency. It is a fine sight, that of a gentleman resolving himself into the primitive constituents of his humanity. Here is a delicate young man now, with an intellectual countenance, a slight figure, a sub-pallid complexion, a most unassuming deportment, a mild adolescent in fact, that any Hiram or Jonathan from between the plough-tails would of course expect to handle with perfect ease. Oh, he is taking off his gold-bowed spectacles! Ah, he is divesting himself of his cravat! Why, he is stripping off his coat! Well, here he is, sure enough, in a tight silk shirt, and with two things that look like batter puddings in the place of his fists. Now see that other fellow with another pair of batter puddings—the big one with the broad shoulders; he will certainly knock the little man's head off, if he strikes him. Feinting, dodging, stopping, hitting, countering—little man's head not off yet. You might as well try to jump upon your own shadow as to hit the little man's intellectual features. He needn't have taken off the gold-bowed spectacles at all. Quick, cautious, shifty, nimble, cool, he catches all the fierce lunges or gets out of their reach, till his turn comes, and then, whack goes one of the batter puddings against the big one's ribs, and bang goes the other into the big one's face, and staggering, shuffling, slipping, tripping, collapsing, sprawling, down goes the big one in a miscellaneous bundle. If my young friend, whose excellent article I have referred to, could only introduce the manly art of self-defence among the clergy, I am satisfied that we should have better sermons and an infinitely less quarrelsome church-militant. A bout with the gloves would let off the ill-nature and cure the indigestion, which, united, have embroiled their subject in a bitter controversy. We should then often hear that a point of difference between an infallible and a heretic, instead of being vehemently discussed in a series of newspaper articles, had been settled by a friendly contest in several rounds, at the close of which the parties shook hands and appeared cordially reconciled.

But boxing you and I are too old for, I am afraid. I was for a moment tempted, by the contagion of muscular electricity last evening, to try the gloves with the Benicia Boy, who looked in as a friend to the noble art; but remembering that he had twice my weight and half my age, besides the advantage of his training, I sat still and said nothing.

There is one other delicate point I wish to speak of with reference to old age. I refer to the use of dioptric media which correct the diminished refracting power of the humors of the eye—in other words, spectacles. I don't use them. All I ask is a large, fair type, a strong daylight or gas-light, and one yard of focal distance, and my eyes are as good as ever. But if your eyes fail, I can tell you something encouraging. There is now living in New York State an old gentleman who, perceiving his sight to fail, immediately took to exercising it on the finest print, and in this way fairly bullied Nature out of her foolish habit of taking liberties at five-and-forty, or thereabout. And now this old gentleman performs the most extraordinary feats with his pen, showing that his eyes must be a pair of microscopes. I should be afraid to say to you how much he writes in the compass of a half-dime—whether the Psalms or the Gospels, or the Psalms and the Gospels, I won't be positive.

But now let me tell you this. If the time comes when you must lay down the fiddle and the bow, because your fingers are too stiff, and drop the ten-foot sculls, because your arms are too weak, and after dallying awhile with eyeglasses, come at last to the undisguised reality of spectacles—if the time comes when that fire of life we spoke of has burned so low that where its flames reverberated there is only the sombre stain of regret, and where its coals glowed, only the white ashes that cover the embers of memory—don't let your heart grow cold, and you may carry cheerfulness and love with you into the teens of your second century, if you can last so long. As our friend, the poet, once said, in some of those old-fashioned heroics of his which he keeps for his private reading—

> Call him not old, whose visionary brain
> Holds o'er the past its undivided reign.
> For him in vain the envious seasons roll
> Who bears eternal summer in his soul.
> If yet the minstrel's song, the poet's lay,
> Spring with her birds, or children with their play,
> Or maiden's smile, or heavenly dream of art
> Stir the few life-drops creeping round his heart—
> Turn to the record where his years are told—
> Count his gray hairs—they cannot make him old!

End of the Professor's paper

[The above essay was not read at one time, but in several instalments, and accompanied by various comments from different persons at the table. The company were in the main attentive, with the exception of a little somnolence on the part of the old gentleman opposite at times, and a few sly, malicious questions about the "old boys" on the part of that forward young fellow who has figured occasionally, not always to his advantage, in these reports.

On Sunday mornings, in obedience to a feeling I am not ashamed of, I have always tried to give a more appropriate character to our conversation. I have never read them my sermon yet, and I don't know that I shall, as some of them might take my convictions as a personal indignity to themselves. But having read our company so much of the Professor's talk about age and other subjects connected with physical life, I took the next Sunday morning to repeat to them the following poem of his, which I have had by me some time. He calls it—I suppose, for his professional friends—"The Anatomist's Hymn"; but I shall name it—]

THE LIVING TEMPLE

Not in the world of light alone,
Where God has built his blazing throne,
Nor yet alone in earth below,
With belted seas that come and go,
And endless isles of sunlit green,
Is all thy Maker's glory seen:
Look in upon thy wondrous frame—
Eternal wisdom still the same!

The smooth, soft air with pulse-like waves
Flows murmuring through its hidden caves,
Whose streams of brightening purple rush
Fired with a new and livelier blush,
While all their burden of decay
The ebbing current steals away,
And red with Nature's flame they start
From the warm fountains of the heart.

No rest that throbbing slave may ask,
Forever quivering o'er his task,
While far and wide a crimson jet
Leaps forth to fill the woven net
Which in unnumbered crossing tides
The flood of burning life divides,
Then kindling each decaying part
Creeps back to find the throbbing heart.

But warned with that unchanging flame
Behold the outward moving frame,
Its living marbles jointed strong
With glistening band and silvery thong,
And linked to reason's guiding reins
By myriad rings in trembling chains,
Each graven with the threaded zone
Which claims it at the master's own.

See how yon beam of seeming white
Is braided out of seven-hued light,
Yet in those lucid globes no ray
By any chance shall break astray.
Hark how the rolling surge of sound
Arches and spirals circling round,
Wakes the hushed spirit through thine ear
With music it is heaven to hear.

Then mark the cloven sphere that holds
All thought in its mysterious folds,
That feels sensation's faintest thrill
And flashes forth the sovereign will;
Think on the stormy world that dwells
Locked in its dim and clustering cells!
The lightning gleams of power it sheds
Along its hollow glassy threads!

O Father! grant thy love divine
To make these mystic temples thine!
When wasting age and wearying strife,
Have sapped the leaning walls of life,
When darkness gathers over all,
And the last tottering pillars fall,
Take the poor dust thy mercy warms
And mould it into heavenly forms!

THE OLD OAK OF ANDOVER

—

BY

HARRIET BEECHER STOWE

HARRIET BEECHER STOWE

1812—1896

Harriet Beecher Stowe was born in 1812 in the little town of Litchfield, Connecticut, where her father, Dr. Lyman Beecher, was a clergyman. Her mother died while Harriet was very young, leaving a family of eight children to the mother's care of her oldest sister Catherine. In 1826 Dr. Beecher received a call to Boston, and Harriet and Catherine went to Hartford, where the latter established a young ladies' school, in which Harriet was first a pupil and later an instructor. Six years later her father became the president of the Lane Theological Seminary at Cincinnati, Ohio, and the two sisters accompanied him to enter on another educational enterprise. It was during her residence in Cincinnati, on the border of the slave State of Kentucky, that Harriet was first deeply impressed by the sorrows of slavery. In 1836 she married Professor Stowe, one of the instructors in the theological seminary, and a man of lofty character and fine intellect. Mrs. Stowe at this period contributed regularly to the magazines, in spite of her numerous household cares.

In 1850 Professor Stowe was called to Bowdoin College, and the family removed to Brunswick. Here, during the next two years, Mrs. Stowe wrote "Uncle Tom's Cabin, or Life among the Lowly," the work appearing in serial form in the "National Era," published in Washington. She received only the paltry sum of three hundred dollars for the serial. In book form the work achieved a most astounding success, three thousand copies being sold on the day of publication, and three hundred thousand more during the first year. It was translated into forty languages, and became the most widely read novel ever written in the English language.

In 1853 the Stowes removed to Andover, where Professor Stowe became one of the leading teachers in the theological seminary. This period was one of the happiest and busiest of Mrs. Stowe's life, and Andover was always very dear to her. In 1856 "Dred" was published, and in 1859 she brought out "The Minister's Wooing," a work in which the author struck a new note, taking New England life instead of slavery for her theme. She made her first trip to Europe in 1853, her reception, especially in England, surpassing that ever accorded to a woman not of royal blood. During the war her literary activity was incessant. She strove especially to stir up sympathy for the Northern cause in England. Her noble "Appeal" to the women of England did perhaps as much for the cause of the Union as the eloquent speeches of her famous brother, Henry Ward Beecher. Her later books include "Agnes of Sorrento," "The Pearl of Orr's Island," and "Oldtown Folks." She also published a book of poems, including many of exquisite beauty. Professor Stowe died in 1886; Mrs. Stowe survived her husband ten years, passing away in 1896 at the age of eighty-five. Both were buried at Andover.

Mrs. Stowe's literary style is marked by intense earnestness, sympathy and religious conviction. Her pen appeals to the human heart with sympathetic and stirring effect. Even in her short sketches some definite purpose is always discernible, as in the charming paper on "The Old Oak of Andover," which begins as a reverie and ends as a sermon. When we consider that most of her life was passed amid household cares that gave little time for reading or meditation, the volume of her literary work and the beauty of her style are, indeed, remarkable.

THE OLD OAK OF ANDOVER

A Revery

SILENTLY, with dreamy languor, the fleecy snow is falling. Through the windows, flowery with blossoming geranium and heliotrope, through the downward sweep of crimson and muslin curtain, one watches it as the wind whirls and sways it in swift eddies.

Right opposite our house, on our Mount Clear, is an old oak, the apostle of the primeval forest. Once, when this place was all wildwood, the man who was seeking a spot for the location of the buildings of Phillips Academy climbed this oak, using it as a sort of green watch tower, from whence he might gain a view of the surrounding country. Age and time, since then, have dealt hardly with the stanch old fellow. His limbs have been here and there shattered; his back begins to look mossy and dilapidated; but after all, there is a piquant, decided air about him, that speaks the old age of a tree of distinction, a kingly oak. To-day I see him standing, dimly revealed through the mist of falling snows; to-morrow's sun will show the outline of his gnarled limbs—all rose color with their soft snow burden; and again a few months, and spring will breathe on him, and he will draw a long breath, and break out once more, for the three hundredth time, perhaps, into a vernal crown of leaves. I sometimes think that leaves are the thoughts of trees, and that if we only knew it, we should find their life's experience recorded in them. Our oak! what a crop of meditations and remembrances must he have thrown forth, leafing out century after century. Awhile he spake and thought only of red deer and Indians; of the trillium that opened its white triangle in his shade; of the scented arbutus, fair as the pink ocean shell, weaving her fragrant mats in the moss at his feet; of feathery ferns, casting their silent shadows on the checkerberry leaves, and all those sweet, wild, nameless, half-mossy things, that live in the gloom of forests, and are only desecrated when brought to scientific light, laid out and stretched on a botanic bier. Sweet old forest days!—when blue jay, and yellow hammer, and bobolink made his leaves merry, and summer was a long opera of such music as Mozart dimly dreamed. But then came human kind bustling beneath; wondering, fussing, exploring, measuring, treading down flowers, cutting down trees, scaring bobolinks—and Andover, as men say, began to be settled.

Stanch men were they—these Puritan fathers of Andover. The old oak must have felt them something akin to himself. Such strong, wrestling limbs had they, so gnarled and knotted were they, yet so outbursting with a green and vernal crown, yearly springing, of noble and generous thoughts, rustling with leaves which shall be for the healing of nations.

These men were content with the hard, dry crust for themselves, that they might sow seeds of abundant food for us, their children; men out of whose hardness in enduring we gain leisure to be soft and graceful, through whose poverty we have become rich. Like Moses, they had for their portion only the pain and weariness of the wilderness, leaving to us the fruition of the promised land. Let us cherish for their sake the old oak, beautiful in its age as the broken statue of some antique wrestler, brown with time, yet glorious in its suggestion of past achievement.

I think all this the more that I have recently come across the following passage in one of our religious papers. The writer expresses a kind of sentiment which one meets very often upon this subject, and leads one to wonder what glamor could have fallen on the minds of any of the descendants of the Puritans, that they should cast nettles on those honored graves where they should be proud to cast their laurels.

"It is hard," he says, "for a lover of the beautiful—not a mere lover, but a believer in its divinity also—to forgive the Puritans, or to think charitably of them. It is hard for him to keep Forefathers' Day, or to subscribe to the Plymouth Monument; hard to look fairly at what they did, with the memory of what they destroyed rising up to choke thankfulness; for they were as one-sided and narrow-minded a set of men as ever lived, and saw one of truth's faces only—the hard, stern, practical face, without loveliness, without beauty, and only half dear to God.

The Puritan flew in the face of facts, not because he saw them and disliked them, but because he did not see them. He saw foolishness, lying, stealing, worldliness—the very mammon of unrighteousness rioting in the world and bearing sway—and he ran full tilt against the monster, hating it with a very mortal and mundane hatred, and anxious to see it bite the dust that his own horn might be exalted. It was in truth only another horn of the old dilemma, tossing and goring grace and beauty, and all the loveliness of life, as if they were the enemies instead of the sure friends of God and man."

Now, to those who say this we must ask the question with which Socrates of old pursued the sophist: What is beauty? If beauty be only physical, if it appeal only to the senses, if it be only an enchantment of graceful forms, sweet sounds, then indeed there might be something of truth in this sweeping declaration that the Puritan spirit is the enemy of beauty.

The very root and foundation of all artistic inquiry lies here. What is beauty? And to this question God forbid that we Christians should give a narrower answer than Plato gave in the old times before Christ arose, for he directs the aspirant who would discover the beautiful to "consider of greater value the beauty existing in the soul, than that existing in the body." More gracefully he teaches the same doctrine when he tells us that "there are two kinds of Venus (beauty), the one, the elder, who had no mother, and was the daughter of Uranus (heaven), whom we name the celestial; the other, younger, daughter of Jupiter and Dione, whom we call the vulgar."

Now, if disinterestedness, faith, patience, piety, have a beauty celestial and divine, then were our fathers worshippers of the beautiful. If high-mindedness and spotless honor are beautiful things, they had those. What work of art can compare with a lofty and heroic life? Is it not better to be a Moses than to be a Michael Angelo making statues of Moses? Is not the life of Paul a sublimer work of art than Raphael's cartoons? Are not the patience, the faith, the undying love of Mary by the cross, more beautiful than all the Madonna paintings in the world? If, then, we would speak truly of our fathers, we should say that, having their minds fixed on that celestial beauty of which Plato speaks, they held in slight esteem that more common and earthly.

Should we continue the parable in Plato's manner, we might say that the earthly and visible Venus, the outward grace of art and nature, was ordained of God as a priestess, through whom men were to gain access to the divine, invisible One; but that men, in their blindness, ever worship the priestess instead of the divinity.

Therefore it is that great reformers so often must break the shrines and temples of the physical and earthly beauty, when they seek to draw men upward to that which is high and divine.

Christ says of John the Baptist, "What went ye out for to see? A man clothed in soft raiment? Behold they which are clothed in soft raiment are in king's palaces." So was it when our fathers came here. There were enough wearing soft raiment and dwelling in kings' palaces. Life in papal Rome and prelatic England was weighed down with blossoming luxury. There were abundance of people to think of pictures, and statues, and gems, and cameos, vases and marbles, and all manner of deliciousness. The world was all drunk with the enchantments of the lower Venus, and it was needful that these men should come, Baptist-like in the wilderness, in raiment of camel's hair. We need such men now. Art, they tell us, is waking in America; a love of the beautiful is beginning to unfold its wings; but what kind of art, and what kind of beauty? Are we to fill our houses with pictures and gems, and to see that even our drinking cup and vase are wrought in graceful pattern, and to lose our reverence for self-denial, honor, and faith?

Is our Venus to be the frail, ensnaring Aphrodite, or the starry, divine Urania?

CHOICE EXAMPLES OF EARLY PRINTING AND ENGRAVING.

Fac-similes from Rare and Curious Books.

EARLY VENETIAN PRINTING.

Design from a book printed at Venice in 1487 by Bartolomeo Miniatore.

As Bernardo was called Pictor, the painter, so the printer Bartolomeo won the title of Miniatore by his drawings in miniatured pigment; he was a miniaturist in the literal sense of the term, and his talent is exhibited to advantage in the example before us. The classic origin of the design is evident, and nothing can be more delicate, more harmonious, and appropriate than the white forms on the red background. The quaint view of Ferrara is interesting, as giving an idea of the fortifications of a sixteenth-century Italian city.

FERARA.

PETER THE GREAT

—

BY

JOHN LOTHROP MOTLEY

JOHN LOTHROP MOTLEY

1814—1877

Born at Dorchester, Massachusetts, in 1814, John Lothrop Motley graduated from Harvard College in 1831, and, like Bancroft, travelled abroad to complete his education. After several years of study in the principal German universities, where he won the warm friendship of Bismarck, at that time a student at Göttingen, Motley returned to Boston and began the study of law. After practising a short time, he retired from the profession and turned his attention to literature. Two novels from his pen proved to be failures, and the young writer concluded that history rather than fiction was the true field for his enterprising genius. He had long been deeply interested in the eventful history of the Netherlands during their long struggle with Spain, and now selected this period as the subject of his investigation. In 1851 he went abroad a second time to study at first hand the wealth of material lying dormant in the libraries of Europe, and especially in the archives of Holland, Belgium, and Spain. Fortunately he was possessed of sufficient means to enable him to carry on this work thoroughly and deliberately. In 1856 the first of the three great divisions, into which the work had gradually shaped itself in his mind, was completed and published under the title " The Rise of the Dutch Republic." The work was at once recognized as one of the most notable historical productions of the day, and translations of it immediately appeared in Germany, France, and Holland.

In 1857 Motley returned to the United States, and assisted in establishing the " Atlantic Monthly." He soon found it necessary, however, to return to Europe, where alone could be found the books and manuscripts necessary for the continuation of his work. His researches carried him through the state papers at Brussels, the Spanish archives at Simancas, and he had occasion to visit the great libraries at London, Paris, Venice, and other European capitals. In 1860 appeared the first part of " The United Netherlands," and in 1868 the second part. In the mean time, in 1861, Motley had been appointed Minister to Austria. He was recalled in 1867, and in 1869 was appointed Minister to Great Britain. A year later he was abruptly called home on account, as is now known, of his friendship for Charles Sumner, at that moment in great disfavor with the administration. Although his recall under these circumstances was no disgrace, Motley looked upon it as such, and felt it keenly. In 1874 he published " The Life and Death of John of Barneveld." It was the historian's intention to make a history of the Thirty Years' War the third division of his historical labors, but death, in 1877, prevented the execution of this plan.

Motley is, perhaps, the most able and successful of American historians. In his skill in delineating character, and in presenting to the reader a comprehensive view of intricate events, he has not many equals, and few superiors. His style is masterly. He is one of the classical historians of the century. Throughout, his pages abound in brilliant description, in vivid, swift-moving narrative; they sparkle with a keen, and sometimes sarcastic humor, and often thrills us with passages of dramatic power.

PETER THE GREAT

ONE day, in the year 1697, the great Duke of Marlborough happened to be in the village of Saardam. He visited the dockyard of one Mynheer Calf, a rich shipbuilder, and was struck with the appearance of a journeyman at work there. He was a large, powerful man, dressed in a red woollen shirt and duck trousers, with a sailor's hat, and seated, with an adze in his hand, upon a rough log of timber which lay on the ground. The man's features were bold and regular, his dark brown hair fell in natural curls about his neck, his complexion was strong and ruddy, with veins somewhat distended, indicating an ardent temperament and more luxurious habits than comported with his station; and his dark, keen eye glanced from one object to another with remarkable restlessness. He was engaged in earnest conversation with some strangers, whose remarks he occasionally interrupted, while he rapidly addressed them in a guttural but not unmusical voice. As he became occasionally excited in conversation, his features twitched convulsively, the blood rushed to his forehead, his arms were tossed about with extreme violence of gesticulation, and he seemed constantly upon the point of giving way to some explosion of passion, or else of falling into a fit of catalepsy. His companions, however, did not appear alarmed by his vehemence, although they seemed to treat him with remarkable deference; and, after a short time, his distorted features would resume their symmetry and agreeable expression, his momentary frenzy would subside, and a bright smile would light up his whole countenance.

The duke inquired the name of this workman, and was told it was one Pieter Baas, a foreign journeyman of remarkable mechanical abilities and great industry. Approaching, he entered into some slight conversation with him upon matters pertaining to his craft. While they were conversing a stranger of foreign mien and costume appeared, holding a voluminous letter in his hand; the workman started up, snatched it from his hand, tore off the seals and greedily devoured its contents, while the stately Marlborough walked away unnoticed. The duke was well aware that, in this thin disguise, he saw the Czar of Muscovy. Pieter Baas, or Boss Peter, or Master Peter, was Peter the despot of all the Russians, a man who, having just found himself the undisputed proprietor of a quarter of the globe with all its inhabitants, had opened his eyes to the responsibilities of his position, and had voluntarily descended from his throne for the noble purpose of qualifying himself to reascend it.

The empire of Russia, at this moment more than twice as large as Europe, having a considerable extent of seacoasts, with flourishing commercial havens both upon the Baltic and the Black Seas, and a chain of internal communication, by canal and river, connecting them both with the Caspian and the Volga, was at the accession of Peter I of quite sufficient dimensions for any reasonable monarch's ambition, but of most unfortunate geographical position. Shut off from civilized western Europe by vast and thinly peopled forests and plains, having for neighbors only "the sledded Polack," the Turk, the Persian, and the Chinese, and touching nowhere upon the ocean, that great highway of civilization—the ancient empire of the Czars seemed always in a state of suffocation. Remote from the sea, it was a mammoth without lungs, incapable of performing the functions belonging to its vast organization, and presenting to the world the appearance of a huge, incomplete, and inert mass, waiting the advent of some new Prometheus to inspire it with life and light.

Its capital, the *bizarre* and fantastic Moscow, with its vast, turreted, and venerable Kremlin—its countless churches, with their flashing spires and clustering and turbaned minarets glittering in green, purple, and gold; its mosques, with the cross supplanting the crescent; its streets swarming with bearded merchants and ferocious janizaries, while its female population were immured and invisible—was a true type of the empire, rather Asiatic than European, and yet compounded of both.

The government, too, was far more Oriental than European in its character. The Normans had, to be sure, in the eleventh century taken possession of the Russian government with the same gentlemanlike effrontery with which, at about the same time, they had seated themselves upon every throne in Europe; and the crown of Ruric had been transmitted like the other European crowns for many generations, till it descended through a female branch upon the head of the Romanoffs, the ancestors of Peter and the present imperial family. But though there might be said to be an established dynasty, the succession to the throne was controlled by the Strelitzes, the licentious and ungovernable soldiery of the capital, as much as the Turkish or Roman Empire by the janizaries or pretorians; and the history of the government was but a series of palace-revolutions, in which the sovereign, the tool alternately of the priesthood and the body-guard, was elevated, deposed, or strangled, according to the prevalence of different factions in the capital. The government was in fact, as it has been epigrammatically characterized, "a despotism tempered by assassination."

The father of Peter I, Alexis Michaelovitch, had indeed projected reforms in various departments of the government. He seems to have been, to a certain extent, aware of the capacity of his empire, and to have had some faint glimmerings of the responsibility which weighed upon him, as the inheritor of this vast hereditary estate. He undertook certain revisions of the laws, if the mass of contradictory and capricious edicts which formed the code deserve that name; and his attention had particularly directed itself to the condition of the army and the church. Upon his death, in 1677, he left two sons, Theodore and John, and four daughters, by his first wife; besides one son, Peter, born in 1672, and one daughter, Natalia, by the second wife, of the house of Narischkin. The eldest son, Theodore, succeeded, whose administration was directed by his sister, the ambitious and intriguing Princess Sophia, assisted by her paramour Galitzin. Theodore died in 1682, having named his half-brother Peter as his successor, to the exclusion of his own brother John, who was almost an idiot. Sophia, who, in the fitful and perilous history of Peter's boyhood, seems like the wicked fairy in so many Eastern fables, whose mission is constantly to perplex, and if possible destroy, the virtuous young prince, who, however, struggles manfully against her enchantments and her hosts of allies, and comes out triumphant at last

—Sophia, assisted by Couvanski, general of the Strelitzes, excited a tumult in the capital. Artfully inflaming the passions of the soldiery, she directed their violence against all those who stood between her and the power she aimed at; many of the Narischkin family (the maternal relatives of Peter), with their adherents, were butchered with wholesale ferocity; many crown-officers were put to death; and the princess at length succeeded in proclaiming the idiot John and the infant Peter as joint Czars, and herself as regent.

From this time forth Sophia, having the reins of government securely in her hand, took particular care to surround the youthful Peter with the worst influences. She exposed him systematically to temptation, she placed about him the most depraved and licentious associates, and seems to have encouraged the germination of every vicious propensity with the most fostering care. In 1689, during the absence of Prince Galitzin upon his second unsuccessful invasion of the Crimea, Peter was married, at the age of seventeen, through the influence of a faction hostile to Sophia, to a young lady of the Lapouchin family. After the return of Galitzin a desperate revolt of the Strelitzes was concerted between their general and Sophia and Galitzin, whose object was to seize and murder Peter. He saved himself for the second time in the convent of the Trinity —the usual place of refuge when the court was beleaguered, as was not unusual, by the janizaries—assembled around him those of the *boiars* and the soldiers who were attached to him, and with the personal bravery and promptness which have descended like an heirloom in his family, defeated the conspirators at a blow, banished Galitzin to Siberia, and locked up Sophia in a convent, where she remained till her death fifteen years afterward. His brother John remained nominally as joint Czar till his death in 1696.

In less than a year from this time Peter made the acquaintance of a very remarkable man, to whom, more than to any other, Russia seems to have been indebted for the first impulse toward civilization. Happening one day to be dining at the house of the Danish minister, he was pleased with the manners and conversation of his excellency's private secretary. This was a certain youthful Genevese adventurer named Lefort. He had been educated for the mercantile profession and placed in a counting-house; but being of an adventurous disposition, with decided military tastes and talents, he had enlisted as a volunteer and served with some distinction in the Low Countries. Still following his campaigning inclinations, he enlisted under a certain Colonel Verstin, who had been commissioned by the Czar Alexis to pick up some German recruits, and followed him to Archangel. Arriving there, he found that the death of Alexis had left no demand for the services either of himself or the colonel, and after escaping with difficulty transportation to Siberia, with which he seems to have been threatened for no particular reason, he followed his destiny to Moscow, where he found employment under the Danish envoy De Horn, and soon after was introduced to the Czar.

It was this young adventurer, a man of no extraordinary acquirements, but one who had had the advantage of a European education, and the genius to know its value and to reap its full benefit—a man of wonderful power of observation, in whom intuition took the place of experience, and who possessed the rare faculty of impressing himself upon other minds with that genial warmth and force which render the impression indelible—it was this truant Genevese clerk who planted the first seeds in the fertile but then utterly fallow mind of the Czar. Geniality and sympathy were striking characteristics of both minds, and they seem to have united by a kind of elective affinity from the first instant they were placed in neighborhood of each other.

It was from Lefort that the Czar first learned the great superiority of the disciplined troops of western Europe over the licentious and anarchical soldiery of Russia. It was in concert with Lefort that he conceived on the instant the daring plan of annihilating the Strelitzes, the body-guard which had set up and deposed the monarchs—a plan that would have inevitably cost a less sagacious and vigorous prince his throne and life, and which he silently and cautiously matured, till, as we shall have occasion to relate, it was successfully executed. Almost immediately after his acquaintance with Lefort, he formed a regiment upon the European plan, which was to be the germ of the reformed army which he contemplated. This regiment was called the Preobrazinski body-guard, from the name of the palace, and Lefort was appointed its colonel, while the Czar entered himself as drummer.

It was to Lefort, also, that the Czar was about this time indebted for the acquaintance of the celebrated Menshikoff. This was another adventurer, who had great influence upon the fortunes of the empire, who sprang from the very humblest origin, and who seemed like Lefort to have been guided from afar by the finger of Providence to become a fit instrument to carry out the plans of Peter. The son of miserable parents upon the banks of the Volga, not even taught to read or write, Menshikoff sought his fortune in Moscow, and at the age of fourteen became apprentice to a pastry-cook, and earned his living as an itinerant vender of cakes and pies; these he offered about the streets, recommending them in ditties of his own composing, which he sang in a very sweet voice. While engaged in this humble occupation he happened one day to attract the attention of Lefort, who entered into some little conversation with him. The Swiss volunteer, who had so lately expanded into the general and admiral of Muscovy, could hardly dream, nor did he live long enough to learn, that in that fair-haired, barefooted, sweet-voiced boy the future prince of the empire, general, governor, regent, and almost autocrat, stood disguised before him. There really seems something inexpressibly romantic in the accidental and strange manner in which the chief actors in the great drama of Peter's career seem to have been selected and to have received their several parts from the great hand of Fate. The youthful Menshikoff was presented by Lefort to the Czar, who was pleased with his appearance and vivacity and made him his page, and soon afterward his favorite and confidant. At about the same time that Peter commenced his model regiment, he had also commenced building some vessels at Voroneje, with which he had already formed the design of sailing down the Don and conquering Azov, the key to the Black Sea, from the Turks.

Nothing indicated the true instinct of Peter's genius more decidedly than the constancy with which he cultivated a love for maritime affairs. He is said in infancy to have had an almost insane fear of water; but, as there was never any special reason assigned for it, this was probably invented to make his naval progress appear more remarkable. At all events, he seems very soon to have conquered his hydrophobia, and in his boyhood appears to have found his chief amusement in paddling about the river Yausa, which passes through Moscow, in a little skiff built by a Dutchman, which had attracted his attention as being capable, unlike the flat-bottomed scows, which were the only boats with which he had been previously familiar, of sailing against the wind. Having solved the mystery of the keel, he became passionately fond of the sport, and not satisfied with the navigation of the Yausa, nor of the lake Peipus, upon which he amused himself for a time, he could not rest till he had proceeded to Archangel, where he purchased and manned a vessel, in which he took a cruise or two upon the Frozen Ocean as far as Ponoi, upon the coast of Lapland.

Peter understood thoroughly the position of his empire the moment he came to the throne. Previous Czars had issued a multiplicity of edicts, forbidding their subjects to go out of the empire. Peter saw that the great trouble was that they could not get out. Both the natural gates of his realm were locked upon him, and the keys were in the hands of his enemies. When we look at the map of Russia now, we do not sufficiently appreciate the difficulties of Peter's position at his accession. To do so is to appreciate his genius and the strength of his will. While paddling in his little skiff on the Yausa he had already determined that this great inland empire of his, whose inhabitants had never seen or heard of the ocean, should become a maritime power. He saw that, without seaports, it could never be redeemed from its barbarism, and he was resolved to exchange its mongrel Orientalism for European civilization. Accordingly, before he had been within five hundred miles of blue water he made himself a sailor, and at the same time formed the plan, which he pursued with iron pertinacity to its completion, of conquering the Baltic from the Swede, and the Euxine from the Turk. Fully to see and appreciate the necessity of this measure was, in the young, neglected barbarian prince, a great indication of genius; but the resolution to set about and accomplish this mighty scheme in the face of ten thousand obstacles constituted him a hero. He was, in fact, one of those few characters whose existence has had a considerable influence upon history. If he had not lived, Russia would very probably have been at the present moment one great Wallachia or Moldavia—a vast wilderness, peopled by the same uncouth barbarians who even now constitute the mass of its population, and governed by a struggling, brawling, confused mob of unlettered *boiars*, knavish priests, and cut-throat janizaries.

It was not so trifling a task as it may now appear for Russia to conquer Sweden and the Sublime Porte. On the contrary, Sweden was so vastly superior in the scale of civilization, and her disciplined troops, trained for a century upon the renowned battle-fields of Europe, with a young monarch at their head who loved war as other youths love a mistress, gave her such a decided military preponderance that she looked upon Russia with contempt. The Ottoman Empire, too, was at that time not the rickety, decrepit state which it now is, holding itself up, like the cabman's horse, only by being kept in the shafts, and ready to drop the first moment its foreign master stops whipping; on the contrary, in the very year in which Peter inherited the empire from his brother Theodore, two hundred thousand Turks besieged Vienna, and drove the Emperor Leopold in dismay from his capital. Although the downfall of the Porte may be dated from the result of that memorable campaign, yet the Sultan was then a vastly more powerful potentate than the Czar, and the project to snatch from him the citadel of Azov, the key of the Black Sea, was one of unparalleled audacity.

But Peter had already matured the project, and was determined to execute it. He required seaports, and, having none, he determined to seize those of his neighbors. Like the "King of Bohemia with his seven castles," he was the "most unfortunate man in the world, because, having the greatest passion for navigation and all sorts of sea affairs, he had never a seaport in all his dominions." Without stopping however, like Corporal Trim, to argue the point in casuistry, whether—Russia, like Bohemia, being an inland country—it would be consistent with Divine benevolence for the ocean to inundate his neighbor's territory in order to accommodate him, he took a more expeditious method. Preferring to go to the ocean, rather than wait for the ocean to come to him, in 1695 he sailed down the Don with his vessels, and struck his first blow at Azov. His campaign was unsuccessful, through the treachery and desertion of an artillery officer named Jacob; but, as the Czar through life possessed the happy faculty of never knowing when he was beaten, he renewed his attack the next year, and carried the place with the most brilliant success. The key of the Palus Mæotis was thus in his hands, and he returned in triumph to Moscow, where he levied large sums upon the nobility and clergy, to build and sustain a fleet upon the waters he had conquered, to drive the Tartars from the Crimea, and to open and sustain a communication with Persia, through Circassia and Georgia.

Thus the first point was gained, and his foot at last touched the ocean. Moreover, the Tartars of the Crimea, who had been from time immemorial the pest of Russia—a horde of savages, who "said their prayers but once a year, and then to a dead horse," and who had yet compelled the Muscovites to pay them an annual tribute, and had inserted in their last articles of peace the ignominious conditions that "the Czar should hold the stirrup of their Khan, and feed his horse with oats out of his cap, if they should chance at any time to meet"—these savages were humbled at a blow, and scourged into insignificance by the master hand of Peter.

A year or two before the capture of Azov, Peter had repudiated his wife. Various pretexts, such as infidelity and jealousy, have been assigned for the step; among others, the enmity of Menshikoff, whom she had incensed by the accusation that he had taken her husband to visit lewd women who had formerly been his customers for pies; but the real reason was that, like every one else connected with the great reformer, she opposed herself with the most besotted bigotry to all his plans. She was under the influence of the priests, and the priests, of course, opposed him. Unfortunately, the Czar left his son Alexis in the charge of the mother, a mistake which, as we shall see, occasioned infinite disaster.

Peter, having secured himself a seaport, sent a number of young Russians to study the arts of civilized life in Holland, Italy, and Germany; but, being convinced that he must do everything for himself, and set the example to his subjects, he resolved to descend from his throne and go to Holland to perfect himself in the arts, and particularly to acquire a thorough practical knowledge of maritime affairs.

Having been hitherto unrepresented in any European court, he fitted out a splendid embassy extraordinary to the States-General of Holland—Lefort, Golownin, Voristzin, and Menshikoff being the plenipotentiaries, while the Czar accompanied them *incognito,* as *attaché* to the mission. The embassy proceeds through Esthonia and Livonia, visits Riga—where the Swedish governor, D'Alberg, refuses permission to visit the fortifications, an indignity which Peter resolves to punish severely—and, proceeding through Prussia, is received with great pomp by the King at Königsberg. Here the Germans and Russians, " most potent at pottery," meet each other with exuberant demonstrations of friendship, and there is much carousing and hard drinking. At this place Peter leaves the embassy, travels privately and with great rapidity to Holland, and never rests till he has established himself as a journeyman in the dockyard of Mynheer Calf. From a seafaring man named Kist, whom he had known in Archangel, he hires lodgings, consisting of a small room and kitchen, and a garret above them, and immediately commences a laborious and practical devotion to the trade which he had determined to acquire. The Czar soon became a most accomplished ship-builder. His first essay was upon a small yacht, which he purchased and refitted upon his arrival, and in which he spent all his leisure moments, sailing about in the harbor, visiting the vessels in port, and astonishing the phlegmatic Dutchmen by the agility with which he flew about among the shipping. Before his departure he laid down and built, from his own draught and model, a sixty-gun ship, at much of the carpentry of which he worked with his own hands, and which was declared by many competent judges to be an admirable specimen of naval architecture.

But, besides his proficiency so rapidly acquired in all maritime matters, he made considerable progress in civil engineering, mathematics, and the science of fortification, besides completely mastering the Dutch language, and acquiring the miscellaneous accomplishments of tooth-drawing, blood-letting, and tapping for the dropsy. He was indefatigable in visiting every public institution, charitable, literary, or scientific, in examining the manufacturing establishments, the corn-mills, saw-mills, paper-mills, oil-factories, all of which he studied practically, with the view of immediately introducing these branches of industry into his own dominions; and, before leaving Holland, he spent some time at Texel, solely for the purpose of examining the whale-ships, and qualifying himself to instruct his subjects in this pursuit after his return. "*Wat is dat? Dat wil ik zien,*" was his eternal exclamation to the quiet Hollanders, who looked with profound astonishment at this boisterous foreign prince, in carpenter's disguise, flying round like a harlequin, swinging his stick over the backs of those who stood in his way, making strange grimaces, and rushing from one object to another with a restless activity of body and mind which seemed incomprehensible. He devoured every possible morsel of knowledge with unexampled voracity; but the sequel proved that his mind had an ostrich-like digestion as well as appetite. The seeds which he collected in Holland, Germany, and England bore a rich harvest in the Scythian wildernesses, where his hand planted them on his return. Having spent about nine months in the Netherlands, he left that country for England.

His purpose in visiting England was principally to examine her navy-yards, dockyards, and maritime establishments, and to acquire some practical knowledge of English naval architecture. He did not design to work in the dockyards, but he preserved his *incognito*, although received with great attention by King William, who furthered all his plans to the utmost, and deputed the Marquis of Caermarthen, with whom the Czar became very intimate, to minister to all his wants during his residence in England. He was first lodged in York Buildings; but afterward, in order to be near the sea, he took possession of a house called Sayes Court, belonging to the celebrated John Evelyn, "with a back door into the King's yard, at Deptford"; there, says an old writer, "he would often take up the carpenters' tools, and work with them; and he frequently conversed with the builders, who showed him their draughts, and the method of laying down, by proportion, any ship or vessel."

It is amusing to observe the contempt with which the servant of the gentle, pastoral Evelyn writes to his master concerning his imperial tenant, and the depredations and desecrations committed upon his "most boscaresque grounds." "There is a house full of people," he says, "right nasty. The Czar lies next your library, and dines in the parlor next your study. He dines at ten o'clock, and six at night; is very seldom at home a whole day; very often in the King's yard, or by water, dressed in several dresses. The best parlor is pretty clean for the King to be entertained in." Moreover, in the garden at Sayes Court, there was, to use Evelyn's own language, "a glorious and refreshing object, an impregnable hedge of about four hundred feet in length, nine feet high, and five feet in diameter, at any time of the year glittering with its armed and variegated leaves; the taller standards, at orderly distances, blushing with their natural coral"; and through this "glorious and refreshing object" the Czar amused himself by trundling a wheelbarrow every morning for the sake of the exercise!

He visited the hospitals, and examined most of the public institutions in England; and particularly directed his attention toward acquiring information in engineering, and collecting a body of skilful engineers and artificers to carry on the great project which he had already matured of opening an artificial communication by locks and canals between the Volga, the Don, and the Caspian—a design, by the way, which was denounced by the clergy and nobility of his empire "as a piece of impiety, being to turn the streams one way which Providence had directed another." His evenings were generally spent with the Marquis of Caermarthen, with pipes, beer, and brandy, at a tavern near Tower Hill, which is still called the "Czar of Muscovy."

During his stay in England he went to see the University of Oxford, and visited many of the cathedrals and churches, and "had also the curiosity to view the Quakers and other Dissenters at their meeting-houses in the time of service." In this connection it is impossible not to quote the egregiously foolish remarks of Bishop Burnet in his "History of His Own Times":

"I waited upon him often," says the bishop, "and was ordered, both by the King and the archbishop, to attend upon him and to offer him such information as to our religion and constitution as he might be willing to receive. I had good interpreters, so I had much free discourse with him. He is a man of a very hot temper, soon influenced, and very brutal in his passion; he raises his natural heat by drinking much brandy, which he rectifies himself with great application; he is subject to convulsive motions all over his body, and his head seems to be affected with these. He wants not capacity, and has a larger measure of knowledge than might be expected from his education, which was very indifferent; a want of judgment, with an instability of temper, appears in him but too often and too evidently. He is mechanically turned, and seems designed by nature rather to be a ship-carpenter than a great prince. This was his chief study and exercise while he staid here; he wrought much with his own hands, and made all about him work at the models of ships. He told me he designed a great fleet at Azov, and with it to attack the Turkish Empire; but he did not seem capable of conducing so great a design, though his conduct in his wars since this has discovered a greater genius in him than appeared at that time. He was desirous to understand our doctrine, but he did not seem disposed to mend matters in Muscovy. He was, indeed, resolved to encourage learning and to polish his people by sending some of them to travel in other countries, and to draw strangers to come and live among them. He seemed apprehensive still of his sister's intrigues. There is a mixture both of passion and severity in his temper. He is resolute, but understands little of war, and seemed not at all inquisitive in that way. After I had seen him often, and had conversed much with him, I could not but adore the depth of the providence of God, that had raised up such a furious man to so absolute an authority over so great a part of the world."

The complacency with which the prelate speaks of this "furious man," "designed by nature rather to be a ship-carpenter than a great prince," who "did not seem disposed to mend matters in Muscovy," is excessively ludicrous. Here was a youth of twenty-five, who had seen with a glance the absolute necessity of opening for his empire a pathway to the ocean, and had secured that pathway by a blow, and who now, revolving in his mind the most daring schemes of conquest over martial neighbors, and vast projects of internal improvement for his domains, had gone forth in mask and domino from his barbarous citadel, not for a holiday pastime, but to acquire the arts of war and peace, and, like a modern Cadmus, to transplant from older regions the seeds of civilization to the barbarous wildernesses of his realm. Here was a crowned monarch, born in the purple, and in the very heyday of his youth, exchanging his diadem and sceptre for the tools of a shipwright, while at the same time in his capacious brain his vast future lay as clearly imaged, and his great projects already to his imagination appeared as palpable as, long years afterward, when completed, they became to the observation of the world; and yet, upon the whole, the churchman thought him "not disposed to mend matters in Muscovy," and rather fitted by nature "to be a ship-carpenter than a great prince."

The Czar, before his departure from England, engaged a large number of scientific persons, at the head of whom was Ferguson, the engineer, to accompany him to Russia, to be employed upon the various works of internal improvement already projected. To all these persons he promised liberal salaries, which were never paid, and perfect liberty to depart when they chose, "with crowns for convoy put into their purse"; although, in the sequel, the poor devils never got a ruble for their pains, and those who escaped assassination by some jealous Russian or other, and were able to find their way "bootless home, and weather-beaten back," after a few profitless years spent upon the Czar's sluices and bridges, were to be considered fortunate.

One of the disadvantages, we suppose, of one man's owning a whole quarter of the globe and all its inhabitants, is a tendency to think lightly of human obligations. It is useless to occupy one's mind with engagements that no human power can enforce. The artificers, being there, might accomplish their part of the Czar's mission to civilize, or at least to Europeanize, Russia. This was matter of consequence to the world; their salaries were of no importance to anybody but themselves. It is odd that these persons were the first to introduce into Russia the science of reckoning by Arabic numerals, accounts having been formerly kept (and, indeed, being still kept by all shop-keepers and retail dealers) by means of balls upon a string, as billiards are marked in America. For the Czar to have introduced an improved method of account-keeping by means of the very men with whom he intended to keep no account at all seems a superfluous piece of irony, but so it was. He had, however, a nicer notion of what was due from one potentate to another; for, upon taking his departure from England, he took from his breeches-pocket a ruby, wrapped in brown paper, worth about ten thousand pounds, and presented it to King William. He also, in return for the agreeable hours passed with Lord Caermarthen at the "Czar of Muscovy" upon Tower Hill, presented that nobleman with the right to license every hogshead of tobacco exported to Russia by an English company who had paid him fifteen thousand pounds for the monopoly, and to charge five shillings for each license.

Upon his return through Vienna, where he was entertained with great pomp, he received news of an insurrection which had broken out in Moscow, but which had already been suppressed by the energy of General Patrick Gordon. This news induced him to give up his intended visit to Italy and to hasten back to his capital. He found upon his arrival that the Strelitzes, who, instigated of course by the Princess Sophia, were the authors of the revolt, had been defeated, and the ringleaders imprisoned. He immediately hung up three or four of them in front of Sophia's window, had half a dozen more hung and quartered, and a few more broken upon the wheel. Under the circumstances, this was quite as little as a Czar who respected himself, and who proposed to remain Czar, could have done by way of retaliation upon a body of men as dangerous as these Strelitzes.

It is not singular, however, that at that day, when the Czar of Muscovy was looked upon by western Europeans as an ogre who habitually breakfasted upon his subjects, these examples of wholesome severity were magnified into the most improbable fables. Korb, the secretary of the Austrian legation at Moscow, entertained his sovereign with minute details of several banquets given by Peter to the nobility and diplomatic corps, at every one of which several dozen Strelitzes were decapitated in the dining-room. He tells of one select dinner-party in particular, in which the Czar chopped off the heads of twenty with his own hands, washing down each head with a bumper of brandy, and then obliging Lefort, and several of the judges, and some of the foreign ministers to try their hand at the sport. In short, if we could believe contemporary memorialists, the Strelitzes were kept in preserves like pheasants, and a grand *battue* was given once a week by the Czar to his particular friends, in which he who bagged the most game was sure to recommend himself most to the autocrat. If we were to rely upon the general tone of contemporary history, or to place any credence in circumstantial and statistical details of persons having facts within their reach, we should believe that there never was so much fun in Moscow as while these Strelitzes lasted. Residents there stated that two thousand of them were executed in all, including those made away with by the Czar and the *dilettanti*.

Perhaps our readers may think that we are exaggerating. We can assure them that the flippancy is not ours, but history's. We should have dwelt less upon the topic had not our friend the Marquis de Custine reproduced some of these fables with such imperturbable gravity.[1]

At all events, the Strelitzes were entirely crushed by these vigorous measures; and from cutting off the heads of the janizaries, the Czar now found leisure to cut off the petticoats and beards of his subjects. The great cause of complaint which De Custine makes against Peter is that he sought to improve his country by importing the seeds of civilization from the older countries of western Europe. He would have preferred to have had the Russians, being a Slavonic race, civilized as it were Slavonically. What this process is, and where it has been successfully put into operation, he does not inform us. As we read the history of the world, it seems to us that the arts have circled the earth, successively implanting themselves in different countries at different epochs, and producing different varieties of intellectual, moral, and physical fruit, corresponding to the myriad influences exercised upon the seed. At all events, if Peter made a mistake in importing the germs of ancient culture from more favored lands, it was a mistake he made in common with Cadmus, and Cecrops, and Theseus, and other semi-fabulous personages—with Solon, and Lycurgus, and Pythagoras, in less crepuscular times.

Right or wrong, however, Peter was determined to occidentalize his empire. The darling wish of his heart was to place himself upon the seashore, in order the more easily to Eu-

[1] On lit dans M. de Ségur les faits suivants: " Pierre, lui-même a interrogé ces criminels (les Strélitz) par la torture; puis à l'imitation d'Iwan le Tyran, il se fait leur juge, leur bourreau; il force ses nobles restés fidèles à trancher les têtes des nobles coupables, qu'ils viennent de condamner. Le cruel, du haut de son trône, assiste d'un œil sec à ces exécutions; il fait plus, il mêle aux joies des festins l'horreur des supplices. Ivre de vin et de sang, le verre d'une main, la hache de l'autre, en une seule heure, vingt libations successives marquent la chute de vingt têtes de Strélitz, qu'il abat à ses pieds, en s'enorgueillissant de son horrible adresse. L'année d'après, le contre coup, soit du soulèvement de ses janissaires, soit de l'atrocité de leur supplice, retentit au loin dans l'empire, et d'autres revoltes éclatent. Quatre-vingt Strélitz, chargés de chaînes, sont trainés d'Azoff à Moscou, et leurs têtes, qu'un boyard tient successivement par les cheveux, tombent encore sous la hache du Czar."—(" Histoire de Russie et de Pierre le Grand," par M. le Général Comte de Ségur.—" La Russie en 1839," par le Marquis de Custine, i. 306.)

" Mais tandis que ce grand précepteur de son peuple enseignait si bien la civilité puérile aux boyards et aux marchands de Moscou, il s'abaissait lui-même à la pratique des métiers les plus vils, à commencer par celui de bourreau; on lui a vu couper vingt têtes de sa main dans une soirée; et on l'a entendu se vanter de son adresse à ce métier, qu'il exerça avec une rare férocité lorsqu'il eut triomphé des coupables, mais encore plus malheureux Strélitz," etc.—(De Custine, iii. 330.)

ropeanize his country. In the mean time, and while awaiting a good opportunity for the " reannexation " of Ingria, Esthonia, and Livonia, provinces which had several centuries before belonged to the Russian crown, but had been ceded to and possessed by Sweden for ages, he began to denationalize his subjects by putting a tax upon their beards and their petticoats. Strange to say, his subjects were so much more patriotic than their master that the tax became very productive. Peter increased his revenue, but could not diminish the beards or petticoats. He was obliged to resort to force, and by " entertaining a score or two of tailors and barbers " at each gate of Moscow, whose business it was to fasten upon every man who entered, and to " cut his petticoats all round about," as well as his whiskers, he at last succeeded in humanizing their costume—a process highly offensive, and which caused the clergy, who naturally favored the Russian nationality upon which they were fattened, to denounce him as Antichrist. At the same time he altered the commencement of the year from the first of September to the first of January, much to the astonishment of his subjects, who wondered that the Czar could change the course of the sun. He also instituted assemblies for the encouragement of social intercourse between the sexes. But his most important undertakings were the building, under his immediate superintendence, assisted by the English officers whom he had brought with him, of a large fleet upon the Don, and the junction of that river with the Volga. About this time he met with an irreparable loss in the death of Lefort, who perished at the early age of forty-six. Peter was profoundly afflicted by this event, and honored his remains with magnificent obsequies.

Both coasts of the Gulf of Finland, together with both banks of the river Neva, up to the lake Ladoga, had been long and were still in possession of the Swedes. These frozen morasses were not a tempting site for a metropolis, certainly; particularly when they happened to be in the possession of the most warlike nation of Europe, governed by the most warlike monarch, as the sequel proved, that had ever sat upon its throne. Still, Peter had determined to take possession of that coast, and already in imagination had built his capital upon those dreary solitudes, peopled only by the elk, the wolf, and the bear. This man, more than anyone perhaps that ever lived, was an illustration of the power of volition. He always settled in his own mind exactly what he wanted, and then put on his wishing-cap. With him to will was to have. Obstacles he took as a matter of course. It never seemed to occur to him to doubt the accomplishment of his purpose. For our own part we do not admire the capital which he built, nor the place he selected; both are mistakes, in our humble opinion, as time will prove and is proving. But it is impossible not to admire such a masterly effort of human volition as the erection of Petersburg.

In the year 1700 was formed the alliance between Augustus the Strong, Elector of Saxony and King of Poland, the King of Denmark, and the Czar Peter, against Charles XII, King of Sweden, then a boy of eighteen, of whose character nothing was known, and who, it was thought probable, might be bullied. The Czar, as we know, desired Ingria and Carelia. Augustus wished to regain Esthonia and Livonia, ceded by Poland to Charles XI of Sweden; and Denmark wished to recover Holstein and Schleswig. It soon appeared that the allied sovereigns had got hold of the wrong man. Charles XII, to the astonishment of his own court no less than of his enemies, in one instant blazed forth a hero. He "smote the sledded Polack," to begin with; then defeated the Danes; and, having thus despatched his two most formidable enemies in appearance, he was at leisure to devote his whole attention to the Czar, whom, however, he treated with the contempt which a thoroughbred soldier, at the head of tried and disciplined troops, naturally felt for the barbarous autocrat of barbarous hordes.

Peter, however, who knew nothing of war but in theory, with the exception of his maiden campaign of Azov, went manfully forward to the encounter. He invaded Ingria at the head of sixty thousand men; and wishing, like Andrew Aguecheek, to "keep on the windy side of the law," and to save appearances, he defended his invasion by the ludicrous pretext that his ambassadors had been charged exorbitant prices for provisions on their tour through the Swedish provinces to Holland, and that he himself had been denied a sight of the citadel at Riga. Not that he wanted Riga himself, or Ingria, or Livonia—"Oh, no, not at all"—but the preposterous charges made by the butchers and bakers of Ingria were insults which could only be washed out in blood. On September 20th he laid siege to Narva, a strongly fortified town on the river Narowa. On November 19th, Charles XII fell upon Peter's army during a tremendous snow-storm, which blew directly in their teeth, and with nine thousand soldiers completely routed and cut to pieces or captured about sixty thousand Russians. Never was a more ignominious defeat. The Russians were slaughtered like sheep, and their long petticoats prevented the survivors from running away half as fast as they wished. The consequence was that, according to the Swedish accounts, the prisoners four times outnumbered the whole Swedish army.

One would have thought that this would have settled the Czar for a little while, and kept him quiet and reasonable. It did so. He preserved the most imperturbable *sang froid* after his return to Moscow, and devoted himself with more zeal than ever to the junction of the Baltic and the Euxine, just at the moment when the former seemed farthest from him, and when a common man would have been "qualmish at the name" of Baltic. At the same time, reversing the commonplace doctrine, he continues in war to prepare for peace—with one hand importing sheep from Saxony, erecting linen and paper factories, building hospitals and founding schools, while with the other he melts all the church and convent bells in Moscow into cannon, and makes every preparation for a vigorous campaign the ensuing season. He had not the slightest suspicion that he was beaten. He was, in fact, one of those intellectual Titans who never feel their strength till they have been fairly struck to the earth. "I know very well," he says in his journal, "that the Swedes will have the advantage of us for a considerable time; but they will teach us at length to beat them." And at a later period he says: "If we had obtained a victory over the Swedes at Narva, being, as we were, so little instructed in the arts of war and policy, into what an abyss might not this good fortune have sunk us! On the contrary, the success of the Swedes cost them very dear afterward at Pultowa."

In the following spring his troops obtained some trifling successes, and General Scherematoff made the memorable capture of Marienburg, in Livonia, memorable not so much in a military point of view as on account of a young and pretty Livonian girl who was captured with the town. This young woman, whose Christian name was Martha, without any patronymic, or any at least that has been preserved, was born near Dorpt, and had been educated by one Dr. Gluck, a Lutheran minister at Marienburg, who pronounced her a "pattern of virtue, intelligence, and good conduct"; she had been married the day before the battle of Marienburg to a Swedish sergeant, who fell in the action, and she now found herself alone, a friendless, helpless widow and orphan of sixteen, exposed without any protector to all the horrors of a besieged and captured town.

If a writer of fiction, with a brain fertile in extravagant and incredible romance, had chosen to describe to us this young peasant-girl, weeping half distracted among the smoking ruins of an obscure provincial town, and then, after rapidly shifting a few brilliant and tumultuous scenes in his phantasmagoria, had presented to us the same orphan girl as a crowned empress, throned upon a quarter of the world, and the sole arbitress and autocrat of thirty millions of human beings, and all this without any discovery of a concealed origin, without crime and without witchcraft, with nothing supernatural in the machinery, and nothing intricate in the plot—should we not all have smiled at his absurdity? And yet, this captive girl became the consort of the Czar Peter, and upon his death the Empress of all the Russias. The Russian General Bauer saw her, and rescued her from the dangers of the siege. She afterward became the mistress of Menshikoff, with whom she lived till 1704, when, in the seventeenth year of her age, the Czar saw her, was captivated by her beauty, and took her for his mistress, and afterward privately, and then publicly, married her.

It is to this epoch that belongs the abolition of the patriarchal dignity in Russia. Peter, having at a blow destroyed the Strelitzes, had long intended to annihilate the ecclesiastical power, the only balance which existed in the country to the autocracy of the sovereign. The superstition of the Russians was and is unbounded. Their principal saint was Saint Anthony, who, says a quaint old author, "came all the way from Rome to Novgorod by water on a millstone, sailing down the Tiber to Cività Vecchia, from thence passing through several seas to the mouth of the Neva, then went up that, and, crossing the lake Ladoga into the Volkhoff, arrived at the city before named. Besides this extraordinary voyage, he wrought several other miracles as soon as he landed where the monastery now stands that is dedicated to him; one was, to order a company of fishermen to cast their nets into the sea; which having done, they immediately drew up, with a great quantity of fish, a large trunk containing several church ornaments, sacred utensils, and priestly vestments for celebrating the liturgy, which the Russians, as well as the Eastern Greeks, believe was first performed at Rome in the same manner and with the same ceremonies as they themselves use at this time. The people tell you further that he built himself a little cell, in which he ended his days. In this place there now stands a chapel, in which they say he was buried, and that his body remains as uncorrupted as at the instant of his death. Over the door of the cell the monks show a millstone, which they endeavor to make the ignorant people believe is the very same that the saint sailed upon from Rome, and to which great devotions were once paid, and many offerings made till the time Peter the Great made himself sovereign pontiff."

To this saint, or to Saint Nicholas, we forget which, letters of introduction were always addressed by the priests, and placed in the hands of the dead when laid in their coffins. The superstition of the Russians is grosser and more puerile than that of any people purporting to be Christians. They would rather starve than eat pigeons, because the Holy Ghost assumed the form of a dove; they dip their new-born children into the Neva in January, through holes cut in the ice, directly after the ceremony of blessing the water has been concluded by the patriarch; and it would be an easy but endless task to enumerate other similar absurdities. It may be supposed that the patriarchal dignity, founded upon superstition as solid as this, would be a difficult power to contend with. It was so. The patriarch's power was enormous. He pronounced sentence of life, and death, and torture, without intervention of any tribunal. On Palm Sunday he rode to church upon an ass "caparisoned in white linen," at the head of a long procession of ecclesiastical and civil dignitaries, with a mitre upon his head, and "skirts of many colors, three or four ells long," borne by a band of young men, while the Czar walked uncovered by his side, holding the bridle of the beast upon his arm.

This dignity, which had been established by a sort of accident in the year 1588, up to which time the Russian Church acknowledged the supremacy of the Patriarch of Constantinople, had grown to be very distasteful to Peter. The Church was the greatest possible enemy to his plans of reformation. The bigotry of its opposition to all his projects was insurmountable. Besides, it was very inconvenient that anyone should have any power or any rights except himself. He determined to annihilate the office of patriarch, and to place himself at the head of the Church. We do not find, however, that he thought it necessary to go through an apprenticeship in this profession, as he had done in others; but, on the contrary, upon the death of the Patriarch Adrian, which happened about this time, he simply appointed himself *pontifex maximus,* and declined nominating any other patriarch. The man who had destroyed the janizaries, cut off the beards of his subjects, and changed the course of the sun, was also strong enough to trample the prelate's mitre in the dust. He was entirely successful in his contest with the Church. The clergy made but a feeble resistance. The printing-press, to be sure, which he had first introduced into Russia, swarmed with libels upon him, and denounced him as Antichrist; but he was defended by others of the clergy, "because the number six hundred and sixty-six was not found in his name, and he had not the sign of the beast."

Before the close of the year 1702 the troops of the Czar had driven the Swedes from the Ladoga and the Neva, and had taken possession of all the ports in Carelia and Ingria. On May 16th, without waiting another moment after having possessed himself of the locality, he begins to build his metropolis. One hundred thousand miserable workmen are consumed in the first twelve months, succumbing to the rigorous climate and the unhealthy position. But "*il faut casser des œufs pour faire une omelette*"; in one year's time there are thirty thousand houses in Petersburg. Never was there such a splendid improvisation. Look for a moment at a map of Russia and say if Petersburg was not a magnificent piece of volition—a mistake, certainly, and an extensive one—but still a magnificent mistake. Upon a delta, formed by the dividing branches of the Neva—upon a miserable morass half under water, without stones, without clay, without earth, without wood, without building materials of any kind—having behind it the outlet of the lake Ladoga and its tributary swamps, and before it the Gulf of Finland contracting itself into a narrow compass, and ready to deluge it with all the waters of the Baltic whenever the southwest wind should blow a gale eight and forty hours—with a climate of polar severity, and a soil as barren as an iceberg—was not Petersburg a bold *impromptu?* We never could look at this capital, with its imposing though monotonous architecture, its colossal squares, its vast colonnades, its endless vistas, its spires and minarets sheathed in barbaric gold and flashing in the sun, and remember the magical rapidity with which it was built, and the hundred thousand lives that were sacrificed in building it, without recalling Milton's description of the building of Pandemonium:

> "Anon out of the earth a fabric huge
> Rose like an exhalation, . . .
> Built like a temple, where pilasters round
> Were set, and Doric pillars overlaid
> With golden architrave; nor did there want
> Cornice or frieze, with bossy sculptures graven;
> The roof was fretted gold. Not Babylon
> Nor great Alcairo such magnificence
> Equalled in all their glories, to enshrine
> Belus or Serapis their gods, or seat
> Their kings, when Egypt with Assyria strove
> In wealth and luxury. The ascending pile
> Stood fixed her stately height; and straight the doors
> Opening their brazen folds discover, wide
> Within, her ample spaces o'er the smooth
> And level pavement."

Within a few months after the foundation of Petersburg and Cronstadt, Peter had the pleasure of piloting into his new seaport with his own hands a vessel belonging to his old friend Cornelius Calf, of Saardam. The transfer of the seat of government, by the removal of the Senate from Moscow to Petersburg, was effected a few years afterward. Since that time the repudiated Oriental capital of the ancient Czars, the magnificent Moscow, with her golden tiara and her Eastern robe, has sat, like Hagar in the wilderness, deserted and lonely in all her barbarian beauty. Yet even now, in many a backward look and longing sigh she reads plainly enough that she is not forgotten by her sovereign, that she is still at heart preferred, and that she will eventually triumph over her usurping and artificial rival.

The building of Petersburg in a year was, however, a mere

aside in the great military drama that was going on. Peter founded this city as soon as he had won a place for it; but the war still went on. While the Czar was erecting his capital, establishing woollen manufactures, and importing sheep from Saxony, Charles XII was knocking the Elector of Saxony off the Polish throne, putting Stanislaus Leckzinsky in his place, and ravaging all Poland and Saxony. The scenes of the great drama which occupied the next few years, but which we have no intention of sketching, opened in Poland, and closed on the confines of Turkey. It is a magnificent, eventful, important drama, a chapter of history which has been often written and is familiar to almost everyone, and yet which would well bear handling again. There is no life of Peter which is in all respects satisfactory, which does not partake too much of eulogium or censure in its estimation of his character; and there is none which develops with sufficient accuracy and impartiality, and in a sufficiently striking manner, the stirring events of the great Northern war. The brilliant drama enacted in the first fifteen years of the present century—forming probably the most splendid chapter in the military history of the world, and which is still so fresh in the minds of men—has thrown into comparative oblivion the very picturesque and imposing scenes which were displayed in the first fifteen years of the eighteenth. And yet what a magnificent subject for the historical painter, what imposing personages, what dramatic catastrophes, what sudden and bewildering reverses, what wild scenery, what Salvator-like *chiaroscuro*—dark Sarmatian forests enveloping the actors in mystery and obscurity, with flashes of light breaking upon the anxious suspense of Europe, and revealing portentous battles, sieges, and hair-breadth escapes—what "dreadful marches" through the wilderness, what pitched combats, upon whose doubtful result hinged, as almost never before or since, the weal or woe of millions, and in which kings fought sword in hand in the hottest of the fight, with their crowns staked upon the issue!

There was always something very exciting to our imagination in the characters of the three kings who were the principal actors in the Northern war. There seemed to be a strange, fitful, mythical character about the war and the men who waged it. The Elector Augustus of Saxony, King of Poland, with his superhuman and almost fabulous physical strength, his personal bravery, his showy, chivalrous character, his world-renowned adventures in a gentler field, familiar to posterity through the records of "*La Saxe galante,*" is a striking personage. It is astonishing that such a magnificent Lothario should have chosen, for the barren honor of being elected to the Polish throne, to exchange the brilliant and voluptuous gayety of his own court for "the bloody noses and cracked crowns" which were "passing current" in Poland. But it is still more astonishing that, having once engaged in the affair, he should have cut such a miserable figure in it. The splendid Augustus, Augustus the Strong, Augustus the Gallant, became merely the anvil for the sledge-hammers of Charles and Peter. He made a fool of himself; he disgraced himself more than it seemed possible for a human being to disgrace himself; he humiliated himself more completely, more stupidly, because more unnecessarily, than it seemed possible for the greatest idiot, as well as the most arrant coward, to humiliate himself. He lost his crown at the very start, went down on his knees in the dirt to pick it up again, made a secret treaty with Charles, renouncing his alliance with the Czar, deserted his ally with incredible folly just as the Russians in conjunction with his own troops were gaining a brilliant victory and entering Warsaw in triumph, concealed his shameful negotiation from his own generals, while at the same time he wrote a letter to Charles, apologizing for having gained a victory, and assuring him that he had intended to have drawn off his troops and deserted to the enemy, but that his orders had not been obeyed, and then sneaked off to Charles's camp, where, in obedience to that monarch's orders, he capped the climax of his shame by writing a letter of sincere and humble congratulation to Stanislaus Leckzinsky for supplanting him upon his own throne. Peter, in the sequel, put his crown on his head again, to be sure; but forever after he looked like

> ". . . the thief,
> Who from the shelf the precious diadem stole,
> And put it in his pocket."

What a pity that this man, who was deficient neither in courage nor, we suppose, in a certain amount of intellect sufficient for all ordinary purposes, should have got himself into such a scrape merely for the sake of carrying an election over the Prince of

Conti and Stanislaus! The truth was that, the moment he got among giants—giants in action, like Charles and Peter—he showed himself the pygmy he was in mind, despite his stature, his strength, and his personal bravery.

And Charles XII, the hero, the crowned gladiator—what had he to do with the eighteenth century? The hero of everybody's boyhood, he remains a puzzle and a mystery to us in our maturer years. He seems an impossibility in the times in which he lived. On the death of Charles XI, and the commencement of the hostile movement by Russia and Denmark, the stripling sovereign seems to dilate into the vast, shadowy proportions of some ancient hero of Scandinavian Sagas. He seems like one of the ancient Norsemen, whose vocation was simply to fight—who conquered the whole earth, not because they wanted it, but because they were sent into the world for no other earthly purpose; a legitimate representative of the old Sea-Kings, or rather an ancient Sea-King himself, reappearing in the eighteenth century, with no specially defined object, and proposing to himself no particular business in the world which he had so suddenly revisited, but to fight as much as possible, and with anybody that came along. Viewed in this light, he can be judged more justly. He was out of place where he was. He would have been a magnificent hero and a useful personage six or seven hundred years earlier. He was a very mischievous character in the eighteenth century. People no longer fought in the same way as before; they no longer fought for the fun of it; they now had always an object in their wars. Sovereigns, however belligerent in taste, had always an eye to their interest. This was preëminently the case with his great antagonist, Peter. He never fought except for an object; but, sooner than relinquish the object, he would have fought till "sun and moon were in the flat sea sunk." He was a creator, a founder, a lawgiver, as well as a warrior. He was constructive; Charles merely destructive. The Czar was a great statesman; Charles only a great gladiator. In war, Peter was always preparing for peace; as for Charles, after he first started upon his career, he never seemed to have had the faintest suspicion that there was such a thing, such a *status,* as peace. He came into the world to fight, and he fought; he lived fighting, he died fighting. He poured himself out, like a fierce torrent from his native mountains, in one wild, headlong, devastating flood. There was nothing beneficent, nothing fertilizing, in his career. His kingdom was neglected, his treasury exhausted, his subjects impoverished; while he himself, from the admiration and wonder of Europe, became, or would have become, but for his timely death, its laughing-stock. The hero at Narva was only Bombastes Furioso at Bender.

While Charles was deposing Augustus and crowning Stanislaus, the troops of Peter were not idle. Keeping his eye ever fixed upon his great object, the Czar was adding to his domain province after province of what was then the Swedish seacoast. Dorpt and Narva are captured, and with them all Ingria, of which Peter makes the pastry-cook's apprentice governor. Courland soon follows, and now the Czar joins his forces to those of Augustus in Poland. While he is called off to quell an insurrection in Astrakhan (distances are nothing to the Czar), Augustus seizes the opportunity to make the ignominious compact with the Swedish king to which we have referred, and—most shameful and perfidious part of his treason—surrenders to the vengeance of the ferocious Charles, *to the torture and the wheel,* the unfortunate General Patkul, ambassador of the Czar at the court of Augustus, who had incurred the hatred of the Swedish monarch for heading a deputation of Livonian nobles, and presenting to him a petition concerning the rights and privileges of their province. The allies of King Augustus take possession of Warsaw, while King Augustus himself is writing his congratulations to King Stanislaus.

Peter, having helped himself to almost as many Swedish provinces as he cared for, while Charles has been bullying Augustus and breaking Patkul on the wheel, is now disposed to treat for peace. The French envoy at Dresden offers his services, but Charles declines treating except at Moscow. "My brother Charles wishes to act Alexander," says the Czar; "but he shall not find me Darius."

Peter now conceives almost exactly the same plan by which the conqueror of the nineteenth century was entrapped and destroyed. He makes his country and climate fight for him, and retreats slowly before his advancing enemy, drawing him on step by step to a barren country, whence he could have no retreat, and where Peter could suddenly advance from his own secure position and overwhelm him at a blow. With masterly generalship he retreats before his hot-headed adversary, still "tempting him to the desert with his sword," marches to Mohilev and Orsha on the eastern bank of the Dnieper, a position in free communication with Smolensk, sends his Cossacks to lay waste the country for thirty miles round, and then orders them to join him beyond the Borysthenes. The two Northern monarchs now disappear from the eyes of anxious Europe among the wildernesses of ancient Scythia. Peter, with a hundred thousand men well provided and in convenient communication with his own cities and magazines, remains quiet. Charles, intent upon dictating terms at Moscow, crosses the Borysthenes with eighty thousand men. A fierce battle without results is fought on the Beresina. Charles pushes on to Smolensk. By order of Peter the country between the Borysthenes and Smolensk had been laid waste. At the approach of winter the Swedish army dwindles and wastes away beneath the horrors of the iron climate. Still Charles advances, when suddenly, and to the Czar inexplicably, he turns aside from his path, abandons his design upon Moscow, and directs his steps to the Ukraine. The mystery is solved by the news of Mazeppa's treason. The old Hetman of the Cossacks deserts to Charles, promising to bring over all his troops: he brings no one but himself; the Cossacks scorn his treachery, and remain faithful to their Czar.

By this time it was December, the cold intense, and the Swedish army perishing by thousands; Count Piper implores his master to halt and go into the best winter-quarters they could find in the Ukraine. The King refuses, resolved to reduce the Ukraine, and then march to Moscow. In the month of May, after a winter spent by the Czar's forces in comfortable quarters and by the King's exposed to all kinds of misery, Charles lays siege to Pultowa with eighteen thousand men, the remnant of his eighty thousand. On June 15, 1709, the Czar appears before Pultowa, and, by feint of attack upon the Swedes, succeeds in throwing two thousand men into the place, and at length, a few days after, gives him battle and utterly routs and destroys his army. Both the King and the Czar, throughout this

> ". . . dread Pultowa's day,
> When fortune left the royal Swede,"

fight in the front of the battle. Several balls pierce the Czar's clothes; while Charles, having been previously wounded in the heel, is carried through the fight upon a litter. After the total overthrow of his army Charles escapes on horseback with a handful of followers, and, entering the confines of Turkey, halts at Bender on the Dniester.

The battle of Pultowa and the final overthrow of Charles are followed during the autumn and winter by the complete conquest of Livonia—Viborg, Elbing, Riga, and Revel being taken early in 1710. At the same time Peter deposes Stanislaus and restores the illustrious Augustus.

In the mean time Charles remains at Bender, the stipendiary of the Sultan, while Poniatowski, his emissary at the Porte, is busily intriguing to bring about a declaration of war from Turkey against the Czar. In conjunction with the Khan of the Crimean Tartars, who appeals to the Sultan's jealousy of the increasing power of Russia, and inspires him with a desire to recover Azov and expel his encroaching neighbors from the Black Sea, the envoy succeeds. The Grand Mufti declares that it is necessary for the Sultan to go to war with the Czar; whereupon the Muscovite ambassador is forthwith "clapped into prison" by way of commencement of hostilities, and the war begins. Peter immediately makes a levy of one man in four, besides one "valet out of every two belonging to the nobility," makes a solemn declaration of war, and then marches at the head of forty thousand men to the frontier of Turkey. Previously to his departure he makes a public proclamation of his previous marriage to Catharine; and the Empress, despite his earnest remonstrances, accompanies the invading army.

It is strange that the Czar on this expedition should have committed the same error, and placed himself in almost the same unfortunate predicament, as his adversary Charles. Trusting to the representations and the friendship of the faithless Hospodar of Moldavia, he advances rapidly at the head of an insufficient force into a hostile and barren country, relying for men and munitions of war upon his ally. Crossing the Pruth, he finds himself near Jassy, in a hostile country between an army of Turks and another of Tartars, with a deep and rapid river between him and his own dominions. Forty thousand Russians are held at bay by two hundred thousand Turks and Tartars.

The situation of the Czar is terrible; annihilation seems to stare him in the face. His enemy Charles visits the Turkish camp in disguise, urging the Czar's destruction upon the Vizier. A destructive battle is going on unceasingly, which in three days costs him eighteen thousand men. Retreat is impossible; no ally is near him, no succor expected. What can possibly extricate him? Shall he dash upon the Turks at the head of his remaining forces and cut his way through them, or die, sword in hand, in the attempt? Shall he surrender to the overwhelming power of the Sultan's army, and be paraded at Constantinople as the captive Czar? Tortured and perplexed, he shuts himself up alone in his tent and falls into terrible convulsions. None of his generals dare approach him; he has forbidden an entrance to all. Suddenly, in spite of the prohibition, the captive of Marienburg stands before him. She who at all times possessed a mysterious power to calm the spasmodic affections, half physical, half mental, to which he was subject, now appears before him like an angel to relieve his agony and to point out an escape from impending ruin. She suggests the idea of negotiation, which had occurred to no one in the desperate situation in which they were placed, and which she instinctively prophesied would still be successful. She strips herself of her jewels, and ransacks the camp for objects of value to form a suitable present for the Grand Vizier. The Vice-Chancellor Shaffiroff is despatched to the enemy's camp, and the apparently impossible result is a treaty of peace. Arms are suspended immediately, and soon afterward honorable articles are signed, of which the principal are the surrender of Azov, the exclusion of the Czar from the Black Sea, the demolition of the fortress of Taganrog, the withdrawal of the Russian soldiers from the neighborhood of the Danube, and the promise of free passage to Charles XII through Russia to his own states.

It is unnecessary to analyze or to criticise the different motives that actuated the Vizier in acceding to an honorable negotiation, when the Czar seemed to be so completely in his power. It is sufficient that this was the surprising and fortunate result of Catharine's counsel. "Her great merit," says Voltaire, "was that she saw the possibility of negotiation at a moment when the generals seem to have seen nothing but an inevitable misfortune." No language can describe the rage and mortification of Charles XII at this unexpected result—at this apparently impossible escape of his hated rival from overwhelming ruin. Hastening to the camp of the Vizier, he upbraids him, as if he had been his master instead of his stipendiary; he expresses his profound disgust that the Czar has not been carried to Constantinople, instead of being allowed to go home so easily. "And who will govern his empire in his absence?" asked the Vizier, with bitter irony, adding that "it would never to do have all the sovereigns away from home." In answer to this retort, Charles grins ferociously in his face, turns on his heel, and tears the Vizier's robe with his spurs. After thus insulting the great functionary of the Sultan, he continues three years longer a pensionary upon his bounty. To the reiterated entreaties of his Senate, that he would return, and attend to the pressing exigencies of his kingdom, he replies, in a style worthy of Bombastes, that he would send one of his boots to govern them, and remains at Bender, still deluded and besotted with the idea that he should yet appear with a Turkish force before Moscow. At last, in 1714, after fighting a pitched battle at the head of his valets, grooms, and house-servants, against a considerable Turkish army, sent to dislodge him by force, he is ignominiously expelled from the country whose hospitality he has so long outraged, and returns in the disguise of a courier to Sweden.

The Czar upon his return to his dominions gains a considerable victory over the Swedish fleet in the Baltic, commanding his own in person in a line-of-battle ship of his own building. On arriving at Petersburg he ordains a great triumphal procession to bring the captured ships with their admirals and officers up the Neva. At this time he transfers the Senate from Moscow to Petersburg, establishes assemblies, at which the penalty for infringement of the rules and regulations is to "empty the great eagle, a huge bowl, filled with wine and brandy," institutes the Academy of Arts and Sciences, founds the public library commenced with the one captured ("conveyed, the wise it call") from the university at Abo, sends a mission through Siberia to China, and draws up a map of his dominions, much of it with his own hand.

In 1715, after taking Stralsund, completing the conquest of Finland and Esthonia, and commanding in person the allied fleets of England, Denmark, and Russia, he makes a second tour in Europe, accompanied by Catharine. He revisits Saardam, where he is received with great enthusiasm, is entertained with great distinction in Paris, and visits the tomb of Cardinal Richelieu, where he exclaims, dropping upon his knees, "Thou great man, I would have given thee half of my dominions to have learned of thee to govern the other half." He drew up with his own hand a treaty of commerce with France, and returned through Berlin to Petersburg. The letters of the Margravine of Baireuth from Berlin present no very flattering picture of the imperial travellers. She describes Peter as dressed plainly in a naval costume, handsome, but rude, uncouth, and of dreadful aspect; and Catharine as fat, frouzy, and vulgar, needing only to be seen to betray her obscure origin, and bedizened with chains, orders, and holy relics, "making such a *Geklinkklank* as if an ass with bells were coming along"; she represents them both as intolerable beggars, plundering the palace of everything they could lay their hands on.

Peter had long ago constituted himself the head of the Church, and treated with contempt the pretensions of the prelates to temporal power. When at Paris, however, he had received an elaborate petition from the Sorbonne, the object of which was to effect a reunion between the Greek and Latin Churches. But the despot who had constituted himself the head, hand, heart, and conscience of his people—who had annihilated throughout his empire every element of power adverse to his own—who had crushed the soldiery, the nobility, and the clergy, deposed the patriarch, and constituted himself the high priest of his empire—was not very likely to comply with the Sorbonne's invitation to acknowledge the supremacy of the Pope in his dominions. Nevertheless, he received their petition with great politeness.

On his return to Petersburg, he was vexed by the importunity of some of his own clergy, who clamored for the appointment of a patriarch, on the ground that it was demanded by the people, and that it was necessary to assert the dignity and independence of the Greek Church. Now there happened to be about Petersburg one Sotoff, a venerable jester of eighty-four, who had been the Czar's writing-master in his younger years, and at the age of seventy had been advanced to the dignity of buffoon. This venerable individual the Czar fixes upon for the office of patriarch, previously creating him a prince and a pope. In order to make the office of patriarch completely ridiculous in the eyes of the people, and to give them a little innocent recreation at the same time, he now ordains a solemn marriage between this patriarch and a "buxom widow of thirty-four." We must ask indulgence while we quote a short description of this funny ceremony from the old author already cited:

"The nuptials of this extraordinary couple were solemnized by the court in masks or mock show. The company consisted of about four hundred persons of both sexes. Every four persons had their proper dress and peculiar musical instruments, so that they represented a hundred different sorts of habits and music, particularly of the Asiatic nations. The four persons appointed to invite the guests were the greatest stammerers that could be found in all Russia. Old, decrepit men, who were not able to walk or stand, had been picked out to serve for bridesmen, stewards, and waiters. There were four running footmen, the most unwieldy fellows, who had been troubled with the gout most of their lives, and were so fat and bulky that they wanted others to lead them. The mock Czar of Moscow, who represented King David in his dress, instead of a harp, had a lyre with a bear-skin to play upon. He, being the chief of the company, was carried on a sort of a pageant placed on a sled, to the four corners of which were tied as many bears, which, being pricked with goads by fellows purposely appointed for it, made such a frightful roaring as well suited the confused and horrible din raised by the disagreeing instruments of the rest of the company. The Czar himself was dressed like a boor of Friesland, and skilfully beat a drum in company with three generals. In this manner, bells ringing everywhere, the ill-matched couple were attended by the masks to the altar of the great church, where they were joined in matrimony by a priest a hundred years old, who had lost his eyesight and his memory; to supply which defect a pair of spectacles were put upon his nose, two candles held before his eyes, and the words sounded into his ears, which he was to pronounce. From church the procession went to the Czar's palace, where the diversion lasted some days. Many strange adventures and comical accidents happened on their riding-sleds through the streets, too long to be related here.

Thus much may suffice to show that the Czar, among all the heavy cares of government, knew how to set apart some days for the relaxation of his mind, and how ingenious he was in the contrivance of those diversions."

We confess that we are unable to agree with the grave conclusion of the author from whom we quote. To us this "ingenious diversion" seems about as sorry a jest as we ever heard of. However, it was considered "most admirable fooling" in Moscow, and, at all events, after two or three repetitions, seems to have quite cured the people of their desire for patriarchs.

"The Czar," says Voltaire, "thus laughingly avenged twenty emperors of Germany, ten kings of France, and a host of sovereigns. This was all the fruit which the Sorbonne gathered from their not very politic idea of reuniting the Greek and Latin Churches."

The darkest chapter in the life of Peter now approaches. After the lapse of a century, no one can read the account of that dreadful tragedy, the trial, condemnation, and death of the Czarevitch Alexis, without a shudder of horror. No one can contemplate the spectacle of a son judicially condemned by his father for no crime—no one can read the record of the solemn farce which represents the trial of the unfortunate victim without feeling all his admiration for the extraordinary qualities of the Czar swallowed up by indignation and abhorrence. Up to this time Peter seems a man—a hard-hearted, despotic, inexorable man, perhaps—but he is still human. He now seems only a machine, a huge engine of unparalleled power, placed upon the earth to effect a certain task, working its mighty arms night and day with ceaseless and untiring energy, crashing through all obstacles, and annihilating everything in its path with the unfeeling precision of gigantic mechanism.

It was hardly to be expected, to be sure, that this tremendous despot, who had recoiled before no obstacle in the path of his settled purpose, who had strode over everything with the step of a giant, who had given two seas to an inland empire, who had conquered the most warlike nation and sovereign of Europe with barbarians in petticoats, who had crushed the nobility, annihilated the janizaries, trampled the patriarch in the dust—who had repudiated his wife because she was attached to the old customs of Muscovy, and had married and crowned a pastry-cook's mistress because it was his sovereign will and pleasure—it was hardly to be expected that such a man would hesitate about disinheriting his own son if he thought proper to do so. But it might have been hoped that he would content himself with disinheriting him, and that the "Pater Patriæ," as by solemn decree he was shortly afterward entitled, would remember that he was also father of Alexis.

This unhappy young man, the son of the repudiated wife of the Czar, seems to have been a very miserable creature. We have the fullest sympathy with the natural disappointment of Peter at the incorrigible, hopeless stupidity and profligacy of his son. Still, he had himself to blame in a great measure for many of his son's defects. His education had been neglected, or rather, worse than neglected; it had been left to the care of monks, to the care of the very order of people most wedded to the ancient state of things, and most desirous of restoring it if possible. The necessary result of such training upon a dull boy might easily have been foreseen. There was, however, not the slightest objection to disinheriting him; he had no claim to the throne, and he was totally unworthy of it. There was no law of Russia designating the eldest son as successor. On the contrary, the genius of the Russian autocracy seems to vest the fee simple of all the Russias and all the Russians in the actual autocrat, to be disposed of as he sees fit, and devised to whomsoever he deems most eligible. This had been, and was then, the law, if it be worth while to talk about law when the will of the sovereign makes and alters the law at any moment. Alexis seems to have been weak, dissolute, and intriguing—a sot, a bigot, a liar, and a coward—the tool of "bushy-bearded" priests and designing women, whose control of the empire had been terminated by Peter's energetic measures. The Czar's predominating fear was that at his death the empire would relapse into the quagmire of barbarism from which he had reclaimed it. Alexis, priest-ridden and ignorant, was sure to become a tool in the hands of priests as soon as he should ascend the throne, and the old order of things would as surely be reinstated.

Peter, soon after the death of his son's wife (a virtuous and intelligent German princess, whose life seems to have been worn out by the neglect, cruelty, and debauchery of her husband), remonstrates with him upon his evil courses, commands him to reform, and threatens else to disinherit him. "Amend your life, or else turn monk," says the Czar. "I intend to embrace the monastic life," replies the son; "I pledge myself to do so, and only ask your gracious permission." The Czar, just before his departure for Germany and France, visits Alexis, who was, or pretended to be, confined to his bed by sickness. The young man again renews his renunciation of the succession and repeats his pledge to become a monk. Peter bids him take six months to consider the matter, takes an affectionate farewell of him, and sets out upon his travels. As soon as his back is turned, Alexis realizes the old distich:

> "The devil was sick, the devil a monk would be;
> The devil got well, the devil a monk was he."

He recovers his health instantaneously, and celebrates his father's departure by getting very drunk with a select party of friends. Seven months afterward the Czar writes to him to join him at Copenhagen, if he had determined to reform his life and make himself fit for the succession; if not, to execute his monastic plans without delay. Alexis accordingly announces his intention of going to Copenhagen, draws a heavy bill on Menshikoff for his travelling expenses, leaves Moscow, and, instead of Copenhagen, sneaks off to Vienna. The Emperor of Germany, however, turns him off, and he goes to Naples. Two envoys of the Czar, Tolstoy and Romanzoff, proceed to Naples and induce him, by ample promises of forgiveness on the part of his father, to return. The following is a part of his father's letter:

"I write to you for the last time, to tell you that you are to execute my will, which Tolstoy and Romanzoff will announce to you on my part. If you obey me, I assure you and I promise, in the name of God, that I will not punish you, and that, if you return, I will love you more than ever; but if you do not, I give you as your father, in virtue of the power which I have received from God, my eternal curse; and as your sovereign, I assure you that I shall find the means of punishing you; in which I hope that God will assist me, and that he will take my just cause in his hand."

Upon the faith of this sacred promise Alexis accompanies the two emissaries to Moscow, where they arrive on February 13, 1718. The day after his arrival the Czar, by way of keeping his promise of pardoning and loving him more than ever, calls a grand council of the senate and all the dignitaries of the empire, and there, in the most solemn, formal, and authentic manner, disinherits Alexis, deprives him of all claim to the succession, and obliges him, and all those present, to take the oath of future allegiance to his and Catharine's son Peter, then an infant, who, however, shortly afterward died. This was the beginning of the fulfilment of his promise; but it was only the beginning of the end. Alexis was worthless, ignorant, stupid, and depraved; but he had committed no crime, and deserved no punishment, certainly not the punishment of death. A comfortable state of things there would be in the world, if every man who happened to have a profligate dunce of a son were to be justified in cutting his head off; and for an autocrat and high priest to do so seems to us a thousand times more atrocious.

However, the Czar seems to have been determined, after his first evasion, to get rid of him, and accordingly produces the charge of a conspiracy. Alexis is formally accused of conspiring against his father's life and throne, and a pack of perfectly contemptible stuff is collected together to make what was called evidence; it consisted of confessions of his mistress, his pot-companions, and his confessor—all upon the rack—that he had been known to express wishes for his father's death, and to throw out hints about receiving assistance, in a certain event, from the Emperor of Germany. But in the whole mess of it there is not the faintest shadow of a shade of evidence that he had ever conspired, that he had ever entertained any design against his father; and the necessary result, upon any candid mind, of a perusal of the evidence is a conviction of his perfect innocence of the crime charged upon him. There is not a country in the world where there is any pretence of administering justice, in which such an accusation, supported by such evidence, would not have been hooted out of court. Still, the accusation was made, and something which they called a trial was instituted. The prince is sworn upon the Holy Evangelists to tell the whole truth, and nothing but the truth; and he immediately begins to utter lies by the wholesale. His weak intellect seems to have been possessed and disordered by one idea—that if he should confess a great deal more than was expected, and make himself out much more guilty than he was supposed to be, he should perhaps obtain his pardon. Having, however, done nothing criminal, and having said nothing that could be fairly considered suspicious, he dives into the bottom of his breast, and brings up and displays his most secret thoughts by way of self-accusation. The truth seems to have been that he was bullied to the last degree. We know the Czar to have been a man who eminently inspired awe, and Alexis was of an uncommonly sneaking disposition. As the event proved, Peter absolutely frightened his son to death. Certainly, never were the forms of judicial investigation so outraged as in this trial. The details are sickening, and we have already transgressed the indulgence of our readers. Let one or two questions, made by the prosecution, and answered by the criminal in writing, suffice as specimens of the Czar's criminal jurisprudence:

"When you saw, in the letter of Beyer" (a gossiping envoy from the German Emperor's Court, who wrote to his sovereign all the news, true or false, as fast as he picked it up), "that there was a revolt in the army of Mecklenburg, you were rejoiced; I believe that you had some view, and that you would have declared for the rebels, even in my lifetime." The answer of Alexis is, "If the rebels had called me in your lifetime, I should probably have joined them, supposing that they had been strong enough." In answer to another question, he avows that "he had accused himself before God, in confession to the priest Jacques, of having wished the death of his father; and that the confessor Jacques had replied: 'God will pardon you for it; we all wish it as much.'"

After this farce of a trial had been enacted, the Czar, waiving his prerogative of life and death, determined to submit the case to the judgment of the clergy, judges, and high officers of state. This always seemed to us very paltry. It was an attempt to shift the responsibility of the murder off his own shoulders, where only it belonged. The council of clergy, after recognizing the Czar's power—*jus vitæ et necis*—which nobody ever doubted, and citing several cases from the Old Testament, recommended mercy, relying principally upon Absalom's case. It was plain they washed their hands of it. Meantime, further investigations, it was pretended, had made the matter worse; and, on July 5th, the ministers, senators, and generals unanimously condemn the prince to death, leaving the sentence, of course, open to the Czar's revision, and prescribing no particular mode of execution. The sentence of death is published, Alexis is informed of it, and seems literally to have been frightened to death by it; for, while the Czar was deliberating what course to take (and the opinion of the most indulgent—we confess not ours—seems to be that he did not intend the execution of the sentence), the unfortunate young man was carried off by a kind of apopletic seizure, and, on July 7th, died contrite, receiving the sacrament and extreme unction, and imploring his father's pardon.

This account seems to be now accepted as the true one. But the Marquis de Custine, in his greediness to devour everything that blackens the character of Russia in general, and of Peter the Great in particular, could not, of course, fail to reproduce the stories that have been told and retold, exploded and reëxploded—and which will continue, we suppose, to be told and exploded, believed in and ridiculed, to the end of time. It was not believed by many people in Europe at the time, and it is not believed by the Comte de Ségur and the Marquis de Custine now, that the prince died a natural death —if the cataleptic convulsive fit, consequent upon extreme and protracted mental agony, which finally ended his life, can be called a natural and not a violent death. All sorts of stories were told at the time, each more incredible than the other, and each disproving the other. The Czar was said to have knouted him to death with his own hands—to have poisoned him with a potion which he sent Marshal Weyde to an apothecary's shop in broad daylight to procure—to have cut off his head, and then to have had it privately sewed on again by Madame Cramer—in short, to have made away with him by a variety of means, all of which could not well have been true, and all of which are, under the circumstances, extremely unlikely. To us it seems ridiculous to add a new horror to this terrible tragedy. We are not sure, either, that the supposed assassination makes the matter any worse. "Murder most foul as at the best it is," we are unable to see that the private murder is a whit more atrocious than the public, solemn, and judicial murder of which the Czar stands accused and condemned to all eternity.

It certainly does not seem to have been in Peter's nature to have taken his son off by poison, or in any private way. The autocrat was a man who gloried in his own actions, in displaying the tremendous, irresistible power of his own will. He had collected all the dignity of his empire to assist at the spectacle; he had invoked the attention of all Europe to the tragedy he proposed to enact; he had determined to execute his son, and he did intend, we have no doubt, to murder him in the most ceremonious manner, and for the good of his country. We have not a doubt of his motives; he thought himself actuated by the purest philanthropy; but these expansive bosoms, which embrace the whole earth, or a third of it, in their colossal affection, are apt to be deficient in the humbler virtues of love and charity when it comes to detail. The truth was, Peter loved his country so well that he determined to sacrifice his son to its welfare; in other words, his heart was as hard as the nether millstone, and he would have sacrificed twenty thousand sons rather than have been thwarted in the cherished projects of his ambitious intellect. But we confess we can conceive of no motive for the alleged assassination. It was not in the character of the Emperor, and it was a piece of stupidity as well as barbarity. "If the assassination had trammelled up the consequence" of all that preceded, "then it were well"; and the deed might have been possible. But the broken faith to his son, the atrocious trial, the deliberate condemnation, could in no manner have been obliterated from the minds of men by the "deep damnation" of a secret "taking off." He had announced to the world his intention of executing his son for alleged disobedience and conspiracy; he had sent to every court in Europe copies of the judicial proceedings, ending in the condemnation of the victim; he had been publicly brandishing the sword of justice over his son's neck, and calling upon the world to witness the spectacle; and why he should have made all this parade for the mere purpose of poisoning him, knouting him, or cutting his head off in secret, seems inexplicable.

Besides, as Voltaire very strongly urges, the different kinds of assassination alleged disprove each other, and the fact that Alexis was never alone from the moment of the condemnation to the hour of his death makes any secret execution impossible. The knouting story has not found many advocates; the poisoning and the beheading are supported about equally, and are both about equally probable. It certainly was not probable that the Czar would have sent a high officer of court to fetch the poison, and a few minutes afterward have despatched another messenger to bid the first make great haste. This is not exactly the way in which poisoning is usually managed. And the other story, that the young man's head was cut off and then sewed on again, is so ludicrous that it would deserve no attention but for the number of writers who have reported it upon the authority of contemporaneous gossip. At what moment the Czar found a secret opportunity to cut the head off—how Madame Cramer found a secret opportunity to sew it on again—how this ingenious lady, who, we suppose, had not practised this kind of needlework as a profession, was able to fit it on so adroitly as to deceive not only the whole court but even the patient himself, for, as far as we can understand the story, Alexis seems to have received extreme unction and the sacrament, in presence of about a hundred witnesses, after Mrs. Cramer's job was finished—are all matters very difficult to explain. Moreover, as we have already observed, we do not see much greater atrocity in the one case than in the other. Peter's will being the only law of the land, he could do what he chose, execute his son as he chose, and by his own hand if he chose. The only law which could have any binding force over the autocrat was the law of nature, and that, to his soul of granite, was weaker than the spider's web. He was determined to sacrifice his son to the welfare of his country, and to insure the continuance of his reformation in Church and State. Sacrifices of this sort have always found advocates and admirers, and are sure to be repeated on great occasions, and at rare intervals, to the end of time.

Dismissing this painful subject, we hasten to conclude this imperfect sketch of the principal events in the Czar's history. We will not dwell upon the extraordinary but abortive intrigues of the two arch-plotters of Europe, Cardinal Alberoni and Baron Görtz, by which the Czar and the Swedish monarch were to be reconciled and combined in a plot against George I of England, and in favor of the Pretender. A chance bullet from "a petty fortress and a dubious hand" at Frederikshald, in Norway, terminates at once the life of Charles and the intrigues of Görtz. The baron, instead of taking the crown from George's head, loses his own head at Stockholm; Alberoni is turned out of Spain; and the Czar remains *in statu quo*, having been careful throughout the whole intrigue, which was perfectly well known in England, to make the most barefaced promises of eternal friendship to the House of Hanover; and "to reiterate," as the diplomatists say, "the assurances of his distinguished consideration" for the English King all the time that he was plotting against his throne.

The death of Charles alters the complexion of Europe. Peace, which was hardly possible during his lifetime, becomes the immediate object of all parties. The Prince of Hesse, husband of Queen Ulrica, and, by cession of his wife, King of Sweden, is desirous of peace upon almost any terms which will allow of an honorable repose to his exhausted and impoverished country. Peter, having obtained possession of all the provinces he required, is ready to sheathe the sword on receiving proper recognition of his title to the property thus acquired; and accordingly, after a good deal of bravado upon the Baltic between the English and the Russian fleets, and the burning of some fifty or sixty Swedish villages, innumerable châteaux, and fifteen or twenty thousand houses, in a descent made by the Russians upon the coasts of Sweden, the war, which continues with ferocity during all the negotiations for peace, is at last brought to a conclusion by the signing of the treaty of Neustadt, on September 10, 1721. By this treaty of peace, the Czar is guaranteed in the possession of Livonia, Esthonia, Ingria, Carelia, Viborg, and the many adjacent islands, and thus reaps the reward of twenty years' hard labor; receiving, moreover, from the senate and synod, by solemn decree—what seems insipid homage for an autocrat—the titles of Great, Emperor, and Pater Patriæ.

After an interval of two years, passed in establishing woollen, paper, and glass manufactories, embellishing his capital, and regulating the internal and foreign commerce of Russia, we suddenly find him, accompanied by the faithful Catharine, descending the Volga at the head of a large army. A revolution which had broken out in Persia, in the course of which the reigning sovereign, the imbecile Hussein, finds himself hard pressed by the Afghan prince, Meer Mahmoud, offers an opportunity to Peter to possess himself of a few maritime provinces on the Caspian, to console him for the loss of Azov consequent upon the disaster of the Pruth. A few hundred Russians, engaged in commerce at the town of Shamakia, having been cut to pieces during some of the hostile movements, he finds therein a pretext for invading Persia, and requiring satisfaction from both sovereign and rebel. Failing in this, of course, he sails from Astrakhan to Derbent, which town he takes possession of, and, soon afterward, being applied to by the unhappy Sophi for protection against the Afghans, he consents to afford it, in consideration of receiving the towns of Baku and Derbent, together with the provinces of Ghilan, Mazanderan, and Astrabad. "It is not land I want, but water," exclaims the Czar, as he snatches these sunny provinces, the whole southern coast of the Caspian, the original kingdom of Cyrus, from the languid hand of the Persian, without the expenditure of the blood, time, and treasure which it had cost him to wrest the frozen swamps of Finland from the iron grasp of Charles.

Peter's conquests are now concluded. The Russian colossus now stands astride, from the "thrilling regions of thick-ribbed ice" on the Baltic to the "fragrant bowers of Astrabad" on the Caspian, with a foot upon either sea. The man who had begun to gratify his passion for maritime affairs by paddling a little skiff on the Yausa, and who became on his accession only the barbaric sovereign of an inland and unknown country, now finds himself the lord of two seas, with a considerable navy, built almost by his own hand. It was upon his return to Petersburg from his Persian expedition that he ordered the very skiff in which he commenced navigation to be brought from Moscow, and took occasion to give to his court an entertainment which was called the "consecration of the Little Grandsire," that being the name he had given to the skiff. At the time of this ceremony of the consecration, the progeny of the Little Grandsire numbered already, according to the returns of the admiralty, "forty-one ships of the line, in a condition for service at sea, carrying twenty-one hundred and six guns, manned with fourteen thousand nine hundred seamen, besides a proportionate number of frigates, galleys, and other small craft." The little cabin which was Peter's house while building Petersburg still stands upon what is now called the Citadel; it is consecrated as a chapel, filled with votive offerings, and inclosed with a brick wall, and the Little Grandsire is religiously preserved within the building.

We are certainly not taken in by the colossal puerility of the Russian marine any more than the Marquis de Custine is; and, although the descendants of the Little Grandsire are now at least double the number they were at the time of the consecration, we have not heard of any very brilliant exploits on any ocean to justify the very imposing and very Roman *rostra* which decorate the exchange at Petersburg. To use a vulgar but expressive phrase, the Russian navy has not yet set the Baltic on fire, and we doubt if it ever will. If it could thaw a little, it would be all the better; for, Cronstadt being blockaded by ice six months in the year, the navy is only paraded during the pleasant weather for the amusement of the autocrat. As long as England stands where it does, and the Russian winter remains as it is, we shall hardly fear much from the descendants of the Little Grandsire, at least till the capital is shifted to the Bosphorus.

At the same time we are far from agreeing with the Marquis de Custine in his sweeping condemnation of Peter's policy in building Petersburg and establishing a marine. It was a thousand times better to have the Black Sea and the Baltic than nothing; and if his successors had taken half as much pains as himself in fostering the maritime trade of the country, and if Russia, instead of all this parade of ships of the line, frigates, and steamers, could create a mercantile marine for itself, and could manage its own considerable foreign trade, now monopolized by foreign vessels, principally the English, she might still obtain the germ of a maritime population while waiting for Constantinople. But till she learns that the strength of a navy consists in sailors and not ships she is not likely to be a very formidable power upon the ocean, let her build as many line-of-battle ships as she chooses.

The only other interesting incident in Peter's life, which now draws rapidly to its close, was the coronation of Catharine as Empress consort. This event was celebrated with extraordinary pomp, and particular stress is laid in the Emperor's proclamation upon her conduct in the affair of the Pruth, and the salvation of himself and his army is attributed to her heroism and presence of mind. There seems to be little doubt that Peter intended this solemn coronation of the Empress during his lifetime—a ceremony which was not usual in Russia—to be an indication of his intention that she should succeed to the throne upon his death.

Very soon after this, having exposed himself when in a feeble state of health by standing in the water a long time and over-exerting himself in saving the lives of some sailors and soldiers who were near being wrecked in a storm upon the Gulf of Finland, he was attacked by a painful disorder, to which he had been subject during the latter years of his life, and expired with calmness and resignation on January 28, 1725. His sufferings during his last illness had been so intense that he was unable to make any intelligible disposition as to the succession; and, strange to say, the possessor of this mighty empire, of which the only fundamental law was the expressed will of the sovereign, died intestate. It is in the highest degree probable that he had intended to appoint his wife as his successor; at any rate, assisted by the promptness of Menshikoff and her own resolution, Catharine ascended the throne without opposition.

The disorder which thus cut off the Czar in the fifty-fourth year of his age was an acute inflammation of the intestines and bladder; but, as a matter of course, his death was attributed to poison. We do not observe that the Marquis de Custine has revived this story, which is matter of surprise to us, particularly as we believe that his friend the Comte de Ségur has adopted it in his history. The temptation to damage the character of the Empress, and to represent her to posterity as an adulteress and a poisoner, was too strong to be resisted by the contemporary chroniclers. Lamberti gives us a detailed account of an intrigue of Catharine with one of her chamberlains, a melodramatic discovery made by Peter in an arbor, and a consequent determination upon his part to shut her up for life in a convent. She escaped her fate, according to the same faithful historian, in a singular manner. Peter, it appears, kept a memorandum-book, and was in the habit of making daily minutes of everything he proposed to do; while one of Catharine's pages was in the habit of secretly bringing His Majesty's tablets from his dressing-room for the daily inspection of the Empress. The intended imprisonment of Catharine, jotted down among other memoranda, was thus revealed to her, whereupon she incontinently poisoned him. This story has been sufficiently disproved. It is hardly worth disproving; for it is not probable that a man who had suddenly made this discovery of the guilt of a woman who had just been crowned as empress, and whom he had now determined to imprison for life, instead of designating her as his successor, would require to make any memorandum of the matter. And yet we are expected to believe that an entry was found upon Peter's tablets almost literally to this effect: "*Mem.* To repudiate my wife, shave her head, and lock her up in a convent"; as if otherwise the matter would have slipped his memory. How is it possible that our friend De Custine has allowed this story to escape him?

In the vast square of the Admiralty at St. Petersburg stands the celebrated colossal statue of Peter the Great. Around him are palaces, academies, arsenals, gorgeous temples with their light and starry cupolas floating up like painted balloons, and tall spires sheathed in gold, and flashing like pillars of fire. This place, which is large enough for half the Russian army to encamp in, is bounded upon one side by the Admiralty building, the Winter Palace, and the Hermitage, the façades of the three extending more than a mile; in front of the Winter Palace rises the red, polished granite column of Alexander, the largest monolith in the world; from the side opposite the palace radiate three great streets lined with stately and imposing buildings, thronged with population, and intersected by canals which are all bridged with iron; across the square, on the side opposite the statue, stands the Isaac's Church, built of marble, bronze, granite, and gold, and standing upon a subterranean forest, more than a million large trees having been driven into the earth to form its foundation. The Emperor faces the Neva, which pours its limpid waters through quays of solid granite, which for twenty-five miles line its length and that of its branches; and beyond the river rise in full veiw the Bourse, the Academy of Arts and Sciences, and other imposing public edifices.

This equestrian statue has been much admired; we think justly so. The action of the horse is uncommonly spirited and striking, and the position of the Emperor dignified and natural. He waves his hand, as if, like a Scythian wizard as he was, he had just caused this mighty, swarming city, with all its palaces and temples, to rise like a vapor from the frozen morasses of the Neva with one stroke of his wand. In winter, by moonlight, when the whole scene is lighted by the still, cold radiance of a polar midnight, we defy anyone to pause and gaze upon that statue without a vague sensation of awe. The Czar seems to be still presiding in sculptured silence over the colossal work of his hand; to be still protecting his capital from the inundations of the ocean, and his empire from the flood of barbarism, which he always feared would sweep over it upon his death.

"How shall we rank him upon glory's page?"

It is impossible not to admire his genius, his indomitable energy, his unconquerable will. He proposed to himself, while yet a youth, the mighty task of civilizing his country, and of converting a mongrel Asiatic empire into a powerful European state. It is difficult to place one's self in the right position to judge him correctly. We are very far from agreeing with the Marquis de Custine, that his mistake was in importing his civilization. Russia had waited in vain quite long enough for the spontaneous and indigenous germination of the arts and sciences. Besides, in these days when steam is so rapidly approximating and assimilating the different parts of the earth to each other, when railroads are opened to the Red Sea, and steamers paddle by the Garden of Eden, it is difficult to say what nation will long retain a peculiar and appropriate civilization of its own. That the Czar opened the door to Europe and the ocean, that he erected a granite portal, a triumphal arch, upon his western frontier, is to us his greatest merit. If Russia is to be civilized, it must be through the influence of the West; if Russia is to be free, the hymn of liberty will never be wafted to her ears from the silent deserts of Asia, or the sepulchral stillness of China. The Emperor did right to descend from his Slavonic throne, and to go abroad to light the torch of civilization in more favored lands.

But while we admire the concentration of purpose which sustained him throughout his labors, we cannot help deploring the great and fundamental mistake which made them all comparatively worthless. A despot by birth, education, and temperament, he had never the most glimmering notion of the existence of a people. In Russia, then and at this day, there is not even the fiction of a people. Peter had a correct idea of the proper sources of civilization: he knew where and how to collect the seeds; but he forgot that there was nobody to civilize. A people may be humanized, cultivated, brought to any degree of perfection in arts, and arms, and sciences; but he undertook to civilize a state in which there was but one man, and that man himself. The root must grow before the branches and the foliage. Of this the autocrat had no idea. He had already annihilated the only class which was not composed of slaves. With one stroke of his sceptre he had demolished the feudal nobility, or what corresponded in a degree to the feudal nobility of Europe, and had made all social rank throughout his empire to depend upon service to himself. What was accomplished at a later day in western Europe, in the midst of long convulsions and struggles, by the upheaving of the democracy, was effected by the autocrat at a blow. This was a fatal error. There were slaves enough before. It was unnecessary to degrade the nobles. But, the more closely we analyze Peter's character, the more cogently we are compelled to conclude that his actuating motive was rather his own fame than the good of his country. A great peculiarity of his ambition was that, though possessed of eminent military talents and highly successful in his campaigns, he seems to have cared but little for the *certaminis gaudia;* to have taken but small delight in battles and victories for themselves; to have cared little for conquest, beyond what he required for his settled purpose. Conquering, he never aspires to be a conqueror; victorious over the greatest general of the age, he is ready to sheathe his sword as soon as the object of the contest is attained. His ambition was to be a founder, and he never, in victory or defeat, was once turned aside from his purpose. He was determined to advance his empire to the ocean, to create a new capital, and to implant there and throughout his empire the elements of European civilization. If his ambition had flown a little higher, had he determined to regenerate his people, the real civilization of his empire would have followed sooner than it is now likely to do. Of this he probably never dreamed. He was a despot throughout. He might have found other matters in England worthy of his attention, other institutions as intimately connected with civilization as the English naval architecture; but he appears to have been completely indifferent to the great spectacle presented to an autocrat by a constitutional kingdom. "Are these all lawyers?" said he, one day, when visiting the courts at Westminster. "What can be the use of so many lawyers? I have but two in my empire, and I mean to hang one of them as soon as I get back." He certainly might as well have hung them both; a country without law has very little need of lawyers.

It was because his country was inhabited by slaves, and not by a people, that it was necessary, in every branch of his great undertaking, to go into such infinitesimal details. Our admiration of the man's power is, to be sure, increased by a contemplation of the extraordinary versatility of his genius, its wide grasp, and its minute perception; but we regret to see so much elephantine labor thrown away. As he felt himself to be the only man in the empire, so in his power of labor he rises to a demigod, a Hercules. He felt that he must do everything himself, and he did everything. He fills every military post, from drummer to general, from cabin-boy to admiral; with his own hand he builds ships of the line, and navigates them himself in storm and battle; he superintends every manufactory, every academy, every hospital, every prison; with his own hand he pulls teeth and draws up commercial treaties—wins all his battles with his own sword, at the head of his army, and sings in the choir as chief bishop and head of his church—models all his forts, sounds all his harbors, draws maps of his own dominions, all with his own hand—regulates the treasury of his empire and the account-books of his shopkeepers, teaches his subjects how to behave themselves in assemblies, prescribes the length of their coat-skirts, and dictates their religious creed. If, instead of contenting himself with slaves who only aped civilization, he had striven to create a people capable and worthy of culture, he might have spared himself all these minute details; he would have produced less striking, instantaneous effects, but his work would have been more durable, and his fame more elevated. His was one of the monarch minds, who coin their age and stamp it with their image and superscription; but his glory would have been greater if he had thought less of himself, and more of the real interests of his country. If he had attempted to convert his subjects from cattle into men, he need not have been so eternally haunted by the phantom of returning barbarism, destroying after his death all the labor of his lifetime, and which he could exorcise only by shedding the blood of his son. Viewed from this position, his colossal grandeur dwindles. It seems to us that he might have been so much more, that his possible seems to dwarf his actual achievements. He might have been the creator and the lawgiver of a people. He was, after all, only a tyrant and a city-builder. Even now, his successors avert their eyes from the West. The city of his love is already in danger from more potent elements than water. New and dangerous ideas fly through that magnificent western gateway. When the portal is closed, the keys thrown into the Baltic, and the discarded Moscow again embraced, how much fruit will be left from the foreign seeds transplanted? When the Byzantine Empire is restored, perhaps we shall see their ripened development; the Russians of the Lower Empire will be a match for the Greeks who preceded them.

Still, we repeat, it is difficult to judge him justly. He seems to have felt a certain mission confided to him by a superior power. His object he accomplished without wavering, without precipitation, without delay. We look up to him as to a giant, as we see him striding over every adversary, over every obstacle in his path. He seems in advance of his country, of his age, of himself. In his exterior he is the great prince, conqueror, reformer; in his interior, the Muscovite, the barbarian. He was conscious of it himself. "I wish to reform my empire," he exclaimed, upon one occasion, "and I cannot reform myself." In early life his pleasures were of the grossest character; he was a hard drinker, and was quarrelsome in his cups. He kicked and cuffed his ministers, on one occasion was near cutting the throat of Lefort in a paroxysm of drunken anger, and was habitually caning Prince Menshikoff. But, after all, he did reform himself, and, in the latter years of his life, his habits were abstemious and simple, and his days and nights were passed in labors for his country and his fame.

It is difficult to judge him justly. Perhaps it would have been impossible to have planted even the germ of civil or even social liberty in such a wilderness as Russia was at his accession. It was something to lift her ever so little above the waves of barbarism, where he found her "many fathoms deep." He accomplished a great deal. He made Russia a maritime country, gave her a navy and a commercial capital, and quadrupled her revenue; he destroyed the Strelitzes, he crushed the patriarch, he abolished the monastic institutions of his empire. If he had done nothing else, he would, for these great achievements, deserve the eternal gratitude of his country.

SOLITUDE

—

BY

HENRY DAVID THOREAU

HENRY DAVID THOREAU

1817—1862

Concord, Massachusetts, so rich in associations both literary and historical, was the birthplace and life-long home of Henry David Thoreau. Born in 1817, he was educated in the schools of his native town and in Boston, and, though his parents were poor, he was enabled to go to Harvard College, graduating with the class of 1837. His reading and the study of Greek literature made a deep impression on him, and later he endeavored to give to his style a classical conciseness and precision, and often with notable success. For a time after his graduation he taught school, but being more or less of a shiftless nature, he soon found another and more congenial occupation. He never married. For two years he lived with Emerson as a member of his family, and although he endeavored not to be a mere follower of the great author, the influence of the literary master was naturally very powerful in shaping his mental development. In 1845 Thoreau built for himself a modest retreat in a bit of woodland belonging to Emerson on the shore of Walden Pond, where he lived for more than two years. He told his friends that in thus secluding himself his object was "to transact some private business," or, to be more plain, that his seclusion concerned no one but himself. What he really wanted was solitude, partly for the sake of studying nature in all her varying moods under conditions wholly removed from human influences, and partly that he might write at leisure and be free from all interruptions. His essay on "Solitude" is not only characteristic of his general style and mode of thought, but is also interesting as indicating his mood in this remarkable hermit life by Walden Pond.

On his return to civilization Thoreau set about to find a publisher for his book, and after a long search succeeded. In 1849 "A Week on the Concord and Merrimac Rivers" appeared. The public, however, did not appreciate this, and a few years later he gathered the greater part of his first editions and stored the books in his garret, writing in his journal, "I have now a library of nearly nine hundred volumes, over seven hundred of which I wrote myself." He was not discouraged, however, and in 1854 published a second book under the title of "Walden." This book is the one by which Thoreau is now best known, and it contains many of his best thoughts and an exposition of his own characteristic philosophy. It was the last of his books published during his lifetime. He died of consumption in 1862 at the age of forty-four. After his death a number of additional volumes were published by collecting the papers he had published in various magazines, and making considerable extracts from the journal he had kept for thirty years, so that now there are eleven volumes in the authorized edition of his works.

Thoreau's reputation rests chiefly on the great gift he possessed as an interpreter of nature. As one of his admirers said, "he talked about nature just as if she'd been born and brought up in Concord." No writer ever had a keener power of observation than Thoreau, and his skill in giving adequate expression to his observations was scarcely less remarkable. His choice of words is always felicitous, his use of quotations strikingly apt, and many of his phrases and sentences are perfect examples of English composition. His chosen field was unique, as was his own personal character. Thus he has given us much in his books which he alone could give, and for the lack of which American literature would be decidedly poorer.

SOLITUDE

THIS is a delicious evening, when the whole body is one sense, and imbibes delight through every pore. I go and come with a strange liberty in nature, a part of herself. As I walk along the stony shore of the pond in my shirt sleeves, though it is cool as well as cloudy and windy, and I see nothing special to attract me, all the elements are unusually congenial to me. The bullfrogs trump to usher in the night, and the note of the whippoorwill is borne on the rippling wind from over the water. Sympathy with the fluttering alder and poplar leaves almost takes away my breath; yet, like the lake, my serenity is rippled but not ruffled. These small waves raised by the evening wind are as remote from storm as the smooth reflecting surface. Though it is now dark, the wind still blows and roars in the wood, the waves still dash, and some creatures lull the rest with their notes. The repose is never complete. The wildest animals do not repose, but seek their prey now; the fox, and skunk, and rabbit now roam the fields and woods without fear. They are nature's watchmen—links which connect the days of animated life.

When I return to my house I find that visitors have been there and left their cards, either a bunch of flowers, or a wreath of evergreen, or a name in pencil on a yellow walnut leaf or a chip. They who come rarely to the woods take some little piece of the forest into their hands to play with by the way, which they leave, either intentionally or accidentally. One has peeled a willow wand, woven it into a ring, and dropped it on my table. I could always tell if visitors had called in my absence, either by the bended twigs or grass, or the print of their shoes, and generally of what sex or age or quality they were by some slight trace left, as a flower dropped, or a bunch of grass plucked and thrown away, even as far off as the railroad, half a mile distant, or by the lingering odor of a cigar or pipe. Nay, I was frequently notified of the passage of a traveller along the highway sixty rods off by the scent of his pipe.

There is commonly sufficient space about us. Our horizon is never quite at our elbows. The thick wood is not just at our door, nor the pond, but somewhat is always clearing, familiar and worn by us, appropriated and fenced in some way, and reclaimed from nature. For what reason have I this vast range and circuit, some square miles of unfrequented forest, for my privacy, abandoned to me by men? My nearest neighbor is a mile distant, and no house is visible from any place but the hill-tops within half a mile of my own. I have my horizon bounded by woods all to myself; a distant view of the railroad where it touches the pond on the one hand, and of the fence which skirts the woodland road on the other. But for the most part it is as solitary where I live as on the prairies. It is as much Asia or Africa as New England. I have, as it were, my own sun and moon and stars, and a little world all to myself. At night there was never a traveller passed my house, or knocked at my door, more than if I were the first or last man; unless it were in the spring, when at long intervals some came from the village to fish for pouts—they plainly fished much more in the Walden Pond of their own natures, and baited their hooks with darkness—but they soon retreated, usually with light baskets, and left "the world to darkness and to me," and the black kernel of the night was never profaned by any human neighborhood. I believe that men are generally still a little afraid of the dark, though the witches are all hanged and Christianity and candles have been introduced.

Yet I experienced sometimes that the most sweet and tender, the most innocent and encouraging society may be found in any natural object, even for the poor misanthrope and most melancholy man. There can be no very black melancholy to him who lives in the midst of nature and has his senses still. There was never yet such a storm but it was Æolian music to a healthy and innocent ear. Nothing can rightly compel a simple brave man to a vulgar sadness. While I enjoy the friendship of the seasons I trust that nothing can make life a burden to me. The gentle rain which waters my beans and keeps me in the house to-day is not drear and melancholy, but good for me, too. Though it prevents my hoeing them, it is of far more worth than my hoeing. If it should continue so long as to cause the seeds to rot in the ground and destroy the potatoes in the low lands, it would still be good for the grass on the uplands, and, being good for the grass, it would be good for me. Sometimes, when I compare myself with other men, it seems as if I were more favored by the gods than they, beyond any deserts that I am conscious of; as if I had a warrant and surety at their hands which my fellows have not, and were especially guided and guarded. I do not flatter myself, but if it be possible they flatter me. I have never felt lonesome, or in the least oppressed by a sense of solitude, but once, and that was a few weeks after I came to the woods, when, for an hour, I doubted if the near neighborhood of man was not essential to a serene and healthy life. To be alone was something unpleasant. But I was at the same time conscious of a slight insanity in my mood, and seemed to foresee my recovery. In the midst of a gentle rain while these thoughts prevailed, I was suddenly sensible of such sweet and beneficent society in nature, in the very pattering of the drops, and in every sound and sight around my house, an infinite and unaccountable friendliness all at once like an atmosphere sustaining me, as made the fancied advantages of human neighborhood insignificant, and I have never thought of them since. Every little pine needle expanded and swelled with sympathy and befriended me. I was so distinctly made aware of the presence of something kindred to me, even in scenes which we are accustomed to call wild and dreary, and also that the nearest of blood to me and humanest was not a person nor a villager, that I thought no place could ever be strange to me again.

> "Mourning untimely consumes the sad;
> Few are their days in the land of the living,
> Beautiful daughter of Toscar."

Some of my pleasantest hours were during the long rain storms in the spring or fall, which confined me to the house for the afternoon as well as the forenoon, soothed by their ceaseless roar and pelting; when an early twilight ushered in a long evening in which many thoughts had time to take root and unfold themselves. In those driving northeast rains which tried the village houses so, when the maids stood ready with mop and pail in front entries to keep the deluge out, I sat behind my door in my little house, which was all entry, and thoroughly enjoyed its protection. In one heavy thunder shower the lightning struck a large pitch-pine across the pond, making a very conspicuous and perfectly regular spiral groove from top to bottom, an inch or more deep, and four or five inches wide, as you would groove a walking-stick. I passed it again the other day, and was struck with awe on looking up and beholding that mark, now more distinct than ever, where a terrific and resistless bolt came down out of the harmless sky eight years ago. Men frequently say to me, "I should think you would feel lonesome down there, and want to be nearer to folks, rainy and snowy days and nights especially." I am tempted to reply to such: This whole earth which we inhabit is but a point in space. How far apart, think you, dwell the two most distant inhabitants of yonder star, the breadth of whose disk cannot be appreciated by our instruments? Why should I feel lonely? Is not our planet in the Milky Way? This which you put seems to me not to be the most important question. What sort of space is that which separates a man from his fellows and makes him solitary? I have found that no exertion of the legs can bring two minds much nearer to one another. What do we want most to dwell near to? Not to many men surely, the depot, the post-office, the bar-room, the meeting-house, the school-house, the grocery, Beacon Hill, or the Five Points, where men most congregate, but to the perennial source of our life, whence in all our experience we have found that to issue, as the willow stands near the water and sends out its roots in that direction. This will vary with different natures, but this is the place where a wise man will dig his cellar. . . . I one evening overtook one of my townsmen, who has accumulated what is called "a handsome property"—though I never got a fair view of it—on the Walden road, driving a pair of cattle to market, who inquired of me how I could bring my mind to give up so many of the comforts of life. I answered that I was very sure I liked it passably well; I was not joking. And so I went home to my bed, and left him to pick his way through the darkness and the mud to Brighton—or Brighttown—which place he would reach some time in the morning.

Any prospect of awakening or coming to life to a dead man makes indifferent all times and places. The place where that may occur is always the same, and indescribably pleasant to all our senses. For the most part we allow only outlying and transient circumstances to make our occasions. They are, in fact, the cause of our distraction. Nearest to all things is that power which fashions their being. Next to us the grandest laws are continually being executed. Next to us is not the workman whom we have hired, with whom we love so well to talk, but the workman whose work we are.

"How vast and profound is the influence of the subtile powers of heaven and of earth!"

"We seek to perceive them, and we do not see them; we seek to hear them, and we do not hear them; identified with the substance of things, they cannot be separated from them."

"They cause that in all the universe men purify and sanctify their hearts, and clothe themselves in their holiday garments to offer sacrifices and oblations to their ancestors. It is an ocean of subtile intelligences. They are everywhere, above us, on our left, on our right; they environ us on all sides."

We are the subjects of an experiment which is not a little interesting to me. Can we not do without the society of our gossips a little while under these circumstances—have our own thoughts to cheer us? Confucius says truly, "Virtue does not remain as an abandoned orphan; it must of necessity have neighbors."

With thinking we may be beside ourselves in a sane sense. By a conscious effort of the mind we can stand aloof from actions and their consequences; and all things, good and bad, go by us like a torrent. We are not wholly involved in nature. I may be either the drift-wood in the stream, or Indra in the sky looking down on it. I may be affected by a theatrical exhibition; on the other hand, I may not be affected by an actual event which appears to concern me much more. I only know myself as a human entity; the scene, so to speak, of thoughts and affections; and am sensible of a certain doubleness by which I can stand as remote from myself as from another. However intense my experience, I am conscious of the presence and criticism of a part of me, which, as it were, is not a part of me, but spectator, sharing no experience, but taking note of it; and that is no more I than it is you. When the play, it may be the tragedy, of life is over, the spectator goes his way. It was a kind of fiction, a work of the imagination only, so far as he was concerned. This doubleness may easily make us poor neighbors and friends sometimes.

I find it wholesome to be alone the greater part of the time. To be in company, even with the best, is soon wearisome and dissipating. I love to be alone. I never found the companion that was so companionable as solitude. We are for the most part more lonely when we go abroad among men than when we stay in our chambers. A man thinking or working is always alone, let him be where he will. Solitude is not measured by the miles of space that intervene between a man and his fellows. The really diligent student in one of the crowded hives of Cambridge College is as solitary as a dervish in the desert. The farmer can work alone in the field or the woods all day, hoeing or chopping, and not feel lonesome, because he is employed; but when he comes home at night he cannot sit down in a room alone, at the mercy of his thoughts, but must be where he can "see the folks," and recreate, and as he thinks remunerate, himself for his day's solitude; and hence he wonders how the student can sit alone in the house all night and most of the day without *ennui* and "the blues"; but he does not realize that the student, though in the house, is still at work in his field, and chopping in his woods, as the farmer in his, and in turn seeks the same recreation and society that the latter does, though it may be a more condensed form of it.

Society is commonly too cheap. We meet at very short intervals, not having had time to acquire any new value for each other. We meet at meals three times a day, and give each other a new taste of that old musty cheese that we are. We have had to agree on a certain set of rules, called etiquette and politeness, to make this frequent meeting tolerable and that we need not come to open war. We meet at the post-office, and at the sociable, and about the fireside every night; we live thick and are in each other's way, and stumble over one another, and I think that we thus lose some respect for one another. Certainly less frequency would suffice for all important and hearty communications. Consider the girls in a factory—never alone, hardly in their dreams. It would be better if there were but one inhabitant to a square mile, as where I live. The value of a man is not in his skin, that we should touch him.

I have heard of a man lost in the woods and dying of famine

and exhaustion at the foot of a tree, whose loneliness was relieved by the grotesque visions with which, owing to bodily weakness, his diseased imagination surrounded him, and which he believed to be real. So also, owing to bodily and mental health and strength, we may be continually cheered by a like but more normal and natural society, and come to know that we are never alone.

I have a great deal of company in my house; especially in the morning, when nobody calls. Let me suggest a few comparisons, that some one may convey an idea of my situation. I am no more lonely than the loon in the pond that laughs so loud, or than Walden Pond itself. What company has that lonely lake, I pray? And yet it has not the blue devils, but the blue angels in it, in the azure tint of its waters. The sun is alone, except in thick weather, when there sometimes appear to be two, but one is a mock sun. God is alone—but the devil, he is far from being alone; he sees a great deal of company; he is legion. I am no more lonely than a single mullein or dandelion in a pasture, or a bean leaf, or sorrel, or a horse-fly, or a humblebee. I am no more lonely than the Mill Brook, or a weathercock, or the north star, or the south wind, or an April shower, or a January thaw, or the first spider in a new house.

I have occasional visits in the long winter evenings, when the snow falls fast and the wind howls in the wood, from an old settler and original proprietor, who is reported to have dug Walden Pond, and stoned it, and fringed it with pine woods; who tells me stories of old time and of new eternity; and between us we manage to pass a cheerful evening with social mirth and pleasant views of things, even without apples or cider—a most wise and humorous friend, whom I love much, who keeps himself more secret than ever did Goffe or Whalley; and though he is thought to be dead, none can show where he is buried. An elderly dame, too, dwells in my neighborhood, invisible to most persons, in whose odorous herb garden I love to stroll sometimes, gathering simples and listening to her fables; for she has a genius of unequalled fertility, and her memory runs back farther than mythology, and she can tell me the original of every fable, and on what fact every one is founded, for the incidents occurred when she was young. A ruddy and lusty old dame, who delights in all weathers and seasons, and is likely to outlive all her children yet.

The indescribable innocence and beneficence of nature—of sun and wind and rain, of summer and winter—such health, such cheer, they afford forever! and such sympathy have they ever with our race, that all nature would be affected, and the sun's brightness fade, and the winds would sigh humanely, and the clouds rain tears, and the woods shed their leaves and put on mourning in midsummer, if any man should ever for a just cause grieve. Shall I not have intelligence with the earth? Am I not partly leaves and vegetable mould myself?

What is the pill which will keep us well, serene, contented? Not my or thy great-grandfather's, but our great-grandmother nature's universal, vegetable, botanic medicines, by which she has kept herself young always, outlived so many old Parrs in her day, and fed her health with their decaying fatness. For my panacea, instead of one of those quack vials of a mixture dipped from Acheron and the Dead Sea, which come out of those long shallow black schooner-looking wagons which we sometimes see made to carry bottles, let me have a draught of undiluted morning air. Morning air! If men will not drink of this at the fountain-head of the day, why, then, we must even bottle up some and sell it in the shops, for the benefit of those who have lost their subscription ticket to morning time in this world. But remember, it will not keep quite till noonday even in the coolest cellar, but drive out the stopples long ere that and follow westward the steps of Aurora. I am no worshipper of Hygeia, who was the daughter of that old herb-doctor Æsculapius, and who is represented on monuments holding a serpent in one hand, and in the other a cup out of which the serpent sometimes drinks; but rather of Hebe, cupbearer to Jupiter, who was the daughter of Juno and wild lettuce, and who had the power of restoring gods and men to the vigor of youth. She was probably the only thoroughly sound-conditioned, healthy, and robust young lady that ever walked the globe, and wherever she came it was spring.

CAMBRIDGE THIRTY YEARS AGO

—

BY

JAMES RUSSELL LOWELL

JAMES RUSSELL LOWELL

1819—1891

Cambridge, inseparably associated with the names of so many of America's men of letters, was the birthplace and, during the greater part of his splendid career, the home of James Russell Lowell. Born in 1819, he was sent to one of the private schools in his native town, and then to Harvard, where he graduated in 1838. Two years later he was admitted to the bar, but never practised, devoting himself almost exclusively to the pursuit of literature. His first volume of poems was published in 1841, the collection containing many verses that he afterwards suppressed. Three years later he married, and went to live at "Elmwood," the beautiful house where he was born. The same year appeared "A Legend of Brittany," one of the most admired of his poems. In 1848 he published "A Fable for Critics," one of the wittiest of literary satires, and also issued in book form the first series of the powerful "Biglow Papers," denouncing the Mexican War. These vigorous poems in the Yankee dialect and bristling with Yankee humor and common-sense remain a noteworthy contribution to American literature.

In 1854 Lowell accepted the professorship of modern languages at Harvard made vacant by the resignation of Longfellow, and after two years spent in Europe entered upon his work. From 1857 to 1862 Lowell was the editor of the newly founded "Atlantic Monthly," and from 1863 to 1872 he was associated with Professor Charles Eliot Norton in editing the "North American Review." In 1864 he published a prose work, "Fireside Travels," containing "Cambridge Thirty Years Ago," and numerous other sketches written in his best vein. In 1866 appeared the second series of the "Biglow Papers," dealing with questions connected with the Civil War. Various volumes of essays in the same vein as "Fireside Travels" soon followed, including "Among my Books" in 1870, "My Study Window" in 1871, and "Among my Books," a second series, in 1876. The fact that Lowell was called upon to write the "Commemoration Ode" in honor of the sons of Harvard slain in the Civil War, two odes celebrating the centennial commemoration of battles in the Revolutionary War, and another ode in honor of the centennial anniversary of the Declaration of Independence, shows us the great regard he enjoyed as a popular poet.

In 1877 Mr. Lowell was sent as Minister to Spain, and in 1880 was transferred to the Court of St. James, where he remained till 1885, becoming a prominent figure in the public and literary life of England, and one of the most popular and respected ambassadors ever sent there from any country in recent times. He was often called upon to deliver public addresses, many of which were collected and published in 1886 under the title of "Democracy, and Other Addresses," a volume in which he displays the mature judgment of the scholar, the man of letters, and the man of affairs. In 1888 he brought out a volume of "Political Essays," and his "Latest Literary Essays and Addresses" was issued in 1891, the year of his death.

Lowell, though not the most popular of American poets, takes the foremost rank in American literature, as a satirist, essayist, and critic. Moreover, he was a most charming representative of the American gentleman and scholar, and all that is best in American life. His poetical writings are of uneven and disputed merit, but in his prose he is always clear and vigorous; scholarly but never pedantic; always inspiring and frequently brilliant.

CAMBRIDGE THIRTY YEARS AGO

A Memoir addressed to the Edelmann Storg in Rome

IN those quiet old winter evenings, around our Roman fireside, it was not seldom, my dear Storg, that we talked of the advantages of travel, and in speeches not so long that our cigars would forget their fire (the measure of just conversation) debated the comparative advantages of the Old and the New Worlds.[1] You will remember how serenely I bore the imputation of provincialism, while I asserted that those advantages were reciprocal; that an orbed and balanced life would revolve between the old and the new as its opposite, but not antagonistic poles, the true equator lying somewhere midway between them. I asserted also that there were two epochs at which a man might travel—before twenty, for pure enjoyment, and after thirty, for instruction. At twenty, the eye is sufficiently delighted with merely seeing; new things are pleasant only because they are not old; and we take everything heartily and naturally in the right way, events being always like knives, which either serve us or cut us, as we grasp them by the blade or the handle. After thirty, we carry with us our scales with lawful weights stamped by experience, and our chemical tests acquired by study, with which to ponder and assay all arts, and institutions, and manners, and to ascertain either their absolute worth, or their merely relative value to ourselves. On the whole, I declared myself in favor of the after-thirty method—was it partly (so difficult is it to distinguish between opinions and personalities) because I had tried it myself, though with scales so imperfect and tests so inadequate? Perhaps so, but more because I held that a man should have travelled thoroughly round himself and the great *terra incognita* just outside and inside his own threshold, before he

[1] This essay is taken from "Putnam's Magazine," vol. iii., 1854.

undertook voyages of discovery to other worlds. Let him first thoroughly explore that strange country laid down on the maps as Seauton; let him look down into its craters and find whether they be burnt out or only sleeping; let him know between the good and evil fruits of its passionate tropics; let him experience how healthful are its serene and high-lying table-lands; let him be many times driven back (till he wisely consent to be baffled) from its metaphysical Northwest passages that lead only to the dreary solitudes of a sunless world, before he think himself morally equipped for travels to more distant regions. But does he commonly even so much as think of this, or, while buying amplest trunks for his corporeal apparel, does it once occur to him how very small a portmanteau will contain all his mental and spiritual outfit? Oftener, it is true, that a man who could scarce be induced to expose his unclothed body, even in a village of prairie-dogs, will complacently display a mind as naked as the day it was born, without so much as a fig-leaf of acquirement on it, in every gallery of Europe. If not with a robe dyed in the Tyrian purple of imaginative culture, if not with the close-fitting active dress of social or business training —at least, my dear Storg, one might provide himself with the merest waist-clout of modesty!

But if it be too much to expect men to traverse and survey themselves before they go abroad, we might certainly ask that they should be familiar with their own villages. If not even that, then it is of little import whither they go, and let us hope that, by seeing how calmly their own narrow neighborhood bears their departure, they may be led to think that the circles of disturbance set in motion by the fall of their tiny drop into the ocean of eternity, will not have a radius of more than a week in any direction; and that the world can endure the subtraction of even a justice of the peace with provoking equanimity. In this way, at least, foreign travel may do them good, may make them, if not wiser, at any rate less fussy. Is it a great way to go to school, and a great fee to pay for the lesson? We cannot pay too much for that genial stoicism which, when life flouts us and says—*Put that in your pipe and smoke it!*—can puff away with as sincere a relish as if it were tobacco of Mount Lebanon in a narghileh of Damascus.

After all, my dear Storg, it is to know things that one has

need to travel, and not men. Those force us to come to them, but these come to us—sometimes whether we will or no. These exist for us in every variety in our own town. You may find your antipodes without a voyage to China; he lives there, just round the next corner, precise, formal, the slave of precedent, making all his tea-cups with a break in the edge, because his model had one, and your fancy decorates him with an endlessness of airy pig-tail. There, too, are John Bull, Jean Crapaud, Hans Sauerkraut, Pat Murphy, and the rest.

It has been well said:

> "He needs no ship to cross the tide,
> Who, in the lives around him, sees
> Fair window-prospects opening wide
> O'er history's fields on every side,
> Rome, Egypt, England, Ind, and Greece.
>
> "Whatever moulds of various brain
> E'er shaped the world to weal or woe—
> Whatever empires wax and wane—
> To him who hath not eyes in vain,
> His village-microcosm can show."

But things are good for nothing out of their natural habitat. If the heroic Barnum had succeeded in transplanting Shakespeare's house to America what interest would it have had for us, torn out of its appropriate setting in softly-hilled Warwickshire, which showed us that the most English of poets must be born in the most English of counties? I mean by a Thing that which is not a mere spectacle, that which the mind leaps forth to, as it also leaps to the mind, as soon as they come within each other's sphere of attraction, and with instantaneous coalition form a new product—knowledge. Such, in the understanding it gives us of early Roman history, is the little territory around Rome, the *gentis cunabula,* without a sight of which Livy and Niebuhr and the maps are vain. So, too, one must go to Pompeii and the Museo Borbonico, to get a true conception of that wondrous artistic nature of the Greeks, strong enough, even in that petty colony, to survive foreign conquest and to assimilate barbarian blood, showing a grace and fertility of invention, whose Roman copies Raffaello himself could only copy, and enchanting even the base utensils of the kitchen with an inevitable sense of beauty to which we subterranean Northmen have not yet so much as dreamed of climbing. Mere sights one can see quite as well at home. Mont Blanc does not tower more grandly in the memory than did the dream-peak which loomed afar on the morning horizon of hope; nor did the smoke-palm of Vesuvius stand more erect and fair, with tapering stem and spreading top, in that Parthenopeian air than under the diviner sky of imagination. I know what Shakespeare says about home-keeping youths, and I can fancy what you will add about America being interesting only as a phenomenon, and uncomfortable to live in, because we have not yet done with getting ready to live. But is not your Europe, on the other hand, a place where men have done living for the present, and of value chiefly because of the men who had done living in it long ago? And if, in our rapidly-moving country, one feel sometimes as if he had his home in a railroad train, is there not also a satisfaction in knowing that one is going somewhere? To what end visit Europe, if people carry with them, as most do, their old parochial horizon, going hardly as Americans even, much less as men? Have we not both seen persons abroad who put us in mind of parlor goldfish in their vase, isolated in that little globe of their own element, incapable of communication with the strange world around them, a show themselves, while it was always doubtful if they could see at all beyond the limits of their portable prison? The wise man travels to discover himself; it is to find himself out that he goes out of himself and his habitual associations, trying everything in turn till he find that one activity, sovran over him by divine right, toward which all the disbanded powers of his nature and the irregular tendencies of his life gather joyfully, as to the common rallying-point of their loyalty.

All these things we debated while the ilex logs upon the hearth burned down to tinkling coals, over which a gray, soft moss of ashes grew betimes, mocking the poor wood with a pale travesty of that green and gradual decay on forest-floors, its natural end. Already the clock at the Capuccini told the morning quarters, and on the pauses of our talk no sound intervened but the muffled hoot of an owl in the near convent-garden, or the rattling tramp of a patrol of that French army which keeps him a prisoner in his own city who claims to lock and unlock the doors of heaven. But still the discourse would eddy round one obstinate rocky tenet of mine, for I maintained, you remember, that the wisest man was he who stayed at home; that to see the antiquities of the Old World was nothing, since the youth of the world was really no farther away from us than our own youth; and that, moreover, we had also in America things amazingly old, as our boys, for example. Add, that in the end this antiquity is a matter of comparison, which skips from place to place as nimbly as Emerson's sphinx, and that one old thing is good only till we have seen an older. England is ancient till we go to Rome. Etruria dethrones Rome, but only to pass this sceptre of antiquity which so lords it over our fancies to the Pelasgi, from whom Egypt straightway wrenches it to give it up in turn to older India. And whither then? As well rest upon the first step, since the effect of what is old upon the mind is single and positive, not cumulative. As soon as a thing is past it is as infinitely far away from us as if it had happened millions of years ago. And if the learned Huet be correct, who reckoned that every human thought and record could be included in ten folios, what so frightfully old as we ourselves, who can, if we choose, hold in our memories every syllable of recorded time, from the first crunch of Eve's teeth in the apple, downward, being thus ideally contemporary with hoariest Eld?

> "Thy pyramids built up with newer might
> To us are nothing novel, nothing strange."

Now, my dear Storg, you know my (what the phrenologists call) inhabitiveness and adhesiveness, how I stand by the old thought, the old thing, the old place, and the old friend, till I am very sure I have got a better, and even then migrate painfully. Remember the old Arabian story, and think how hard it is to pick up all the pomegranate-seeds of an opponent's argument, and how, as long as one remains, you are as far from the end as ever. Since I have you entirely at my mercy (for you cannot answer me under five weeks) you will not be surprised at the advent of this letter. I had always one impregnable position, which was, that however good other places might be, there was only one in which we could be born, and which therefore possessed a quite peculiar and inalienable virtue. We had the fortune, which neither of us has had reason to call other than good, to journey together through the green, secluded valley of boyhood; together we climbed the mountain wall which shut it in, and looked upon those Italian plains of early manhood; and, since then, we have met sometimes by a well, or broken bread together at an oasis in the arid desert of life, as it truly is. With this letter I propose to make you my fellow-traveller in one of those fireside voyages which, as we grow older, we make oftener and oftener through our own past. Without leaving your elbow-chair, you shall go back with me thirty years, which will bring you among things and persons as thoroughly preterite as Romulus or Numa. For, so rapid are our changes in America, that the transition from old to new, the shifting from habits and associations to others entirely different, is as rapid almost as the pushing in of one scene and the drawing out of another on the stage. And it is this which makes America so interesting to the philosophic student of history and man. Here, as in a theatre, the great problems of anthropology, which in the old world were ages in solving, but which are solved, leaving only a dry net result; are compressed, as it were, into the entertainment of a few hours. Here we have I know not how many epochs of history and phases of civilization contemporary with each other, nay, within five minutes of each other by the electric telegraph. In two centuries we have seen rehearsed the dispersion of man from a small point over a whole continent; we witness with our own eyes the action of those forces which govern the great migration of the peoples, now historical in Europe; we can watch the action and reaction of different races, forms of government, and higher or lower civilizations. Over there, you have only the dead precipitate, demanding tedious analysis; but here the elements are all in solution, and we have only to look to know them all. History, which every day makes less account of governors and more of man, must find here the compendious key to all that picture-writing of the past. Therefore it is, my dear Storg, that we Yankees may still esteem our America a place worth living in. But calm your apprehensions: I do not propose to drag you with me on such a historical circumnavigation of the globe, but only to show you that (however needful it may be to go abroad for the study of æsthetics) a man who uses the eyes of his heart may find also pretty bits of what may be called the social picturesque, and little landscapes over which that Indian summer atmosphere of the past broods as sweetly and tenderly as over a Roman ruin. Let us look at the Cambridge of thirty years since.

The seat of the oldest college in America, it had, of course, some of that cloistered quiet which characterizes all university towns. But, underlying this, it had an idiosyncrasy of its own. Boston was not yet a city, and Cambridge was still a country village, with its own habits and traditions, not yet feeling too strongly the force of suburban gravitation. Approaching it from the west by what was then called the New Road (it is so called no longer, for we change our names whenever we can, to the great detriment of all historical association) you would pause on the brow of Symonds' Hill to enjoy a view singularly soothing and placid. In front of you lay the town, tufted with elms, lindens, and horse-chestnuts, which had seen Massachusetts a colony, and were fortunately unable to emigrate with the Tories by whom, or by whose fathers, they were planted. Over it rose the noisy belfry of the college, the square, brown tower of the church, and the slim, yellow spire of the parish meeting-house, by no means ungraceful, and then an invariable characteristic of New England religious architecture. On your right the Charles slipped smoothly through green and purple salt-meadows, darkened, here and there, with the blossoming black-grass as with a stranded cloud-shadow. Over these marshes, level as water, but without its glare, and with softer and more soothing gradations of perspective, the eye was carried to a horizon of softly-rounded hills. To your left hand, upon the Old Road, you saw some half-dozen dignified old houses of the colonial time, all comfortably fronting southward. If it were spring-time the rows of horse-chestnuts along the fronts of these houses showed, through every crevice of their dark heap of foliage, and on the end of every drooping limb, a cone of pearly flowers, while the hill behind was white or rosy with the crowding blooms of various fruit-trees. There is no sound, unless a horseman clatters over the loose planks of the bridge, while his antipodal shadow glides silently over the mirrored bridge below, or unless

"O winged rapture, feathered soul of spring,
Blithe voice of woods, fields, waters, all in one,
Pipe blown through by the warm, mild breath of June,
Shepherding her white flocks of woolly clouds,
The bobolink has come, and climbs the wind
With rippling wings, that quaver, not for flight,
But only joy, or, yielding to its will,
Runs down, a brook of laughter, through the air."

Such was the charmingly rural picture which he who, thirty years ago, went eastward over Symonds' Hill, had given him for nothing to hang in the gallery of memory. But we are a city now, and Common Councils have as yet no notion of the truth (learned long ago by many a European hamlet) that picturesqueness adds to the actual money value of a town. To save a few dollars in gravel, they have cut a kind of dry ditch through the hill, where you suffocate with dust in summer, or flounder through waist-deep snow-drifts in winter, with no prospect but the crumbling earth-walls on each side. The landscape was carried away, cart-load by cart-load, and, deposited on the roads, forms a part of that unfathomable pudding, which has, I fear, driven many a teamster and pedestrian to the use of phrases not commonly found in English dictionaries.

We called it "the village" then (I speak of Old Cambridge), and it was essentially an English village, quiet, unspeculative, without enterprise, sufficing to itself, and only showing such differences from the original type as the public school and the system of town government might superinduce. A few houses, chiefly old, stood around the bare common, with ample elbow-room, and old women, capped and spectacled, still peered through the same windows from which they had watched Lord Percy's artillery rumble by to Lexington, or caught a glimpse of the handsome Virginia general who had come to wield our homespun Saxon chivalry. People were still living who regretted the late unhappy separation from the mother island, who had seen no gentry since the Vassalls went, and who thought that Boston had ill kept the day of her patron saint, Botolph, on June 17, 1775. The hooks were to be seen from which had swung the hammocks of Burgoyne's captive red-coats. If memory does not deceive me, women still washed clothes in the town-spring, clear as that of Bandusia. One coach sufficed for all the travel to the metropolis. Commencement had not ceased to be the great holiday of the Puritan Commonwealth, and a fitting one it was—the festival of Santa Scolastica, whose triumphal path one may conceive strewn with leaves of spelling-book instead of bay. The students (scholars they were called then) wore their sober uniform, not ostentatiously distinctive nor capable of rousing democratic envy, and the old lines of caste were blurred rather than rubbed out, as servitor was softened into beneficiary. The Spanish king was sure that the gesticulating student was either mad or reading Don Quixotte, and if, in those days, you met a youth swinging his arms and talking to himself, you might conclude that he was either a lunatic or one who was to appear in a "part" at the next commencement. A favorite place for the rehearsal of these orations was the retired amphitheatre of the Gravelpit, perched unregarded on whose dizzy edge, I have heard many a burst of *plus-quam-Ciceronian* eloquence, and (often repeated) the regular *saluto vos præstantissimas*, etc., which every year (with a glance at the gallery) causes a flutter among the fans innocent of Latin, and delights to applauses of conscious superiority the youth almost as innocent as they. It is curious, by the way, to note how plainly one can feel the pulse of self in the plaudits of an audience. At a political meeting, if the enthusiasm of the lieges hang fire, it may be exploded at once by an allusion to their intelligence or patriotism, and at a literary festival, the first Latin quotation draws the first applause, the clapping of hands being intended as a tribute to our own familiarity with that sonorous tongue, and not at all as an approval of the particular sentiment conveyed in it. For if the orator should say, "Well has Tacitus remarked, *Americani omnes sunt naturaliter fures et stulti*," it would be all the same. But the Gravelpit was patient, if irresponsive; nor did the declaimer always fail to bring down the house, bits of loosened earth falling now and then from the precipitous walls, their cohesion perhaps overcome by the vibrations of the voice, and happily satirizing the effect of most popular discourses, which prevail rather with the clay than with the spiritual part of the hearer. Was it possible for us in those days to conceive of a greater potentate than the president of the university, in his square doctor's cap, that still filially recalled Oxford and Cambridge? If there was a doubt, it was suggested only by the Governor, and even by him on artillery election days alone, superbly martial with epaulets and buckskin breeches, and bestriding the war-horse, promoted to that solemn duty for his tameness and steady habits.

Thirty years ago the town had indeed a character. Railways and omnibuses had not rolled flat all little social prominences and peculiarities, making every man as much a citizen everywhere as at home. No Charlestown boy could come to our annual festival without fighting to avenge a certain traditional porcine imputation against the inhabitants of that historic locality, to which our youth gave vent, in fanciful imitations of the dialect of the sty, or derisive shouts of "Charlestown hogs!" The penny newspaper had not yet silenced the tripod of the barber, oracle of news. Everybody knew everybody, and all about everybody, and village wit, whose high 'change was around the little market-house in the town-square, had labelled every more marked individuality with nick-names that clung like burs. Things were established then, and men did not run through all the figures on the dial of society so swiftly as now, when hurry and competition seem to have quite unhung the modulating pendulum of steady thrift, and competent training. Some slow-minded persons even followed their father's trade, a humiliating spectacle, rarer every day. We had our established loafers, topers, proverb-mongers, barber, parson, nay, postmaster, whose tenure was for life. The great political engine did not then come down at regular quadrennial intervals, like a nail-cutting machine, to make all official lives of a standard length, and to generate lazy and intriguing expectancy. Life flowed in recognized channels, narrower, perhaps, but with all the more individuality and force.

There was but one white-and-yellow-washer, whose own cottage, fresh-gleaming every June through grape-vine and creeper, was his only sign and advertisement. He was said to possess a secret, which died with him like that of Luca della Robbia, and certainly conceived all colors but white and yellow to savor of savagery, civilizing the stems of his trees annually with liquid lime, and meditating how to extend that candid baptism even to the leaves. His pie-plants (the best in town), compulsory monastics, blanched under barrels, each in his little hermitage, a vegetable Certosa. His fowls, his ducks, his geese, could not show so much as a gray feather among them, and he would have given a year's earnings for a white peacock. The flowers which decked his little door-yard were whitest China-asters and goldenest sunflowers, which last, backsliding from their traditional Parsee faith, used to puzzle us urchins not a little by staring brazenly every way except towards the sun. Celery, too, he raised, whose virtue is its paleness, and the silvery onion, and turnip, which, though outwardly conforming to the green heresies of summer, nourish a purer faith subterraneously, like early Christians in the catacombs. In an obscure corner grew the sanguine beet, tolerated only for its usefulness in allaying the asperities of Saturday's salt fish. He loved winter better than summer, because nature then played the whitewasher, and challenged with her snows the scarce inferior purity of his overalls and neck-cloth. I fancy that he never rightly liked commencement, for bringing so many black coats together. He founded no school. Others might essay his art, and were allowed to try their 'prentice hands on fences and the like coarse subjects, but the ceiling of every housewife waited on the leisure of Newman (*ichneumon* the students called him for his diminutiveness), nor would consent to other brush than his. There was also but one brewer—Lewis, who made the village beer, both spruce and ginger, a grave and amiable Ethiopian, making a discount always to the boys, and wisely, for they were his chiefest patrons. He wheeled his whole stock in a white-roofed handcart, on whose front a signboard presented at either end an insurrectionary bottle, yet insurgent after no mad Gallic fashion, but soberly and Saxonly discharging itself into the restraining formulary of a tumbler, symbolic of orderly prescription. The artist had struggled manfully with the difficulties of his subject, but had not succeeded so well that we did not often debate in which of the twin bottles spruce was typified, and in which ginger. We always believed that Lewis mentally distinguished between them, but by some peculiarity occult to exoteric eyes. This ambulatory chapel of the Bacchus that gives the colic, but not inebriates, only appeared at the commencement holidays. The lad who bought of Lewis laid out his money well, getting respect as well as beer, three " sirs " to every glass—" Beer, sir? yes, sir: spruce or ginger, sir?" I can yet recall the innocent pride with which I walked away after that somewhat risky ceremony (for a bottle sometimes blew up), dilated not alone with carbonic-acid gas, but with the more ethereal fixed air of that titular flattery. Nor was Lewis proud. When he tried his fortunes in the capital on election days, and stood amid a row of rival venders in the very flood of custom, he never forgot his small fellow-citizens, but welcomed them with an assuring smile, and served them with the first.

The barber's shop was a museum, scarce second to the larger one of Greenwoods in the metropolis. The boy who was to be clipped there was always accompanied to the sacrifice by troops of friends, who thus inspected the curiosities gratis. While the watchful eye of R—— wandered to keep in check these rather unscrupulous explorers, the unpausing shears would sometimes overstep the boundaries of strict tonsorial prescription, and make a notch through which the phrenological developments could be distinctly seen. As Michael Angelo's design was modified by the shape of his block, so R——, rigid in artistic proprieties, would contrive to give an appearance of design to this aberration, by making it the key-note of his work, and reducing the whole head to an appearance of premature baldness. What a charming place it was, how full of wonder and delight! The sunny little room, fronting southwest upon the common, rang with canaries and Java sparrows, nor were the familiar notes of robin, thrush, and bobolink wanting. A large white cockatoo harangued vaguely, at intervals, in what we believed (on R——'s authority) to be the Hottentot language. He had an unveracious air, but in what inventions of former grandeur he was indulging in, what sweet South-African Argos he was remembering, what tropical heats and giant trees by unconjectured rivers, known only to the wallowing hippopotamus, we could only guess at. The walls were covered with curious old Dutch prints, bills of albatross and penguin, and whales' teeth fantastically engraved. There was Frederick the Great, with head drooped plottingly, and keen side-long glance from under the three-cornered hat. There hung Bonaparte, too, the long-haired, haggard general of Italy, his eyes sombre with prefigured destiny; and there was his island grave; the dream and the fulfilment. Good store of sea-fights there was also; above all, Paul Jones in the Bonhomme

Richard, the smoke rolling courteously to leeward, that we might see him dealing thunderous wreck to the two hostile vessels, each twice as large as his own, and the reality of the scene corroborated by streaks of red paint leaping from the mouth of every gun. Suspended over the fireplace, with the curling-tongs, were an Indian bow and arrows, and in the corners of the room stood New Zealand paddles and war-clubs quaintly carved. The model of a ship in glass we variously estimated to be worth from a hundred to a thousand dollars, R—— rather favoring the higher valuation, though never distinctly committing himself. Among these wonders, the only suspicious one was an Indian tomahawk, which had too much the peaceful look of a shingling-hatchet. Did any rarity enter the town, it gravitated naturally to these walls, to the very nail that waited to receive it, and where, the day after its accession, it seemed to have hung a lifetime. We always had a theory that R—— was immensely rich (how could he possess so much and be otherwise?) and that his pursuing his calling was an amiable eccentricity. He was a conscientious artist and never submitted it to the choice of his victim whether he would be perfumed or not. Faithfully was the bottle shaken and the odoriferous mixture rubbed in, a fact redolent to the whole school-room in the afternoon. Sometimes the persuasive tonsor would impress one of the attendant volunteers and reduce his poll to shoe-brush crispness, at cost of the reluctant ninepence hoarded for Fresh Pond and the next half-holiday.

Shall the two groceries want their *vates sacer,* where E. & W. I. goods and country prod*ooce* were sold with an energy mitigated by the quiet genius of the place, and where strings of urchins waited, each with cent in hand, for the unweighed dates (thus giving an ordinary business transaction all the excitement of a lottery), and buying, not only that cloying sweetness, but a dream also of Egypt, and palm-trees, and Arabs, in which vision a print of the Pyramids in our geography tyrannized like that taller thought of Cowper's?

At one of these the unwearied students used to ply a joke handed down from class to class. *Enter A,* and asks gravely, "Have you any sour apples, Deacon?"

"Well, no, I haven't any just now that are exactly sour; but there's the bell-flower apple, and folks that like a sour apple generally like that." (*Exit A.*)

Enter B. "Have you any sweet apples, Deacon?"

"Well, no, I haven't any just now that are exactly sweet; but there's the bell-flower apple, and folks that like a sweet apple generally like that." (*Exit B.*)

There is not even a tradition of any one's ever having turned the wary deacon's flank, and his Laodicean apples persisted to the end, neither one thing nor another. Or shall the two town-constables be forgotten, in whom the law stood worthily and amply embodied, fit either of them to fill the uniform of an English beadle? Grim and silent as Ninevite statues they stood on each side of the meeting-house door at commencement, propped by long staves of blue and red, on which the Indian with bow and arrow, and the mailed arm with the sword, hinted at the invisible sovereignty of the State ready to reinforce them, as

> "For Achilles' portrait stood a spear
> Grasped in an armed hand."

Stalwart and rubicund men they were, second only, if second, to S——, champion of the county, and not incapable of genial unbendings when the fasces were laid aside. One of them still survives in octogenarian vigor, the Herodotus of village and college legend, and may it be long ere he depart, to carry with him the pattern of a courtesy, now, alas! old-fashioned, but which might profitably make part of the instruction of our youth among the other humanities!

In those days the population was almost wholly without foreign admixture. Two Scotch gardeners there were—Rule, whose daughter (glimpsed perhaps at church, or possibly the mere Miss Harris of fancy) the students nicknamed Anarchy or Miss Rule—and later Fraser, whom whiskey sublimed into a poet, full of bloody histories of the Forty-twa, and showing an imaginary French bullet, sometimes in one leg, sometimes in the other. With this claim to a military distinction he adroitly contrived to mingle another to a natural one, asserting double teeth all round his jaws, and having thus created two sets of doubts, silenced both at once by a single demonstration, displaying the grinders to the confusion of the infidel.

The old court-house stood then upon the square. It has shrunk back out of sight now, and students box and fence where Parsons once laid down the law, and Ames and Dexter showed their skill in the fence of argument. Times have changed, and manners, since Chief Justice Dana (father of Richard the First, and grandfather of Richard the Second) caused to be arrested for contempt of court a butcher who had come in without a coat to witness the administration of his country's laws, and who thus had his curiosity exemplarily gratified. Times have changed also since the cellar beneath it was tenanted by the twin brothers Snow. Oyster-men were they indeed, silent in their subterranean burrow, and taking the ebbs and floods of custom with bivalvian serenity. Careless of the months with an R in them, the maxim of Snow (for we knew them but as a unit) was, " When 'ysters are good, they are good; and when they ain't, they isn't." Grecian F—— (may his shadow never be less!) tells this, his great laugh expected all the while from deep vaults of chest, and then coming in at the close, hearty, contagious, mounting with the measured tread of a jovial but stately butler who brings ancientest good-fellowship from exhaustless bins, and enough, without other sauce, to give a flavor of stalled ox to a dinner of herbs. Let me preserve here an anticipatory elegy upon the Snows, written years ago by some nameless college rhymer:

DIFFUGERE NIVES

" Here lies, or lie—decide the question, you,
If they were two in one or one in two—
P. & S. Snow, whose memory shall not fade,
Castor and Pollux of the oyster-trade:
Hatched from one egg, at once the shell they burst,
(The last, perhaps, a P. S. to the first,)
So homoöusian both in look and soul,
So undiscernibly a single whole,
That, whether P. was S., or S. was P.,
Surpassed all skill in etymology;
One kept the shop at once, and all we know
Is that together they were the Great Snow,
A snow not deep, yet with a crust so thick
It never melted to the son of Tick;
Perpetual? nay, our region was too low,
Too warm, too southern, for perpetual Snow;
Still, like fair Leda's sons, to whom 'twas given
To take their turns in Hades and in Heaven,

Our Dioscuri new would bravely share
The cellar's darkness and the upper air;
Twice every year would each the shades escape,
And, like a sea-bird, seek the wave-washed Cape,
Where (Rumor voiced) one spouse sufficed for both;
No bigamist, for she upon her oath,
Unskilled in letters, could not make a guess
At any difference twixt P. and S.—
A thing not marvellous, since Fame agrees
They were as little different as two peas,
And she, like Paris, when his Helen laid
Her hand 'mid snows from Ida's top conveyed
To cool their wine of Chios, could not know,
Between those rival candors, which was Snow.
Whiche'er behind the counter chanced to be
Oped oysters oft, his clam-shells seldom he;
If e'er he laughed, 'twas with no loud guffaw,
The fun warmed through him with a gradual thaw:
The nicer shades of wit were not his gift,
Nor was it hard to sound Snow's simple drift;
His were plain jokes, that many a time before
Had set his tarry messmates in a roar,
When floundering cod beslimed the deck's wet planks—
The humorous specie of Newfoundland Banks.

"But Snow is gone, and, let us hope, sleeps well,
Buried (his last breath asked it) in a shell;
Him on the Stygian shore my fancy sees
Noting choice shoals for oyster colonies,
Or, at a board stuck full of ghostly forks,
Opening for practice visionary Yorks.
And whither he has gone, may we too go—
Since no hot place were fit for keeping Snow!"

Cambridge has long had its port, but the greater part of its maritime trade was, thirty years ago, intrusted to a single Argo, the sloop Harvard, which belonged to the college, and made annual voyages to that vague Orient known as Down East, bringing back the wood that, in those days, gave to winter life at Harvard a crackle and a cheerfulness, for the loss of which the greater warmth of anthracite hardly compensates. New England life, to be genuine, must have in it some sentiment of the sea—it was this instinct that printed the device of the pine-tree on the old money and the old flag—and these periodic ventures of the sloop Harvard made the old viking fibre vibrate in the hearts of all the village boys. What a vista of mystery

CHOICE EXAMPLES OF EARLY PRINTING AND ENGRAVING.

Fac-similes from Rare and Curious Books.

PAGE FROM A BOOK OF HOURS.

Simon Vostre, who published many "Books of Hours" at Paris toward the end of the fifteenth century, was noted for the woodcuts of his works. Bold, clear Gothic lettering and rich borders characterize this page, and the woodcuts of the borders are especially rich and bright. The marginal border is decorated with colonettes and scrolls, rising one above the other, and forming the frame for a graceful and spirited series of figures: a shepherd playing on the bagpipes; below him another shepherd seated on the bough of a tree in an easy swinging attitude; lower down a maiden walks through the wood, raising her hand as if praying or reciting; and lowest of all in this border is a shepherd vigorously pushing his way through the thick trees. A grotesque figure, elf or gnome, with sword and target, occupies the corner. The composition is completed by a merry troop of youths and maidens hand in hand skipping and dancing on their way. The miniature, itself, presents a figure of Christ rising from a stone sarcophagus, and addressing the Pope and Cardinals who are kneeling at the altar in front of a sacramental chalice

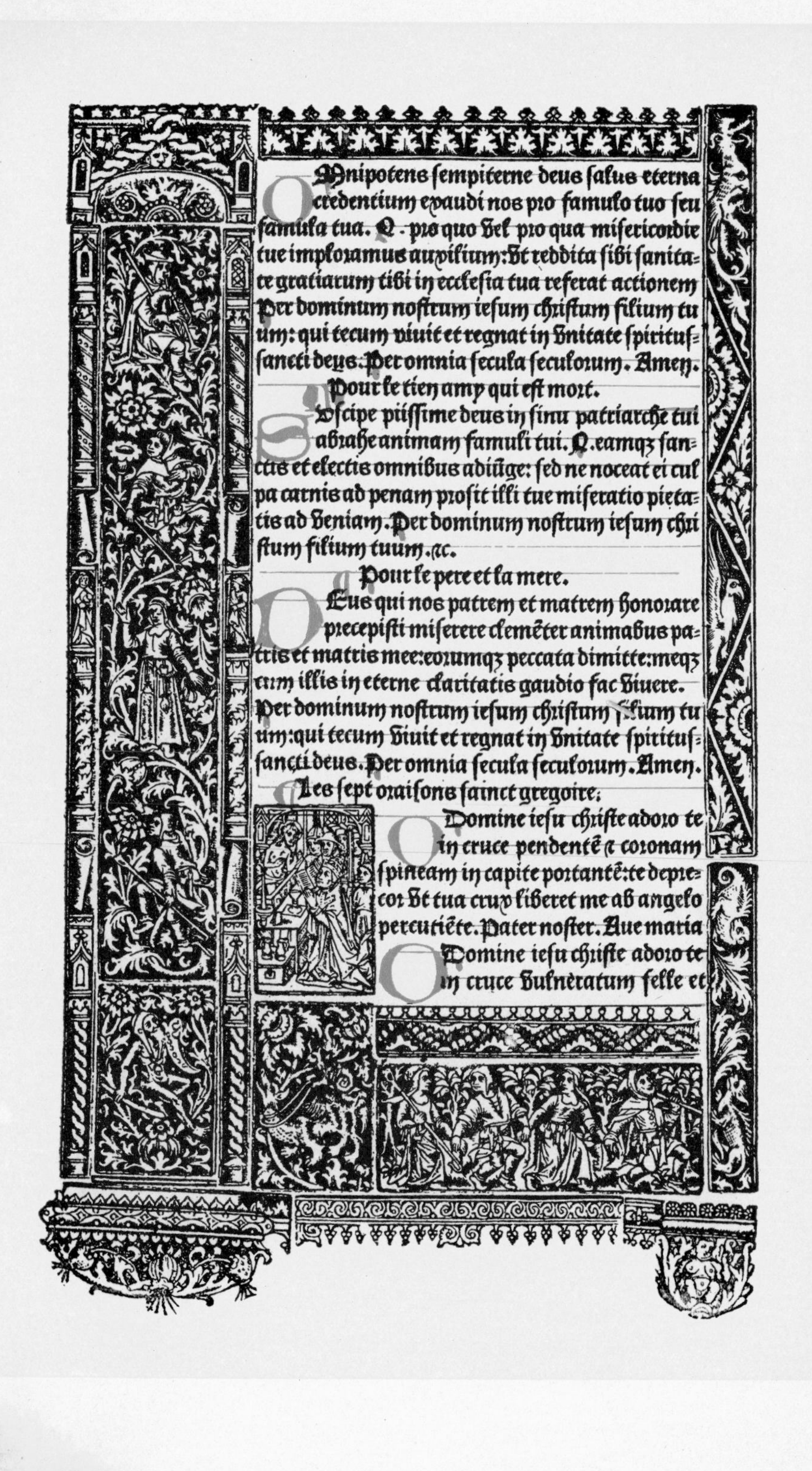

Omnipotens sempiterne deus salus eterna
credentium exaudi nos pro famulo tuo seu
famula tua. N. pro quo vel pro qua misericordie
tue imploramus auxilium: Vt reddita sibi sanita-
te gratiarum tibi in ecclesia tua referat actionem
Per dominum nostrum iesum christum filium tuum: qui tecum viuit et regnat in Vnitate spiritus-
sancti deus. Per omnia secula seculorum. Amen.

Pour le tien amy qui est mort.

Suscipe piissime deus in sinu patriarche tui
abrahe animam famuli tui. N. eamqz san-
ctis et electis omnibus adiunge: sed ne noceat ei cul
pa carnis ad penam prosit illi tue miseratio pieta-
tis ad Veniam. Per dominum nostrum iesum christum filium tuum. &c.

Pour le pere et la mere.

Deus qui nos patrem et matrem honorare
precepisti miserere clemēter animabus pa-
tris et matris mee: eorumqz peccata dimitte: meqz
cum illis in eterne claritatis gaudio fac Viuere.
Per dominum nostrum iesum christum filium tuum: qui tecum Viuit et regnat in Vnitate spiritus-
sancti deus. Per omnia secula seculorum. Amen.

Les sept oraisons sainct gregoire.

O Domine iesu christe adoro te
in cruce pendentē & coronam
spineam in capite portantē: te depre-
cor Vt tua crux liberet me ab angelo
percutiēte. Pater noster. Aue maria

O Domine iesu christe adoro te
in cruce Vulneratum felle et

and adventure did her sailing open to us! With what pride did we hail her return! She was our scholiast upon Robinson Crusoe and the mutiny of the Bounty. Her captain still lords it over our memories, the greatest sailor that ever sailed the seas, and we should not look at Sir John Franklin himself with such admiring interest as that with which we enhaloed some larger boy who had made a voyage in her, and had come back without braces to his trousers (gallowses we called them), and squirting ostentatiously the juice of that weed which still gave him little private returns of something very like sea-sickness. All our shingle vessels were shaped and rigged by her, who was our glass of naval fashion and our mould of aquatic form. We had a secret and wild delight in believing that she carried a gun, and imagined her sending grape and canister among the treacherous savages of Oldtown. Inspired by her were those first essays at navigation on the Winthrop duck-pond, of the plucky boy who was afterwards to serve two famous years before the mast.

The greater part of what is now Cambridgeport was then (in the native dialect) a "huckleberry pastur." Woods were not wanting on its outskirts, of pine, and oak, and maple, and the rarer tupelo with downward limbs. Its veins did not draw their blood from the quiet old heart of the village, but it had a distinct being of its own, and was rather a great caravansary than a suburb. The chief feature of the place was its inns, of which there were five, with vast barns and court yards, which the railroad was to make as silent and deserted as the palaces of Nimroud. Great white-topped wagons, each drawn by double files of six or eight horses, with its dusty bucket swinging from the hinder axle, and its grim bull-dog trotting silent underneath, or in midsummer panting on the lofty perch beside the driver (how elevated thither baffled conjecture), brought all the wares and products of the country to their mart and seaport in Boston. Those filled the inn-yards, or were ranged side by side under broad-roofed sheds, and far into the night the mirth of their lusty drivers clamored from the red-curtained bar-room, while the single lantern, swaying to and fro in the black cavern of the stables, made a Rembrandt of the group of hostlers and horses below. There were, beside the taverns, some huge square stores where groceries were sold, some houses, by whom or why inhabitd was to us boys a problem, and, on the edge of the marsh, a currier's shop, where, at high tide, on a floating platform, men were always beating skins in a way to remind one of Don Quixote's fulling-mills. Nor did these make all the port. As there is always a Coming Man who never comes, so there is a man who always comes (it may be only a quarter of an hour) too early. This man, so far as the port is concerned, was Rufus Davenport. Looking at the marshy flats of Cambridge, and considering their nearness to Boston, he resolved that there should grow up a suburban Venice. Accordingly, the marshes were bought, canals were dug, ample for the commerce of both Indies, and four or five rows of brick houses were built to meet the first wants of the wading settlers who were expected to rush in—whence? This singular question had never occurred to the enthusiastic projector. There are laws which govern human migrations quite beyond the control of the speculator, as many a man with desirable building-lots has discovered to his cost. Why mortal men will pay more for a chess-board square in that swamp, than for an acre on the breezy upland close by, who shall say? And again, why, having shown such a passion for your swamp, they are so coy of mine, who shall say? Not certainly any one who, like Davenport, had got up too early for his generation. If we could only carry that slow, imperturbable old clock of Opportunity, that never strikes a second too soon or too late, in our fobs, and push the hands forward as we can those of our watches! With a foreseeing economy of space which now seems ludicrous, the roofs of this forlorn-hope of houses were made flat, that the swarming population might have a place to dry their clothes. But A. U. C. 30 showed the same view as A. U. C. 1—only that the brick blocks looked as if they had been struck by a malaria. The dull weed upholstered the decaying wharves, and the only freight that heaped them was the kelp and eel-grass left by higher floods. Instead of a Venice, behold a Torzelo! The unfortunate projector took to the last refuge of the unhappy—book-making, and bored the reluctant public with what he called a Right-aim Testament, prefaced by a recommendation from General Jackson, who perhaps, from its title, took it for some treatise on ball-practice.

But even Cambridge, my dear Storg, did not want associations poetic and venerable. The stranger who took the "Hourly" at Old Cambridge, if he were a physiognomist and student of character might perhaps have had his curiosity excited by a person who mounted the coach at the port. So refined was his whole appearance, so fastidiously neat his apparel—but with a neatness that seemed less the result of care and plan than a something as proper to the man as whiteness to the lily—that you would have at once classed him with those individuals, rarer than great captains and almost as rare as great poets, whom nature sends into the world to fill the arduous office of gentleman. Were you ever emperor of that Barataria which under your peaceful sceptre would present, of course, a model of government, this remarkable person should be Duke of Bienséance and Master of Ceremonies. There are some men whom destiny has endowed with the faculty of external neatness, whose clothes are repellent of dust and mud, whose unwithering white neck-cloths persevere to the day's end, unappeasably seeing the sun go down upon their starch, and whose linen makes you fancy them heirs in the maternal line to the instincts of all the washerwomen from Eve downward. There are others whose inward natures possess this fatal cleanness, incapable of moral dirt-spot. You are not long in discovering that the stranger combines in himself both these properties. A *nimbus* of hair, fine as an infant's and early white, showing refinement of organization and the predominance of the spiritual over the physical, undulated and floated around a face that seemed like pale flame, and over which the flitting shades of expression chased each other, fugitive and gleaming as waves upon a field of rye. It was a countenance that, without any beauty of feature, was very beautiful. I have said that it looked like pale flame, and can find no other words for the impression it gave. Here was a man all soul, whose body seemed a lamp of finest clay, whose service was to feed with magic oils, rare and fragrant, that wavering fire which hovered over it. You, who are an adept in such matters, would have detected in the eyes that artist-look which seems to see pictures ever in the air, and which, if it fall on you, makes you feel as if all the world were a gallery, and yourself the rather indifferent portrait of a gentleman hung therein. As the stranger brushes by you in alighting, you detect a single incongruity—a smell of dead tobacco-smoke. You ask his name, and the answer is, "Mr. Allston."

"Mr. Allston!" and you resolve to note down at once in your diary every look, every gesture, every word of the great painter?[2] Not in the least. You have the true Anglo-Norman indifference, and most likely never think of him again till you hear that one of his pictures has sold for a great price, and then contrive to let your grandchildren know twice a week that you met him once in a coach, and that he said, "Excuse me, sir," in a very Titianesque manner, when he stumbled over your toes in getting out. Hitherto Boswell is quite as unique as Shakespeare. The country gentleman, journeying up to London, inquires of Mistress Davenant at the Oxford inn the name of his pleasant companion of the night before. "Master Shakespeare, an 't please your worship." And the justice, not without a sense of the unbending, says, "Truly, a merry and conceited gentleman!" It is lucky for the peace of great men that the world seldom finds out contemporaneously who its great men are, or, perhaps, that each man esteems the fortunate he who shall draw the lot of memory from the helmet of the future. Had the eyes of some Stratford burgess been achromatic telescopes, capable of a perspective of two hundred years! But, even then, would not his record have been fuller of *say I's* than of *says he's?* Nevertheless, it is curious to consider from what infinitely varied points of view we might form our estimate of a great man's character, when we remember that he had his points of contact with the butcher, the baker, and the candlestick-maker, as well as with the ingenious A, the sublime B, and the Right Honorable C. If it be true that no man ever clean forgets everything, and that the act of drowning (as is asserted) forthwith brightens up all those o'er-rusted impressions, would it not be a curious experiment, if, after a remarkable person's death, the public, eager for minutest particulars, should gather together all who had ever been brought into relations with him, and, submerging them to the hair's-breadth hitherward of the drowning-point, subject them to strict cross-examination by the Humane Society, as soon as they become

[2] [This refers to Washington Allston, one of the greatest of American painters. He was born in South Carolina in 1779, and died at Cambridge in 1843. He studied abroad at the Royal Academy and in Rome, and his work acquired a world-wide reputation.—EDITOR.]

conscious between the resuscitating blankets? All of us probably have brushed against destiny in the street, have shaken hands with it, fallen asleep with it in railway carriages, and knocked heads with it in some one or other of its yet unrecognized incarnations.

Will it seem like presenting a tract to a colporteur, my dear Storg, if I say a word or two about an artist to you over there in Italy? Be patient, and leave your button in my grasp yet a little longer. A——, a person whose opinion is worth having, once said to me, that, however one's opinions might be modified by going to Europe, one always came back with a higher esteem for Allston. Certainly he is thus far the greatest English painter of historical subjects. And only consider how strong must have been the artistic bias in him to have made him a painter at all under the circumstances. There were no traditions of art, so necessary for guidance and inspiration. Blackburn, Smibert, Copley, Trumbull, Stuart—it was, after all, but a Brentford sceptre which their heirs could aspire to, and theirs were not names to conjure with, like those through which Fame, as through a silver trumpet, had blown for three centuries. Copley and Stuart were both remarkable men, but the one painted like an inspired silk-mercer, and the other seems to have mixed his colors with the claret of which he and his generation were so fond. And what could a successful artist hope for at that time, beyond the mere wages of his work? His pictures would hang in cramped back-parlors, between deadly cross-fires of lights, sure of the garret or the auction-room erelong, in a country where the nomad population carry no household gods with them but their five wits and their ten fingers. As a race, we care nothing about art, but the Puritan and the Quaker are the only Anglo-Saxons who have had pluck enough to confess it. If it were surprising that Allston should have become a painter at all, how almost miraculous that he should have been a great and original one! We call him original deliberately, because, though his school is essentially Italian, it is of less consequence where a man buys his tools, than what use he makes of them. Enough English artists went to Italy and came back painting history in a very Anglo-Saxon manner, and creating a school as melodramatic as the French, without its perfection in technicalities. But Allston carried thither a nature open on the southern side, and brought it back so steeped in rich Italian sunshine that the east winds (whether physical or intellectual) of Boston and the dusts of Cambridgeport assailed it in vain. To that bare wooden studio one might go to breathe Venetian air, and, better yet, the very spirit wherein the elder brothers of art labored, etherealized by metaphysical speculation, and sublimed by religious fervor. The beautiful old man! Here was genius with no volcanic explosions (the mechanic result of vulgar gunpowder often), but lovely as a Lapland night; here was fame, not sought after nor worn in any cheap French fashion as a ribbon at the button-hole, but so gentle, so retiring, that it seemed no more than an assured and emboldened modesty; here was ambition, undebased by rivalry and incapable of the downward look; and all these massed and harmonized together into a purity and depth of character, into a tone, which made the daily life of the man the greatest masterpiece of the artist.

But let us go to the Old Town. Thirty years since the muster and the Cornwallis allowed some vent to those natural instincts which Puritanism scotched, but not killed. The Cornwallis had entered upon the estates of the old Guy Fawkes procession, confiscated by the Revolution. It was a masquerade, in which that grave and suppressed humor, of which the Yankees are fuller than other people, burst through all restraints, and disported itself in all the wildest vagaries of fun. It is a curious commentary on the artificiality of our lives, that men must be disguised and masked before they will venture into the obscurer corners of their individuality, and display the true features of their nature. One remarked it in the carnival, and one especially noted it here among a race naturally self-restrained; for Silas, and Ezra, and Jonas were not only disguised as Redcoats, Continentals, and Indians, but not unfrequently disguised in drink also. It is a question whether the lyceum, where the public is obliged to comprehend all vagrom men, supplies the place of the old popular amusements. A hundred and fifty years ago, Cotton Mather bewails the carnal attractions of the tavern and the training field, and tells of an old Indian who imperfectly understood the English tongue, but desperately mastered enough of it (when under sentence of death) to express a desire for instant hemp rather than listen to any more ghostly consolations. Puritanism—I am perfectly aware how great a debt we owe it—tried over again the old experiment of driving out nature with a pitchfork, and had the usual success. It was like a ship inwardly on fire, whose hatches must be kept hermetically battened down, for the admittance of an ounce of Heaven's own natural air would explode it utterly. Morals can never be safely embodied in the constable. Polished, cultivated, fascinating Mephistopheles! it is for the ungovernable breakings-away of the soul from unnatural compression that thou waitest with a patient smile. Then it is that thou offerest thy gentlemanly arm to unguarded youth for a pleasant stroll through the city of destruction, and, as a special favor, introducest him to the bewitching Miss Circe, and to that model of the hospitable old English gentleman, Mr. Comus.

But the muster and the Cornwallis were not peculiar to Cambridge. Commencement day was. Saint Pedagogus was a worthy whose feast could be celebrated by men who quarrelled with minced pies, and blasphemed custard through the nose. The holiday preserved all the features of an English fair. Stations were marked out beforehand by the town constables, and distinguished by numbered stakes. These were assigned to the different vendors of small wares, and exhibitors of rarities, whose canvas booths, beginning at the market-place, sometimes half encircled the Common with their jovial embrace. Now all the Jehoiada-boxes in town were forced to give up their rattling deposits of specie, if not through the legitimate orifice, then to the brute force of the hammer. For hither were come all the wonders of the world, making the Arabian Nights seem possible, and which we beheld for half price, not without mingled emotions—pleasure at the economy, and shame at not paying the more manly fee. Here the mummy unveiled her withered charms—a more marvellous Ninon, still attractive in her three thousandth year. Here were the Siamese twins; ah! if all such enforced and unnatural unions were made a show of! Here were the flying horses (their supernatural effect injured—like that of some poems—by the visibility of the man who turned the crank), on which, as we tilted at the ring, we felt our shoulders tingle with the accolade, and heard the clink of golden spurs at our heels. Are the realities of life ever worth half so much as its cheats? And are there any feasts half so filling at the price as those Barmecide ones spread for us by imagination? Hither came the Canadian giant, surreptitiously seen, without price, as he alighted, in broad day (giants were always foolish), at the tavern. Hither came the great horse Columbus, with shoes two inches thick, and more wisely introduced by night. In the trough of the town-pump might be seen the mermaid, its poor monkey's head carefully sustained above water, for fear of drowning. There were dwarfs, also, who danced and sang, and many a proprietor regretted the transaudient properties of canvas, which allowed the frugal public to share in the melody without entering the booth. Is it a slander of H——, who reports that he once saw a deacon, eminent for psalmody, lingering near one of those vocal tents, and, with an assumed air of abstraction, furtively drinking in, with unhabitual ears, a song, not secular merely, but with a dash of libertinism! The New England proverb says, "All deacons are good, but—there's a difference in deacons." On these days Snow became super-terranean, and had a stand in the square, and Lewis temperately contended with the stronger fascinations of egg-pop. But space would fail me to make a catalogue of everything. No doubt, Wisdom also, as usual, had her quiet booth at the corner of some street, without entrance-fee, and, even at that rate, got never a customer the whole day long. For the bankrupt afternoon there were peep-shows, at a cent each.

But all these shows and their showers are as clean gone now as those of Cæsar and Timour and Napoleon, for which the world paid dearer. They are utterly gone out, not leaving so much as a snuff behind—as little thought of now as that John Robins, who was once so considerable a phenomenon as to be esteemed the last great Antichrist and son of perdition by the entire sect of Muggletonians. Were commencement what it used to be, I should be tempted to take a booth myself, and try an experiment recommended by a satirist of some merit, whose works were long ago dead and (I fear) deedeed to boot:

"Menenius, thou who fain wouldst know how calmly men can pass
Those biting portraits of themselves, disguised as fox or ass,
Go borrow coin enough to buy a full-length psyche-glass,
Engage a rather darkish room in some well-sought position,
And let the town break out with bills, so much per head admission,
Great natural curiosity! The biggest living fool!
Arrange your mirror cleverly, before it set a stool,

Admit the public one by one, place each upon the seat,
Draw up the curtain, let him look his fill, and then retreat:
Smith mounts and takes a thorough view, then comes serenely down,
Goes home and tells his wife the thing is curiously like Brown;
Brown goes and stares, and tells his wife the wonder's core and pith
Is that 'tis just the counterpart of that conceited Smith.
Life calls us all to such a show: Menenius, trust in me,
While thou to see thy neighbor smil'st, he does the same for thee."

My dear Storg, would you come to my show, and, instead of looking in my glass, insist on taking your money's worth in staring at the exhibitor?

Not least among the curiosities which the day brought together were some of the graduates, posthumous men, as it were, disentombed from country parishes and district schools, but perennial also, in whom freshly survived all the college jokes, and who had no intelligence later than their senior year. These had gathered to eat the college dinner, and to get the triennial catalogue (their *libro d'oro*), referred to oftener than any volume but the Concordance. Aspiring men they were certainly, but in a right unworldly way; this scholastic festival opening a peaceful path to the ambition which might else have devastated mankind with prolusions on the Pentateuch, or genealogies of the dormouse family. For since in the academic processions the classes are ranked in the order of their graduation, and he has the best chance at the dinner who has the fewest teeth to eat it with, so, by degrees, there springs up a competition in longevity, the prize contended for being the oldest surviving graduateship. This is an office, it is true, without emolument, but having certain advantages, nevertheless. The incumbent, if he come to commencement, is a prodigious lion, and commonly gets a paragraph in the newspapers once a year with the (fiftieth) last survivor of Washington's life guard. If a clergyman, he is expected to ask a blessing and return thanks at the dinner, a function which he performs with centenarian longanimity, as if he reckoned the ordinary life of man to be fivescore years, and that a grace must be long to reach so far away as heaven. Accordingly, this silent race is watched, on the course of the catalogue, with an interest worthy of Newmarket; and as star after star rises in the galaxy of death, till one name is left alone, an oasis of life in the stellar desert, it grows solemn. The natural feeling is reversed, and it is the solitary life that becomes sad and monitory, the Stylites there on the lonely top of his century-pillar, who has heard the passing-bell of youth, love, friendship, hope—of everything but immitigable eld.

Dr. K—— was president of the university then, a man of genius, but of genius that evaded utilization, a great water-power, but without rapids, and flowing with too smooth and gentle a current to be set turning wheels and whirling spindles. His was not that restless genius, of which the man seems to be merely the representative, and which wreaks itself in literature or politics, but of that milder sort, quite as genuine, and perhaps of more contemporaneous value, which *is* the man, permeating the whole life with placid force, and giving to word, look, and gesture a meaning only justifiable by our belief in a reserved power of latent reinforcement. The man of talents possesses them like so many tools, does his job with them, and there an end; but the man of genius is possessed by it, and it makes him into a book or a life according to its whim. Talent takes the existing moulds, and makes its castings, better or worse, of richer or baser metal, according to knack and opportunity; but genius is always shaping new ones, and runs the man in them, so that there is always that human feel in its results which gives us a kindred thrill. What it will make we can only conjecture, contented always with knowing the infinite balance of possibility against which it can draw at pleasure. Have you ever seen a man whose check would be honored for a million pay his toll of one cent? and has not that bit of copper, no bigger than your own, and piled with it by the careless toll-man, given you a tingling vision of what golden bridges he could pass—into what Elysian regions of taste and enjoyment and culture, barred to the rest of us? Something like it is the impression made by such characters as K——'s on those who come in contact with them.

There was that in the soft and rounded (I had almost said melting) outlines of his face which reminded one of Chaucer. The head had a placid yet dignified droop like his. He was an anachronism, fitter to have been abbot of fountains or Bishop Golias, courtier and priest, humorist and lord spiritual, all in one, than for the mastership of a provincial college which combined, with its purely scholastic functions, those of accountant and chief of police. For keeping books he was incompetent (unless it were those he borrowed), and the only discipline he exercised was by the unobtrusive pressure of a gentlemanliness which rendered insubordination to him impossible. But the world always judges a man (and rightly enough, too) by his little faults, which he shows a hundred times a day, rather than by his great virtues which he discloses perhaps but once in a lifetime, and to a single person—nay, in proportion as they are rarer, and he is nobler, is shyer of letting their existence be known at all. He was one of those misplaced persons whose misfortune it is that their lives overlap two distinct eras, and are already so impregnated with one that they can never be in healthy sympathy with the other. Born when the New England clergy were still an establishment and an aristocracy, and when office was almost always for life, and often hereditary, he lived to be thrown upon a time when avocations of all colors might be shuffled together in the life of one man, like a pack of cards, so that you could not prophesy that he who was ordained to-day might not accept a colonelcy of filibusters to-morrow. Such temperaments as his attach themselves, like barnacles, to what seems permanent, but presently the good ship Progress weighs anchor, and whirls them away from drowsy tropic inlets to arctic waters of unnatural ice. To such crustaceous natures, created to cling upon the immemorial rock amid softest mosses, comes the bustling nineteenth century and says, "Come, come, bestir yourself to be practical: get out of that old shell of yours forthwith!" Alas, to get out of the shell is to die!

One of the old travellers in South America tells of fishes that built their nests in trees (*piscium et summa hæsit genus ulmo*), and gives a print of the mother fish upon her nest, while her mate mounts perpendicularly to her without aid of legs or wings. Life shows plenty of such incongruities between a man's place and his nature (not so easily got over as by the traveller's undoubting engraver), and one cannot help fancying that K—— was an instance in point. He never encountered, one would say, the attraction proper to draw out his native force. Certainly, few men who impressed others so strongly, and of whom so many good things are remembered, left less behind them to justify contemporary estimates. He printed nothing, and was, perhaps, one of those the electric sparkles of whose brains, discharged naturally and healthily in conversation, refuse to pass through the non-conducting medium of the inkstand. His ana would make a delightful collection. One or two of his official ones will be in place here. Hearing that Porter's flip (which was exemplary) had too great an attraction for the collegians, he resolved to investigate the matter himself. Accordingly, entering the old inn one day, he called for a mug of it, and, having drunk it, said, "And so, Mr. Porter, the young gentlemen come to drink your flip, do they?" "Yes, sir—sometimes." "Ah, well, I should think they would. Good day, Mr. Porter," and departed, saying nothing more; for he always wisely allowed for the existence of a certain amount of human nature in ingenuous youth. At another time the "Harvard Washington" asked leave to go into Boston to a collation which had been offered them. "Certainly, young gentlemen," said the president, "but have you engaged anyone to bring home your muskets?"—the college being responsible for these weapons, which belonged to the State. Again, when a student came with a physician's certificate, and asked leave of absence, K—— granted it at once and then added, "By the way, Mr. ——, persons interested in the relation which exists between states of the atmosphere and health, have noticed a curious fact in regard to the climate of Cambridge, especially within the college limits—the very small number of deaths in proportion to the cases of dangerous illness." This is told of Judge W——, himself a wit, and capable of enjoying the humorous delicacy of the reproof.

Shall I take Brahmin Alcott's favorite word and call him a dæmonic man? No, the Latin *genius* is quite old-fashioned enough for me, means the same thing, and its derivative geniality expresses, moreover, the base of K——'s being. How he suggested cloistered repose, and quadrangles mossy with centurial associations! How easy he was, and how without creak was every movement of his mind! This life was good enough for him, and the next not too good. The gentleman-like pervaded even his prayers. His were not the manners of a man of the world, nor of a man of the other world either; but both met in him to balance each other in a beautiful equilibrium. Praying, he leaned forward upon the pulpit-cushion as for conversation, and seemed to feel himself (without irreverence) on terms of friendly but courteous familiarity with Heaven. The expression of his face was that of tranquil contentment, and he appeared less to be supplicating expected mercies than thankful for those already found, as if he were saying the *gratias* in the refectory of the Abbey of Theleme. Under him flourished the Harvard Washington Corps, whose gyrating banner, inscribed *Tam Marti quam Mercurio* (*atqui magis Lyæo* should have been added), on the evening of training-days, was an accurate dynamometer of Willard's punch or Porter's flip. It was they who, after being royally entertained by a maiden lady of the town, entered in their orderly book a vote that Miss Blank was a gentleman. I see them now, returning from the imminent deadly breach of the law of Rechab, unable to form other than the serpentine line of beauty, while their officers, brotherly rather than imperious, instead of reprimanding, tearfully embraced the more eccentric wanderers from military precision. Under him the Med. Facs. took their equal place among the learned societies of Europe, numbering among their grateful honorary members Alexander, Emperor of all the Russias, who (if college legends may be trusted) sent them in return for their diploma a gift of medals confiscated by the authorities. Under him the college fire-engine was vigilant and active in suppressing any tendency to spontaneous combustion among the freshmen, or rushed wildly to imaginary conflagrations, generally in a direction where punch was to be had. All these useful conductors for the natural electricity of youth, dispersing it or turning it harmlessly into the earth, are taken away now—wisely or not, is questionable.

An academic town, in whose atmosphere there is always something antiseptic, seems naturally to draw to itself certain varieties and to preserve certain humors (in the Ben Jonsonian sense) of character—men who come not to study so much as to be studied. At the headquarters of Washington once, and now of the muses, lived C——, but before the date of these recollections. Here for seven years (as the law was then) he made his house his castle, sunning himself in his elbow-chair at the front-door, on that seventh day, secure from every arrest but that of death's. Here long survived him his turbaned widow, studious only of Spinoza, and refusing to molest the canker-worms that annually disleaved her elms, because we were all vermicular alike. She had been a famous beauty once, but the canker years had left her leafless, too, and I used to wonder, as I saw her sitting always alone at her accustomed window, whether she were ever visited by the reproachful shade of him who (in spite of Rosalind) died broken-hearted for her in her radiant youth.

And this reminds me of F——, who, also crossed in love, allowed no mortal eye to behold his face for many years. The eremitic instinct is not peculiar to the Thebais, as many a New England village can testify, and it is worthy of consideration that the Romish Church has not forgotten this among her other points of intimate contact with human nature. F—— became purely vespertinal, never stirring abroad till after dark. He occupied two rooms, migrating from one to the other, as the necessities of housewifery demanded, and when it was requisite that he should put his signature to any legal instrument (for he was an anchorite of ample means), he wrapped himself in a blanket, allowing nothing to be seen but the hand which acted as scribe. What impressed us boys more than anything was the rumor that he had suffered his beard to grow, such an anti-Sheffieldism being almost unheard of in those days, and the peculiar ornament of man being associated in our minds with nothing more recent than the patriarchs and apostles, whose effigies we were obliged to solace ourselves with weekly in the family Bible. He came out of his oysterhood at last, and I knew him well, a kind-hearted man, who gave annual sleigh-rides to the town-paupers, and supplied the poorer children with school-books. His favorite topic of conversation was eternity, and, like many other worthy persons, he used to fancy that meaning was an affair of aggregation, and that he doubled the intensity of what he said by the sole aid of the multiplication-table. "Eternity!" he used to say, "it is not a day; it is not a year; it is not a hundred years; it is not a thousand years; it is not a million years; no, sir" (the *sir* being thrown in to recall wandering attention), "it is not ten million years!" and so on, his enthusiasm becoming a mere frenzy when he got among his sextillions, till I sometimes wished he had continued in retirement. He used to sit at the open window during thunder-storms, and had a Grecian feeling about death by lightning. In a certain sense he had his desire, for he died suddenly—not by fire from heaven, but by the red flash of apoplexy, leaving his whole estate to charitable uses.

If K—— were out of place as president, that was not P—— as Greek professor. Who that ever saw him can forget him, in his old age, like a lusty winter, frosty but kindly, with great silver spectacles of the heroic period, such as scarce twelve noses of these degenerate days could bear? He was a natural celibate, not dwelling "like the fly in the heart of the apple," but like a lonely bee, rather, absconding himself in Hymettian flowers, incapable of matrimony as a solitary palm-tree. There was not even a tradition of youthful disappointment. I fancy him arranging his scrupulous toilet, not for Amaryllis or Neæra, but, like Machiavelli, for the society of his beloved classics. His ears had needed no prophylactic wax to pass the Sirens' isle, nay, he would have kept them the wider open, studious of the dialect in which they sang, and perhaps triumphantly detecting the Æolic digamma in their lay. A thoroughly single man, single-minded, single-hearted, buttoning over his single heart a single-breasted surtout, and wearing always a hat of a single fashion—did he in secret regard the dual number of his favorite language as a weakness? The son of an officer of distinction in the Revolutionary War, he mounted the pulpit with the erect port of soldier, and carried his cane more in the fashion of a weapon than a staff, but with the point lowered in token of surrender to the peaceful proprieties of his calling. Yet sometimes the martial instincts would burst the cerements of black coat and clerical neck-cloth, as once when the students had got into a fight upon the training-field, and the licentious soldiery, furious with rum, had driven them at point of bayonet to the college-gates, and even threatened to lift their arms against the muses' bower. Then, like Major Goffe at Deerfield, suddenly appeared the gray-haired P——, all his father resurgent in him, and shouted, "Now, my lads, stand your ground, you're in the right now! don't let one of them get inside the college grounds!" Thus he allowed arms to get the better of the toga, but raised it, like the prophet's breeches, into a banner, and carefully ushered resistance with a preamble of infringed right. Fidelity was his strong characteristic, and burned equably in him through a life of eighty-three years. He drilled himself till inflexible habit stood sentinel before all those postern-weaknesses which temperament leaves unbolted to temptation. A lover of the scholar's herb, yet loving freedom more, and knowing that the animal appetites ever hold one hand behind them for Satan to drop a bribe in, he would never have two cigars in his house at once, but walked every day to the shop to fetch his single diurnal solace. Nor would he trust himself with two on Saturdays, preferring (since he could not violate the Sabbath even by that infinitesimal traffic) to depend on providential ravens, which were seldom wanting in the shape of some black-coated friend who knew his need and honored the scruple that occasioned it. He was faithful also to his old hats, in which appeared the constant service of the antique world, and which he preserved forever, piled like a black pagoda under his dressing-table. No scarecrow was ever the residuary legatee of his beavers, though one of them in any of the neighboring peach-orchards would have been sovran against an attack of freshmen. He wore them all in turn, getting through all in the course of the year, like the sun through the signs of the Zodiac, modulating them according to seasons and celestial phenomena, so that never was spider-web or chickweed so sensitive a weather-gage as they. Nor did his political party find him less loyal. Taking all the tickets, he would seat himself apart and carefully compare them with the list of regular nominations as printed in his "Daily Advertiser" before he dropped his ballot in the box. In less ambitious moments it almost seems to me that I would rather have had that slow, conscientious vote of P——'s alone than have been chosen alderman of the ward!

If you had walked to what was then sweet Auburn by the pleasant Old Road, on some June morning thirty years ago, you would, very likely, have met two other characteristic persons, both phantasmagoric now, and belonging to the past. Fifty years earlier the scarlet-coated, rapiered figures of Vassall, Oliver, and Brattle, creaked up and down there on red-heeled shoes, lifting the ceremonious three-cornered hat and offering the fugacious hospitalities of the snuff-box. They are all shadowy alike now, not one of your Etruscan Lucumos or Roman Consuls more so, my dear Storg. First is W——, his queue slender and tapering like the tail of a violet crab, held out horizontally by the high collar of his shepherd's-gray overcoat, whose style was of the latest when he studied at Leyden in his hot youth. The age of cheap clothes sees no more of those faithful old garments, as proper to their wearers and as distinctive as the barks of trees, and by long use interpenetrated with their very nature. Nor do we see so many humors (still in the old sense) now that every man's soul belongs to the public, as when social distinctions were more marked, and men felt that their personalities were their castles, in which they could entrench themselves against the world. Nowadays men are shy of letting their true selves be seen, as if in some former life they had committed a crime, and were all the time afraid of discovery and arrest in this. Formerly they used to insist on your giving the wall to their peculiarities, and you may still find examples of it in the parson or the doctor of retired villages. One of W——'s oddities was touching. A little brook used to run across the street, and the sidewalk was carried over it by a broad stone. Of course, there is no brook now. What use did that little glimpse of ripple serve, where the children used to launch their chip fleets? W——, in going over this stone, which gave a hollow resonance to the tread, used to strike upon it three times with his cane, and mutter "Tom! Tom! Tom!" I used to think he was only mimicking with his voice the sound of the blows, and possibly it was that sound which suggested his thought—for he was remembering a favorite nephew prematurely dead. Perhaps Tom had sailed his boats there; perhaps the reverberation under the old man's foot hinted at the hollowness of life; perhaps the fleeting eddies of the water brought to mind the *fugaces annos*. W——, like P——, wore amazing spectacles, fit to transmit no smaller image than the page of mightiest folios of Dioscorides or Hercules de Saxoniâ, and rising full-disked upon the beholder like those prodigies of two moons at once, portending change to monarchs. The great collar disallowing any independent rotation of the head, I remember he used to turn his whole person in order to bring their *foci* to bear upon an object. One can fancy that terrified nature would have yielded up her secrets at once, without cross-examination, at their first glare. Through them he had gazed fondly into the great mare's-nest of Junius, publishing his observations upon the eggs found therein in a tall octavo. It was he who introduced vaccination to this Western World. He used to stop and say good-morning kindly, and pat the shoulder of the blushing school-boy who now, with the fierce snow-storm wildering without, sits and remembers sadly those old meetings and partings in the June sunshine.

Then, there was S——, whose resounding "Haw! haw! haw! by George!" positively enlarged the income of every dweller in Cambridge. In downright, honest good cheer and good neighborhood it was worth five hundred a year to every one of us. Its jovial thunders cleared the mental air of every sulky cloud. Perpetual childhood dwelt in him, the childhood of his native Southern France, and its fixed aid was all the time bubbling up and sparkling and winking in his eyes. It seemed as if his placid old face were only a mask behind which a merry Cupid had ambushed himself, peeping out all the while, and ready to drop it when the play grew tiresome. Every word he uttered seemed to be hilarious, no matter what the occasion. If he were sick and you visited him, if he had met with a misfortune (and there are few men so wise that they can look even at the back of a retiring sorrow with composure), it was all one; his great laugh went off as if it were set like an alarm-clock, to run down, whether he would or no, at a certain nick. Even after an ordinary "Good morning!" (especially if to an old pupil, and in French), the wonderful "Haw! haw! haw! by George!" would burst upon you unexpectedly like a salute of artillery on some holiday which you had forgotten. Everything was a joke to him—that the oath of allegiance had been administered to him by your grandfather—that he had taught Prescott his first Spanish (of which he was proud)—no matter what. Everything came to him marked by nature—right side up, with care, and he kept it so. The world to him, as to all of us, was like a medal, on the obverse of which is stamped the image of Joy, and on the reverse that of Care. S—— never took the foolish pains to look at that other side, even if he knew its existence; much less would it have occurred to him to turn it into view and insist that his friends should look at it with him. Nor was this a mere outside good-humor; its source was deeper in a true Christian kindliness and amenity. Once when he had been knocked down by a tipsily-driven sleigh, and was urged to prosecute the offenders—"No, no," he said, his wounds still fresh, "young blood! young blood! it must have its way; I was young myself." *Was!* few men come into life so young as S—— went out. He landed in Boston (then the front door of America) in '93, and, in honor of the ceremony, had his head powdered afresh, and put on a suit of court-mourning before he set foot on the wharf. My fancy always dressed him in that violet silk, and his soul certainly wore a full court-suit. What was there ever like his bow? It was as if you had received a decoration, and could write yourself gentleman from that day forth. His hat rose, regreeting your own, and, having sailed through the stately curve of the old *régime,* sank gently back over that placid brain which harbored no thought less white than the powder which covered it. I have sometimes imagined that there was a graduated arc over his head, invisible to other eyes than his, by which he meted out to each his rightful share of castorial consideration. I carry in my memory three exemplary bows. The first is that of an old beggar, who already carrying in his hand a white hat, the gift of benevolence, took off the black one from his head also, and profoundly saluted me with both at once, giving me, in return for my alms, a dual benediction, puzzling as a nod from Janus Bifrons. The second I received from an old cardinal who was taking his walk just outside the Porta San Giovanni at Rome. I paid him the courtesy due to his age and rank. Forthwith rose—first, *the* hat; second, the hat of his confessor; third, that of another priest who attended him; fourth, the fringed cocked-hat of his coachman; fifth and sixth, the ditto, ditto, of his two footmen. Here was an investment, indeed; six hundred per cent. interest on a single bow! The third bow, worthy to be noted in one's almanac among the other *mirabilia,* was that of S——, in which courtesy had mounted to the last round of her ladder —and tried to draw it up after her.

But the genial veteran is gone even while I am writing this, and I will play Old Mortality no longer. Wandering among these recent graves, my dear friend, we may chance to—— But no, I will not end my sentence. I bid you heartily farewell.

PREFACE TO "LEAVES OF GRASS"

—

BY

WALT WHITMAN

WALT WHITMAN

1819—1892

The "good gray poet," as his admirers loved to call him, was born at West Hills, Long Island, in 1819. Walt Whitman's father was a carpenter, and the family had little time and still less inclination for books. When he was a child his parents removed to Brooklyn, where he attended the public schools. At the age of thirteen he began to support himself by setting type. When less than twenty he edited a small Long Island paper. He contributed for a time stories and sketches to various papers. These he afterwards gathered into a volume entitled "Specimen Days and Collect," but they are devoid of any literary merit, and are of interest only in connection with his later work. In 1849 Whitman travelled through the West and South. He edited a paper in New Orleans for a year, afterwards allowing himself to drift around in an indescribably careless and happy-go-lucky manner. On his return to the East he resumed in New York a Bohemian existence among reporters, literary men, actresses, omnibus drivers, laboring men, mingling with all sorts and conditions of men in metropolitan life. When in Brooklyn he devoted himself to the more serious occupation of a carpenter and builder, building and selling small houses for working-people.

He spent a large part of his time, however, in what was then New York City exclusive of Brooklyn, and his huge and striking figure was a familiar sight on the ferries and omnibuses. Here he delighted to spend hours watching the crowds, and meditating on the themes to which he was soon to give such striking and original expression. He read much during this period, especially in the Bible, but his reading was desultory, and left him in absolute ignorance of much that would be familiar enough to a high-school boy of to-day. In 1855 he published the book that contained the outcome of his musings and observations under the title of "Leaves of Grass." The work made a sensation, and aroused a sharp literary controversy as to whether its author was the greatest poet in America or an egotistic and ignorant charlatan, a genius or an idiot. As the echoes of this controversy have not yet died away it is too soon to attempt a final estimate. In his own statement, contained in the preface to the "Leaves of Grass," Whitman disclaims much that the more reckless of his admirers have claimed for him.

During the Civil War, Whitman went to Washington and became a volunteer nurse and an occasional correspondent to the New York "Times." This portion of his career was strikingly unselfish and noble. A record of some of his observations and impressions was published in a volume entitled "Drum Taps." On the death of President Lincoln he wrote two of his finest poems, "When Lilacs last in the Door-yard Bloomed," and "O Captain! My Captain!" In 1873 he removed to Camden, New Jersey, where he lived until his death in 1892. He published a number of other books, none of which added materially to the reputation he won by his first.

Whitman's style constitutes one of the subjects of the controversy aroused by his work. His poetry is without rhyme or rhythm, and violates every rule of poetical art and tradition. His prose is clumsy, at times unintelligible. Yet, in spite of this utter indifference to form, Whitman in his prose sometimes rises to poetic grandeur, and many passages of his work possess a rough, moving eloquence and beauty. He himself appealed to posterity to be the final judge of his work, and to this appeal modern criticism can take no well-founded exception.

PREFACE* TO "LEAVES OF GRASS"

AMERICA does not repel the past, or what the past has produced under its forms, or amid other politics, or the idea of castes, or the old religions—accepts the lesson with calmness—is not impatient because the slough still sticks to opinions and manners and literature, while the life which served its requirements has passed into the new life of the new forms—perceives that the corpse is slowly borne from the eating and sleeping rooms of the house—perceives that it waits a little while in the door—that it was fittest for its days—that its action has descended to the stalwart and well-shaped heir who approaches—and that he shall be fittest for his days.

The Americans, of all nations at any time upon the earth, have probably the fullest poetical nature. The United States themselves are essentially the greatest poem. In the history of the earth hitherto, the largest and most stirring appear tame and orderly to their ampler largeness and stir. Here at last is something in the doings of man that corresponds with the broadcast doings of the day and night. Here is action untied from strings, necessarily blind to particulars and details, magnificently moving in masses. Here is the hospitality which forever indicates heroes. Here the performance, disdaining the trivial, unapproached in the tremendous audacity of its crowds and groupings, and the push of its perspective, spreads with crampless and flowing breadth, and showers its prolific and splendid extravagance. One sees it must indeed own the riches of the summer and winter, and need never be bankrupt while corn grows from the ground, or the orchards drop apples, or the bays contain fish.

Other States indicate themselves in their deputies—but the genius of the United States in not best or most in its executives

* This is the preface to the first edition of "Leaves of Grass," published in 1855.

or legislatures, nor in its ambassadors or authors, or colleges or churches or parlors, nor even in its newspapers or inventors—but always most in the common people, south, north, west, east, in all its States, through all its mighty amplitude. The largeness of the nation, however, were monstrous without a corresponding largeness and generosity of the spirit of the citizen. Not swarming States, nor streets and steamships, nor prosperous business, nor farms, nor capital, nor learning, may suffice for the ideal of man—nor suffice the poet. No reminiscences may suffice either. A live nation can always cut a deep mark, and can have the best authority the cheapest—namely, from its own soul. This is the sum of the profitable uses of individuals or States, and of present action and grandeur, and of the subjects of poets. (As if it were necessary to trot back generation after generation to the Eastern records! As if the beauty and sacredness of the demonstrable must fall behind that of the mythical! As if men do not make their mark out of any times! As if the opening of the Western continent by discovery, and what has transpired in North and South America, were less than the small theatre of the antique, or the aimless sleep-walking of the Middle Ages!) The pride of the United States leaves the wealth and finesse of the cities, and all returns of commerce and agriculture, and all the magnitude of geography or shows of exterior victory, to enjoy the sight and realization of full-sized men, or one full-sized man unconquerable and simple.

The American poets are to enclose old and new, for America is the race of races. The expression of the American poet is to be transcendent and new. It is to be indirect, and not direct or descriptive or epic. Its quality goes through these to much more. Let the age and wars of other nations be chanted, and their eras and characters be illustrated, and that finish the verse. Not so the great psalm of the republic. Here the theme is creative, and has vista. Whatever stagnates in the flat of custom or obedience or legislation, the great poet never stagnates. Obedience does not master him; he masters it. High up out of reach he stands, turning a concentrated light—he turns the pivot with his finger—he baffles the swiftest runners as he stands, and easily overtakes and envelops them. The time straying toward infidelity and confections and persiflage he withholds by steady faith. Faith is the antiseptic of the soul—it pervades the com-

. . .

mon people and preserves them—they never give up believing and expecting and trusting. There is that indescribable freshness and unconsciousness about an illiterate person, that humbles and mocks the power of the noblest expressive genius. The poet sees for a certainty how one not a great may be just as sacred and perfect as the greatest artist.

The power to destroy or remould is freely used by the greatest poet, but seldom the power of attack. What is past is past. If he does not expose superior models, and prove himself by every step he takes, he is not what is wanted. The presence of the great poet conquers—not parleying, or struggling or any prepared attempt. Now he has passed that way, see after him! There is not left any vestige of despair, or misanthropy or cunning, or exclusiveness, or the ignominy of a nativity, or color, or delusion of hell, or the necessity of hell—and no man thenceforward shall be degraded for ignorance or weakness or sin. The greatest poet hardly knows pettiness or triviality. If he breathes into anything that was before thought small, it dilates with the grandeur and life of the universe. He is a seer—he is individual—he is complete in himself—the others are as good as he, only he sees it, and they do not. He is not one of the chorus—he does not stop for any regulation—he is the president of regulation. What the eyesight does to the rest, he does to the rest. Who knows the curious mystery of the eyesight? The other senses corroborate themselves, but this is removed from any proof but its own, and foreruns the identities of the spiritual world. A single glance of it mocks all the investigations of man, and all the instruments and books of the earth, and all reasoning. What is marvellous? What is unlikely? What is impossible or baseless or vague—after you have once just opened the space of a peach-pit, and given audience to far and near, and to the sunset, and had all things enter with electric swiftness, softly and duly, without confusion or jostling or jam?

The land and sea, the animals, fishes, and birds, the sky of heaven and the orbs, the forests, mountains and rivers, are not small themes—but folks expect of the poet to indicate more than the beauty and dignity which always attach to dumb real objects—they expect him to indicate the path between reality and their souls. Men and women perceive the beauty well enough—probably as well as he. The passionate tenacity of hunters, woodmen, early risers, cultivators of gardens and orchards and fields, the love of healthy women for the manly form, seafaring persons, drivers of horses, the passion for light and the open air, all is an old varied sign of the unfailing perception of beauty, and of a residence of the poetic in out-door people. They can never be assisted by poets to perceive—some may, but they never can. The poetic quality is not marshalled in rhyme or uniformity, or abstract addresses to things, nor in melancholy complaints or good precepts, but is the life of these and much else, and is in the soul. The profit of rhyme is that it drops seeds of a sweeter and more luxuriant rhyme, and of uniformity that it conveys itself into its own roots in the ground out of sight. The rhyme and uniformity of perfect poems show the free growth of metrical laws, and bud from them as unerringly and loosely as lilacs and roses on a bush, and take shapes as compact as the shapes of chestnuts and oranges, and melons and pears, and shed the perfume impalpable to form. The fluency and ornaments of the finest poems or music or orations or recitations, are not independent but dependent. All beauty comes from beautiful blood and a beautiful brain. If the greatnesses are in conjunction in a man or woman, it is enough—the fact will prevail through the universe; but the gaggery and gilt of a million years will not prevail. Who troubles himself about his ornaments or fluency is lost. This is what you shall do: Love the earth and sun and the animals, despise riches, give alms to everyone that asks, stand up for the stupid and crazy, devote your income and labor to others, hate tyrants, argue not concerning God, have patience and indulgence towards the people, take off your hat to nothing known or unknown, or to any man or number of men—go freely with powerful uneducated persons, and with the young and with the mothers of families—reëxamine all you have been told in school or church or in any book, and dismiss whatever insults your own soul; and your very flesh shall be a great poem, and have the richest fluency, not only in its words, but in the silent lines of its lips and face, and between the lashes of your eyes, and in every motion and joint of your body. The poet shall not spend his time in unneeded work. He shall know that the ground is already ploughed and manured; others may not know it, but he shall. He shall go directly to the creation. His trust shall master the trust of everything he touches—and shall master all attachment.

The known universe has one complete lover, and that is the greatest poet. He consumes an eternal passion, and is indifferent which chance happens, and which possible contingency of fortune or misfortune, and persuades daily and hourly his delicious pay. What balks or breaks others is fuel for his burning progress to contact and amorous joy. Other proportions of the reception of pleasure dwindle to nothing to his proportions. All expected from heaven or from the highest, he is *rapport* within the sight of the daybreak, or the scenes of the winter woods, or the presence of children playing, or with his arm round the neck of a man or woman. His love above all love has leisure and expanse—he leaves room ahead of himself. He is no irresolute or suspicious lover—he is sure—he scorns intervals. His experience and the showers and thrills are not for nothing. Nothing can jar him—suffering and darkness cannot—death and fear cannot. To him complaint and jealousy and envy are corpses buried and rotten in the earth—he saw them buried. The sea is not surer of the shore, or the shore of the sea, than he is the fruition of his love, and of all perfection and beauty.

The fruition of beauty is no chance of miss or hit—it is as inevitable as life—it is exact and plumb as gravitation. From the eyesight proceeds another eyesight, and from the hearing proceeds another hearing, and from the voice proceeds another voice, eternally curious of the harmony of things with man. These understand the law of perfection in masses and floods—that it is profuse and impartial—that there is not a minute of the light or dark, nor an acre of the earth and sea, without it—nor any direction of the sky, nor any trade or employment, nor any turn of events. This is the reason that about the proper expression of beauty there is precision and balance. One part does not need to be thrust above another. The best singer is not the one who has the most lithe and powerful organ. The pleasure of poems is not in them that take the handsomest measure and sound.

Without effort, and without exposing in the least how it is done, the greatest poet brings the spirit of any or all events and passions and scenes and persons, some more and some less, to bear on your individual character as you hear or read. To do this well is to compete with the laws that pursue and follow Time. What is the purpose must surely be there, and the clew of it must be there—and the faintest indication is the indication of the best, and then becomes the clearest indication. Past and present and future are not disjoined but joined. The greatest poet forms the consistence of what is to be, from what has been and is. He drags the dead out of their coffins and stands them again on their feet. He says to the past, Rise and walk before me that I may realize you. He learns the lesson—he places himself where the future becomes present. The greatest poet does not only dazzle his rays over character and scenes and passions—he finally ascends, and finishes all—he exhibits the pinnacles that no man can tell what they are for, or what is beyond—he glows a moment on the extremest verge. He is most wonderful in his last half-hidden smile or frown; by that flash of the moment of parting the one that sees it shall be encouraged or terrified afterward for many years. The greatest does not moralize or make application of morals—he knows the soul. The soul has that measureless pride which consists in never acknowledging any lessons or deductions but its own. But it has sympathy as measureless as its pride, and the one balances the other, and neither can stretch too far while it stretches in company with the other. The inmost secrets of art sleep with the twain. The greatest poet has lain close betwixt both, and they are vital in his style and thoughts.

The art of art, the glory of expression and the sunshine of the light of letters, is simplicity. Nothing is better than simplicity—nothing can make up for excess, or for the lack of definiteness. To carry on the heave of impulse and pierce intellectual depths and give all subjects their articulations, are powers neither common nor very uncommon. But to speak in literature with the perfect rectitude and *insouciance* of the movements of animals, and the unimpeachableness of the sentiment of trees in the woods and grass by the roadside, is the flawless triumph of art. If you have looked on him who has achieved it you have looked on one of the masters of the artists of all nations and times. You shall not contemplate the flight of the gray gull over the bay, or the mettlesome action of the blood horse, or the tall leaning of sunflowers on their stalk, or the appearance of the sun journeying through heaven or the appearance of the moon afterward, with any more satisfaction than you shall contemplate him. The great poet has less a marked style, and is more the channel of thoughts and things without increase or diminution, and is the free channel of himself. He swears to his art, I will not be meddlesome, I will not have in my writing any elegance, or effect, or originality, to hang in the way between me and the rest like curtains. I will have nothing hang in the way, not the richest curtains. What I tell I tell for precisely what it is. Let who may exalt or startle or fascinate or soothe, I will have purposes as health or heat or snow has, and be as regardless of observation. What I experience or portray shall go from my composition without a shred of my composition. You shall stand by my side and look in the mirror with me.

The old red blood and stainless gentility of great poets will be proved by their unconstraint. A heroic person walks at his ease through and out of that custom or precedent or authority that suits him not. Of the traits of the brotherhood of first-class writers, savans, musicians, inventors, and artists nothing is finer than silent defiance advancing from new free forms. In the need of poems, philosophy, politics, mechanism, science, behavior, the craft of art, an appropriate native grand opera, ship-craft, or any craft, he is greatest forever and ever who contributes the greatest original practical example. The cleanest expression is that which finds no sphere worthy of itself, and makes one.

The messages of great poems to each man and woman are, Come to us on equal terms, only then can you understand us. We are no better than you. What we inclose you inclose, what we enjoy you may enjoy. Did you suppose there could be only one Supreme? We affirm there can be unnumbered Supremes, and that one does not countervail another any more than eye-sight countervails another—and that men can be good or grand only of the consciousness of their supremacy within them. What do you think is the grandeur of storms and dismemberments, and the deadliest battles and wrecks, and the wildest fury of the elements, and the power of the sea, and the motion of nature, and the throes of human desires, and dignity and hate and love? It is that something in the soul which says, Rage on, whirl on, I tread master here and everywhere—Master of the spasms of the sky and of the shatter of the sea, Master of nature and passion and death, and of all terror and all pain.

The American bards shall be marked for generosity and affection, and for encouraging competitors. They shall be Kosmos, without monopoly or secrecy, glad to pass anything to anyone—hungry for equals night and day. They shall not be careful of riches and privilege—they shall be riches and privilege—they shall perceive who the most affluent man is. The most affluent man is he that confronts all the shows he sees by equivalents out of the stronger wealth of himself. The American bard shall delineate no class of persons, nor one or two out of the strata of interests, nor love most nor truth most, nor the soul most, nor the body most—and not be for the Eastern States more than the Western, or the Northern States more than the Southern.

Exact science and its practical movements are no checks on the greatest poet, but always his encouragement and support. The outset and remembrance are there—there the arms that lifted him first, and braced him best—there he returns after all his goings and comings. The sailor and traveller—the anatomist, chemist, astronomer, geologist, phrenologist, spiritualist, mathematician, historian, and lexicographer, are not poets, but they are the lawgivers of poets, and their construction underlies the structure of every perfect poem. No matter what rises or is uttered, they sent the seed of the conception of it—of them and by them stand the visible proofs of souls. If there shall be love and content between the father and the son, and if the greatness of the son is the exuding of the greatness of the father, there shall be love between the poet and the man of demonstrable science. In the beauty of poems are henceforth the tuft and final applause of science.

Great is the faith of the flush of knowledge, and of the investigation of the depths of qualities and things. Cleaving and circling here swells the soul of the poet, yet is president of itself always. The depths are fathomless, and therefore calm. The innocence and nakedness are resumed—they are neither modest nor immodest. The whole theory of the supernatural, and all that was twined with it or educed out of it, departs as a dream. What has ever happened—what happens, and whatever may or shall happen, the vital laws inclose all. They are sufficient for any case and for all cases—none to be hurried or retarded—any special miracle of affairs or persons inadmissible in the vast clear scheme where every motion and every spear of grass, and the frames and spirits of men and women and all that concerns them, are unspeakably perfect miracles, all referring to all, and each distinct and in its place. It is also not consistent with the reality of the soul to admit that there is anything in the known universe more divine than men and women.

Men and women, and the earth and all upon it, are to be taken as they are, and the investigation of their past and present and future shall be unintermitted, and shall be done with perfect candor. Upon this basis philosophy speculates, ever looking towards the poet, ever regarding the eternal tendencies of all towards happiness, never inconsistent with what is clear to the senses and to the soul. For the eternal tendencies of all towards happiness make the only point of sane philosophy. Whatever comprehends less than that—whatever is less than the laws of light and of astronomical motion—or less than the laws that follow the thief, the liar, the glutton, and the drunkard, through this life and doubtless afterward—or less than vast stretches of time, or the slow formation of destiny, or the patient upheaving of strata—is of no account. Whatever would put God in a poem or system of philosophy as contending against some being or influence, is also of no account. Sanity and *ensemble* characterize the great master—spoilt in one principle, all is spoilt. The great master has nothing to do with miracles. He sees health for himself in being one of the mass—he sees the hiatus in singular eminence. To the perfect shape comes common ground. To be under the general law is great, for that is to correspond with it. The Master knows that he is unspeakably great, that all are unspeakably great—that nothing, for instance, is greater than to conceive children, and bring them up well—that to *be* is just as great as to perceive or tell.

In the make of the great masters the idea of political liberty is indispensable. Liberty takes the adherence of heroes wherever man and woman exist—but never takes any adherence or welcome from the rest more than from poets. They are the voice and exposition of liberty. They out of ages are worthy the grand idea—to them it is confided, and they must sustain it. Nothing has precedence of it and nothing can warp or degrade it.

As the attributes of the poets of the Kosmos concentre in the real body, and in the pleasure of things, they possess the superiority of genuineness over all fiction and romance. As they emit themselves, facts are showered over with light—the daylight is lit with more volatile light—the deep between the setting and rising sun goes deeper many fold. Each precise object or condition or combination or process exhibits a beauty—the multiplication table its—old age its—the carpenter's trade its—the grand opera its—the huge-hulled clean-shaped New York clipper at sea under steam or full sail gleams with unmatched beauty—the American circles and large harmonies of government gleam with theirs—and the commonest definite intentions and actions with theirs. The poets of the Kosmos advance through all interpositions and coverings and turmoils and stratagems to first principles. They are of use—they dissolve poverty from its need, and riches from its conceit. You large proprietor, they say, shall not realize or perceive more than anyone else. The owner of the library is not he who holds a legal title to it, having bought and pair for it. Anyone and everyone is owner of the library (indeed he or she alone is owner), who can read the same through all the varieties of tongues and subjects and styles, and in whom they enter with ease, and make supple and powerful and rich and large.

These American States, strong and healthy and accomplished, shall receive no pleasure from violations of natural models, and must not permit them. In paintings or mouldings or carvings in mineral or wood, or in the illustrations of books or newspapers, or in the patterns of woven stuffs, or anything to beautify rooms or furniture or costumes, or to put upon cornices or monuments, or on the prows or sterns of ships, or to put anywhere before the human eye indoors or out, that which distorts honest shapes, or which creates unearthly beings or places or contingencies, is a nuisance and revolt. Of the human form especially, it is so great it must never be made ridiculous. Of ornaments to a work nothing *outre* can be allowed—but those ornaments can be allowed that conform to the perfect facts of the open air, and that flow out of the nature of the work, and come irrepressibly from it, and are necessary to the completion of the work. Most works are most beautiful without ornament. Exaggerations will be revenged in human physiology. Clean and vigorous, children are born only in those communities where the models of natural forms are public every day. Great genius and the people of these States must never be demeaned to romances. As soon as histories are properly told, no more need of romances.

The great poets are to be known by the absence in them of tricks, and by the justification of perfect personal candor. All faults may be forgiven of him who has perfect candor. Henceforth let no man of us lie, for we have seen that openness wins the inner and outer world, and that there is no single exception, and that never since our earth gathered itself in a mass has deceit or subterfuge or prevarication attracted its smallest particle or the faintest tinge of a shade—and that through the enveloping wealth and rank of a State, or the whole republic of States, a sneak or sly person shall be discovered and despised—and that the soul has never once been fooled and never can be fooled—and thrift without the loving nod of the soul is only a fetid puff—and there never grew up in any of the continents of the globe, nor upon any planet or satellite, nor in that condition which precedes the birth of babes, nor at any time during the changes of life, nor in any stretch of abeyance or action of vitality, nor in any process of formation or reformation anywhere, a being whose instinct hated the truth.

Extreme caution or prudence, the soundest organic health, large hope and comparison and fondness for women and children, large alimentiveness and destructiveness and causality, with a perfect sense of the oneness of nature, and the propriety of the same spirit applied to human affairs, are called up of the float of the brain of the world to be parts of the greatest poet from his birth out of his mother's womb, and from her birth out of her mother's. Caution seldom goes far enough. It has been thought that the prudent citizen was the citizen who applied himself to solid gains, and did well for himself and for his family, and completed a lawful life without debt or crime. The greatest poet sees and admits these economies as he sees the economies of food and sleep, but has higher notions of prudence than to think he gives much when he gives a few slight attentions at the latch of the gate. The premises of the prudence of life are not the hospitality of it, or the ripeness and harvest of it. Beyond the independence of a little sum laid aside for burial-money, and of a few clap-boards around and shingles overhead on a lot of American soil owned, and the easy dollars that supply the year's plain clothing and meals, the melancholy prudence of the abandonment of such a great being as a man is, to the toss and pallor of years of money-making, with all their scorching days and icy nights, and all their stifling deceits and underhand dodgings, or infinitesimals of parlors, or shameless stuffing while others starve, and all the loss of the bloom and odor of the earth, and of the flowers and atmosphere, and of the sea, and of the true taste of the women and men you pass or have to do with in youth or middle age, and the issuing sickness and desperate revolt at the close of a life without elevation or *naïveté* (even if you have achieved a secure $10,000 a year, or election to Congress or the Governorship), and the ghastly chatter of a death without serenity or majesty, is the great fraud upon modern civilization and forethought, blotching the surface and system which civilization undeniably drafts, and moistening with tears the immense features it spreads and spreads with such velocity before the reached kisses of the soul.

Ever the right explanation remains to be made about prudence. The prudence of the mere wealth and respectability of the most esteemed life appears too faint for the eye to observe at all, when little and large alike drop quietly aside at the thought of the prudence suitable for immortality. What is the wisdom that fills the thinness of a year, or seventy or eighty years—to the wisdom spaced out by ages, and coming back at a certain time with strong reinforcements and rich presents, and the clear faces of wedding-guests as far as you can look, in every direction, running gayly towards you? Only the soul is of itself—all else has reference to what ensues. All that a person does or thinks is of consequence. Nor can the push of charity or personal force ever be anything else than the profoundest reason, whether it brings argument to hand or no. No specification is necessary—to add or subtract or divide is in vain. Little or big, learned or unlearned, white or black, legal or illegal, sick or well, from the first inspiration down the windpipe to the last expiration out of it, all that a male or female does that is vigorous and benevolent and clean is so much sure profit to him or her in the unshakable order of the universe, and through the whole scope of it forever. The prudence of the greatest poet answers at last the craving and glut of the soul, puts off nothing, permits no let-up for its own case or any case, has no particular Sabbath or Judgment Day, divides not the living from the dead, or the righteous from the unrighteous, is satisfied with the present, matches every thought or act by its correlative, and knows no possible forgiveness or deputed atonement.

The direct trial of him who would be the greatest poet is to-day. If he does not flood himself with the immediate age as with vast oceanic tides—if he be not himself the age transfigured and if to him is not opened the eternity which gives similitude to all periods and locations and processes, and animate and inanimate forms, and which is the bond of time, and rises up from its conceivable vagueness and infiniteness in the swimming shapes of to-day, and is held by the ductile anchors of life, and makes the present spot the passage from what was to what shall be, and commits itself to the representation of this wave of an hour, and this one of the sixty beautiful children of the wave—let him merge in the general run, and wait his development.

Still the final test of poems, or any character or work, remains. The prescient poet projects himself centuries ahead, and judges performer or performance after the changes of time. Does it live through them? Does it still hold on untired? Will the same style, and the direction of genius to similar points, be satisfactory now? Have the marches of tens and hundreds and thousands of years made willing detours to the right hand and the left hand for his sake? Is he beloved long and long after he is buried? Does the young man think often of him? and the young woman think often of him? and do the middle-aged and the old think of him?

A great poem is for ages and ages in common, and for all degrees and complexions, and all departments and sects, and for a woman as much as a man, and a man as much as a woman. A great poem is no finish to a man or woman, but rather a beginning. Has anyone fancied he could sit at last under some due authority, and rest satisfied with explanations, and realize, and be content and full? To no such terminus does the greatest poet bring—he brings neither cessation nor sheltered fatness and ease. The touch of him, like nature, tells in action. Whom he takes he takes with firm, sure grasp into live regions previously unattained—thenceforward is no rest—they see the space and ineffable sheen that turn the old spots and lights into dead vacuums. Now there shall be a man cohered out of tumult and chaos—the elder encourages the younger and shows him how—they too shall launch off fearlessly together till the new world fits an orbit for itself, and looks unabashed on the lesser orbits of the stars, and sweeps through the ceaseless rings, and shall never be quiet again.

There will soon be no more priests. Their work is done. A new order shall arise, and they shall be the priests of man, and every man shall be his own priest. They shall find their inspiration in real objects to-day, symptoms of the past and future. They shall not deign to defend immortality or God, or the perfection of things, or liberty, or the exquisite beauty, and reality of the soul they shall arise in America, and be responded to from the remainder of the earth.

The English language befriends the grand American expression—it is brawny enough, and limber and full enough. On the tough stock of a race who through all change of circumstance was never without the idea of political liberty, which is the animus of all liberty, it has attracted the terms of daintier and gayer and subtler and more elegant tongues. It is the powerful language of resistance—it is the dialect of common-sense. It is the speech of the proud and melancholy races, and of all who aspire. It is the chosen tongue to express growth, faith, self-esteem, freedom, justice, equality, friendliness, amplitude, prudence, decision, and courage. It is the medium that shall well-nigh express the inexpressible.

No great literature, nor any like style of behavior or oratory or social intercourse or household arrangements or public institutions, or the treatment by bosses of employed people, nor executive detail, or detail of the army and navy, nor spirit of legislation or courts, or police or tuition or architecture, or songs or amusements, can long elude the jealous and passionate instinct of American standards. Whether or no the sign appears from the mouths of the people, it throbs a live interrogation in every freeman's and freewoman's heart, after that which passes by or this built to remain. Is it uniform with my country? Are its disposals without ignominious distinctions? Is it for the ever-growing communes of brothers and lovers, large, well united, proud beyond the old models, generous beyond all models? Is it something grown fresh out of the fields or drawn from the sea for use to me to-day here? I know that what answers for me, an American, in Texas, Ohio, Canada, must answer for any individual or nation that serves for a part of my materials. Does this answer? Is it for the nursery of the young of the republic? Does it solve readily with the sweet milk of the nipples of the breasts of the Mother of Many Children?

America prepares with composure and good-will for the visitors that have sent word. It is not intellect that is to be their warrant and welcome. The talented, the artist, the ingenious, the editor, the statesman, the erudite, are not unappreciated—they fall in their places and do their work. The soul of the nation also does its work. It rejects none, it permits all. Only towards the like of itself will it advance half way. An individual is as superb as a nation when he has the qualities which make a superb nation. The soul of the largest and wealthiest and proudest nation may well go half way to meet that of its poets.

JAMES FENIMORE COOPER

—

BY

FRANCIS PARKMAN

FRANCIS PARKMAN

1823—1893

Francis Parkman was born at Boston in 1823. His family were people of wealth and education, and thus he was from childhood surrounded by influences favorable to a scholarly development. His health, however, was far from strong, and for several years during his boyhood he lived in the Middlesex Fells, a wild tract not far from the city, hunting, fishing, living a real frontier existence. From time to time he set out on extensive expeditions, roaming through the Maine woods and the region about Lake George and Lake Champlain, localities abounding in historical interest. Already he had determined to devote his life to telling the story of the great struggle between the English colonists and the French and Indians. Soon after graduating from Harvard College in 1844 Parkman set out for the far distant Black Hills, where he shared the hardships and privations incident to life among the Indians, with a view to learning their manner of living and thinking. His constitution, unfortunately, was ill adapted to this rough life, and his health broke down completely. On his return home he was too feeble to write, but dictated an account of his experiences which, after being printed in a magazine, was published in a volume entitled "The California and Oregon Trail." This book was published in 1849. Two years later appeared the first volume of the great historical work that had already shaped itself in Parkman's mind. This was the "History of the Conspiracy of Pontiac." Chronologically this should have been the last volume in the series. Parkman, however, appears to have written it first, as the material for it was most vivid in his memory, and probably he was in the mood best adapted for that portion of his work.

The physical difficulties under which he labored were always great, and at times almost insupportable. There were times when he could read only at intervals, times when he could not read at all. The bulk of the work had to be done for him by an amanuensis, and many of the authorities had to be read to him, as he was unable to read them himself. Under these depressing circumstances his courage never faltered, and steadily one by one the volumes of his great history were issued from the press. "Pioneers of France in the New World," in chronological order the first of the series, was published in 1865; then at intervals of two years came "The Jesuits in North America" and "La Salle, and the Discovery of the Great West." Other volumes followed at intervals of from three to five years until 1892, when the great task was completed. The following year Mr. Parkman died, at the age of seventy, while still engaged in revising his earlier volumes, and happy in the consciousness that the task he had set out to accomplish more than fifty years before was done.

In his chosen field Parkman has no rivals, and his work is likely to remain, for a long time, the standard authority on the period of which it treats. His style is vivid and pleasing, displaying great descriptive powers and skill in narrating the stirring events and romantic incidents of his history. Of Parkman's other writings, which are few, his essay on "James Fenimore Cooper" is one of the most interesting. Here Parkman records some of his impressions of the man who has given us such a vivid portrayal of the North American Indian.

JAMES FENIMORE COOPER

NO American writer has been so extensively read as James Fenimore Cooper. His novels have been translated into nearly every European language. Nay, we are told—but hardly know how to believe it—that they may be had duly rendered into Persian at the bazaars of Ispahan. We have seen some of them well thumbed and worn at a little village in a remote mountainous district of Sicily; and in Naples and Milan the bookstalls bear witness that " L'Ultimo dei Mohecanni " is still a popular work. In England these American novels have been eagerly read and transformed into popular dramas; while cheap and often stupidly mutilated editions of them have been circulated through all her colonies, garrisons, and naval stations, from New Zealand to Canada.

Nor is this widely-spread popularity undeserved. Of all American writers Cooper is the most original, the most thoroughly national. His genius drew aliment from the soil where God had planted it, and rose to a vigorous growth, rough and gnarled, but strong as a mountain cedar. His volumes are a faithful mirror of that rude transatlantic nature which to European eyes appears so strange and new. The sea and the forest have been the scenes of his countrymen's most conspicuous achievements; and it is on the sea and in the forest that Cooper is most thoroughly at home. Their spirit inspired him, their images were graven on his heart; and the men whom their embrace has nurtured, the sailor, the hunter, the pioneer, move and act upon his pages with all the truth and energy of real life.

There is one great writer with whom Cooper has been often compared, and the comparison is not void of justice; for though, on the whole, far inferior, there are certain high points of literary excellence in regard to which he may contest the palm with Sir Walter Scott. It is true that he has no claim to share the humor and pathos, the fine perception of beauty and delicacy in character, which add such charms to the romances of Scott. Nor can he boast that compass and variety of power which could deal alike with forms of humanity so diverse; which could portray with equal mastery the Templar Bois Guilbert, and the Jewess Rebecca; the manly heart of Henry Morton, and the gentle heroism of Jeanie Deans. But notwithstanding this unquestioned inferiority on the part of Cooper, there were marked affinities between him and his great contemporary. Both were practical men, able and willing to grapple with the hard realities of life. Either might have learned with ease to lead a regiment, or command a line-of-battle ship. Their conceptions of character were no mere abstract ideas, or unsubstantial images, but solid embodiments in living flesh and blood. Bulwer and Hawthorne —the conjunction may excite a smile—are writers of a different stamp. Their conceptions are often exhibited with consummate skill, and, in one of these examples at least, with admirable truthfulness; but they never cheat us into a belief in their reality. We may marvel at the skill of the artist, but we are prone to regard his creations rather as figments of art than as reproductions of nature—as a series of vivified and animate pictures, rather than as breathing men and women. With Scott and with Cooper it is far otherwise. Dominie Sampson and the antiquary are as distinct and familiar to our minds as some eccentric acquaintance of our childhood. If we met Long Tom Coffin on the wharf at New Bedford, we should wonder where we had before seen that familiar face and figure. The tall, gaunt form of Leather-stocking, the weather-beaten face, the bony hand, the cap of fox-skin, and the old hunting-frock, polished with long service, seem so palpable and real, that in some moods of mind one may easily confound them with the memories of his own experiences. Others have been gifted to conceive the elements of far loftier character, and even to combine these in a manner equally truthful; but few have rivalled Cooper in the power of breathing into his creations the breath of life, and turning the phantoms of his brain into seeming realities. It is to this, in no small measure, that he owes his widely spread popularity. His most successful portraitures are drawn, it is true, from humble walks and rude associations; yet they are instinct with life, and stamped with the impress of a masculine and original genius.

The descriptions of external nature with which Cooper"s works abound bear a certain analogy to his portraitures of character. There is no glow upon his pictures, no warm and varied coloring, no studied contrast of light and shade. Their virtue consists in their fidelity, in the strength with which they impress themselves upon the mind, and the strange tenacity with which they cling to the memory. For our own part, it was many years since we had turned the pages of Cooper, but still we were haunted by the images which his spell had evoked—the dark gleaming of hill-embosomed lakes, the tracery of forest boughs against the red evening sky, and the raven flapping his black wings above the carnage-field near the Horicon. The descriptions have often, it must be confessed, the grave fault of being overloaded with detail; but they are utterly mistaken who affirm, as some have done, that they are but a catalogue of commonplaces—mountains and woods, rivers and torrents, thrown together as a matter of course. A genuine love of nature inspired the artist's pen; and they who cannot feel the efficacy of its strong picturing have neither heart nor mind for the grandeur of the outer world.

Before proceeding, however, we must observe that, in speaking of Cooper's writings, we have reference only to those happier offsprings of his genius which form the basis of his reputation; for, of that numerous progeny which have of late years swarmed from his pen, we have never read one, and therefore, notwithstanding the ancient usage of reviewers, do not think ourselves entitled to comment upon them.

The style of Cooper is, as style must always be, in no small measure the exponent of the author's mind. It is not elastic or varied, and is certainly far from elegant. Its best characteristics are a manly directness, and a freedom from those prettinesses, studied turns of expression, and petty tricks of rhetoric, which are the pride of less masculine writers. Cooper is no favorite with *dilettanti* critics. In truth, such criticism does not suit his case. He should be measured on deeper principles, not by his manner, but by his pith and substance. A rough diamond—and he is one of the roughest—is worth more than a jewel of paste, though its facets may not shine so clearly.

And yet, try Cooper by what test we may, we shall discover in him grave defects. The field of his success is, after all, a narrow one; and even in his best works he often oversteps its limits. His attempts at sentiment are notoriously unsuccessful. Above all, when he aspires to portray a heroine, no words can express the remarkable character of the product. With simple country girls he succeeds somewhat better; but, when he essays a higher flight, his failure is calamitous. The most rabid asserter of the rights of woman is scarcely more ignorant of woman's true power and dignity. This is the more singular, as his novels are very far from being void of feeling. They seldom, however—and who can wonder at it?—find much favor with women, who for the most part can see little in them but ghastly stories of shipwrecks, ambuscades, and bush-fights, mingled with prolix descriptions and stupid dialogues. Their most appreciating readers may perhaps be found, not among persons of sedentary and studious habits, but among those of a more active turn, military officers and the like, whose tastes have not been trained into fastidiousness, and who are often better qualified than literary men to feel the freshness and truth of the author's descriptions.

The merit of a novelist is usually measured less by his mere power of description than by his skill in delineating character. The permanency of Cooper's reputation must, as it seems to us, rest upon three or four finely conceived and admirably executed portraits. We do not allude to his Indian characters, which, it must be granted, are for the most part either superficially or falsely drawn; while the long conversations which he puts into their mouths are as truthless as they are tiresome. Such as they are, however, they have been eagerly copied by a legion of the smaller poets and novel writers; so that, jointly with Thomas Campbell, Cooper is responsible for the fathering of those aboriginal heroes, lovers, and sages, who have long formed a petty nuisance in our literature. The portraits of which we have spoken are all those of white men, from humble ranks of society, yet not of a mean or vulgar stamp. Conspicuous before them all stands the well-known figure of Leatherstocking. The life and character of this personage are contained in a series of five independent novels, entitled, in honor of him, the "Leatherstocking Tales." Cooper has been censured, and even ridiculed, for this frequent reproduction of his favorite hero, which, it is affirmed, argues poverty of invention; and yet there is not one of the tales in question with which we would willingly part. To have drawn such a character is in itself sufficient honor; and, had Cooper achieved nothing else, this alone must have insured him a wide and merited renown. There is something admirably felicitous in the conception of this hybrid offspring of civilization and barbarism, in whom uprightness, kindliness, innate philosophy, and the truest moral perceptions are joined with the wandering instincts and the hatred of restraints which stamp the Indian or the Bedouin. Nor is the character in the least unnatural. The white denizens of the forest and the prairie are often among the worst though never among the meanest of mankind; but it is equally true that where the moral instincts are originally strong they may find nutriment and growth among the rude scenes and grand associations of the wilderness. Men as true, generous, and kindly as Leatherstocking may still be found among the perilous solitudes of the West. The quiet, unostentatious courage of Cooper's hero had its counterpart in the character of Daniel Boone; and the latter had the same unaffected love of nature which forms so pleasing a feature in the mind of Leatherstocking.

Civilization has a destroying as well as a creating power. It is exterminating the buffalo and the Indian, over whose fate too many lamentations, real or affected, have been sounded for us to renew them here. It must, moreover, sweep from before it a class of men, its own precursors and pioneers, so remarkable both in their virtues and their faults, that few will see their extinction without regret. Of these men Leatherstocking is the representative; and though in him the traits of the individual are quite as prominent as those of the class, yet his character is not on this account less interesting, or less worthy of permanent remembrance. His life conveys in some sort an epitome of American history, during one of its most busy and decisive periods. At first we find him a lonely young hunter in what was then the wilderness of New York. Ten or twelve years later he is playing his part manfully in the old French war. After the close of the Revolution we meet him again on the same spot where he was first introduced to us; but now everything is changed. The solitary margin of the Otsego Lake is transformed into the seat of a growing settlement, and the hunter, oppressed by the restraints of society, turns his aged footsteps westward in search of his congenial solitude. At length we discover him, for the last time, an octogenarian trapper, far out on the prairies of the West. It is clear that the successive stages of his retreat from society could not well be presented in a single story, and that the repetition which has been charged against Cooper as a fault was indispensable to the development of his design.

"The Deerslayer," the first novel in the series of Leatherstocking tales, seems to us one of the most interesting of Cooper's productions. He has chosen for the scene of his story the Otsego Lake, on whose banks he lived and died, and whose scenery he has introduced into three, if not more, of his novels. The Deerslayer, or Leatherstocking, here makes his first appearance as a young man, in fact scarcely emerged from boyhood, yet with all the simplicity, candor, feeling, and penetration which mark his riper years. The old buccaneer in his aquatic habitation, and the contrasted characters of his two daughters, add a human interest to the scene, for the want of which the highest skill in mere landscape painting cannot compensate. The character of Judith seems to us the best drawn, and by far the most interesting, female portrait in any of Cooper's novels with which we are acquainted. The story, however, is not free from the characteristic faults of its author. Above all, it contains, in one instance at least, a glaring exhibition of his aptitude for describing horrors. When he compels his marvellously graphic pen to depict scenes which would disgrace the shambles or the dissecting-table, none can wonder that ladies and young clergymen regard his pages with abhorrence. These, however, are but casual defects in a work which bears the unmistakable impress of genius.

"The Pathfinder" forms the second volume of the series,

and is remarkable, even among its companions, for the force and distinctness of its pictures. For ourselves—though we diligently perused the despatches—the battle of Palo Alto and the storming of Monterey are not more real and present to our mind than some of the scenes and characters of "The Pathfinder," though we have not read it for nine years—the little fort on the margin of Lake Ontario, the surrounding woods and waters, the veteran major in command, the treacherous Scotchman, the dogmatic old sailor, and the Pathfinder himself. Several of these scenes are borrowed in part from Mrs. Grant's "Memoirs of an American Lady"; but, in borrowing, Cooper has transmuted shadows into substance. Mrs. Grant's facts—for as such we are to take them—have an air of fiction; while Cooper's fiction wears the aspect of solid fact. His peculiar powers could not be better illustrated than by a comparison of the passages alluded to in the two books.

One of the most widely known of Cooper's novels is "The Last of the Mohicans," which forms the third volume of the series, and which, with all the elements of a vulgar popularity, combines excellences of a far higher order. It has, nevertheless, its great and obtrusive faults. It takes needless liberties with history; and, though it would be folly to demand that an historical novelist should always conform to received authorities, yet it is certainly desirable that he should not unnecessarily set them at defiance; since the incidents of the novel are apt to remain longer in the memory than those of the less palatable history. But whatever may be the extent of the novelist's license, it is at all events essential that his story should have some semblance of probability, and not run counter to nature and common-sense. In "The Last of the Mohicans" the machinery of the plot falls little short of absurdity. Why a veteran officer, pent up in a little fort, and hourly expecting to be beleaguered by a vastly superior force, consisting in great part of bloodthirsty savages, should at that particular time desire or permit a visit from his two daughters, is a question not easy to answer. Nor is the difficulty lessened when it is remembered that the young ladies are to make the journey through a wilderness full of Indian scalping-parties. It is equally difficult to see why the lover of Alice should choose, merely for the sake of a romantic ride, to conduct her and her sister by a circuitous and most perilous by-path through the forests, when they might more easily have gone by a good road under the safe escort of a column of troops who marched for the fort that very morning. The story founded on these gross inventions is sustained by various minor improbabilities, which cannot escape the reader unless his attention is absorbed by the powerful interest of the narrative.

It seems to us a defect in a novel or a poem when the heroine is compelled to undergo bodily hardship, to sleep out at night in the woods, drenched by rain, stung by mosquitoes, and scratched by briars—to forego all appliances of the toilet, and above all, to lodge in an Indian wigwam. Women have sometimes endured such privation, and endured it with fortitude; but it may be safely affirmed that, for the time, all grace and romance were banished from their presence. We read Longfellow's "Evangeline" with much sympathy in the fortunes of the errant heroine, until, as we approached the end of the poem, every other sentiment was lost in admiration of the unparalleled extent of her wanderings, at the dexterity with which she contrived to elude at least a dozen tribes of savages at that time in a state of war, at the strength of her constitution, and at her marvellous proficiency in woodcraft. When, however, we had followed her for about two thousand miles on her forest pilgrimage, and reflected on the figure she must have made, so tattered and bepatched, bedrenched and bedraggled, we could not but esteem it a happy circumstance that she failed, as she did, to meet her lover; since, had he seen her in such plight, every spark of sentiment must have vanished from his breast, and all the romance of the poem been ingloriously extinguished. With Cooper's heroines, Cora and Alice, the case is not so hard. Yet, as it does not appear that, on a journey of several weeks, they were permitted to carry so much as a valise or a carpet-bag, and as we are expressly told that, on several occasions, they dropped by the wayside their gloves, veils, and other useful articles of apparel, it is certain that at the journey's end they must have presented an appearance more calculated to call forth a Christian sympathy than any emotion of a more romantic nature.

In respect to the delineation of character, "The Last of

the Mohicans" is surpassed by several other works of the author. Its distinguishing merit lies in its descriptions of scenery and action. Of the personages who figure in it, one of the most interesting is the young Mohican, Uncas, who, however, does not at all resemble a genuine Indian. Magua, the villain of the story, is a less untruthful portrait. Cooper has been criticised for representing him as falling in love with Cora; and the criticism is based on the alleged ground that passions of this kind are not characteristic of the Indian. This may, in some qualified sense, be true; but is well known that Indians, in real life as well as in novels, display a peculiar partiality for white women, on the same principle by which Italians are prone to admire a light complexion, while the Swedes regard a brunette with highest esteem. Cora was the very person to fascinate an Indian. The coldest warrior would gladly have received her into his lodge, and promoted her to be his favorite wife, wholly dispensing, in honor of her charms, with flagellation or any of the severer marks of conjugal displeasure.

The character of Hawkeye or Leatherstocking is, in "The Last of the Mohicans" as elsewhere, clearly and admirably drawn. He often displays, however, a weakness which excites the impatience of the reader—an excessive and ill-timed loquacity. When, for example, in the fight at Glenn's Falls, he and Major Heywood are crouching in the thicket, watching the motions of four Indians, whose heads are visible above a log at a little distance, and who, in the expression of Hawkeye himself, are gathering for a rush, the scout employs the time in dilating upon the properties of the "long-barrelled, soft-metalled rifle." The design is, no doubt, to convey an impression of his coolness in moments of extreme danger; but, under such circumstances, the bravest man would judge it the part of good sense to use his eyes rather than his tongue. Men of Hawkeye's class, however talkative they may be at the camp-fire, are remarkable for preserving a close silence while engaged in the active labors of their calling.

It is easy to find fault with "The Last of the Mohicans," but it is far from easy to rival or even approach its excellences. The book has the genuine game flavor; it exhales the odors of the pine-woods and the freshness of the mountain wind. Its dark and rugged scenery rises as distinctly on the eye as the images of the painter's canvas, or rather as the reflection of nature herself. But it is not as the mere rendering of material forms that these wood-paintings are most highly to be esteemed; they breathe the sombre poetry of solitude and danger. In these achievements of his art, Cooper, we think, has no equal, unless it may be the author of that striking romance, "Wacousta; or, The Prophecy," whose fine powers of imagination are, however, even less under the guidance of a just taste than those of the American novelist.

The most obvious merit of "The Last of the Mohicans" consists in its descriptions of action, in the power with which the author absorbs the reader's sympathies, and leads him, as it were, to play a part in the scene. One reads the accounts of a great battle—aside from any cause or principle at issue—with the same kind of interest with which he beholds the grand destructive phenomena of nature, a tempest at sea, or a tornado in the tropics; yet with a feeling far more intense, since the conflict is not a mere striving of insensate elements, but of living tides of human wrath and valor. With descriptions of petty skirmishes or single combats the feeling is of a different kind. The reader is enlisted in the fray—a partaker, as it were, in every thought and movement of the combatants, in the alternations of fear and triumph, the prompt expedient, the desperate resort, the palpitations of human weakness, or the courage that faces death. Of this species of description, the scene of the conflict at Glenn's Falls is an admirable example, unsurpassed, we think, even by the combat of Balfour and Bothwell, or by any other passage of the kind in the novels of Scott. The scenery of the fight, the foaming cataract, the little islet with its stout-hearted defenders, the precipices and the dark pine-woods, add greatly to the effect. The scene is conjured before the reader's eye, not as a vision or a picture, but like the tangible presence of rock, river, and forest. His very senses seem conspiring to deceive him. He seems to feel against his cheek the wind and spray of the cataract, and hear its sullen roar, amid the yells of the assailants and the sharp crack of the answering rifle. The scene of the strife is pointed out to travellers as if this fictitious combat were a real event of history. Mills, factories, and bridges have marred the native wildness of the spot, and a village has usurped the domain of the forest; yet still those foaming waters and black sheets of limestone rock are clothed with all the interest of an historic memory; and the *cicerone* of the place can show the caves where the affrighted sisters took refuge, the point where the Indians landed, and the rock whence the despairing Huron was flung into the abyss. Nay, if the lapse of a few years has not enlightened his understanding, the guide would as soon doubt the reality of the battle of Saratoga as that of Hawkeye's fight with the Mingoes.

"The Pioneers," the fourth volume of the series, is, in several respects, the best of Cooper's works. Unlike some of its companions, it bears every mark of having been written from the results of personal experience; and, indeed, Cooper is well known to have drawn largely on the recollections of his earlier years in the composition of this novel. The characters are full of vitality and truth, though, in one or two instances, the excellence of the delineation is impaired by a certain taint of vulgarity. Leatherstocking, as he appears in "The Pioneers," must certainly have had his living original in some gaunt, gray-haired old woodsman, to whose stories of hunts and Indian fights the author may perhaps have listened in his boyhood with rapt ears, unconsciously garnering up in memory the germs which time was to develop into a rich harvest. The scenes of the Christmas turkey-shooting, the fish-spearing by firelight on Otsego Lake, the rescue from the panther, and the burning of the woods, are all inimitable in their way. Of all Cooper's works, "The Pioneers" seems to us most likely to hold a permanent place in literature, for it preserves a vivid reflection of scenes and characters which will soon have passed away.

"The Prairie," the last of the "Leatherstocking Tales," is a novel of far inferior merit. The story is very improbable, and not very interesting. The pictures of scenery are less true to nature than in the previous volumes, and seem to indicate that Cooper had little or no personal acquaintance with the remoter parts of the West. The book, however, has several passages of much interest, one of the best of which is the scene in which the aged trapper discovers, in the person of a young officer, the grandson of Duncan Heywood and Alice

Munro, whom, half a century before, he had protected in such imminent jeopardy on the rocks of Glenn's Falls and among the mountains of Lake George. The death of Abiram White is very striking, though reminding one of a similar scene in "The Spy." The grand deformity in the story is the wretched attempt at humor in the person of Dr. Obed Battius. David Gamut, in "The Mohicans," is bad enough; but Battius out-Herods Herod, and great must be the merit of the book which one such incubus would not sink beyond redemption.

The novel which first brought the name of Cooper into distinguished notice was "The Spy"; and this book, which gave him his earliest reputation, will contribute largely to preserve it. The story is full of interest, and the character of Harvey Birch is drawn with singular skill.

"The Pilot" is usually considered the best of Cooper's sea-tales. It is in truth a masterpiece of his genius; and although the reader is apt to pass with impatience over the long conversations among the ladies at Saint Ruth's, and between Alice Dunscombe and the disguised Paul Jones, yet he is amply repaid when he follows the author to his congenial element. The description of the wreck of the Ariel, and the death of Long Tom Coffin, can scarcely be spoken of in terms of too much admiration. Long Tom is to Cooper's sea-tales what Leatherstocking is to the novels of the forest—a conception so original and forcible that posterity will hardly suffer it to escape from remembrance. "The Red Rover," "The Water-Witch," and the remainder of the sea-tales, are marked with the same excellences and defects with the novels already mentioned, and further comments would therefore be useless.

The recent death of the man who had achieved so much in the cause of American literature has called forth, as it should have done, a general expression of regret; and the outcries, not unprovoked, which of late have been raised against him, are drowned in the voice of sorrow. The most marked and original of American writers has passed from among us. It was an auspicious moment when his earlier works first saw the light; for their promise in their rude vigor—a good hope that from such rough beginnings the country might develop a literary progeny which, taking lessons in the graces, and refining with the lapse of years, might one day do honor to its parentage; and when the chastened genius of Bryant arose it seemed that the fulfilment of such a hope was not far remote. But this fair promise has failed, and to this hour the purpose, the energy, the passion of America have never found their adequate expression on the printed page. The number of good writers truly American, by which we mean all those who are not imitators of foreign modes, might be counted on the fingers of the two hands; nor are the writers of this small class, not excepting even Bryant himself, in any eminent degree the favorites of those among their countrymen who make pretensions to taste and refinement. As in life and manners the American people seem bent on aping the polished luxury of another hemisphere, so likewise they reserve their enthusiasm and their purses for the honeyed verse and sugared prose of an emasculate and supposititious literature.

Some French writer—Chateaubriand, we believe—observes that the only portion of the American people who exhibit any distinctive national character are backwoodsmen of the West. The remark is not strictly true. The whole merchant marine, from captains to cabin-boys, the lumbermen of Maine, the farmers of New England, and indeed all the laboring population of the country, not of foreign origin, are marked with strong and peculiar traits. But when we ascend into the educated and polished classes these peculiarities are smoothed away, until, in many cases, they are invisible. An educated Englishman is an Englishman still; an educated Frenchman is often intensely French; but an educated American is apt to have no national character at all. The condition of the literature of the country is, as might be expected, in close accordance with these peculiarities of its society. With but few exceptions, the only books which reflect the national mind are those which emanate from, or are adapted to, the unschooled classes of the people—such, for example, as Dr. Bird's "Nick of the Woods," "The Life of David Crockett," "The Big Bear of Arkansas," with its kindred legends, and, we may add, the earlier novels of Cooper. In the politer walks of literature we find much grace of style, but very little originality of thought—productions which might as readily be taken for the work of an Englishman as of an American.

This lack of originality has been loudly complained of, but

it seems to us inevitable under the circumstances. The healthful growth of the intellect, whether national or individual, like healthful growth of every other kind, must proceed from the action of internal energies, not from foreign aid. Too much assistance, too many stimulants, weaken instead of increasing it. The cravings of the American mind, eager as they are, are amply supplied by the copious stream of Euglish current literature. Thousands, nay, millions of readers and writers drink from this bounteous source, and feed on this foreign aliment, till the whole complexion of their thoughts is tinged with it, and by a sort of necessity they think and write at second hand. If this transatlantic supply were completely cut off, and the nation abandoned to its own resources, it would eventually promote, in a high degree, the development of the national intellect. The vitality and force, which are abundantly displayed in every department of active life, would soon find their way into a higher channel, to meet the new and clamorous necessity for mental food; and, in the space of a generation, the oft-repeated demand for an original literature would be fully satisfied.

In respect to every department of active life, the United States are fully emancipated from their ancient colonial subjection. They can plan, invent, and achieve for themselves, and this, too, with a commanding success. But in all the finer functions of thought, in all matters of literature and taste, we are essentially provincial. England once held us in a state of political dependency. That day is past; but she still holds us in an intellectual dependency far more complete. Her thoughts become our thoughts, by a process unconscious but inevitable. She caters for our mind and fancy with a liberal hand. We are spared the labor of self-support; but by the universal law, applicable to nations no less than to individuals, we are weakened by the want of independent exercise. It is a matter of common remark that the most highly educated classes among us are far from being the most efficient either in thought or action. The vigorous life of the nation springs from the deep rich soil at the bottom of society. Its men of greatest influence are those who have studied men before they studied books, and who, by hard battling with the world, and boldly following out the bent of their native genius, have hewed their own way to wealth, station, or knowledge from the ploughshare or the forecastle. The comparative shortcomings of the best educated among us may be traced to several causes; but, as we are constrained to think, they are mainly owing to the fact that the highest civilization of America is communicated from without instead of being developed from within, and is therefore nerveless and unproductive.

"OUR BEST SOCIETY"

—

BY

GEORGE WILLIAM CURTIS

GEORGE WILLIAM CURTIS

1824—1892

George William Curtis, born February 24, 1824, was a descendant of one of the oldest New England families. After receiving his early education in his native town he was sent to a school in Jamaica Plain, Massachusetts. When his father moved to New York in 1838 young Curtis entered the counting-room of a commercial house to fit himself for a business career. Commercial pursuits proving distasteful to him he, in company with his elder brother, in 1842 joined the Brook Farm Association in West Roxbury, Massachusetts. Here he came into friendly relations with Thoreau, Hawthorne, George Ripley, Margaret Fuller, and Emerson. The brothers spent eighteen months in study and tilling the soil and another year in similar pursuits with a farmer near Concord. In 1846 Curtis went abroad and after spending two years in Italy attended lectures at the University of Berlin. Another two years were spent in travelling in Egypt and Syria. On his return to America, in 1850, he became a member of the editorial staff of the New York "Tribune," of which his friend George Ripley was at that time the literary editor. Curtis published "Nile Notes of a Howadji" in 1851 and "The Howadji in Syria" in 1852, both interesting books of travel. "Lotus-Eating," a series of letters written to the "Tribune" while abroad, were collected and brought out in book form shortly afterwards.

Curtis, who had by this time acquired considerable literary reputation, was now invited to join Parke Godwin and Charles F. Briggs in the editorship of "Putnam's Monthly," when it was first issued in 1853. By a series of essays, including "Our Best Society," written in a satirical vein, he contributed much to the popularity and success of this publication. In 1857 the publishers of "Putnam's" failed in business and Curtis, although he was under no legal obligation to the firm, assumed personally a large share of the indebtedness in order to save the creditors from pecuniary loss. For twenty years he labored incessantly to lift the self-imposed burden, deriving his chief income by lecturing. The Harpers had, in the mean time, published his books on travel, and John Harper was so favorably impressed with his ability as a writer that he engaged him to edit the department of the "Easy Chair" in "Harper's New Monthly Magazine." It is in this capacity that he developed and perfected a prose style which entitles him to a place in the foremost rank of American writers. In 1860 he assumed the editorial direction of "Harper's Weekly," a position which, in conjunction with his department in "Harper's Magazine," he retained until his death.

Of his political career, though Curtis was prominent on many occasions and rendered excellent services to his party, we need make but cursory mention. He never accepted office. His name is closely connected with the movement of civil service reform, and it was under his guidance that the Social Reform League was founded in 1881. For many years, especially before and after the war, Curtis was a prominent and popular lecturer. His manner as a speaker was peculiarly attractive, as his delivery was not fiery nor impassionate, but rather graceful and winning, with a touch of satire and of humor. His voice was musical and pleasing, his bearing in public always dignified. By his many speeches on public occasions, notably his eulogies on Sumner, Brooks, Bryant, and his friend, Lowell, he will long be remembered by those who heard him. He died at his Staten Island home on August 31, 1892.

"OUR BEST SOCIETY"*

IF gilt were only gold, or sugar-candy common-sense, what a fine thing our society would be! If to lavish money upon *objets de vertu,* to wear the most costly dresses, and always to have them cut in the height of fashion; to build houses thirty feet broad, as if they were palaces; to furnish them with all the luxurious devices of Parisian genius; to give superb banquets, at which your guests laugh, and which make you miserable; to drive a fine carriage and ape European liveries, and crests, and coats-of-arms; to resent the friendly advances of your baker's wife, and the lady of your butcher (you being yourself a cobbler's daughter); to talk much of the "old families" and of your aristocratic foreign friends; to despise labor; to prate of "good society"; to travesty and parody, in every conceivable way, a society which we know only in books and by the superficial observation of foreign travel, which arises out of a social organization entirely unknown to us, and which is opposed to our fundamental and essential principles: if all these were fine, what a prodigiously fine society would ours be!

This occurred to us upon lately receiving a card of invitation to a brilliant ball. We were quietly ruminating over our evening fire, with Disraeli's Wellington speech, "all tears," in our hands, with the account of a great man's burial, and a little man's triumph across the channel. So many great men gone, we mused, and such great crises impending! This democratic movement in Europe; Kossuth and Mazzini waiting for the moment to give the word; the Russian bear watchfully sucking his paws; the Napoleonic empire redivivus; Cuba, and annexation, and slavery; California and Australia, and the consequent considerations of political economy; dear me! exclaimed we, putting on a fresh hodful of coal, we must look a little into the state of parties.

As we put down the coal-scuttle, there was a knock at the

* This essay was originally published in "Putnam's Magazine" for February, 1853.

door. We said, "Come in," and in came a neat Alhambra-watered envelope, containing the announcement that the queen of fashion was "at home" that evening week. Later in the evening, came a friend to smoke a cigar. The card was lying upon the table, and he read it with eagerness. "You'll go, of course," said he, "for you will meet all the 'best society.'"

Shall we truly? Shall we really see the "best society of the city," the picked flower of its genius, character, and beauty? What makes the "best society" of men and women? The noblest specimens of each, of course. The men who mould the time, who refresh our faith in heroism and virtue, who make Plato, and Zeno, and Shakespeare, and all Shakespeare's gentlemen, possible again. The women, whose beauty, and sweetness, and dignity, and high accomplishment, and grace, make us understand the Greek mythology, and weaken our desire to have some glimpse of the most famous women of history. The "best society" is that in which the virtues are the most shining, which is the most charitable, forgiving, long-suffering, modest, and innocent. The "best society" is, by its very name, that in which there is the least hypocrisy and insincerity of all kinds, which recoils from, and blasts, artificiality, which is anxious to be all that it is possible to be, and which sternly reprobates all shallow pretence, all coxcombery and foppery, and insists upon simplicity as the infallible characteristic of true worth. That is the "best society" which comprises the best men and women.

Had we recently arrived from the moon, we might, upon hearing that we were to meet the "best society," have fancied that we were about to enjoy an opportunity not to be overvalued. But unfortunately we were not so freshly arrived. We had received other cards, and had perfected our toilette many times, to meet this same society, so magnificently described, and had found it the least "best" of all. Who compose it? Whom shall we meet if we go to this ball? We shall meet three classes of persons: first, those who are rich, and who have all that money can buy; second, those who belong to what are technically called "the good old families," because some ancestor was a man of mark in the State or country, or was very rich, and has kept the fortune in the family; and, thirdly, a swarm of youths who can dance dexterously, and who are invited for that purpose. Now these are all arbitrary and factitious distinctions upon which to found so profound a social difference as that which exists in American, or, at least in New York, society. First, as a general rule, the rich men of every community, who make their own money, are not the most generally intelligent and cultivated. They have a shrewd talent which secures a fortune, and which keeps them closely at the work of amassing from their youngest years until they are old. They are sturdy men of simple tastes often. Sometimes, though rarely, very generous, but necessarily with an altogether false and exaggerated idea of the importance of money. They are a rather rough, unsympathetic, and, perhaps, selfish class, who, themselves, despise purple and fine linen, and still prefer a cot-bed and a bare room, although they may be worth millions. But they are married to scheming, or ambitious, or disappointed women, whose life is a prolonged pageant, and they are dragged hither and thither in it, are bled of their golden blood, and forced into a position they do not covet and which they despise. Then there are the inheritors of wealth. How many of them inherit the valiant genius and hard frugality which built up their fortunes; how many acknowledge the stern and heavy responsibility of their opportunities; how many refuse to dream their lives away in a Sybarite luxury; how many are smitten with the lofty ambition of achieving an enduring name by works of a permanent value; how many do not dwindle into dainty *dilettanti,* and dilute their manhood with factitious sentimentality instead of a hearty, human sympathy; how many are not satisfied with having the fastest horses and the "crackest" carriages, and an unlimited wardrobe, and a weak affectation and puerile imitation of foreign life?

And who are these of our secondly, these "old families"? The spirit of our time and of our country knows no such thing, but the *habitué* of "society" hears constantly of "a good family." It means simply the collective mass of children, grandchildren, nephews, nieces, and descendants, of some man who deserved well of his country, and whom his country honors. But sad is the heritage of a great name! The son of Burke will inevitably be measured by Burke. The niece of Pope must show some superiority to other women (so to speak), or her equality is inferiority. The feeling of men attributes some magical charm to blood, and we look to see the daughter of Helen as fair as her mother, and the son of Shakespeare musical as his sire. If they are not so, if they are merely names, and common persons—if there is no Burke, nor Shakespeare, nor Washington, nor Bacon, in their words, or actions, or lives, then we must pity them, and pass gently on, not upbraiding them, but regretting that it is one of the laws of greatness that it dwindles all things in its vicinity, which would otherwise show large enough. Nay, in our regard for the great man, we may even admit to a compassionate honor, as pensioners upon our charity, those who bear and transmit his name. But if these heirs should presume upon that fame, and claim any precedence of living men and women because their dead grandfather was a hero—they must be shown the door directly. We should dread to be born a Percy, or a Colonna, or a Bonaparte. We should not like to be the second Duke of Wellington, nor Charles Dickens, Jr. It is a terrible thing, one would say, to a mind of honorable feeling, to be pointed out as somebody's son, or uncle, or granddaughter, as if the excellence were all derived. It must be a little humiliating to reflect that if your great uncle had not been somebody, you would be nobody—that, in fact, you are only a name, and that, if you should consent to change it for the sake of a fortune, as is sometimes done, you would cease to be anything but a rich man. "My father was President, or Governor of the State," some pompous man may say. But, by Jupiter! king of gods and men, what are you? is the instinctive response. Do you not see, our pompous friend, that you are only pointing your own unimportance? If your father was Governor of the State, what right have you to use that fact only to fatten your self-conceit? Take care, good care; for whether you say it by your lips or by your life, that withering response awaits you—"then what are you?" If your ancestor was great, you are under bonds to greatness. If you are small, make haste to learn it betimes, and, thanking heaven that your name has been made illustrious, retire into a corner and keep it, at least, untarnished.

Our thirdly is a class made by sundry French tailors, bootmakers, dancing-masters, and Mr. Brown. They are a *corps de ballet,* for the use of private entertainments. They are fostered by society for the use of young debutantes, and hardier damsels, who have dared two or three years of the "tight" polka. They are cultivated for their heels, not their heads. Their life begins at ten o'clock in the evening, and lasts until four in the morning. They go home and sleep until nine; then they reel, sleepy, to counting-houses and offices, and doze on desks until dinner-time. Or, unable to do that, they are actively at work all day, and their cheeks grow pale, and their lips thin, and their eyes blood-shot and hollow, and they drag themselves home at evening to catch a nap until the ball begins, or to dine and smoke at their club, and be very manly with punches and coarse stories; and then to rush into hot and glittering rooms, and seize very *décolleté* girls closely around the waist, and dash with them around an area of stretched linen, saying, in the panting pauses, "How very hot it is!" "How very pretty Miss Podge looks!" "What a good redowa!" "Are you going to Mrs. Potiphar's?"

Is this the assembled flower of manhood and womanhood, called "best society," and to see which is so envied a privilege? If such are the elements, can we be long in arriving at the present state and necessary future condition of parties?

"Vanity Fair" is peculiarly a picture of modern society. It aims at English follies, but its mark is universal, as the madness is. It is called a satire, but, after much diligent reading, we cannot discover the satire. A state of society not at all superior to that of "Vanity Fair" is not unknown to our experience; and, unless truth-telling be satire; unless the most tragically real portraiture be satire; unless scalding tears of sorrow, and the bitter regret of a manly mind over the miserable spectacle of artificiality, wasted powers, misdirected energies, and lost opportunities, be satirical, we do not find satire in that sad story. The reader closes it with a grief beyond tears. It leaves a vague apprehension in the mind, as if we should suspect the air to be poisoned. It suggests the terrible thought of the enfeebling of moral power, and the deterioration of noble character, as a necessary consequence of contact with "society." Every man looks suddenly and sharply around him, and accosts himself and his neighbors, to ascertain if they are all parties to this corruption. Sentimental youths and maidens, upon velvet sofas, or in calf-bound libraries, resolve that it is an insult to human nature—are sure that their velvet and calf-bound friends are not like the *dramatis personæ* of "Vanity Fair," and that the drama is therefore hideous and unreal. They should remember, what they uniformly and universally forget, that we are not invited, upon the rising of the curtain, to behold a cosmorama, or picture of the world, but a representation of that part of it called Vanity Fair. What its just limits are—how far its poisonous purlieus reach—how much of the world's air is tainted by it, are questions which every thoughtful man will ask himself, with a shudder, and look sadly around, to answer. If the sentimental objectors rally again to the charge, and declare that if we wish to improve the world its virtuous ambition must be piqued and stimulated by making the shining heights of "the ideal" more radiant; we reply, that none shall surpass us in honoring the men whose creations of beauty inspire and instruct mankind. But if they benefit the world, it is no less true that a vivid apprehension of the depths into which we are sunken or may sink nerves the soul's courage quite as much as the alluring mirage of the happy heights we may attain. "To hold the mirror up to nature" is still the most potent method of shaming sin and strengthening virtue.

If "Vanity Fair" be a satire, what novel of society is not? Are "Vivian Grey," and "Pelham," and the long catalogue of books illustrating English, or the host of Balzacs, Sands, Sues, and Dumas, that paint French society, less satires? Nay, if you should catch any dandy in Broadway, or in Pall Mall, or upon the Boulevards, this very morning, and write a coldly true history of his life and actions, his doings and undoings, would it not be the most scathing and tremendous satire?—if by satire you mean the consuming melancholy of the conviction that the life of that pendant to a mustache is an insult to the possible life of a man.

We have read of a hypocrisy so thorough that it was surprised you should think it hypocritical: and we have bitterly thought of the saying when hearing one mother say of another mother's child, that she had "made a good match," because the girl was betrothed to a stupid boy whose father was rich. The remark was the key of our social feeling.

Let us look at it a little, and, first of all, let the reader consider the criticism, and not the critic. We may like very well, in our individual capacity, to partake of the delicacies prepared by our hostess's *chef,* we may not be averse to *paté* and myriad *objets de goût,* and if you caught us in a corner at the next ball, putting away a fair share of *dinde aux truffes,* we know you would have at us in a tone of great moral indignation, and wish to know why we sneaked into great houses, eating good suppers, and drinking choice wines, and then went away with an indigestion, to write dyspeptic disgusts at society.

We might reply that it is necessary to know something of a subject before writing about it, and that if a man wished to describe the habits of South Sea Islanders it is useless to go to Greenland; we might also confess a partiality for *paté,* and a tenderness for *truffes,* and acknowledge that, considering our single absence would not put down extravagant, pompous parties, we were not strong enough to let the morsels drop into unappreciating mouths; or we might say, that if a man invited us to see his new house, it would not be ungracious nor insulting to his hospitality, to point out whatever weak parts we might detect in it, nor to declare our candid conviction, that it was built upon wrong principles and could not stand. He might believe us if we had been in the house, but he certainly would not if we had never seen it. Nor would it be a very wise reply upon his part that we might build a better if we didn't like that. We are not fond of David's pictures, but we certainly could never paint half so well; nor of Pope's poetry, but posterity will never hear of our verses. Criticism is not construction, it is observation. If we could surpass in its own way everything which displeased us, we should make short work of it, and instead of showing what fatal blemishes deform our present society, we should present a specimen of perfection, directly.

We went to the brilliant ball. There was too much of everything—too much light, and eating, and drinking, and dancing, and flirting, and dressing, and feigning, and smirking, and much too many people. Good taste insists first upon fitness. But why had Mrs. Potiphar given this ball? We inquired industriously, and learned it was because she did not give one last year. Is it then essential to do this thing biennially? inquired we with some trepidation. "Certainly," was the bland reply, "or society will forget you." Everybody was unhappy at Mrs. Potiphar's, save a few girls and boys, who danced violently all the evening. Those who did not dance walked up and down the rooms as well as they could, squeezing by non-dancing ladies, causing them to swear in their hearts as the brusque broadcloth carried away the light outworks of gauze and gossamer. The dowagers, ranged in solid phalanx, occupied all the chairs and sofas against the wall, and fanned themselves until supper-time, looking at each other's diamonds, and critcising the toilettes of the younger ladies, each narrowly watching her peculiar Polly Jane, that she did not betray too much interest in any man who was not of a certain fortune. It is the cold, vulgar truth, madam, nor are we in the slightest degree exaggerating. Elderly gentlemen, twisting single gloves in a very wretched manner, came up and bowed to the dowagers, and smirked, and said it was a pleasant party, and a handsome house, and then clutched their hands behind them, and walked miserably away, looking as affable as possible. And the dowagers made a little fun of the elderly gentlemen, among themselves, as they walked away.

Then came the younger non-dancing men—a class of the community who wear black cravats and waistcoats, and thrust their thumbs and forefingers in their waistcoat-pockets, and are called "talking men." Some of them are literary, and affect the philosopher; have, perhaps, written a book or two, and are a small species of lion to very young ladies. Some are of the *blasé* kind—men who affect the extremest elegance, and are reputed "so aristocratic," and who care for nothing in particular, but wish they had not been born gentlemen, in which case they might have escaped *ennui*. These gentlemen stand with hat in hand, and their coats and trousers are unexceptionable. They are the "so gentlemanly" persons of whom one hears a great deal, but which seems to mean nothing but cleanliness. Vivian Grey and Pelham are the models of their ambition, and they succeed in being Pendennis. They enjoy the reputation of being "very clever," and "very talented fellows," and "smart chaps"; but they refrain from proving what is so generously conceded. They are often men of a certain cultivation. They have travelled, many of them—spending a year or two in Paris and a month or two in the rest of Europe. Consequently they endure society at home, with a smile, and a shrug, and a graceful superciliousness, which is very engaging. They are perfectly at home, and they rather despise Young America, which, in the next room, is diligently earning its invitation. They prefer to hover about the ladies who did not come out this season, but are a little used to the world, with whom they are upon most friendly terms, and they criticise together, very freely, all the great events in the great world of fashion.

These elegant Pendennises we saw at Mrs. Potiphar's, but not without a sadness which can hardly be explained. They had been boys once, all of them, fresh and frank-hearted, and full of a noble ambition. They had read and pondered the histories of great men; how they resolved, and struggled, and achieved. In the pure portraiture of genius, they had loved and honored noble women, and each young heart was sworn to truth and the service of beauty. Those feelings were chivalric and fair. Those boyish instincts clung to whatever was lovely, and rejected the specious snare, however graceful and elegant. They sailed, new knights, upon that old and endless crusade against hypocrisy and the devil, and they were lost in the luxury of Corinth, nor longer seek the difficult shores beyond. A present smile was worth a future laurel. The ease of the moment was worth immortal tranquillity. They renounced the stern worship of the unknown God, and acknowledged the deities of Athens. But the seal of their shame is their own smile at their early dreams, and the high hopes of their boyhood, their sneering infidelity of simplicity, their scepticism of motives and of men. Youths, whose younger years were fervid with the resolution to strike and win, to deserve, at least, a gentle remembrance, if not a dazzling fame, are content to eat, and drink, and sleep well; to go to the opera and all the balls; to be known as "gentlemanly," and "aristocratic," and "dangerous," and "elegant"; to cherish a luxurious and enervating indolence, and to "succeed," upon the cheap reputation of having been "fast" in Paris. The end of such men is evident enough from the beginning. They are snuffed out by a "great match," and become an appendage to a rich woman; or they dwindle off into old *roués,* men of the world in sad earnest, and not with elegant affectation, *blasé;* and as they began Arthur Pendennises, so they end the Major. But, believe it, that old fossil heart is wrung sometimes by a mortal pang, as it remembers those squandered opportunities and that lost life.

From these groups we passed into the dancing-room. We have seen dancing in other countries, and dressing. We have certainly never seen gentlemen dance so easily, gracefully, and well, as the American. But the style of dancing, in its whirl, its rush, its fury, is only equalled by that of the masked balls at the French opera, and the balls at the Salle Valentino, the Jardin Mabille, the Château Rouge, and other favorite resorts of Parisian grisettes and lorettes. We saw a few young men looking upon the dance very soberly, and, upon inquiry, learned that they were engaged to certain ladies of the *corps de ballet.* Nor did we wonder that the spectacle of a young woman whirling in a *décolleté* state, and in the embrace of a warm youth around a heated room, induced a little sobriety upon her lover's face, if not a sadness in his heart. Amusement, recreation, enjoyment! There are no more beautiful things. But this proceeding falls under another head. We watched the various toilets of these bounding belles. They were rich and tasteful. But a man at our elbow, of experience and shrewd observation, said, with a sneer, for which we called him to account: " I observe that American ladies are so rich in charms that they are not at all chary of them. It is certainly generous to us miserable black coats. But, do you know, it strikes me as a generosity of display that must necessarily leave the donor poorer in maidenly feeling." We thought ourselves cynical, but this was intolerable; and in a very crisp manner we demanded an apology.

" Why," responded our friend with more of sadness than of satire in his tone, " why are you so exasperated? Look at this scene! Consider that this is, really, the life of these girls. This is what they ' come out ' for. This is the end of their ambition. They think of it, dream of it, long for it. Is it amusement? Yes, to a few, possibly. But listen and gather, if you can, from their remarks (when they make any), that they have any thought beyond this, and going to church very rigidly on Sunday. The vigor of polking and church-going are proportioned; as is the one so is the other. My young friend, I am no ascetic, and do not suppose a man is damned because he dances. But life is not a ball (more's the pity, truly, for these butterflies), nor is its sole duty and delight, dancing. When I consider this spectacle—when I remember what a noble and beautiful woman is, what a manly man—when I reel, dazzled by this glare, drunken by these perfumes, confused by this alluring music, and reflect upon the enormous sums wasted in a pompous profusion that delights no one—when I look around upon all this rampant vulgarity in tinsel and Brussels lace, and think how fortunes go, how men struggle and lose the bloom of their honesty, how women hide in a smiling pretence, and eye with caustic glances their neighbor's newer house, diamonds, or porcelain, and observe their daughters, such as these—why, I tremble, and tremble, and this scene to-night, every 'crack' ball this winter, will be, not the pleasant society of men and women, but—even in this young country—an orgie such as rotting Corinth saw, a frenzied festival of Rome in its decadence."

There was a sober truth in this bitterness, and we turned away to escape the sombre thought of the moment. Addressing one of the panting houris who stood melting in a window, we spoke (and confess how absurdly) of the Düsseldorf Gallery. It was merely to avoid saying how warm the room was, and how pleasant the party was, facts upon which we had already enlarged. "Yes, they are pretty pictures; but, la! how long it must have taken Mr. Düsseldorf to paint them all," was the reply.

By the Farnesian Hercules! no Roman sylph in her city's decline would ever have called the sun-god, Mr. Apollo. We hope that houri melted entirely away in the window; but we certainly did not stay to see.

Passing out toward the supper-room we encountered two young men. "What, Hal," said one, "you at Mrs. Potiphar's?" It seems that Hal was a sprig of one of the "old families." "Well, Joe," said Hal, a little confused, "it is a little strange. The fact is I didn't mean to be here, but I concluded to compromise by coming, and not being introduced to the host." Hal could come, eat Potiphar's supper, drink his wines, spoil his carpets, laugh at his fashionable struggles, and affect the puppyism of a foreign lord, because he disgraced the name of a man who had done some service somewhere, while Potiphar was only an honest man who made a fortune.

The supper-room was a pleasant place. The table was covered with a chaos of supper. Everything sweet and rare, and hot and cold, solid and liquid, was there. It was the very apotheosis of gilt gingerbread. There was a universal rush and struggle. The charge of the guards at Waterloo was nothing to it. Jellies, custard, oyster-soup, ice-cream, wine and water, gushed in profuse cascades over transparent precipices of tulle, muslin, gauze, silk, and satin. Clumsy boys tumbled against costly dresses and smeared them with preserves; when clean plates failed, the contents of plates already used were quietly "chucked" under the table—heel-taps of champagne were poured into the oyster tureens or overflowed upon plates to clear the glasses—wine of all kinds flowed in torrents, particularly down the throats of very young men, who evinced their manhood by becoming noisy, troublesome, and disgusting, and were finally either led, sick, into the hat-room, or carried out of the way, drunk. The supper over, the young people, attended by their matrons, descended to the dancing-room for the "german." This is a dance commencing usually at midnight or a little after, and continuing indefinitely toward daybreak. The young people were attended by their matrons, who were there to supervise the morals and manners of their charges. To secure the performance of this duty, the young people took good care to sit where the matrons could not see them, nor did they, by any chance, look toward the quarter in which the matrons sat. In that quarter, through all the varying mazes of the prolonged dance, to two o'clock, to three, to four, sat the bediamonded dowagers, the mothers, the matrons—against nature, against common-sense. They babbled with each other, they drowsed, they dozed. Their fans fell listless into their laps. In the adjoining room, out of the waking sight, even, of the then sleeping mammas, the daughters whirled in the close embrace of partners who had brought down bottles of champagne from the supper-room, and put them by the side of their chairs for occasional refreshment during the dance. The dizzy hours staggered by—"Azalia, you must come now," had been already said a dozen times, but only as by the scribes. Finally it was declared with authority. Azalia went—Amelia—Arabella. The rest followed. There was prolonged cloaking, there were lingering farewells. A few papas were in the supper-room, sitting among the *débris* of the game. A few young non-dancing husbands sat beneath gas unnaturally bright, reading whatever chance book was at hand, and thinking of the young child at home waiting for mamma, who was dancing the "german" below. A few exhausted matrons sat in the robing-room, tired, sad, wishing Jane would come up; assailed at intervals by a vague suspicion that it was not quite worth while; wondering how it was they used to have such good times at balls; yawning, and looking at their watches; while the regular beat of the music below, with sardonic sadness, continued. At last Jane came up, had had the most glorious time, and went down with mamma to the carriage, and so drove home. Even the last Jane went—the last noisy youth was expelled, and Mr. and Mrs. Potiphar, having duly performed their biennial social duty, dismissed the music, ordered the servants to count the spoons, and an hour or two after daylight went to bed. Enviable Mr. and Mrs. Potiphar!

We are now prepared for the great moral indignation of the friend who saw us eating our *dinde aux truffes* in that remarkable supper-room. We are waiting to hear him say in the most moderate and "gentlemanly" manner that it is all very well to select flaws and present them as specimens, and to learn from him, possibly with indignant publicity, that the present condition of parties is not what we have intimated. Or, in his quiet and pointed way, he may smile at our fiery assault upon edged flounces and nugat pyramids, and the kingdom of Liliput in general.

Yet, after all, and despite the youths who are led out, and carried home, or who stumble through the "german," this is a sober matter. My friend told us we should see the "best society." But he is a prodigious wag. Who make this country? From whom is its character of unparalleled enterprise, heroism, and success derived? Who have given it its place in the respect and the fear of the world? Who, annually, recruit its energies, confirm its progress, and secure its triumph? Who are its characteristic children, the pith, the sinew, the bone, of its prosperity? Who found, and direct, and continue its manifold institutions of mercy and education? Who are, essentially, Americans? Indignant friend, these classes, whoever they may be, are the "best society," because they alone are the representatives of its character and cultivation. They are the "best society" of New York, of Boston, of Baltimore, of St. Louis, of New Orleans, whether they live upon six hundred or sixty thousand dollars a year—whether they inhabit princely houses in fashionable streets (which they often do), or not—whether their sons have graduated at Celarius's and the Jardin Mabille, or have never been out of their father's shops—whether they have "air" and "style," and are "so gentlemanly," and "so aristocratic," or not. Your shoemaker, your lawyer, your butcher, your clergyman—if they are simple and steady, and, whether rich or poor, are unseduced by the sirens of extravagance and ruinous display—help make up the "best society." For that mystic communion is not composed of the rich, but of the worthy; and is "best" by its virtues, and not by its vices. When Johnson, Burke, Goldsmith, Garrick, Reynolds, and their friends, met at supper in Goldsmith's rooms, where was the "best society" in England? When George IV outraged humanity and decency in his treatment of Queen Caroline, who was the first scoundrel in Europe?

Pause yet a moment, indignant friend. Whose habits and principles would ruin this country as rapidly as it has been made? Who are enamored of a puerile imitation of foreign splendors? Who strenuously endeavor to graft the questionable points of Parisian society upon our own? Who pass a few years in Europe and return sceptical of republicanism and human improvement, longing and sighing for more sharply emphasized social distinctions? Who squander, with profuse recklessness, the hard-earned fortunes of their sires? Who diligently devote their time to nothing, foolishly and wrongly supposing that a young English nobleman has nothing to do? Who, in fine, evince by their collective conduct, that they regard their Americanism as a misfortune, and are so the most deadly enemies of their country? None but what our wag facetiously termed "the best society."

If the reader doubts, let him consider its practical results in any great emporiums of "best society." Marriage is there regarded as a luxury, too expensive for any but the sons of rich men, or fortunate young men. We once heard an eminent divine assert, and only half in sport, that the rate of living was advancing so incredibly, that weddings in his experience were perceptibly diminishing. The reasons might have been many and various. But we all acknowledge the fact. On the other hand and about the same time, a lovely damsel (ah! Clorinda!) whose father was not wealthy, who had no prospective means of support, who could do nothing but polka to perfection, who literally knew almost nothing, and who constantly shocked every fairly intelligent person by the glaring ignorance betrayed in her remarks, informed a friend at one of the Saratoga balls, whither he had made haste to meet "the best society," that there were "not more than three good matches in society." *La dame aux camélias,* Marie Duplessis, was to our fancy a much more feminine, and admirable, and moral, and human person, than the adored Clorinda. And yet what she said was the legitimate result of the state of our fashionable society. It worships wealth, and the pomp which wealth can purchase, more than virtue, genius, or beauty. We may be told that it has always been so in every country, and that the fine society of all lands is as profuse and flashy as our own. We deny it, flatly. Neither English, nor French, nor Italian, nor German society, is so unspeakably barren as that which is technically called "society" here. In London, and Paris, and Vienna, and Rome, all the really eminent men and women help make up the mass of society. A party is not a mere ball, but it is a congress of the wit, beauty, and fame of the capital. It is worth while to dress if you shall meet Macaulay, or Hallam, or Guizot, or Thiers, or Landseer, or Delaroche—Mrs. Norton, the Misses Berry, Madame Récamier, and all the brilliant women and famous foreigners. But why should we desert the pleasant pages of those men, and the recorded gossip of those women, to be squeezed flat against a wall while young Doughface pours oyster-gravy down our shirt-front, and Caroline Pettitoes wonders at "Mr. Düsseldorf's" industry?

If intelligent people decline to go, you justly remark, it is their own fault. Yes, but if they stay away, it is very certainly their great gain. The elderly people are always neglected with us, and nothing surprises intelligent strangers more than the tyrannical supremacy of Young America. But we are not surprised at this neglect. How can we be, if we have our eyes open? When Caroline Pettitoes retreats from the floor to the sofa, and instead of a "polker" figures at parties as a matron, do you suppose that "tough old Joes" like ourselves are going to desert the young Caroline upon the floor, for Madame Pettitoes upon the sofa? If the pretty young Caroline, with youth, health, freshness, a fine, budding form, and wreathed in a semitransparent haze of flounced and flowered gauze, is so vapid that we prefer to accost her with our eyes alone, and not with our tongues, is the same Caroline married into a Madame Pettitoes, and fanning herself upon a sofa—no longer particularly fresh, nor young, nor pretty, and no longer budding, but very fully blown—likely to be fascinating in conversation? We cannot wonder that the whole connection of Pettitoes, when advanced to the matron state, is entirely neglected. Proper homage to age we can all pay at home, to our parents and grandparents. Proper respect for some persons is best preserved by avoiding their neighborhood.

And what, think you, is the influence of this extravagant expense and senseless show upon these same young men and women? We can easily discover. It saps their noble ambition, assails their health, lowers their estimate of men, and their reverence for women, cherishes an eager and aimless rivalry, weakens true feeling, wipes away the bloom of true modesty, and induces an *ennui,* a satiety, and a kind of dilettante misanthropy, which is only the more monstrous because it is undoubtedly real. You shall hear young men of intelligence and cultivation, to whom the unprecedented circumstances of this country offer opportunities of a great and beneficent career, complaining that they were born within this blighted circle; regretting that they were not bakers and tallow-chandlers, and under no obligation to keep up appearances; deliberately surrendering all the golden possibilities of that future which this country, beyond all others, holds before them; sighing that they are not rich enough to marry the girls they love, and bitterly upbraiding fortune that they are not millionaires; suffering the vigor of their years to exhale in idle wishes and pointless regrets; disgracing their manhood by lying in wait behind their "so gentlemanly" and "aristocratic" manners, until they can pounce upon a "fortune" and ensnare an heiress into matrimony: and so, having dragged their gifts—their horses of the sun—into a service which shames out of them all their native pride and power, they sink in the mire; and their peers and emulators exclaim that they have "made a good thing of it."

Are these the processes by which a noble race is made and perpetuated? At Mrs. Potiphar's we heard several Pendennises longing for a similar luxury, and announcing their firm purpose never to have wives nor houses until they could have them as splendid as jewelled Mrs. Potiphar, and her palace, thirty feet front. Where were their heads, and their hearts, and their arms? How looks this craven despondency, before the stern virtues of the ages we call dark? When a man is so voluntarily imbecile as to regret he is not rich, if that is what he wants, before he has struck a blow for wealth; or so dastardly as to renounce the prospect of love, because sitting sighing, in velvet dressing-gown and slippers, he does not see his way clear to ten thousand a year: when young women coiffed *à merveille* of unexceptionable " style," who, with or without a prospective penny, secretly look down upon honest women who struggle for a livelihood, like noble and Christian beings, and, as such, are rewarded; in whose society a man must forget that he has ever read, thought, or felt; who destroy in the mind the fair ideal of women, which the genius of art, and poetry, and love, their inspirer has created; then, it seems to us, it is high time that the subject should be regarded, not as a matter of breaking butterflies upon the wheel, but as a sad and sober question, in whose solution, all fathers and mothers, and the state itself, are interested. When keen observers, and men of the world, from Europe, are amazed and appalled at the giddy whirl and frenzied rush of our society—a society singular in history for the exaggerated prominence it assigns to wealth, irrespective of the talents that amassed it, they and their possessor being usually hustled out of sight—is it not quite time to ponder a little upon the Court of Louis XIV, and the " merrie days " of King Charles II? Is it not clear that, if what our good wag, with caustic irony, called " best society," were really such, every thoughtful man would read upon Mrs. Potiphar's softly tinted walls the terrible *" mene, mene "* of an imminent destruction.

Venice in her purple prime of luxury, when the famous law was passed making all gondolas black, that the nobles should not squander fortunes upon them, was not more luxurious than New York to-day. Our hotels have a superficial splendor, derived from a profusion of gilt and paint, wood and damask. Yet, in not one of them can the traveller be so quietly comfortable as in an English inn, and nowhere in New York can a stranger procure a dinner, at once so neat and elegant, and economical, as at scores of *cafés* in Paris. The fever of display has consumed comfort. A gondola plated with gold was no easier than a black wooden one. We could well spare a little gilt upon the walls for more cleanliness upon the public table; nor is it worth while to cover the walls with mirrors to reflect a want of comfort. One prefers a wooden bench to a greasy velvet cushion, and a sanded floor to a soiled and threadbare carpet. An insipid uniformity is the Procrustes-bed upon which " society " is stretched. Every new house is the counterpart of every other, with the exception of more gilt, if the owner can afford it. The interior arrangement, instead of being characteristic, instead of revealing something of the tastes and feelings of the owner, is rigorously conformed to every other interior. The same hollow and tame complaisance rules in the intercourse of society. Who dares say precisely what he thinks upon a great topic? What youth ventures to say sharp things, of slavery, for instance, at a polite dinner-table? What girl dares wear curls, when Martelle prescribes puffs or bandeaux? What specimen of Young America dares have his trousers loose or wear straps to them? We want individuality, heroism, and, if necessary, an uncompromising persistence in difference.

This is the present state of parties. They are wildly extravagant, full of senseless display; they are avoided by the pleasant and intelligent, and swarm with reckless regiments of " Brown's men." The ends of the earth contribute their choicest products to the supper, and there is everything that wealth can purchase, and all the specious splendor that thirty feet front can afford. They are hot, and crowded, and glaring. There is a little weak scandal, venomous, not witty, and a stream of weary platitude, mortifying to every sensible person. Will any of our Pendennis friends intermit their indignation for a moment, and consider how many good things they have said or heard during the season? If Mr. Potiphar's eyes should chance to fall here, will he reckon the amount of satisfaction and enjoyment he derived from Mrs. Potiphar's ball, and will that lady candidly confess what she gained from it beside weariness and disgust? What eloquent sermons we remember to have heard in which the sins and sinners of Babylon, Jericho, and Gomorrah were scathed with holy indignation. The cloth is very hard upon Cain, and completely routs the erring kings of Judah. The Spanish Inquisition, too, gets frightful knocks, and there is much eloquent exhortation to preach the gospel in the interior of Siam. Let it be preached there and God speed the Word. But also let us have a text or two in Broadway and the Avenue.

The best sermon ever preached upon society, within our knowledge, is "Vanity Fair." Is the spirit of that story less true of New York than of London? Probably we never see Amelia at our parties, nor Lieutenant George Osborne, nor good gawky Dobbin, nor Mrs. Rebecca Sharp Crawley, nor old Steyne. We are very much pained, of course, that any author should take such dreary views of human nature. We, for our parts, all go to Mrs. Potiphar's to refresh our faith in men and women. Generosity, amiability, a catholic charity, simplicity, taste, sense, high cultivation, and intelligence, distinguish our parties. The statesman seeks their stimulating influence; the literary man, after the day's labor, desires the repose of their elegant conversation; the professional man and the merchant hurry up from down town to shuffle off the coil of heavy duty, and forget the drudgery of life in the agreeable picture of its amenities and graces presented by Mrs. Potiphar's ball. Is this account of the matter, or "Vanity Fair," the satire? What are the prospects of any society of which that tale is the true history?

There is a picture in the Luxembourg gallery at Paris, "The Decadence of the Romans," which made the fame and fortune of Couture, the painter. It represents an orgie in the court of a temple, during the last days of Rome. A swarm of revellers occupy the middle of the picture, wreathed in elaborate intricacy of luxurious posture, men and women intermingled, their faces, in which the old Roman fire scarcely flickers, brutalized with excess of every kind; their heads of dishevelled hair bound with coronals of leaves, while, from goblets of an antique grace, they drain the fiery torrent which is destroying them. Around the bacchanalian feast stand, lofty upon pedestals, the statues of old Rome, looking with marble calmness and the severity of a rebuke beyond words, upon the revellers. A youth of boyish grace, with a wreath woven in his tangled hair, and with red and drowsy eyes, sits listless upon one pedestal, while upon another stands a boy insane with drunkenness, and proffering a dripping goblet to the marble mouth of the statue. In the corner of the picture, as if just quitting the court—Rome finally departing—is a group of Romans with care-worn brows, and hands raised to their faces in melancholy meditation. In the foreground of the picture, which is painted with all the sumptuous splendor of the Venetian art, is a stately vase, around which hangs a festoon of gorgeous flowers, its end dragging upon the pavement. In the background, between the columns, smiles the blue sky of Italy—the only thing Italian not deteriorated by time. The careful student of this picture, if he have been long in Paris, is some day startled by detecting, especially in the faces of the women represented, a surprising likeness to the women of Paris, and perceives, with a thrill of dismay, that the models for this picture of decadent human nature are furnished by the very city in which he lives.